Gerry Faust:
The Golden Dream

**Gerry Faust
and
Steve Love**

SAGAMORE PUBLISHING
Champaign, IL 61820

Book design, editor: Susan M. McKinney
Dustjacket, photo insert design: Julie L. Denzer

ISBN:1-57167-118-8

Printed in the United States.

For my parents, Alma and Fuzzy, who are with God but who taught me right from wrong and did it with so much love.

For Marlene, my wife of 33 years, who has been my guiding light and friend.

For my three children, Julie Marie, Gerry and Steve, who are the greatest wins of my life.

For Brother Lawrence Eveslage, S.M., who believed in me and hired me as Moeller's first football coach.

For Father Lawrence Krusling and Father James Rieble, C.S.C., both men of God whose friendship and guidance I cherish.

For Father Theodore M. Hesburgh, C.S.C., and Father Edmund P. Joyce, C.S.C., who gave me the opportunity to live The Golden Dream.

—G.F.

For Jacquelyn, my wife, my editor and, above all, my best friend.

—S.L.

Contents

ACKNOWLEDGMENTS

The authors offer their heartfelt thanks to the following persons who relived good times and bad for the sake of *The Golden Dream*:

From the Notre Dame years: Father Edmund P. Joyce, Father James Riehle, Brian Boulac, Bob Crable, Gene Corrigan, Art Decio, John Heisler, Roger Valdiserri and Mike Leep.

And from the Akron years, where truths were seldom close to the surface and not always without pain: Dr. William V. Muse, Dave Adams, Jim Dennison, Ray Meyo, Bill Greenzalis, Ralph Staub, Rudy Sharkey and Bob LaCivita.

In a category by themselves are two persons who shared all the years and have heard all the stories before, because they were part of most of them: Marlene Faust, wife and friend, and Ken Schneider, attorney and friend.

For their support, their patience and their assistance in the editorial process, the authors, singularly or together, owe a debt of gratitude to the following persons: Jacquelyn B. Love, Karen Heisler, Ken Krause, Father Edmund P. Joyce, John Heisler, Ted Mallo, Marion Ruebel and, most of all, Ray Meyo. Whatever is right about *The Golden Dream*, they made it so. Whatever is wrong is no fault of theirs.

FOREWORD

Every Notre Dame fan remembers the story. How a high school football coach had a dream. How he got on his knees every day and prayed to the Blessed Mother for a chance to coach football at Notre Dame. Unheard of they said. A high school coach, even from powerful Moeller High in Cincinnati, would never get the job. But Gerry Faust kept praying and yes, miracles do happen, and one day he became the head coach of Notre Dame.

It is impossible not to like Gerry Faust. He bounds into your life and overwhelms you with good feelings. He always seems to be there on the campus, at the banquets, at practice, at the games. He is as much a part of Notre Dame as anyone I know. Sure, I wish his record was better. He does too. I remember sports publicity chief, Roger Valdiserri describing Faust's joy at getting the job. It was like a fairy tale come true. How he loved it. How he loved being a part of Notre Dame. It was such an exciting, heartwarming story. But today most of us only remember his record. Those five years. The 30 wins, 26 defeats, and one tie. It wasn't easy for him or for Notre Dame. The fans were restless. The alumni were grumbling. They kept hoping every year would be different. Unfortunately, it wasn't. If there ever was a story you wanted to have a happy ending, this was it. He was such a good guy. You hated the way it was coming down. And then one day it was over.

But Gerry Faust didn't go away and hide. He didn't complain. He didn't make excuses. Only now in this book do you get to know what it was really like. That dream. Those feelings. Sky high one minute. Lower than low the next. But always that chin up. This enormous leap in a profession based on wins and losses. What a ride.

Gerry Faust will tell you he may not have been the right coach for Notre Dame but he was the right man. He still is.

Regis Philbin
Notre Dame Class of 1953

Left to right: Lank Smith, Terry Brennan, Lou Holtz, Gerry Faust, Hank Stram, Roger Valdiserri, Regis Philbin.

1

■ THE GOLDEN DREAM ■

The skirt stopped me cold and turned me into a puddle of sweat. I could see it beneath one of the Indianapolis restaurant restroom stalls. There were legs under this skirt, and they didn't look like any legs I'd ever seen in a men's room. They weren't hairy.

Jiminy! This was all I needed.

Off the road and in this restaurant, I thought I would be safe. I thought I had escaped. I thought, finally, I could relax with my wife and celebrate a lifelong dream come true. It hadn't been easy getting there, and I don't mean the years of coaching football. We were being followed.

Reporters in a helicopter had been buzzing like bumblebees above I-74, the interstate highway between Cincinnati and Indianapolis, searching for our car, for me. When Notre Dame announced I had been chosen to become the 24th coach in its storied football history, the media began a frantic search for me. I couldn't hide, but I could run. These people were serious. They blitzed my home with calls, one after another. The ringing wouldn't stop. My son, Gerry, answered them.

"Where's your dad?" the reporters asked him.

"He's in a car with Mom," Gerry said.

"Where? What kind of car? What color?"

My dad was standing nearby, listening. I'd called him and my mom and asked them to come to Cincinnati from Dayton to take care of the kids for a couple of days. Now they had to take care of this too. Gerry was ready to spill it all to the reporters. They didn't even have to pull out his fingernails. He was young then and as honest as he is today. But my dad, my old football coach, the only person who knew what had been going on during all those months of clandestine conversations and waiting, stepped in and saved both of his namesakes.

"Gerry," he told my son, "give me the phone."

Then my dad informed the reporters how much he appreciated their interest in me. He thanked them. He told them he knew they were just trying to do their jobs.

"But," he said, gently, "I don't think the model of Gerry's car or its color is important. You can see Gerry tomorrow in South Bend."

I was going to make headlines all right, but not the ones my dad expected.

As I stood frozen to the floor in Indianapolis I could see the headlines in the next day's papers: New Notre Dame head coach caught in women's restroom!

What would Father Edmund Joyce and Father Theodore Hesburgh say? They run Notre Dame, Father Joyce as executive vice president and Father Hesburgh as president. And hey, what would my wife say? I leave her at a table in the dining room to make some telephone calls and the calls I end up having to make are to my attorney, Ken Schneider, and a bail bondsman.

How had I gotten myself into this mess?

During the next five years, other people would ask me that question. They still ask me. But they aren't talking about how I ended up in a women's restroom on the November Monday in 1980 on which Notre Dame announced it would write the name of a high school coach from Cincinnati alongside Knute Rockne's and Ara Parseghian's.

There is a simple explanation about that women's restroom. I wish the rest of the story were as simple—and funny.

The restaurant hadn't labeled its restrooms Men and Women. Instead, it had put those cute little figures on the doors. You know the ones—they're supposed to look like a man and woman, but they don't look like either one. They look like the Pat character on "Saturday Night Live." I can never tell whether it's a man or a woman.

I wasn't paying much attention to restroom doors that evening. I'd just made my first recruiting calls for Notre Dame, and I was so excited I needed a restroom.

On our way to South Bend, where the next day there would be a massive press conference to introduce me as the Notre Dame coach, my wife, Marlene, and I had stopped at about 6 o'clock to eat. The place had class. A nice steak house. I'd eaten there before, but my mind was on a different sort of beef this night.

"Marlene," I said, "I've got to use the phone. I've got to call a couple of my players. I'll be right back."

I hadn't even gotten to South Bend, where we were supposed to meet Father Ned Joyce at 8 or 8:30 p.m. at the Morris Inn, but I felt I had to be on the telephone to three of my players at Moeller High School. I called offensive tackle Doug Williams, fullback Mark Brooks and linebacker Mike Larkin, the older brother of Barry Larkin of the Cincinnati Reds.

"This is Mr. Faust," I told them.

I know it sounds formal, but that's what my players always called me. They never called me Coach, always Mr. Faust. I never asked them to. It was just one of the things the kids at Moeller did, as a sign of respect. Respect is one thing I can understand. Our principal at Moeller wanted me to call him Larry, but I never could.

He is like a brother to me. I love the man. But to me, he was and is Father Krusling. Same with Father Joyce and Father Hesburgh. I couldn't even bring myself to call them Father Ned and Father Ted.

Father Joyce had telephoned me just before 3 that Monday afternoon, and I hadn't had a chance to talk to my Moeller players before leaving Cincinnati for South Bend. Father Joyce wanted me to get on the road as soon as possible after he called to offer me the job. He knew the media would be on my heels, and, boy, were they! I felt as if we were playing hide-and-seek. For a while there, Richard Kimball, the Fugitive, wasn't the only man on the run in Indiana.

When I called my players, I didn't have to play games. Though I hadn't talked to them directly about leaving Moeller after 18 seasons, they knew. We had discussed it in a roundabout way during the season that had just ended. I'd told them that despite the fact the newspapers were speculating I would be going to Notre Dame, I was their coach. Now that the speculation had proved true, I still wanted to be their coach.

"Congratulations, Mr. Faust," the players said, one after another.

"I want you to come with me," I told them. "I want you to go from Moeller to Notre Dame and let's win together there the way we have at Moeller. I'm offering you room and board, tuition, books and fees."

All three players told me the same thing.

"Mr. Faust," they said, "we'd love to be with you."

Two of the three, Larkin and Brooks, did come to South Bend. I got so excited at the prospect that I ended up in the women's restroom. When I saw that skirt and those legs beneath the stall, I said to myself: "Oh my gosh. I'm in the wrong place." If I cussed, this would have been a good time for something stronger than "Oh my gosh."

I did an about-face and got out of there. It was a great move —but one I never thought I'd have to make at Notre Dame.

I'd loved Notre Dame as long as I can remember. When I was in the fifth or sixth grade and playing Catholic Youth Organization football, I'd ride my bike to practice with my cleats slung over my handlebars, my helmet on my head, whistling the Notre Dame Victory March. Even in the fourth grade I knew what I wanted and I wasn't bashful about telling others. Ask my friend, Paul Taulbee. My dad was coaching Dayton Chaminade High School, and Paul and I were arguing over who was the best coach in the city. I told him my dad was and there wasn't any question about it. What's more, I told Paul, one day I was going to be the head coach at Notre Dame.

Paul's mouth dropped open.

"Yeah, sure," he said. "And I'm going to be the President of the United States."

When I first wrote to Father Joyce to express my interest in being his coach at Notre Dame, I didn't tell him that choosing me was pre-ordained. That was in 1977. I don't know why I decided to write that letter. I just did.

Father Joyce didn't think I was crazy, but other people did.

Andy Urbanic was coaching at Penn Hills in those days, and Penn Hills was one of the outstanding Pittsburgh teams that we played when I was at Moeller. Well, Andy heard before our game that I wanted to be the Notre Dame coach.

"Not only do we have to play Moeller, and they're good," Urbanic told everyone, "but we have to play a crazy guy. He thinks he's going to be the coach at Notre Dame some day. I'm telling you, the guy's nuts."

Most people probably felt the way Andy did. I know it sounded crazy, this high school coach with no college coaching experience thinking he could jump right to Notre Dame. But Father Joyce wrote a nice reply to that first letter. He said they were very happy with Coach Dan Devine and that he was doing an excellent job, but that he appreciated my interest and also he appreciated the quality of the young men we had sent to Notre Dame to be a part of its football program.

I'd talked to Father Joyce once before on the phone. He had called to ask if it would be a good idea for him to call Tim Koegel, a quarterback of ours that Notre Dame was recruiting. I said: "Father, if you call Tim, you'll get him. Tim's uncle is a priest and if a priest from Notre Dame calls, it will really mean something to him."

So Father Joyce called, and Tim went to Notre Dame.

The year after I wrote that first letter to Father Joyce—it was 1978—I invited him to speak at the 50th Anniversary banquet of the Greater Cincinnati League. We had some more correspondence about his appearance, and when he was giving what I thought was a great speech, he seemed to look over at me a couple of times in an unusual way. We made eye contact as if there were a bond between us. But that was the end of it. At least, I thought it was.

"I remember meeting Gerry in mingling with the crowd," Father Joyce says today. "But I'm sure even before that time I had been interested in his career and following him at Moeller from a distance."

I found out later that Father Joyce couldn't help but follow my career.

"I don't know when all this started," Father Joyce says, "but I used to get letters from some guy in Cincinnati. He'd send me all these clippings on Moeller, and I would read them with some curiosity. I didn't know the person writing the letters. It was some lawyer."

Some lawyer? It was my lawyer. But I didn't know at the time that he was doing this. He was just being a friend. He knew the dream and believed in it.

"Quite a few things came from me," Cincinnati attorney Ken Schneider says. "I felt they ought to be aware of Gerry and the value he would be to Notre Dame, the value I saw in him. Gerry is a way of life. He's an example of the way life ought to be lived, a life we all should emulate. I thought I could be of assistance."

"Obviously," Father Joyce says, "he thought Gerry would be a great coach at Notre Dame. That came out in the letters. They were always well-written and on nice stationery. He planted that bug in my ear. But the thing that interested me most in Gerry was the kids whom we had gotten from Moeller. They were all, I thought, outstanding young men, the kind of guys we'd like to have at Notre Dame as student-athletes. I thought Gerry was giving the proper kind of leadership to them."

I'd been to South Bend only two or three times before we drove into the city the night of November 24, 1980, and headed for the Morris Inn, where Father Joyce was to meet Marlene and me. The first time I was in South Bend, I had been a high school senior from Chaminade High School. It was a Friday before Notre Dame played the University of Southern California and there were a hundred recruits on campus. It was a different time. Colleges could put high school players through workouts in those days. So we stayed in the dorms. They gave us football shoes and divided us by position. I can still hear the coaches.

"Quarterbacks over here," one of them shouted.

I started trotting to the spot the coach indicated and 18 other guys began to run along with me. Someone once asked me how many of them were better than I was, and I told him 18. He laughed. I wasn't trying to be funny. It sure wasn't funny at the time. I think Len Dawson was there. He ended up in the Pro Football Hall of Fame. I don't know who else. All I know is that I watched the other quarterbacks throw the football and when it came my turn, I knew I wasn't in their class. Those were the days when schools could offer partial scholarships and that's what they offered me. I think they did it because my dad had great teams at Chaminade, and Notre Dame wanted to continue to have his support when it tried to recruit his players.

I turned down that scholarship, but not because I knew I wasn't good enough. I'd have gone to Notre Dame just to be part of the team and to graduate from the University. I turned it down because my dad was a Catholic high school teacher. We didn't have much money to pay for college. We had something more important, though. They call it family values today. We just called it love. The only thing that love couldn't do was pay the tuition. I needed a full scholarship. That's how I ended up at the University of Dayton, which I don't regret one bit. I love Dayton to this day.

Because we approached preparation for each game of the season at Moeller as a seven-day-a-week job, just as college coaching staffs do, there had been no time in the fall to sneak away to South Bend to visit my former Moeller players who had gone on to contribute so much to Notre Dame's success.

During his speech at that GCL Banquet, the one during which Father Joyce looked in my direction several times, he said something about me and the 14 players we had sent to Notre Dame during the 1970s that, at least as I look at it in retrospect, hinted at his willingness to see a high school coach in a Notre Dame frame of reference. "We owe him a lot," Father Joyce said. "He has sent us many fine young men. He is the kind of man we want our coaches to be."

The kind of man we want our coaches to be.

Maybe if we hadn't just lost 13-12 to Cincinnati Princeton—our only regular-season loss in eight years—I would have heard in those generous words the hope of a dream to be fulfilled. I didn't. I was too upset. And even those as close to me as Denny Dressman, who wrote a book about my years at Moeller, only recognized after the fact that Notre Dame is the kind of place to factor the principles of a person into the equation of choosing a coach. Coaches can't always control what happens on the field, even when they've prepared their teams properly. But their values, the way they conduct their lives, can remain a constant.

We lost that Princeton game to a last-second, 37-yard field goal that hit one of the uprights and bounced between them. You could say I lost that game. We were leading 12-10 with a minute to go and I decided we should punt from Princeton's 40-yard line. I wanted to bury Princeton as deep in its own territory as possible, to make it impossible for it to score a touchdown or even get into field-goal position with so little time remaining. I was confident our defense could protect against the big play.

There was one thing I didn't know.

The play before we were to punt, our center had lost a contact lens. All of a sudden, he came running to the sideline. I didn't realize why and before I could get to him and ask what the problem was, he had run back onto the field to snap the ball to the punter. He had removed his other lens and was snapping without them. He couldn't see. He sails the ball over our punter's head. Princeton gets it and throws one pass. A kid makes an unbelievable catch. They kick the field goal and win. I wasn't in any mood for a banquet, even a couple of days later. I felt bad not only for myself and the other coaches but also for our players. Dog-gone it! If we had won that game, we could have won six straight state championships. You remember those things. But more than that, you remember the kids who were a part of the championships.

That's why in the spring of 1980 when Marlene said, "Let's go to Notre Dame to the spring game and see the kids play," I agreed, if only after arguing that I was too busy. Marlene knew what was important. She became close to all the players at Moeller.

While we went to South Bend to visit with and watch Tim Koegel, Bob Crable and Harry Oliver, Tony Hunter, and Rick Naylor in the spring game, I had someone else I wanted to visit. The first place I went was the Grotto. It's my favorite spot on campus. I find such peace there. I have a special devotion to the Blessed Mother. For as long as I can remember, I've prayed to her to intercede for me with Her Son, Our Lord. So I lit candles for my family and my parents. Then I lit another candle and made a promise to the Blessed Mother. I told her that if I ever became coach at Notre Dame, I would visit the Grotto every day I was in South Bend. I would never be too busy. I would never forget. Three weeks later, Father Joyce, who was also chairman of the Faculty Board in Control of Athletics, telephoned me at school. That call changed my life.

"Gerry," someone said, "you've got a call. Some priest."

I was in the Moeller locker room with the other coaches and I went to a phone having no idea that the priest would be Father Joyce.

"Gerry Faust," I said.

"Gerry," the voice replied, "this is Father Joyce. I'll be in Cincinnati on business and I'd like to meet with you. Could you make it?"

"Father, I'd love to see you."

So on a May day in 1980, I drove downtown to the Clarion Hotel. I had no idea why Father Joyce wanted to see me. There wasn't anything going on at Notre Dame, as far as I knew. I rode the elevator up to his room and knocked on the door. I never gave a thought to my promise to the Blessed Mother three weeks earlier.

Father Joyce invited me into his hotel room. He's a man who fills you with awe every time you meet him. He commands respect, as does Father Hesburgh, by the way he carries himself. People tell me—even some who like me—that I'm not in danger of winning an endorsement contract with Brooks Brothers. I look more comfortable in a sweatshirt with a whistle around my neck than in a blue pinstriped suit and Jaccard tie. Not Father Joyce. He's good-looking. Clean-cut. Tall. Self-assured. But when he met me at the door, he had on a turtleneck sweater. I'd never seen him in anything except a Roman collar. It shocked me. The real shock, however, was still to come.

Even in casual clothes, Father Joyce is an impressive man, the kind to whom you listen carefully, worried you might miss something important. He has a set of principles that don't change when his clothes do. Both he and Father Hesburgh can be very firm, even dogmatic. But they are two of the best men I've ever known. Because of all we've gone through together, I have the greatest respect and deepest love for both of them.

Father Joyce and I talked for a half hour before he came to the point of why he had asked to see me.

"Gerry," he said, "I'm going to talk to you confidentially. Are you interested in being the Notre Dame football coach?"

The question was so unexpected it stunned me. I hardly knew what to say.

Sure, I'd written that letter to Father Joyce in 1977, but I'd never told anyone about it. I never made a secret that my ambition was to coach Notre Dame. Not since the fourth grade. I'd said so during interviews with the media. I'd told friends. In fact, for eight or nine years, I had told Father Krusling that I wouldn't sign my Moeller contract unless he'd give me permission to leave during the school year if Notre Dame ever offered me the job of head coach. He'd just laugh.

"Here," Father Krusling would say, shoving the contract to me, "just sign this."

In the last couple of years, though, he had stopped laughing.

"You know, Gerry," Father Krusling said, "I think it might happen."

Now, Father Joyce was telling me the same thing.

"Father Joyce," I said, "that would be a dream come true."

"Gerry," Father Joyce continued, "there's a possibility that the job may open after next football season. Coach Devine's wife has been sick. She needs a warm climate in order to live a more normal life. Coach Devine has expressed some concern about this, but we haven't sat down and discussed it fully. I don't know where it is at this stage. So I'd appreciate it if you didn't say a word about this to anybody."

"Father, I won't," I said.

There were no promises that I'd get the job. But what happened next may have been the most important moment in my life.

"I have a couple of questions I'd like to ask you," Father Joyce said.

"Sure, Father."

"Gerry," he said, "recruiting is the lifeblood of college football, of all college athletics, and you've never recruited before. This is a great concern I have, because it is a very difficult phase of college athletics."

I knew what I wanted to say. I didn't hesitate. Unconsciously I had been preparing for years to be able to answer this question, to allay these very concerns.

"Father," I said, "recruiting is the least of my problems. I've had an opportunity very few coaches in the country have ever had. I've been at Moeller High School, where we've had so many great athletes that all the best head coaches in the country have had to make visits. I've observed for 18 years every head coach, every top assistant. The Bear Bryants. The John Robinsons. The Woody Hayeses. The Joe Paternos. They've all walked through our door to recruit, because I've guided every young man in our football program through the process.

"I've seen how those coaches turn kids on and how they turn them off. I've made mental notes of how to be the best recruiter in college athletics. For 18 years, I've had the best schooling anyone could have. Couple that with Notre Dame's mystique and prestige and I can out-recruit anybody."

Father Joyce didn't say anything. And he never asked me his second question. Years later, Father Joyce remembered that moment.

"That was a good answer," Father Joyce recalls. "I decided with his personality that it wouldn't be that difficult. With his salesmanship, Gerry could recruit."

During the next six months I kept the promise of confidentiality I had made to Father Joyce—with one exception. I didn't tell my wife or my children, and I didn't take any of my coaches into my confidence. I didn't even tell Father Krusling, though I did make sure that my Moeller contract contained the no-longer-laughable Golden Dome Clause. Some guys have golden parachute clauses. I had something better, and I had to tell at least one person: My high school coach—my dad.

I knew it would go no further. I told him he couldn't even tell Mom.

"Dad," I said, "there is a slight chance that I could be the next coach at Notre Dame. I wanted to let you know because of what you've done for me as a father and as a coach."

There was another reason I told dad. A selfish one.

"What do you think?" I asked.

Maybe I was dreaming and playing the fool. Maybe it was impossible to jump from high school—even a high school as successful and as big-time as Moeller—to Notre Dame. Maybe I didn't know enough. Maybe I thought I knew too much. I wasn't sure.

"Gerry," Dad told me, "you've always wanted to go there. If you get the opportunity, take it."

That was all I needed to hear.

I don't know what I would have done had Dad expressed reservations. I never had to think about it, because Dad never hesitated and I knew if he had had doubts, he would have shared them with me. We had not only a special father-son relationship but also a relationship deepened by our mutual commitment to coaching and making a difference in the lives of young men.

Father Joyce had said he would get back to me, but weeks and months passed and I heard nothing. May turned to June and June to July and then it was August and we had begun to prepare another Moeller team, one that would prove special in more ways than I could know during those dog days of summer.

It may sound Pollyannish, but I wasn't thinking about Notre Dame football. I was thinking about Moeller. That's what I told the media when writers showed up en masse the Saturday morning we were to scrimmage Louisville St. X, the best team in Kentucky. There had been no leaks about my conversation with Father Joyce, but because of my long-time avowed interest in Notre Dame the halftime show during the preceding night's National Football League preseason game had created a media parade to Nippert Stadium. The television cameras weren't focused on the scrimmage. They were on me. I knew it would happen the minute I received a phone call in the locker room that Friday afternoon. It was from an old friend whose son was then a Notre Dame player. He told his father there was something interesting happening at Notre Dame and to watch the halftime show of the NFL exhibition game.

It was one of our few nights off during the Moeller season, and I had promised to take Mar to a movie. The movie could wait. I thought the reason why could wait, too.

"Mar," I said, "there's a heck of a football game on TV tonight. Can we stay home and watch it?"

Even then, Marlene had been a coach's wife a long time. She's smart and knows the game. So she knew there wasn't any NFL preseason game worth breaking my promise and our date. She wanted to dropkick me.

"Mar," I told her, "I'll take you to the movie next Saturday. I'd really like to watch this game."

She gave in. She always gave in to me on things like that. She's a great wife, but not because she lets me win more often than my on-field opponents. She's a great wife because she supports me in a way that has always made me feel I could be anything and do anything I want. Our vows should have included the phrase that we would love, honor and run interference for each other. But, like I said, Mar is smart.

When halftime came, she got up to go upstairs from our family room, which was in the basement of a house in Cincinnati that she adored. I stopped her.

"Mar, there's supposed to be something interesting at halftime," I said. "I got a call today. I'm curious."

So she sat back down beside me and we watched as Dave Dials came on ABC with Dan Devine, who announced that he would retire as Notre Dame coach after the upcoming season. I never said a word, but Marlene started to cry.

"Mar," I said, "what's wrong?"

"Gerry," she said, "you're going to get that job, and I don't want to leave Cincinnati."

Right then, I knew. I said to myself: I can't tell her anything about what's going on. Of course, it was already too late. She didn't know, yet she did. She knew, because she knew me.

We didn't talk any more about the fact Notre Dame would be looking for a coach. I had to talk to the media, though. I told them that I wasn't interested in Notre Dame at that moment. I was interested only in Moeller.

"We're trying to win another state championship," I explained. "These kids have worked hard and I'm not going to take my attention away from them. The seniors have dedicated themselves to winning a state championship, and I've dedicated myself to them." It was true. Every word. I didn't know what my status was as far as Notre Dame was concerned, but I knew where I stood with the kids at Moeller. They trusted me.

Five or six weeks after Dan Devine's announcement, Father Joyce called me again. He asked a few questions, which I've forgotten now, and one I haven't. He wanted to know when our season would be over.

"I hope it won't be over until November 23," I told him. "That's the Sunday of the state championship game."

"Gerry," he said, "it's about 50 percent certain that you're going to be the next Notre Dame coach."

He hadn't mentioned my chances before. He had mentioned, however, what he would repeat often and that was that I shouldn't say anything about this to anybody. And I didn't. At the time I was cooperating with Denny Dressman, an assistant managing editor at the *Cincinnati Enquirer,* on the book he was writing about Moeller football and me. Denny had been a sportswriter when I started the Moeller program, and he had gotten to know me and my teams. I liked Denny. I considered him a trusted friend. But I didn't tell Denny. I didn't tell anyone except my dad, and I knew that Father Joyce would understand that.

Keeping quiet didn't quell the rumors. They would get hot, then cool, then rise again and boil over in the media. If the rumors had been mercury in a thermometer, they would have burst out the top in late October or early November. I don't recall the exact date, but I know it was two days after Bill Gleason from the *Chicago Sun-Times* had called.

I didn't know Gleason. But I liked the guy right away. He was gruff on the phone. No polish. He sounded dogmatic but straightforward. No pussy-footing around for this guy. He just hit you with it. Jiminy, did he hit me with it.

"Putting in the paper tomorrow morning," Gleason said, "a headline that you're the next football coach at Notre Dame. What's your reaction?"

What's my reaction? My reaction was that this could sabotage everything. This could kill me. If I said the wrong thing, Father Joyce might wonder if he had the right man. But I don't lie. I knew that saying I had no comment would be as good as confirming Gleason was right. And I didn't know if he was right. My mind raced.

"I think it's stupid," I finally told Gleason.

"Why?"

Like I said, this guy doesn't waste words.

"Why?" I said. "Well, because I've not been offered the job and I think you're making a big mistake and putting your neck on the line."

I hoped that would cause him enough doubt that he wouldn't go with the story. I should have known better. I did know better.

Gleason wasn't backing off.

"All my sources up here tell me it's a lock," he said.

"Well, you know more than I know. If you put that in the paper, you're making a big mistake. But you have to do what you have to do."

Unlike some of my colleagues in coaching, I have had what I consider a good relationship with most members of the media. Not perfect. But pretty dog-gone good. I think it's because I try to understand their jobs. I would learn later it was easier to appreciate the media's role when you're winning as often as we won at Moeller and more difficult when you weren't winning as often as people thought you should at Notre Dame. Which was every Saturday in the fall.

Gleason, who's now the columnist at the *South Bend Tribune*, didn't chew me up the way he does those cigars of his. He could have by asking if I had talked to Father Joyce about the job. I wouldn't have lied. I'd have told him that I had talked with Father Joyce and that I often do about many things. But it would have provided another grain of information on the scale that tipped toward the headline: Faust Next Notre Dame Coach. I was worried.

I called Father Joyce right away. I told his secretary, Pat Roth, who answered the phone, that it was an emergency. When Father Joyce came on the line, I told him what had happened and explained what I had said.

"Gerry," he said, "that was perfect. You have not been offered the job. You were up-front. Honest. You answered well."

Then he said something else that made me feel the way I felt that evening in the Cincinnati hotel room when he said he had two questions to ask me and after I answered his first about recruiting, the second question was forgotten.

"One thing you'll find out on the college level," Father Joyce told me, "is that you have to deal with the press a lot. It doesn't look like you're going to have a problem with that."

I had another problem, though. I knew that the day after that headline and story appeared in the *Chicago Sun-Times*, it also would be plastered across the front of the *Cincinnati Enquirer* and the

Cincinnati Post sports sections and on every Cincinnati television sportscast. I got the call from Gleason on a Thursday and we had a big game the next night against Roger Bacon High School. I didn't want the team to be distracted, but neither did I want the players to pick up the papers and see the headlines without having been warned. Notre Dame wasn't going away. So I brought it up.

"You're probably going to see in the newspapers Saturday that I'm going to be the next Notre Dame football coach," I told the players and coaches. "There isn't any more truth to that right now than the man in the moon. I'm only interested in one thing right now and that is to help you win the state championship. You've dedicated four years to that dream and I owe it to you to help you. Right now, the only thing I'm concerned about is what I've always been concerned about and that is Moeller football.

"Whatever you hear or read, don't believe. The only thing right now is Moeller. Things are written that never come true. So let's drop it. Just forget that and work each week toward our goal of winning the state championship."

I must have set a record for the number of "right nows" I used.

Even if I had to use a hedge that could be interpreted as con-firmation that something was going on between Notre Dame and me, I'm glad I did. Saturday morning's papers—both of them—read: Gerry Faust—Next Coach at Notre Dame? I got blitzed with it. At least they used a question mark, and neither the kids nor the coaches brought it up again. To take their minds off Notre Dame, I pushed the players even harder during the next weeks. But I couldn't get my own mind totally off my dream. The phone wouldn't let me.

Two weeks after Gleason had called, Father Joyce called and said he'd like to meet with me again. He said he'd come to Cincin-nati, but I told him he didn't have to do that, that I'd meet him half way. So we set a time: Sunday evening in Indianapolis, following our last regular-season game. We had beaten Princeton 14-13 in a sold-out stadium to finish the season with a 10-0 record. The coach-ing staff had spent Sunday preparing to play Princeton again in the first round of the playoffs. It wasn't as difficult as it might have been had we not held back some plays on offense and a number of defensive schemes. We knew that win or lose that regular-season game, we were going to have to play Princeton again in the play-offs. It made sense not to show Princeton everything it might see on the road to the state championship.

The game plan fell together quickly. When we were finished, I slipped away to Blue Ash Airport, where I had made arrangements to be flown to Indianapolis in a small private plane. It was the first plane I'd ever rented. They didn't know why I was going to Indianapolis. They thought it was for a speech or a meeting.

I got a cab to the hotel where Father Joyce awaited me in a room upstairs. He was having dinner.

"Would you like something?" he asked me. "I can have dinner sent up."

"Father," I said, "my stomach is too nervous."

It wasn't from the plane ride.

For two hours, Father Joyce and I talked. When the subject became assistant coaches and salaries, I knew it was serious. Then, he offered me a salary. He never offered me the job. Just a salary. I think Father Joyce and I had that in common. He didn't lie, either, and with this approach he wouldn't have to lie if someone asked him whether I had been offered the job. His choice also had to be approved by the Notre Dame Faculty Board in Control of Athletics, a formality which, I understand, proved an example of the strong leadership Father Joyce can provide.

When we talked about salary, Father Joyce said: "What would it take if we decided to hire you?"

Well, I couldn't have cared less about the money. That may seem naive, and maybe it was, but I wanted the job more than anything in the world. More than any amount of money. If you've ever been lucky enough to have been offered your dream job, you understand.

"Father," I said, "just give me whatever you think is right. I don't care. I just want to be at Notre Dame."

"What about this amount?" he asked, and showed me a figure.

I told him that was fine.

Notre Dame, I would discover, never pays its coaches a higher base salary than its highest-paid professor receives. I like that. Sure, coaches can earn a lot more, what with television and radio shows and other outside deals, but the concept is sound. A coach should not be worth more to a university than an equally good professor.

"What do you make at Moeller?" Father Joyce asked me.

"Father, you don't want to know."

At Moeller, I could have been called Gerry Faust Enterprises. It wasn't that I was trying to make a lot of money. I just had a lot of jobs. I was football coach, athletic director, fund raiser and moderator of the booster club meetings. A car dealer provided me with a car. I arranged that on my own. But the most lucrative arrangement I had was giving motivational speeches all over the country. Moeller let me do this because it was good for the school. I wasn't earning the $20,000 and $30,000 per speech you hear about today, but I was well paid.

"I spoke 36 times last year," I told Father Joyce. Then I told him what I had made with all my jobs.

"I'll add $10,000 to the contract," he said.

"No, Father," I told him, "we made a deal. I'm happy with that. I just want my coaches to be well paid, because I think you're only as good as the coaches around you."

I must have said the right thing again. When we parted, we shook hands and Father Joyce said: "Gerry, I'll get back to you. It's about 80 percent."

The percentage kept creeping up. During the next three weeks, each time Father Joyce called, my odds improved. But he never offered me the job. I didn't even know who else was in the running. I didn't care. And I didn't tell a soul. Nobody. I had calls from all over the country regarding the speculation.

If any of those interested had happened upon Gene Corrigan and me at the Greater Cincinnati Airport, the speculation would have been heightened even further. But when, at Father Joyce's request, I drove out to meet Mr. C, I wasn't sure whether our meeting would be a step toward finalizing my selection as coach or the beginning of its unraveling.

I didn't know Gene Corrigan. Heck, I hadn't even known he was going to become the Notre Dame athletic director. Things are kept quiet before they happen at Notre Dame. Father Joyce hadn't said that the University would be hiring Virginia's athletic director and that he'd be taking over a month before a new coach would be named.

"Father Joyce had pretty well made up his mind that he was going to hire Gerry," Gene Corrigan says. "I told him that the one thing I wanted to do before I told him I was going to come to Notre Dame was to meet Gerry. If I did not like Gerry, that was going to affect my decision. I was concerned about a high school coach coming in and taking the job. I would be in any college,

Notre Dame or not. But I went to meet Gerry and how can you not like Gerry Faust?"

The feeling was mutual. We hit it off immediately. We met at the hotel at the airport for two-and-a-half hours. We didn't talk much football or even coaching. We talked more about our families and philosophies of how a man should live his life. I didn't know what kind of athletic director Mr. C was, but I knew a little more about him after our talk. I was impressed. So this is what I told Gene Corrigan:

"If you don't feel comfortable with my candidacy, Mr. Corrigan, I'm willing to step aside right now."

As I had with my father, I wanted to give Mr. C the opportunity to tell me if he thought I was the wrong man or coach for Notre Dame, if he foresaw the leap from Moeller to Notre Dame as too great a leap to make.

"Gerry," Mr. Corrigan said, "I don't have a problem."

"Great," I said.

Gene Corrigan, however, was not the only person who had to be won over. While we were winning playoff games at Moeller, Father Joyce was winning over the Faculty Board in Control of Athletics.

I was told this story by a Notre Dame faculty member: When Father Joyce met with the Faculty Board in Control of Athletics, there were five or six candidates on whom he had information in manila folders. Each board member received a folder for each candidate.

"This is coach so-and-so," Father Joyce would say.

And in each folder there would be two or three sheets of paper.

Then he said: "This is Coach Gerry Faust."

The folders he distributed were an inch thick.

They knew Father Joyce's choice without him saying a word.

"We don't have too much of a democracy here," Father Joyce says. "But in Gerry's case, before we closed in at the final moment, I did convene a group of about six or eight people whom I thought were objective and would be good advisors and were important to Notre Dame in one way or another. Some were professors. Several were trustees. I never did say, when Gerry didn't work out, that we had this committee and we all agreed. I was acting so unilaterally that everybody could say this was just one man's choice."

During the two weeks following my meeting with Father Joyce in Indianapolis, we beat Princeton again, this time by a more impressive 28-3, and shut out Upper Arlington, a Columbus suburb, 36-0. Those victories created the perfect state championship game, the first final between the all-time power of the North, legendary Massillon, and the power of the South, Moeller. That week would have been dramatic enough had the telephone not rung at my home on Tuesday night.

It was the first time Father Joyce had called my house. Marlene answered.

"Gerry," she said, "Father Joyce is on the phone."

"Thanks, Marlene."

I went into the other room and shut the door. It didn't stay shut for long.

Father Joyce asked me at what time and at what number he could call me the following Monday, the day after the championship game. He said he wanted to call between 2 and 3 p.m., and I said 3 would be fine.

"I'll call you then," he said. "And good luck against Massillon."

As soon as I got off the phone, Marlene said: "What's going on?"

During all the time the stories were appearing in the papers and I was being asked all these questions, she hadn't said a word. Not since that night when we watched Dan Devine announce his retirement and she began to cry. Father Joyce's phone call confirmed what she already knew in her heart. She'd have to leave the home she loved for the man she loved even more.

Marlene may have had reservations about leaving Cincinnati, but she hated it when anybody suggested that Notre Dame was not my destiny. On one of the days after Father Joyce's call, Mark Purdy, then the *Cincinnati Enquirer* sports columnist, wrote a column explaining why I was never going to be the coach at Notre Dame. It was long. He had reasons piled on top of reasons. Some of them were pretty good. I just chuckled. Marlene, on the other hand, got upset, and she does not forget such a story, as she was to prove following the championship game against Massillon.

We played the championship game in a gray mist at the University of Cincinnati's Nippert Stadium. The game had sold out in 24 hours. We sold 17,000 tickets at Moeller and Massillon sold 12,000. We both could have sold more. I had lines down the hallways and streaming outside the school, where the tickets were sold. They weren't buying tickets to see Gerry Faust coach his last game. They were buying them because this was the biggest game in high school football. Not just in Ohio; it was the biggest game anywhere. Paul Brown, late owner and coach of the Cincinnati Bengals, had made Massillon famous when it was a steel town. Now, in the age of playoff football, Moeller had taken Massillon's throne and the Tigers wanted it back.

Massillon and the Fausts have a history. In 1946, my dad took one of his great, unbeaten Chaminade teams to Massillon and lost, 35-12. Though it had been a while, I wanted a Faust to beat Massillon. I wanted it for my dad. I wanted it for my players, who had turned a Moeller team less talented than some into one they could take pride in forever. And I wanted it for myself and the coaches. It would be our last game together. They didn't know that, at least not with any certainty, as we dressed at Moeller and boarded the buses for the drive to Nippert Stadium.

It was an early-arriving crowd, drawn to the stadium not only by the lure of the game itself but also by geography. The Massillon fans had had a 200-mile drive, and they didn't want to miss a moment of this day. They started early. They were there, 12,000 of them, in their black and orange rain gear, when we arrived, and they rose as one and began a chant that cut through that mist like a beacon.

It was simple, direct, confident.

"We want Moeller. We want Moeller. We want Moeller."

To reach our locker room, which was halfway up the stands, we had to walk through those Massillon fans who wanted us so badly. I told the players to walk single file with their helmets on, to keep their mouths shut and their ears open. I wanted them to hear it ...

"We want Moeller. We want Moeller. We want Moeller."

In the locker room I met the seniors privately, as I always had done before their last game at Moeller. I knew it was my last game, too, but I never said a word. It was their game, their team. I just told them that this was the game they would remember and live with for the rest of their lives.

They played as if they understood. With 10 seconds to go in the first half, Tony Melink kicked a 47-yard field goal to give us a 24-0 lead. As we ran off the field toward the locker room, it was the 17,000 Moeller fans who stood in unison this time and chanted over and over and over.

"You've got Moeller. You've got Moeller. You've got Moeller."

It was music to our ears.

After we'd won 30-7, Marlene rushed down to the field for what had become a tradition for us: a hug, a kiss and reminder of how much I love her. She had company. The writers had come down to the field and they were firing questions about the game. No one brought up Notre Dame, except Marlene. Mark Purdy was there, and she just couldn't resist.

"See if you ever get tickets to Notre Dame," she said, loud enough for Mark to hear.

I gave her a nudge and told her to be quiet. Mark must not have heard her. If he did, he didn't catch her meaning. I was really sweating it. At least I thought that was sweat in my eyes.

As I climbed the steps to the locker room where the championship trophy would be presented, I stopped and watched the players cavorting in the end zone, still celebrating. I can whistle like crazy and, usually, I would have whistled them off the field. This time, I just stood there and watched them in their joy, and tears streamed down my face.

In the locker room, I asked my dad to accept the championship trophy for us. He deserved it. He was the reason a Faust had beaten Massillon. When he took the trophy, he gave a speech I'll never forget.

"Starting out, you were the poorest Moeller team in the last 10 years," Fuzzy Faust told these young men. "But you made more improvement than any Moeller team in history. You worked hard and you worked together. You showed what hard work can do. You played the toughest schedule we've ever had. You beat some outstanding teams. You've earned this championship and you should be proud of it."

That night, in a celebration at the high school, I had to give what I knew would be my last speech as Moeller's coach. The gym was jammed. There had been so many great speeches before I got up, but I knew I had to get across one point: Moeller wasn't Gerry Faust or any other one person. It was all of the people in that gym, all the people at the school and all those who supported and believed in it. They made Moeller.

"No matter what obstacle Moeller may face," I told the crowd, "it always will be a special school, because of its make-up and because of the unique people it attracts."

I wanted to assure everyone that they would go on and do well but I didn't want to be obvious about it. I think the speech worked. Only one person of the 3,000 there picked up on exactly what I was saying. That was Joe Meale, who still teaches chemistry at Moeller. I'd taught Joe in high school. I guess he had studied me as well as his class work. When I came back from Notre Dame he told me: "Gerry, I had a feeling that Sunday night that you were gone." No one else knew. But a lot of people suspected.

When I got to the office that Monday morning at 7:30, I was greeted by Gordon White of the *New York Times*, Phil Hersh of the *Chicago Sun-Times*, Denny Dressman, Enos Pennington from the *Cincinnati Post*, a reporter from the *Cincinnati Enquirer* and a couple of others. I was like the Pied Piper.

When I went to the cafeteria, the writers went to the cafeteria. When the phone rang and I picked it up, they listened. When I went to chapel, they went to chapel. They wouldn't leave me alone. They were waiting for something to happen. What they didn't know is that something already had.

That weekend one of our seniors and a buddy had been driving across an unmarked railroad crossing and their car was hit by a train. The passenger was killed. I didn't know the Moeller student personally but when I checked in the office, I found out he had come to school. I went to the classroom to see if I could help him.

"How are you doing?" I asked after I'd led him into the hallway. "You must be having a rough time."

"I am," the student said.

I asked if he'd like to talk to a priest, and he said that would help. So I got Father Putka. I took over his class, and when I told the writers, they decided class was too much for them so they left. They shouldn't have if they wanted their story.

At 2:30 I was in the physics lab, where we were going to show the film of the Massillon game to the players. Twenty minutes later the phone rang in the athletic department and someone came to get me. It was the call.

"Gerry Faust," I said.

"Coach?" Father Joyce answered. "This is Father Ned."

"Yes, Father."

I'll never forget what he said next.

"Before I offer you the Notre Dame job and you accept," Father Joyce continued, "I want to tell you two things."

"Go ahead, Father."

"Number one, this job is demanding. It's going to change your lifestyle. It's going to change your family situation. You're not going to see your kids or your family much. Do you want to sacrifice that?"

"Father, I don't have a problem with that."

And, as I reflect on it now, it was no different from Moeller, because at Moeller I was traveling to speak all around the country, I was athletic director, football coach, booster club moderator, fund raiser and in charge of salary negotiations with the faculty. That meant a lot of hours. I told Father Joyce that.

"There won't be any change in the hours I spend at my job," I said.

The only difference was that at Notre Dame I was on a plane almost every day. Looking back, I made the correct assumption, and I knew that Marlene would understand, because she wanted me to be at Notre Dame.

The second thing he told me was a different matter.

"Gerry," Father Joyce said, "the Notre Dame football job is the toughest in America and you have to understand that."

I didn't. I was thinking to myself: That's not right. It's the easiest job in America. I didn't say that, though. What I said was: "Father, I accept the job."

"Congratulations," he said, "you're now the 24th head football coach at Notre Dame."

Then Father Joyce told me he wanted me in my car and on the road when Notre Dame made the announcement at 4 o'clock. The chase was about to begin, but before it did, I asked Father Joyce if I could call my parents, talk to my principal and tell one of my coaches that he'd have to take over the team.

"Go ahead," Father Joyce said. "Your principal already knows, but you go see him."

Upstairs in the principal's office, Father Krusling was waiting for me. He got up from his chair and hugged me.

"Gerry," Father Krusling said, "you belong there."

Tears filled my eyes. We were so close and had been through so much together. I'll never forget the day we were in the gym at a basketball game and I had told Father Krusling how much Moeller needed him and that he should never leave.

"Gerry," he replied, "Moeller needs you. Don't you ever leave. I'll never leave as long as you stay."

"Father," I said, "I'll never leave unless it's to go to Notre Dame."

Now, it *was* Notre Dame, and we had worked so closely and so well together and I was having a really tough time. Not only did

I consider Father Krusling to be like a brother, but I also compare our working relationship to that of Father Hesburgh and Father Joyce. They were the perfect team. We were the perfect team.

"Gerry," Father Krusling said, "I told you I'd stay as long as you were here, but if we both leave now, it'll hurt Moeller. So I'll stay one more year and then I'm going to step down."

And that's what he did.

After I talked to Father Krusling, I went back to the room where the team was watching the film and pulled my line coach, Jim Higgins, out of the room and told him: "Jim, you're going to have to take care of the team. I've got to leave. I've got to go to South Bend."

"What are you going to South Bend for?" Higgins asked. Then it clicked.

"You've got to be kidding," he said.

When I called home, Marlene knew what it meant when I said: "We've got to go, Mar. I got the job."

She knew I had gotten more than that. I had gotten my dream. The next day, having avoided the media and their helicopter, having escaped the women's restroom without being arrested, I would try to explain at the press conference how much this opportunity meant to me. That would be easy. The challenge would be to convince people that this opportunity was as good for Notre Dame as it was for me.

I couldn't sleep that Monday night. I sleep before games. Some fans have accused me of sleeping during games. The only time I can't sleep is after a game. I never sleep then, win or lose. A coach replays so many decisions in his head. This was like that.

Father Joyce had met us at the Morris Inn, but not before we had our own special welcoming committee of one—my niece Anne Marie Oberheu. A student at Saint Mary's then, she greeted us with candy and flowers, just so excited her uncle had been named Notre Dame's coach. I gave her big hug and told her I'd see her soon.

"But right now, Anne Marie," I said, "you've got to get out of here."

No one knew me then, and Father Joyce wanted to keep it that way until the Tuesday press conference. He swept in just as I saw a guy I recognized as a writer but who didn't recognize me. Father Joyce spirited us out of the Morris Inn, onto the campus and across back roads to the home of Roger Valdiserri, who was Notre Dame's assistant athletic director and sports information director.

We'd never met Roger or his wife, Elaine, but we stayed up and talked so long I should have been exhausted and able to sleep. I wasn't.

Reality had begun to set in. I was really at Notre Dame. The coach. I didn't know if I had done the right thing. I had no idea of what lay ahead. Not an inkling. I just knew I was excited because it was Notre Dame.

The morning of Tuesday, November 25, 1980, dawned bright and cold. In a private chapel set aside for Father Hesburgh and Father Joyce, Marlene and I joined new athletic director Gene Corrigan and his wife, Lena, and outgoing athletic director Moose Krause and his wife, Elise, for Mass. It was one of the most beautiful experiences I've ever had. It was quiet and moving, a stark contrast in setting to the one I would walk into at the Athletic and Convocation Center.

There were more than 100 members of the media there and, though I don't remember it and didn't dwell on it, I know skepticism set the tone of the questioning. Everyone wanted to know whether a successful high school coach without college experience could make the transition to what Father Joyce had warned would be the most demanding coaching job in America.

I live my faith, religious and athletic. I answered as honestly as I could. I told them what I had told Father Joyce about having at Moeller the best learning laboratory possible. I tried to allay their concerns, but these were persons such as Joe Doyle, sports editor of the *South Bend Tribune*, who had called me a 50-to-1 longshot to be named Notre Dame coach. The fact I had beaten Doyle's odds didn't necessarily convince everyone that I would be able to beat USC.

I understood how they felt and why. They didn't know me as well as someone like Bob Trumpy, the former NFL tight end who had gone on to become a top-notch sports broadcaster on television and radio. Trump and I were close then and still are. I'd go on his show on WLW radio in Cincinnati before Moeller was to play a big-name opponent such as Penn Hills or Brother Rice High School from Detroit. I'd been on with him that fall and he'd been kidding me about something or other, giving me a hard time, and during a commercial break, I told him: "Trump, some day I'm going to be the head coach at Notre Dame."

He laughed.

"That'll never happen," he said. "And I'll tell you what: If you are ever named coach at Notre Dame, I'll buy you a new pair of shoes, because the shoes you wear in here are terrible."

I looked down. They were just shoes. Black. Nothing fancy. A little scuffed. I guess Trump had a point. GQ wasn't going to be begging me to be the centerfold in any best-dressed coaches fashion layouts.

On the way back to Cincinnati from South Bend that night, I was listening to Trump on WLW and he was saying: "Gerry, I know you're listening. Call me. I've got to talk to you."

Hey, this was Trump. What the heck. I figured I'd stop and give him a call. I always enjoyed talking with him and he'd tried to help us at Moeller. Now I'd repay his kindnesses. I'd give him the first exclusive radio interview since I'd gotten the job he said I'd never get. There was only one problem: I couldn't find a phone for 90 miles.

Finally, I did.

"Trump," I said, "this is Gerry Faust."

"Where are you, Coach?"

"Trump, I'm in Kokomo, Indiana, at a Shell gas station, and by the way, I wear size 11D."

Before I'd left South Bend, I'd done some interviewing of my own. I'd talked briefly to Dan Devine and then I'd spent 45 minutes with Ara Parseghian. Ara, who's from Akron, Ohio, told me his perception of Notre Dame and its uniqueness. At that time Ara had separated himself from the football team, but I invited him to come back to practice, to be on the field, to talk to the team. I knew I would need all the resources I could muster, and Ara Parseghian is one of Notre Dame's greatest. So I had resources. My own and the resources of others. But I was naive, too. I know that now.

In some ways, it didn't matter. Like with my contract for instance.

After the press conference, I went to Father Joyce's office and he handed me a sheet of paper with one line on it. He signed. I signed. It said: "You have a five-year contract at Notre Dame as head football coach." That was it. That was my contract. I never had Ken Schneider, my lawyer, look at that sentence. Didn't need to. I had a handshake. At Notre Dame, that meant everything.

Father Hesburgh, Notre Dame's president, had not attended the press conference, but I did see him in Father Joyce's office. He shook my hand, congratulated me and then pointed a finger right at me.

"Gerry," Father Hesburgh said, "don't you ever cheat at Notre Dame. Win more games than you lose. I'll keep the alumni off your back, and you've got a job forever."

I never cheated. I won more games than I lost. The rest wouldn't turn out to be that easy or simple or I wouldn't be writing this while working with development and admissions at the University of Akron. As promised, however, Father Joyce and Father Hesburgh always supported me. I remember that once an alumnus wrote Father Hesburgh a letter and told him to get rid of me or he was going to stop his donations. Father Hesburgh checked what the donation was, and it was $250. He wrote the guy a short, sweet note. It read: "You keep your donation. I'll keep my coach."

"But Father," I asked, "what if it had been $2.5 million?"

He just looked at me and started laughing.

In the days, weeks, months and years ahead, I would learn that Father Joyce's description of the Notre Dame job was not blarney. I had believed the same thing everyone believes: That it's easy to recruit for Notre Dame, easy to win, that mystique makes it a football machine that anyone can run.

I was dead wrong.

That realization would come soon enough. But on the sunniest morning of my life, the day I was introduced to the world as Notre Dame coach, I walked across campus, looked up at the Golden Dome—which for so long had been my golden dream—and there stood the Blessed Mother, bathed in a yellow-orange glow that matched the golden glow in my heart.

2

■ THE GREAT LEAP ■

 I'm a rah-rah guy. I've got rah-rah in my veins. I had it when I coached in high school, and I took it to Notre Dame with me. I couldn't discard it. It would have been like chopping off my right arm. Everyone wanted to believe in the Golden Dream then. Friends. Strangers. Alumni. Students. Townspeople. Especially my family and former players. Former players like Bob Crable. In that sea of faces at my introductory press conference, there was Crabes. That big smile on his face. He looked a little older than when he played for me at Moeller High School. I know he was a lot wiser. No more Mr. Faust. He called me Fuzzy now, which is what everyone called my dad. Crabes already was an All-America linebacker and one of the reasons I thought this transition to college football would be easy.

Crabes thought so, too.

"I was really optimistic and very excited," Bob Crable recalls. "What I remember most vividly was the press conference in the Athletic and Convocation Center. Tim Koegel, who had been our quarterback at Moeller, was there with me. And there were all these people. I remember all the people. I don't remember everything that was said. But I remember, afterwards, Fuzzy coming down and grabbing me and it was just like it always had been."

My voice, part wood rasp on hard oak, part fog horn, cut through the crowd.

"Hey! Crabes!" I hollered. "How ya doin'?"

"He was slapping me on the shoulder," Crable says. "All that stuff he does. But there was something different, too. Something special. As my personality had developed at Notre Dame, I had become almost businesslike in my attitude toward football. Southern Cal would come in and I'd get pumped up for that. But you played Pitt or Michigan and it didn't matter if they came to South Bend or if you went there. It was businesslike."

I knew I could change that.

"And he did," Crable says. "I thought: Wow! This is going to be fun. I knew how intense Fuzzy could be. I wanted that enthusiasm of his to rub off on everyone. The excitement that Fuzzy brought in really got me going. I was extremely optimistic."

He wasn't alone. Among the Notre Dame coaches, Brian Boulac knew me better than anyone. He'd been to Moeller a hundred times as an assistant coach, recruiting some of our better players. We had talked for hours.

"I didn't have any reservations," Boulac says. "Not after having been with Gerry at Moeller. I thought he could come into Notre Dame and be successful. He had a good work ethic. He was very sincere."

It was more than a work ethic and sincerity that won me the job, though. I found this out from Moose Krause, whom Gene Corrigan had replaced as athletic director. After I'd been at Notre Dame for a while, Moose confided that he had checked me out with someone who not only knew me but also knew more than any man alive about the great leap I was attempting.

"You know," Moose told me, "you've got a really good friend in Paul Brown."

"I know," I said.

I will always remember the day when Paul came up to me after one of our Moeller teams had beaten Cincinnati Elder 24-21. By then, of course, Paul was running the Cincinnati Bengals. He was a legend, the former Massillon High School coach who went straight to Ohio State and then started the Cleveland Browns and coached them to championship after championship. I'd become friends with Paul during our years in Cincinnati, and I knew he liked the way our teams played.

"Gerry," Paul told me after that Elder game, "that's the greatest high school football game I've ever seen."

I couldn't believe it. Given the great high school record Paul Brown had achieved—he was 80-8-2 in nine seasons at Massillon —and the games he had coached, I considered that as meaningful a compliment as I could ever receive. Then Moose told me what Paul Brown had told him.

"Let me tell you why he's a good friend," Moose said. "I contacted him before we hired you. Since he had gone from Massillon to Ohio State, we wanted to get his feeling of whether or not this jump could be made in this day and age. He said unequivocally: 'There's no question. It can be done.' "

And Paul Brown thought I was a coach who could do it.

"All of us knew it was going to be a big gamble, taking a high school coach without college experience," says Father Joyce, Notre Dame executive vice president. "But it seemed a reasonable gamble to take, because Gerry had all the other qualities we were looking for.

"Our No. 1 concern is always absolute integrity. Notre Dame can't tolerate a coach who is willing to cut corners. We know the temptations. We've been involved in big-time football for a long time. I'm well aware of a coach rationalizing cutting corners because everybody else is doing it. How is he going to compete unless he does it? It's easy to rationalize."

There would be plenty for me to rationalize before the lights went out for me at Notre Dame, but taking shortcuts would never be one of those rationalizations. I never cheated; I can prove it. Just ask yourself: How could he lose to Air Force and Purdue so often if he was cheating?

"This guy just fit in," Father Joyce says. "Of course we were very much influenced by what Gerry had put together at Moeller. It was just the best in the country. He seemed to have the powers of organization. His staff at Moeller was bigger than Notre Dame's, twice as big (19 assistant coaches and 25 student managers). And I looked into his motivational ability and everything came back that he motivated kids. The ones he had sent to Notre Dame certainly were motivated.

"He could speak, too. I'd never heard him then. But others I knew had, and I knew he had spoken at IBM and Procter & Gamble business conferences. He has his own style. He doesn't speak like Ara Parseghian or Lou Holtz or some of the others who have coached at Notre Dame, but he has this sincerity. And he was a fine Catholic, a really devout Catholic, and I just trusted him totally. We expect our coaches to be above suspicion—like Caesar's wife. We just don't want anything to blemish our hard-earned reputation."

While part of Notre Dame's reputation is built on doing things the right way, the other part is built on winning. It isn't a coincidence that one of the greatest college coaches I ever knew, Woody Hayes, titled his autobiography *You Win With People.* The first of those people are your coaches.

More than one person has told me that that was my biggest mistake at Notre Dame. I didn't understand the chemistry involved in putting a staff together. There's no equation, no formula. Without experience, you discover what works by experimenting. Sometimes experiments fail. If I had to do it over, I would look at the staff in a different way, and I wouldn't have moved so fast to hire coaches so we could get on the road recruiting. I would find myself two or three young whippersnappers. Guys so enthusiastic you'd have to hold them back, chain them down. I'd hire them for enthusiasm alone. If it were a staff of nine, I'd hire four others with enough college coaching experience that they could get a job anywhere, and then I'd hire three graybeards, guys with wrinkles, guys who have seen it all, done it all, been through it all. Guys like Ralph Staub.

If I had had Staubie at Notre Dame, we might have grown old together in South Bend. He would have been my confidant, the man who wouldn't have let me make the mistakes I made. My timing was rotten. I know others tried to play that role, but...

"He came to us and said: 'I'm going to need help,'" says Brian Boulac, former assistant head coach and now assistant athletic director. "But when the time came, he threw himself into the job and didn't really seek help. Gerry had to have a hand in coaching. He had to make decisions. I don't think he would have been comfortable in a situation where he would have relied more on his assistant coaches. With his personality and because of his experience, he had always been the one making those decisions."

The person who knows me best agrees with Brian's assessment.

"Gerry likes to be in control," Marlene Faust says. "He never wanted to be out of the spotlight. He takes over every room, every situation. That's his personality."

Staubie could have made me listen. I didn't think he would be available, though. He was the head coach at Cincinnati. The situation at Cincinnati looked difficult for him but not impossible. Then, he lost his job. But by that time, I had moved so quickly to name the staff that there was no place for the man who might have helped me more than any other.

Like so many decisions I made during the Notre Dame years, this one taught me a valuable and unforgettable lesson. When I got to South Bend, I interviewed all the assistants and kept several— Brian Boulac, Bill Meyers, George Kelly, Jim Johnson, our defensive coordinator, and Joe Yonto, who became our administrative assistant. The ones who had been very loyal to Dan Devine were also loyal to me. But some of them were critical of Devine during my interviews with them and they turned out to be the same coaches who were critical of me. I learned that anytime in an interview a person is critical of another head coach, he'll be the same about you. Just wait.

Most of the coaches I hired at Moeller came right out of college. That was a much better situation, because you moved people up from the freshman and sophomore teams when you had a varsity opening. The assistant coaches learned your system and what you expected of them. You, in turn, learned about the assistant coaches and could monitor their progress and learn their pluses and minuses. It was a lab setting. Experiments didn't blow up in your face. Because the structure allowed them to move up when someone left to take a head coaching job, your new, young assistants were loyal. In that sense, they were like Staubie.

"I think Gerry's biggest problem," Staub says, "was that when he took the Notre Dame job, he didn't know enough quality college coaches. He didn't surround himself with enough quality. I'm not trying to throw cold water or, worse, ice on some of the coaches he had, but I think his downfall was that he didn't have a good staff. If he had picked the right staff, I think he would still be at Notre Dame."

I'd like to think Staubie is right. But I had all the choices in the football world. I made them. I live with them. I still think I chose good coaches. I just think the chemistry could have been better. Putting a college staff together was foreign to me. On the college level, coaches move more often to advance—or save—their careers. The more coaches and athletic administrators they get to know, the broader their opportunities. That gives you access to some coaches and costs you the services of others, including those you may want to keep.

Past association did more than get me in the door with Tom Lichtenberg, the first of my three offensive coordinators. In fact, the chemistry was so good between us that I didn't even have to talk to Tom to offer him the job.

He was the head coach at Morehead State in Kentucky, but I knew Lichty from the days when he was coaching at Cincinnati Purcell. We were close. How close? Well, after I'd gotten permission from the Morehead State athletic director to talk to Tom about a job, I called his house. His wife, Sue Ann, answered. She said Tom was on the road, recruiting. Since I knew Sue Ann, I told her why I was calling, that I wanted to hire him.

"Well, Gerry," Sue Ann said, "Tom won't be in until late tonight but he accepts the job."

I don't know if that has ever happened in college football. I know it never happened to me again. I didn't even talk to Tom. I offered Sue Ann the job, and she accepted.

"Gerry's greatest strength," attorney and longtime friend Ken Schneider says, "is his greatest weakness. It's love. And his love comes from the heart. So often Gerry has made decisions from the heart, particularly in picking people around him. They were great people. Some he came to recognize couldn't do the job and they were gone, but others continued for long periods of time. In his college career, Gerry made too many decisions from the heart rather than from the head when it came to people. He did the same thing in high school, but it worked there. Harsh decisions were tough for Gerry. He's a darn good coach, but one person cannot do what is necessary to win a ball game. You have to have the right people making the right decisions and questioning decisions to make them better the next time. Love can only go so far. You have to face harsh reality and hard decisions. That was very tough for Gerry."

Ken is right. I hated to fire coaches. I did it only three times in 14 years as a college head coach. Two of those occasions came after the first Notre Dame season and one of them proved a terrible mistake. Ironically, it happened because I *didn't* follow my heart. But as bad a mistake as it was to fire Tom Backhus, who had played for me at Moeller, more perplexing was the fact I ended up with three offensive coordinators—Lichty, who left to become an assistant athletic director at Iowa State; Ron Hudson; and Mike Stock —in five years. The offensive players needed and deserved more continuity than I gave them.

"The one criticism I would have of Fuzzy," says Crable after several years of coaching at Moeller High School himself, "is that you have to have continuity on a staff. Three offensive coordinators in five years? That's awfully tough."

Both Crabes and Ken Schneider are right. There was too much change. Not enough heart in the case of Tom Backhus. Too much heart at other times. But I'll never be sorry I thought with my heart most of the time, because people responded to me the same way.

"He was the kind of person," says Roger Valdiserri, retired Notre Dame associate athletic director and sports information director, "whom people wanted to see succeed. He's a sweetheart, really."

If I was a sweetheart, I was one who had never been kissed. I was such a raw rookie in more ways than just hiring a staff. I had been at Notre Dame about three weeks when I called my office from the road one day while recruiting. Jan Blazi, my secretary, said the president's secretary had called and that Father Hesburgh would like to have lunch with me. She gave me the date. I checked my calendar and I told her that I couldn't. I'd be recruiting that day.

"Jan," I said, "call Helen Hosinski back and ask if Father Hesburgh can meet me on a different date."

She said she would, and I thought everything was fine. But when I got back to South Bend, which was before I was supposed to have met with Father Hesburgh, our team chaplain, Father James Riehle, came into my office, plopped down in a chair and said: "Gerry, you just accomplished another first."

There was a twinkle in Father Riehle's eye. He could sound gruff, but he was as warm as an old pot-bellied stove. And about as smoky, too. He loves his cigars. He had been involved with the team for years, but the school used to send different priests on the road as a get-away weekend from their duties as residence hall rectors. When I arrived, I asked Father Joyce if Father Riehle could be with us on a full-time basis. I felt it was important for the players to get to know one priest really well so they'd feel comfortable with him and have someone to go to. I'd let other priests be with us on the sidelines at home games, but I felt especially comfortable with Father Riehle. So I said:

"What did I do this time, Father?"

He was always the first to tell me things I didn't know, and he was set to do it again. He said he had gone to Sunday supper at Corby Hall, as all the priests did. They get together there weekly to pray, enjoy some fellowship and dine. Father Hesburgh had gotten up to say a few words after dinner and I was the subject. He said a first had happened to him.

"In all my years as president of the University," he told the priests, "I've never been turned down for lunch. But our new football coach, Gerry Faust, told me he was too busy."

The priests broke up in laughter.

I wasn't laughing, though, when I heard this. I must have signed the shortest, sweetest contract—one sentence saying I was hired for five years—of any football coach in the country. Now, it looked to me like it might just be the shortest in another way. Notre Dame doesn't fire its coaches. Usually.

"Father," I asked Father Riehle, "do you think I should keep that appointment?"

"Gerry," he said, "I think that would be the smart thing to do."

So I asked Jan to call Father Hesburgh's secretary and say I would meet him on the day he had originally suggested. I canceled everything and we met at the Morris Inn. Our lunch lasted for two hours and I said maybe five words. Anyone who knows me knows this is a record. I like to talk. Sometimes the words don't all come out in quite the right order, but that doesn't stop me. What I lack in oratorical quality, I make up for in quantity. But not at this lunch. I listened. Father Hesburgh is a man to whom a person wants to listen no matter what the subject, but in this case it was Notre Dame football. He was giving me a short course on how to coach the Fighting Irish.

He started talking with the Rockne era and ran through the Devine era. The strengths and weaknesses of each coach, each program. He never missed a beat. Never told me how to coach. Never told me how to represent Notre Dame. Never told me what was expected of a Notre Dame football coach. But when I walked away from lunch that day, I knew.

Everything was just the way I had thought it would be and wanted it to be. Just the way it had been in my dreams. I still didn't fully appreciate the immense responsibility of what I had walked into until a year later, when I saw "Wake Up the Echoes." The movie premiered in South Bend, so we got to see it before anyone else. Afterward, I said to Marlene: "I never realized how tough this job is." That was the first moment I was intimidated by it. I saw what the job had done to Ara, how it had aged him even though he had won. How he took the job to heart. You have to take it to heart—and I did.

The difficulty of the job wasn't the only thing I didn't understand. I didn't even know how long the games were. Oh sure, I knew they were 60 minutes. But I didn't understand how long 60 minutes could be until I was standing on the sideline in Notre Dame Stadium for the first game, against Louisiana State. We played as if we were enchanted. It was beautiful. We did far more right than wrong. We played really well. There had been such a build-up, so much emotion. The hype around campus was unbelievable and the outcome lived up to it.

The night before that LSU game, what was supposed to be an indoor pep rally had to be moved outside to accommodate the largest crowd—there were 14,000 people there—ever at a Notre Dame pep rally to that date. It must have been payback. I'd been accepting invitations to visit the dorms and talk to the students. Now, they were coming out to visit me and the team.

I didn't think much about it. It was like Moeller. Just more people. A lot more people. Now I look back and it seems so unbelievable. It was a token of love and acceptance that I'll always cherish. But at the time, I was so busy that I didn't have the opportunity to reflect and appreciate what was happening.

There was so much to do, so much to learn. I'd talked for a short time with Dan Devine after I was announced as his replacement but I didn't know the right questions to ask. I wish we had talked about scripting, which is the predetermination of a series of plays with which you test the opponent's defense in various situations at the beginning of a game. I'd never scripted plays at Moeller. At least not on paper. I called the plays and scripted in my head. In college, it was more complicated. The hash marks were different. Blocking schemes were more complex. Pass routes were more intricate and dependent on the defense. At Notre Dame we scripted everything from the hash marks and from the center of the field because of the sophistication of the defenses and because everything just moved faster. There was less time to think.

I thought a lot about time during that opening 27-9 victory over LSU. We led 20-0 at the half and 27-3 after three quarters. When there were about 10 minutes to go in the fourth quarter, I found myself on the sideline next to Jim Higgins, our offensive line coach who had come with me from Moeller. I'm not like Coach Devine. I'm high strung. I look nervous on the sideline even when I'm not. But at this moment, looks didn't lie. We were playing well. We had a commanding lead. But I had a question.

"Jim," I asked, "when is this game going to be over?"

The simple answer was in 10 minutes. But it wasn't that simple.

After the game I realized the difference between 48 minutes in a high school game and 60 minutes in a college game. It isn't just

12 minutes. It's another quarter in a high school game. I knew that, of course. I just didn't realize the difference until I coached my first college game. Those last 10 minutes turned into an eternity.

I would discover soon enough that losses last even longer.

What did not require any adjustment was dealing with people, including the media.

"Gerry was a natural," says John Heisler, who succeeded Valdiserri as sports information director and assistant athletic director. "He was tremendous from Day One. He was so bubbly to start with and then he made himself so available. Anyone who comes here as a coach in football, or any sport, has to understand that media access and relationships are important. It may be different here from other places.

"The media really liked Gerry. I think they wanted to see him succeed. Everybody was just so caught up with the enthusiasm of Gerry being here. Just the way he did business. Anybody who was around the guy for any length of time found his enthusiasm contagious. We used to kid Joe O'Brien, our former assistant athletic director and business manager. He was unabashed about telling people after the very first game that we might never lose another football game. That's how optimistic people were, even within the athletic department."

No one, of course, was more optimistic than me. The only difference was, my optimism lasted a heckuva lot longer than everyone else's. I just knew a high school coach could do this. It wasn't the first time that Notre Dame had turned to one, but in the previous case, Terry Brennan's great leap was bridged by a year as coach of the Notre Dame freshman team.

Terry had played for Frank Leahy, graduating in 1949. Before returning to South Bend in 1953, he had coached Mount Carmel High School in Chicago to three straight city championships. We played against his 1952 team when my dad was coach at Dayton Chaminade. They won, 28-21.

"Like Gerry," says Father Joyce, "Terry seemed a perfect fit. Terry was a Notre Dame graduate and a good friend of Father Hesburgh's. Father Hesburgh was more involved in the decision to hire Terry than I was, although I agreed with it. I'd say we split that decision 50-50.

"We brought Terry in as freshman coach to train him to take Frank Leahy's place. Terry had all the qualities. Just what we'd like to think of as a Notre Dame man. Very bright. Good student. Good football player. A man of integrity. We had hoped that Frank Leahy would be coaching for another four or five years and that Terry would have all that seasoning. Instead, Frank gets sick and the question becomes: Do we move Terry in right now or lose him if we bring in another head coach who would have his own staff? So we took a gamble, and it didn't work. That didn't discourage us, obviously, from hiring Gerry."

In the euphoria of a great beginning, I could see as far as forever and in that vision I was still at Notre Dame, still getting the opportunity to be around great people like Mike Leep, who is one of the owners of several South Bend auto dealerships. Mike became my car coach, the person who supplies cars for the coaching staff.

"I met Gerry probably the third day he was in town," Leep says, "and it has been a great relationship ever since, through all the ups and downs. The community as a whole thought he was the savior when he came to town. It thought the same way Joe O'Brien did: that we might never lose another game. That was just about the headline in the *Chicago Tribune*: Will Notre Dame Ever Lose Again?"

Good thing they added the question mark.

The week before our second game, a game at Michigan in which a fake field goal may have been the most important of my career, it felt like a dream world. And it was. Brian Boulac sensed that.

I remember during recruiting season going for the first time into the room in which Brian, who was our recruiting coordinator, had boards filled with prospective recruits. I almost fell flat on the floor when I got a look at the number of offensive linemen he had listed who were 6-5 or taller and about as wide as an Indiana barn. I had no idea there were so many big athletes in the country. I felt elated—and stupid.

"Geez," I remember thinking, "for 18 years I've been blasting these coaches when they wouldn't take my 6-foot-3 offensive linemen. How could they screw up on that? I used to get flaming mad and climb up on my soap box and tell them that they were missing out on the greatest linemen ever."

But I learned. When I saw that board, I realized why they didn't take my 6-foot-3 linemen from Moeller. They were looking for height and size. I got to be the same way. You could measure those qualities. You couldn't measure a person's will. If you could, I would never have turned down Bernie Kosar from Boardman, Ohio. I don't feel too stupid, though. Woody Hayes turned him down. Joe Paterno turned him down. Bo Schembechler turned him down.

Tom Lichtenberg brought me this film of Bernie and said: "Coach, you've got to look at this guy."

I did.

What I saw was a guy who threw sidearm and clanked around on the field like the Tin Man running from the Scarecrow in "The Wizard of Oz." I'd never seen a quarterback who threw sidearm who was any good. Heck, I'm a lousy old quarterback, and even I didn't throw sidearm.

"Tom," I said, "he can't play at this level. No way."

Smart, huh?

The University of Miami had two scholarships left and it had gotten only one quarterback during recruiting so it took Bernie. Bernie and I kid about that now. I tell Bernie, who won a national championship for Howard Schnellenberger in Miami and has had a rewarding professional career, that if I had taken him, I might still be at Notre Dame.

I didn't take into account the other factors about Bernie. The ones you can't see. Bernie Kosar might be the brightest on-the-field player ever to play quarterback. And he is a great competitor. I don't care how slow he is or whether or not he throws off the right foot or the wrong foot, the guy is outstanding on the field and that's what I didn't understand. I said he couldn't play. Boy, was I wrong. I should know you can't weigh and measure heart.

"Gerry," Brian Boulac says, "was intrigued because he knew these were better athletes at Notre Dame than he had had at Moeller. I think he just felt there would be the same kind of progression as a team, not realizing that everybody we played against had the same kind of players. They were going to be physical and good. Everybody has the same number of scholarships, and there are some very good football players out there to give them to."

It was easy to forget in the wonder of that great beginning.

"That first year," Boulac says, "we were on a high after the first game and that wasn't the time to be on a high. We had started something, but we had to prepare. There's an adage in coaching: A good football team will make its most improvement between the first and second games. We didn't do that. And that was the first sign we were going to have problems."

I couldn't see the problems. All I could see were the head-lines. That Tuesday after the LSU game, we were in the locker room getting ready to practice for Michigan, which had been upset the week before by Wisconsin. Michigan had been the No. 1-ranked team going into the game. We had been fifth or sixth in the polls, but after we looked so good beating LSU, we vaulted all the way to No. 1.

When Jim Higgins and I were alone in the quiet of the locker room, he turned to me and said: "Coach, do you know we're No. 1 in both polls?"

"Can you believe it, Jim? I can't. We've played one game and we're No. 1. You know what?"

"No, what?"

"Last year, we were the No. 1 high school team in the country and now we're the No. 1 college team. We must be the only two coaches who have been No. 1 in high school and college in back-to-back seasons. We both ought to retire right now."

We laughed about it then. I still laugh about it. But truer words were never spoken.

3

■ THE MYSTIQUE ■

After one week as coach, I tossed a pebble onto the mountain of Notre Dame mystique with that No. 1 ranking. The University stands among the nation's finest academically, and academics always will come first. Many caring parents send their children to Notre Dame because of its academic reputation. But that reputation, the University's name, its mystique would never have reached the level it has today without Knute Rockne, football coach. He made America take note of this struggling Catholic university on the flatlands of north central Indiana.

The man remains a legend on the campus to this day.

In fact, he is such an influence that Digger Phelps, Notre Dame's basketball coach during my years in South Bend, bought Knute Rockne's cottage on Lake Michigan. I mean, if a coach slept where Knute slept, walked where Knute walked, saw what Knute saw, maybe the mystique would rub off—even on Digger, who coached a sport in which the ball has no points.

Digger, like so many people at Notre Dame, became my friend. He dressed better than I did. He wore that flower in his lapel when he coached. Very snappy. He also won more games than I did. If you ignore those minor differences, we both loved Notre Dame and wanted to do well for it, to bring it honor.

That's why, during a particularly difficult stretch of games in 1984 in which we lost three consecutive home games, Digger suggested I do something I would never have thought of on my own. It was beyond the mystique. It was downright mystical.

For inspiration and solace, I visited the Grotto daily, keeping my promise to the Blessed Mother whom I had asked to intercede on my behalf when I wanted so badly the chance to coach Notre Dame. Though Her solace washed over me, the victories did not come. I had been to church. I had been to visit the Blessed Mother. I had even put the team back into the traditional blue jerseys, our Mother's color, after Dan Devine had switched to kelly green. Nothing worked. I visited the Grotto not once but three times a day. Still nothing. So when Digger walked into my office one day and sat down, I was ready to listen to anything.

"Gerry," Digger said, "did you ever think of going over to the Stadium, looking up to the heavens and asking Knute to help you?"

Sounds crazy, doesn't it? But Digger was serious, and I was desperate.

If the Rock could call upon the Gipper—remember the legend of George Gipp on his deathbed telling Rockne to one day ask the team to win one for him?—then why couldn't I call upon the Rock?

It sounded reasonable to me in light of the circumstances.

"Gerry," Father Edmund Joyce says, "has such a devotion to our Blessed Mother, but She sure didn't help him one bit in football. When he gets up to Heaven, he's going to have to ask Her: 'Where were you when I needed you?'" (I'm glad he thinks I'm going to heaven.)

I knew the Blessed Mother was there for me, if not in the way I thought I needed, then in the way that mattered most. It would be years and require a pilgrimage to such holy places as Fatima, Lourdes and Medjugorje for me to appreciate the fruitlessness of praying for victory—not even for victory, really, just to do well for Notre Dame—but at that moment, I was willing to try anything. Even Digger's idea.

When Knute Rockne died in that plane crash in Kansas, they found him with a rosary in his hand. He was, I would assume, praying the Rosary as the plane was going down. If a man has that much faith, he is a man I could turn to in an hour of need. I didn't do it right away. But after we lost 36-32 in the Stadium to undefeated South Carolina in '84, I figured I was ready to try anything. I thought Digger's idea might be the answer.

So on a cloudy day I walked over to the Stadium, down through the tunnel and onto the field. The stands stood empty and I was alone out there on the grass in the middle of the field, the place where my future would be decided. Above the far end of the Stadium, I could see Touchdown Jesus on the library. I looked up to the heavens.

"Rock," I said, "if you can help me—please do it."

I know what it sounds like, that I'm more than three bricks shy of a load. But to me, it was no joke. I was sincere.

I don't know if Rock had anything to do with it, but we won our next four games and they came during the most difficult part of that year's schedule—LSU, which was ranked sixth in the country, Penn State, USC 14th, and the Naval Academy in a game at the Meadowlands in New Jersey. Four games. Only one of them at home. Those victories might make the 1984 team the greatest comeback team in Notre Dame history—another pebble on the mystique.

There is, of course, one problem with that pebble. If we'd been winning as we should have, we'd have been adding to the mystique in a way that wouldn't have caused some of the Notre Dame faithful to beg for another coach. If you're the coach, the mystique of Notre Dame football sometimes gets lost in the day-to-day aspects of preparing for the game. It's your job. You don't think about it. You're too happy to try to dissect the mystique and examine all the parts of it that create this happiness. You're with the people you want to be with, in the place you want to be. You're engrossed. Today, I wonder why I wasn't more enthralled, more taken by my circumstances. I think it was because I so thoroughly believed that this was always meant to be. But now, with the distance of the years, it seems unbelievable that I had the chance to live this dream, to be even a small footnote to the mystique.

Much of the mystique of Notre Dame, especially for me, is the Catholic heritage that is so much a presence, particularly the Blessed Mother, who overlooks and, I think, oversees it all. I believe she brought Cheryl Cook, Notre Dame class of '85, to the Grotto. Her story appears in a wonderful book titled *The Grotto Stories*.

"In the fall of 1981 when I had been at Notre Dame for only a couple of weeks, I was feeling a little homesick," Cheryl says in her story. "So I went to the Grotto for a few quiet moments. My father, a Notre Dame grad, told me it was the best place to be when you needed a friend.

"When I arrived there, I noticed a man praying alone and I stood silently next to him until he turned to leave. It was then I recognized him. Gerry Faust. It was the night before the first home game of his first season at Notre Dame. I suppose he was feeling homesick, too. I wished him luck in the game and he thanked me and left. He didn't have the best record but we did win the LSU game the next day and I knew someone was helping him."

No doubt about it: visiting the Grotto always helped me. It gave me strength, comfort, peace of mind, and sometimes it led to absolute wonders. One such wonder, if you believe loving families are the greatest of gifts, began to germinate a year after I met Cheryl Cook at the Grotto. I'd gone to the Grotto again late one evening and there was a girl sitting on the steps. She was very pretty, but she was crying. It was the second day of classes for the freshmen. So I assumed, as I walked down the steps to the Grotto, that she was lonely and sick at heart.

"Are you homesick?" I asked her.

"Yes," she said.

"I'm Gerry Faust, the football coach. It's nice to meet you. What's your name?"

"Laura Lee. It's nice to meet you, too."

"Well, Laura, it's my pleasure. Where are you from?"

"I'm from the Los Angeles area and I'm going to play tennis here at the University."

"That's great. But you're a long way from home, aren't you?"

"Yes. And I really miss my family."

"Well that's understandable. You chose the best place to come, though. The Grotto. I come here every day. It gives me peace. And sometimes ideas. Would you like to meet a football player from Orange County?"

"I'd love to," Laura said.

"I think it would be good for you to meet someone, and this young man is a great person. His name is Larry Williams. What dorm do you live in?"

"Lyons Hall."

"Well, Laura, I'll have Larry stop over tomorrow night after practice so you can meet him and maybe he can help you get through this homesickness. You can talk about things back home."

"That would be great, Coach Faust."

When I knelt to say my prayers, I included Laura in them, and the next afternoon when I walked into the locker room, I went over to Larry's locker, where he was standing. Some people would consider this butting into the lives of the players. But I never thought of it that way. I saw someone who needed help and I helped. I thought Larry would want to help too.

"Larry," I said, "I want you to do me a favor."

I'd written Laura's name and residence hall on a sheet of paper. I handed it to Larry.

"I want you to go over and see this girl after practice. She's homesick. She's from the LA area, like you. She has come here to play tennis. I saw her at the Grotto last night. Would you go over and just sit and talk with her? You've been there. You've been far from home and in a new place. You know what it's like."

"Coach," Larry said, "I'd be glad to do that for you."

After practice we had meetings among the coaches. I didn't know what had happened during Larry's visit to Lyons Hall to see Laura. In fact, with so much football on my mind, I had gone on to the next thing that needed to be done and had forgotten all about Larry and Laura until the next afternoon when I saw Larry.

"Hey, Coach!" Larry yelled from across the locker room.

"Yeah, Larry?"

"Come here, will ya?"

"Sure. How ya doin'?"

"Coach, you didn't tell me she's good looking!"

"Larry, I'm not going to fix you up with someone who isn't, am I?"

"Coach, she's not only a nice girl but she's *REALLY* good looking!"

Larry's right. Laura is good looking. But she was so much more than that, and I sensed it immediately. She was like Larry, and he was special. He became the captain of the 1984 team and ended up playing for the Cleveland Browns. He's a lawyer now and lives in South Bend. So does Laura. They're married and have four children. You know what? The Blessed Mother works in funny ways. She may not have helped me win as many games as I would like to have won, but, I think, She helped me bring Laura and Larry together. If I get the chance to ask the Blessed Mother why She didn't help me win more games, I bet She'll say She was too busy helping me with more important matters of the heart and soul.

The Grotto also was at the heart of another story that not many people know. I used to receive 50 to 100 letters a day. We had five secretaries, including my personal secretary, Jan Blazi. If how well she did her job were reflected on the scoreboard, that headline about never losing another game might have come true. Roger Valdiserri recommended Jan to me and I'll always be grateful. She was loyal, competent and helped guide me and keep me out of trouble. She became Lou Holtz's secretary, and now works for new head coach Bob Davie. It may not seem as if a secretary would contribute to Notre Dame's mystique, but to me a secretary such as Jan is what the Notre Dame mystique is all about—good people doing wonders in their work.

Jan and a couple of other secretaries would sift through the phone messages and letters, locating the most important ones and putting them under a crystal apple given to me by Frank O'Brien, a Notre Dame guy from Albany, N.Y., just up the road from the Big Apple itself. One night there was a letter under the apple from a family in Cincinnati. It was late, probably 10 o'clock. But if something was under the apple, it meant I needed to read it right away.

The Arlings were writing to tell me that their son, Brad, was in a coma and had been for 2 1/2 months and their neurosurgeons were encouraging them to try anything they could to bring him out of the coma. Since Brad was a big fan of Notre Dame, they wondered if I could come to visit him in the hospital. I called the Arlings that night.

Brad, Mrs. Arling explained to me, had been about to enter St. Xavier High School as a freshman. He had made the soccer team and was a straight-A student. Then, as summer came to an end, the family was on an outing and while playing softball, Brad was hit in the left side of his head as he ran to first base. He collapsed and later the doctors placed him into a barbiturate coma in hopes the swelling would go down. It didn't, and they had to operate to remove a blood clot. It was two months later and Brad still was in the coma.

As I listened to the story, I knew that we had no game that week and all the coaches were heading out of town to recruit, including me. I had planned to go to Chicago, but I told the Arlings I would switch to Cincinnati. We were recruiting a number of Cincinnati players, so this was no hardship. Bill Corbett, the pilot who flew me everywhere during those days and became a great friend, got us to Cincinnati the next day and I met Brad's parents at Children's Hospital.

As we rode the elevator up to the fourth floor, I could see a ray of hope in the Arlings' eyes. They were excited, but when I saw Brad lying in his hospital bed, I didn't know what to say. The only time I'd been around a young man in a coma was when one of our freshman players at Moeller got hurt. He fell in the locker room, passed out and we rushed him to the hospital. We thought he was going to die, but he snapped out of his coma in four days. Those were the longest, toughest four days I spent in high school coaching. Now, here was another young man in a coma and it had lasted so much longer. All I could do was talk to Brad. I talked and talked, which for me is not hard. Ten minutes passed. Fifteen. There was no response.

Finally, I told Brad that I had brought something for him. I laid Allen Pinkett's jersey over his chest and told him that Allen, Notre Dame's star running back, had said he wanted Brad to have the jersey. Still no movement. No sign of understanding. Nothing.

I spent a few more minutes before telling the Arlings that I had to leave. As they walked with me to the hospital elevator, tears came to Mrs. Arling's eyes. She had been hoping something good would happen. Nothing had. I had this feeling. I didn't want to create false hope but I had to tell Brad's parents what was in my heart.

"I'll get back to Notre Dame about 2 o'clock this morning," I said, "and the first place I'm going to go is to the Grotto. I'll light a candle for Brad and for you, and you let me know when something good happens."

I didn't say if. I said when.

Three weeks later, there was a phone-message slip under the crystal apple. It was from Mrs. Arling. Though it was 10 at night, I called.

"Mrs. Arling," I said, "this is Gerry Faust."

Mrs. Arling's voice quaked with emotion.

"Coach, it's great to hear from you. Something good has happened. Brad came out of his coma three days ago."

"Jeez! That's great! How's he doing?"

"Coach, he was tested today. You know he was a straight-A student. Well, he has some problems now. He tests only at the third- or fourth-grade level. His neurosurgeon says he'll never be back to the level he was, but that if he works at it, he will be able to live a normal life, have a family, raise children and work. But, Coach, Brad's problems aren't what I wanted to tell you about. His father and I were both there when Brad woke. He looked up at us and said: 'Mom, Dad, I love you.' And we said: 'Brad, we love you, too.' Coach, he knows us. He loves us, and he knows we love him. That's what I wanted to tell you."

As she spoke, I didn't say a word. I couldn't. My throat had frozen shut. I couldn't stop crying. This, I thought, is what life and families are about. Sticking together, through good and bad. Being there for one another.

"Coach," Mrs. Arling said, "you know what else?"

"No, what, Mrs. Arling?"

"Brad wanted to know where the Notre Dame jersey came from. So we told him you had come to visit him and he wants to meet you and to thank you."

"Well, I'll be in Cincinnati in three weeks. We're recruiting Hiawatha Francisco. Can you bring Brad over to Moeller High School?"

"Sure."

When Brad and I met, he was in the early stage of his recovery. He reminded me of the wonderful kids in the Special Olympics program. At both Moeller and Notre Dame, I liked to be what they call a Yell Guy during the Special Olympics competition. I'd cheer those kids and put medals around their necks. You've never seen people so happy to receive a medal. They are God's little angels. I love being around them, and now Brad was one of them. When he saw me, he came over and jumped on me. It embarrassed his parents, but I told them not to worry. I just turned into The Hugger and swallowed him up in the biggest hug I'd ever given anyone.

"Brad," I told him, "I love you."

"I love you," he said.

"Brad, I've got a coaching hat for you. Now you're an official coach at Notre Dame. Every Saturday at Notre Dame Stadium I have 59,075 coaches up in the stands. But when you come to visit me, you'll be the only *official* coach up there, because you have the hat."

He put the hat on his head and a smile on his face. I told Brad that I had to leave.

"Coach," he said, "would you do me a favor?"

"Brad," I said, "I'll do anything I can for you."

"Will you write to me?"

"Brad, not only will I write to you but I'll also call you. And you call me. Here's my number. Call me collect."

That was 13 years ago. Brad lives by himself now. He has his own apartment. He has a full-time job. He's doing great. He still calls me collect every three or four weeks. We still correspond, too. On June 6, 1996, he carried the Olympic torch as it passed through Cincinnati on its way to the Summer Games in Atlanta, then we went out to eat in Cincinnati at my friend Ted Gregory's Montgomery Inn. Brad kept saying that they were the best ribs he had ever eaten. I just smiled. He has come so far.

In fact, probably the greatest, most heart-wrenching letter I've ever received came from Brad. During my years of coaching at the University of Akron, Father Tom Kuhn, who was principal at Elder High School in Cincinnati, asked me to come and speak to the student body. Brad was a junior at Elder then. He wrote and said he wanted to spend some time with me after I talked. Then in a postscript, he wrote the most powerful thing I've ever read, something I've tried to always remember. He wrote:

"Coach, you know I've been on the swim team this last year. Every time I've swum, I've come in last. But each race, my times have gotten better. Next year, I'm going to be a better swimmer. Brad is going to make it."

The "Brad is going to make it" reference was Brad's adaptation of a cover story that appeared in *Sports Illustrated*. It was about my Notre Dame days and the title was: "I'm Going to Make It." Brad had read that in 1984 and remembered. What he wrote meant that he understood what I had been trying to say in that story. He wasn't afraid to fail. He wasn't afraid of life. He got up on that starting platform and he swam every race even though he had come in last every race before. He couldn't care less what people thought. He got up there and tried again. He had determination. He had a goal. When you are not afraid to fail in life, you'll succeed. When you're not afraid to take something on even though the odds are against you, you are going to emerge a success in one way or another.

When I reflect on my stay at Notre Dame, I know how Brad felt. I don't regret the experience one bit. I don't regret trying. And I don't care what people think of my coaching ability. I got up on that starting platform, like Brad, and I swam every race. I gave it my best. That's what Brad was doing. He said he was going to make it. And he did. You make it by having family, friends and faith.

I think of Brad's journey and mine as parallel. We're friends. We stick by each other still. And probably the only reason I got to know Brad was that I was the Notre Dame football coach. I don't think it was a coincidence that he came out of his coma after I lit that candle at the Grotto and put him in my prayers to the Blessed Mother.

I'll always associate Brad Arling with the Notre Dame mystique. It made a Notre Dame fan of him and caused our lives to converge. Defining the mystique isn't easy. Lou Holtz says he can't do it. He can't describe it. He just knows it's there. So does anyone touched in any way by Notre Dame.

My friend Frank Eck, chairman of the board of Advanced Drainage System Co. in Columbus, says Notre Dame's mystique is something he has felt since he was 10 years old, growing up in Redbank, New Jersey, cheering for ol' Notre Dame. "It stayed with me when I graduated from Notre Dame," Frank told me, "and remains with me today."

The mystique may be indefinable but it has a voice, and that voice is the voice of Pat O'Brien, the actor who played Knute Rockne in the movie. I met Pat when the Notre Dame Touchdown Club of Washington, D.C., invited me to give what was my first speech for Notre Dame. It was an afternoon event, right after the 1981 recruiting season and the place was jammed. There must have been 500 people. I asked Pat if he would give his famous Rockne locker room speech about the Gipper and he did. He still knew it word for word, and he did it exactly like in the movie. He got a standing ovation. That was the mystique—and its voice.

To make sure I understood as much about Notre Dame as I could, that I knew its lore by heart, I went to Steve Sylvester, who was one of my captains at Moeller, played at Notre Dame and went on to a career with the Oakland Raiders. Steve had moved back to Cincinnati and had launched a real-estate career. Through Steve I got to know a guy named Don Cisle, who also was a Notre Dame graduate, and his son, Murph, who graduated from Notre Dame and was there at the same time as Steve. Steve told me that Don had every book ever written on Notre Dame. So I called Don.

"How many books do you have on Notre Dame?" I asked.

"Nineteen," he said.

At this point I was still just talking with Father Joyce about the job. There had been no offer, and I had made the promise I wouldn't even hint that I might be the next Notre Dame coach. So I couldn't tell Don, who owns a paving company in Hamilton, Ohio, why I was interested in his books.

"I'm going on vacation to Florida," I told Don. "Could I borrow those books?"

"Sure," Don said.

I read every book. I'd stay up late at night, reading them after the rest of the family had gone to bed. Neither Don nor Steve had any idea why I had borrowed the books, why I wanted to know everything I could about Notre Dame and its football.

It didn't require any reading for me to know that Ara Parseghian still belonged in and to Notre Dame football. Before I came to South Bend, Ara had kept his distance from the football program since resigning as coach in 1974. So on Day One, I asked Roger Valdiserri if he would take me to see Ara, who still had an office in South Bend where he worked in the insurance business. It had been six years since Ara had coached, but he could tell me the problems and the uniqueness of being at Notre Dame. We talked for quite a while that day, and I invited Ara back, asked if he would come to practice, talk to the team, be around when he could. I needed Ara's help.

I'd always respected and loved Ara because of a moment that occurred when he coached at Miami of Ohio and I was playing for Dayton. In those days, coaches were allowed to come to other teams' spring games. So Ara was visiting Dayton. I was the quarterback but was on the sideline in street clothes because of a knee injury. When Ara saw me, he came over and talked with me, asked how my leg was, how I was feeling. He probably doesn't even remember this, but it made a big impression on me, that he would go out of his way to inquire about how I was doing. I became a big Ara fan right then.

When I look back now, I think one of the things that I was successful in doing at Notre Dame was similar to what Ara Parseghian did for me that day in Dayton. I tried to bring to Notre Dame coaching an accessibility and friendliness. Maybe that was my real contribution to the mystique—to be there for as many people and as many causes as I could. I know this openness led to my most memorable moment at Notre Dame.

During the honeymoon period before I'd coached—or lost —a game, everyone was willing to do anything I wanted. I don't think anyone disagreed when I suggested that we open spring practice to fans who wanted to watch. We always closed practices in the fall, and I felt we should give people a chance to see us, that maybe it would create an even closer bond between the community and the University.

On the first day of spring practice, people were lined up deep around the practice fields. We thought we'd draw 400 or 500 people.

There were more than 5,000. It was cold and windy. That didn't matter. It was as if we were playing a game instead of practicing. Some coaches don't draw that many people on Saturdays in the fall. I know. I became one of them at Akron. That's years of Notre Dame mystique. People just want a glimpse of Notre Dame football.

I had gone to the field early with the kickers and punters that day. I wanted to get a look at what kind of kicking game we had. Fifteen or 20 minutes later the team began to come out and to follow a tradition it had under Coach Devine. It assembled at the gate and then the players came running onto the field, with the captains leading them. I didn't know about the tradition, but when I saw the players forming at the gate and starting to run onto the field, I knew I wanted to be there waiting for them, out on the field where the head coach of Notre Dame should be. So I starting running.

I was in the northeast corner of the practice fields and I began sprinting as hard as I could run. I didn't have the speed to beat the players to the main practice field—I never had any speed—so I had to beat them on pure willpower. It wasn't easy. When the players saw all the people waiting there to greet them and to watch them work out, they were pumped up, flying like young Adonises across that field.

As I raced to meet them, cold wind whipped and stung my face. Then, suddenly, the sun broke through the clouds and struck that sea of golden helmets coming in waves toward me. I remember looking up to the heavens. There, before me, stood the Golden Dome and the Blessed Mother, bathed in sun that looked as if it were God's spotlight, a gift to his Mother. Tears streamed down my face, because it was at that moment that I realized what had happened to me.

"Dear Lady, Dear Lord," I said, "thank you for giving me the unbelievable opportunity of being here at Notre Dame."

People ask what my greatest moment at Notre Dame was. Was it leading the team out of the tunnel and onto the field at Notre Dame Stadium? Beating USC or No. 1-ranked Pitt? Winning the Liberty Bowl against Doug Flutie and Boston College?

Those things were wonderful, but none of them was my greatest moment.

My greatest moment was running onto that practice field to meet the team and my destiny, realizing what God had given me. It was an opportunity that few men have in life—to see their dreams turn to gold before their very eyes. I cherish the moment still.

If I was filled with the Notre Dame mystique, Rock Roggeman was practically born into it. He grew up in South Bend, the son of a coach. When his father moved to accept another coaching position, it didn't diminish Rock's love for Notre Dame. He lived and died for the place. So he thought he had gone straight to heaven when Brian Boulac brought him in for a recruiting visit.

Rock had grown up to become a *Parade* magazine All-American while playing linebacker for a high school in Tucson, Arizona. His dad Tom was an assistant coach at the University of Arizona, but Rock Roggeman didn't want to play for Arizona. He wanted to play for just one school. His only school. Notre Dame.

During these recruiting visits the players would arrive on Friday night and we would meet them and talk with all of them. Rock, according to *USA Today*, was 5-foot-11, maybe even 6 feet, and 225 pounds. Well, up close and in person, he was more like 5-9 or 5-10. So right away, size became a question and issue. Our linebackers had to drop into and protect the dead area between their position and the free safety's. Because of the threat of the run, they could only drop so deep, say 8 to 10 yards. The taller the linebacker —especially those playing inside—the better the chance of knocking down a pass thrown into the vulnerable zone behind them. Before we meet with the recruits individually on Saturday, the coaches gather as a staff to discuss them. With Rock, we were looking at this 5-foot-9 kid and we decided we couldn't offer him a scholarship. I had to tell him the next day.

That Saturday morning we had breakfast with Rock and the other recruits. I talked with them as a group and we took them on a tour, stopping early on in the locker room at the Stadium. In the lockers we had hung jerseys with their names on the back. The Notre Dame Victory March was playing. It's a memorable moment for a player. He walks in and sees the jersey with his name on it in the room that Knute Rockne once haunted, this room with so much rich tradition. The walls are the same as when Rockne was there. Even the old heater is the same. It impresses most recruits, but Rock Roggeman wasn't most recruits.

He had literally lived for this moment. The moment he'd see his name on a Notre Dame jersey. The moment he could see his future on the field in Notre Dame Stadium. He may have been only 5-9 and 225 pounds but he was 5-9 and 225 pounds of white-hot intensity. As the Victory March played, this great young man was standing under a crucifix on the wall, his fists clinching and pumping, the veins on his arms popping out, tears coming down his face. When I walked by him, I saw what Notre Dame meant to him.

"Coach," he said, "I'm ready to play for you."

What could I do? I offered Rock a scholarship.

He loved Notre Dame so much that I couldn't turn him down. I never regretted it. Not to this day. He didn't play in a lot of games but in practice he gave his all. They didn't make a movie about Rock as they did about Rudy—Dan Ruettiger—but they could have. Rock and Rudy are what Notre Dame mystique is about. Rock's practice habits made us a better team. He was on the kickoff and other special teams and did a great job for us. Rock cost us a scholarship which we could have given to a player who might have made a greater contribution toward winning games. A Notre Dame coach can't take many of these kids, but he should always take one to whom it means as much to play for Notre Dame as it meant to Rock. Rock is the mystique of Notre Dame and the mystique of Notre Dame is why I ignored the decision we had reached in our coaches' meeting.

Rock Roggeman is now a coach himself. A few years ago we coached against each other, he at Eastern Michigan, where he was defensive coordinator, and me at Akron. That was a special moment for me. Now, Rock is at Louisville as defensive coordinator. He's a great coach, because he loves the kids and will do for them what I tried to do for him.

If mystique got Rock Roggeman in Notre Dame's door, it opens even more doors for Notre Dame. It worked unbelievably in recruiting. When the Notre Dame coach walks in the door, the principal, the football coach, the athletic director, the guidance counselor, everyone wants to meet him. That isn't different from the reaction to the Michigan coach in Michigan or the Ohio State coach in Ohio. When Woody Hayes came to Moeller High School, I had to introduce him to all the teachers. They all wanted to meet him. The reasons were obvious: Ohio State is Ohio State and Woody was Woody. There is one difference for me or any other Notre Dame coach. The doors aren't just open in one state. They're open nationwide.

But once you got in the door and got to meet the young man and his parents, the mystique vanished and the realities of recruiting set in. Those realities could turn the mystique against you. Players and parents would say: But Notre Dame has so many great athletes. When you walked into a house to recruit a quarterback, he knew every quarterback on the team. When I was at Notre Dame, the Mutual Radio Network carried our games to the largest number of stations on any network—150 to 200 then. We also appeared on television often. Now, of course, Notre Dame's games are on TV every week. That offers prospects even more opportunities to get to know your team. Notre Dame is America's team and its mystique can make a player seem better than he is. It can scare away some young men. Other schools use that against you.

Another part of Notre Dame's mystique that can become a double-edged sword might not be obvious. It wasn't to me. Notre Dame looks like a billion dollars. It's beautiful. The men and women who take care of the campus are like artists with huge hearts when it comes to caring for the place. It looks like a country club, but at the same time it exudes learning and faith. Some young men don't want that or can't relate to it, especially low-income athletes who have come up hard on the mean streets of our cities or in the smallest hardscrabble towns. They've never been in an environment like that and when they walk onto campus the things that most people find beautiful and inspiring create for them a psychological barrier. They don't realize that low-income young people go to school at Notre Dame, too. All they see is wealth. They feel miscast and misplaced.

When I was recruiting Tony Woods at Seton Hall Prep in New Jersey, I couldn't understand when he chose Pitt. I'd visited him personally three times. The priest who also was the principal at Seton Hall Prep loved Notre Dame. Tony was a Catholic. It seemed like a perfect match. I loved Tony. Not only was he an All-America player, but I thought he was also an All-America person. So when he visited Notre Dame and then chose Pitt, I called him.

"Tony, you're a Catholic," I said. "You went to a Catholic high school. You have a chance to go to Notre Dame and get a heckuva education. I personally recruited you because you are really important to us and I truly like you. Why aren't you coming?"

"Coach," Tony said, "I'm from Newark. I've lived here all my life. In the city of Pittsburgh I felt more comfortable than I did in South Bend."

"You know what, Tony? I never thought of that. I can understand that. I want to wish you the best. You picked an excellent university."

If the mystique of Notre Dame being a Catholic university does not always convert the Catholic player to Notre Dame, neither does it always scare away a young man whom you might think it would. When we recruited a non-Catholic player, which we did often, we had to overcome the thought that everybody was going to try to convert him to Catholicism. I had that concern when I went to Atlanta with Mal Moore to recruit Wes Pritchett, who was a great linebacker from a fine family. It was, however, a Baptist family and so we didn't know if we were going to have a chance. Baptists are God-fearing people. They don't believe in smoking or drinking. I don't either, but I'm a Catholic. So I didn't know how we'd be received. That's why I took Mal. He shared the Pritchetts' faith. He coached with Bear Bryant at Alabama. He knew the South. Wes had narrowed his possible choices to Georgia Tech and us—and maybe Georgia. That didn't stop me from worrying.

We knocked on the door of this impressive home of this well-to-do Baptist family, and I didn't have to wait long to feel better about our chances of signing Wes. His dad, Ken, came to the door with a cigar in one hand and a drink in the other. I said to myself: He's a Baptist but we're going to get Wes. This is a family with broad views.

For most players who came to visit the campus, players like Rock Roggeman, the mystique would take over. The family atmosphere they found on the Notre Dame campus captured the hearts of most potential recruits. It should. It's real. A person can touch it, and be touched by it.

The best weekend we ever had in recruiting was a weekend when we had a blizzard and the players and their parents could not leave South Bend. It was January. The secondary roads were closed. The turnpike had been shut down. Visits are supposed to last only 48 hours, but we had no choice but to extend that a day. People couldn't even get their cars started. Our planned recruiting schedule had ended. The families sat around and talked, laughed and really got to know one another. We got 14 of the 18 players who were visiting. That was the 1982 recruiting class that included Ron Plantz, Kevin Jennings, John Askin and Eric Dorsey.

Mystique can win recruits but I'm not sure it can win games. I couldn't take advantage of it, in any case. I had no trouble getting the team emotionally ready to play the biggest games. USC, for instance.

"We beat Southern Cal three years under Gerry," Father Joyce says. "Nobody can believe that when I tell them. That's probably because Air Force beat us four years in a row."

That's the problem I had, trying to get players ready for games they should win. The Notre Dame athlete is a very bright person. You're not going to mislead him when it comes to knowing whether or not he is physically more talented than his opponent. We had our teams fundamentally prepared but I couldn't seem to convince them that emotion—the very essence of my being as a coach— could matter enough to turn a game in favor of all these teams for whom Notre Dame was the star on their schedule. Every team keys for Notre Dame and people don't understand this. Lou Holtz was much better at these should-win games than I was.

When you lose the wrong games, it exacerbates the problem of your record and other problems as well.

"Winning would have solved all the little complaints about Gerry," says Father James Riehle, team chaplain. "The Notre Dame fan is a very fickle fan. The only thing that matters is that you win and beat the point spread. I've been around here a long time and I've said publicly before that our fans are not the greatest fans in the world. That's not only true for football but also for other sports. That's not to our credit. But that's the nature of the beast.

"Maybe we've been spoiled by having too many successful years, too many successful coaches and too many great players. I'll go out and play golf and some guy will holler all the way across the course: Tell those guys not to fumble! A grown man hollering as if he had never made a mistake in his life. And we're talking about 18-year-old kids. I don't have much patience for people like that."

But that, too, is part of the Notre Dame mystique, and if it is not the best part, it is not what I remember when today I fly over South Bend and think about what was and what might have been. Instead, I think about the Blessed Mother on top of the Dome. I flew over it hundreds of times in private planes and I've always looked out the window to see if I could see the Blessed Mother. Even today when I'm on a commercial flight that takes me over South Bend, I look for Her. In the car driving up the interstate, you can see the Dome from about two miles before the exit. I always looked for Her. The Blessed Mother on the Dome, the high point of the University, has always fascinated me and given me peace.

The day I got the job I'd always dreamed of having, I looked up at the Dome. Just as I did, the sun appeared through the gray and shone on the Blessed Mother. That's mystique.

4

▪ RECRUITING AS IF YOUR ▪ LIFE DEPENDED ON IT

On a beautiful September Saturday in 1981,
I rode into Notre Dame lore—but not on a
horse as the Fifth Horseman. I took a golf
cart on my crusade. The mystique and the
future of my recruiting at Notre Dame rode
with me.

It was Game Day No. 1.

In a few hours, we would defeat Louisiana State University.
For one shining moment, my name would fit in the same sentence
with Stuhldreher, Miller, Crowley and Layden without catching in
the throat. We were Notre Dame winners, all. Grantland Rice once
compared Notre Dame's Four Horsemen to famine, pestilence, destruction and death. That's nothing. Some Irish fans used to mention Faust right up there with famine, pestilence, destruction and
death, too. But not on this day.

Not on September 12, 1981. On this day, everything was
golden.

Besides making myself accessible to Notre Dame students,
alumni and fans and getting to know as many of them as possible, I
had a reason for deciding to become the first Notre Dame coach to
take a golf cart on a campus tour two hours before coaching the
first college football game of my life. Other than the day I visited
Notre Dame as a high school recruit, I'd never been on the campus
on Game Day. People say it's the most exciting campus atmosphere
in the country. There is such a great love for Notre Dame, you can
touch it.

People visit the Grotto. They go to Sacred Heart Church. They
walk the campus. They drop in on dorm cookouts. They line up for

two blocks to buy Notre Dame paraphernalia at the bookstore. They give new meaning to serious tailgating. By 9 a.m. on a football Saturday, the campus is electrified and energized.

I had to see it, feel it.

So I asked Col. John Stephens, who was Notre Dame's associate athletic director, to take me on the golf-cart tour. I wanted to soak up the atmosphere, to remember it, to share it in the weeks to come with the high school players we would be recruiting. I hadn't been able to do that for the first recruiting class. The players deserved to know what Game Day would be like, the excitement that they would help to generate, what it meant to be a Notre Dame football player or a Domer of any stripe.

The campus was packed. The crowd was so large that Col. Stephens ran into a tree at one point as he attempted to turn the golf cart around without hitting anyone. Everyone was stopping us, eager to say hello.

I wanted to see the band. It played on the steps of the Administration Building a couple of hours before the game and then marched down to the Stadium and in through the tunnel. The band is led by the Irish Guard, its crack marching unit in bearskin shakos and kilts. I don't know what guy would want to wear a skirt, but they fight for the chance. The band adds to Notre Dame pride and tradition. There must have been a thousand people there listening to it when I ran into my brother, Fred, whom I hadn't seen in a couple of months. I got out of the cart, put a big hug on him and told him I loved him. Fred had been the great athlete in our family and here his brother was the coach at Notre Dame. It was a moment filled with nostalgia. That passed soon enough, though, as Col. Stephens wheeled us through the parking lot. Tailgaters often get filled with something other than nostalgia, and I think I ran into some who had had a few too many ounces of liquid refreshment. People were screaming and waving. Then these guys stepped in front of us and stopped the golf cart. They were big. Very big. Chicago guys. Could have been Bears linemen.

"Coach," they demanded, "what are you doing out here? You ought to be getting ready for the game."

"We'll be ready," I promised.

This was great. I hadn't coached my first game yet and the fans already were on me. You should do this. You shouldn't do that. They weren't kidding, either. I talked to them for a while, and they shook my hand.

"Good luck, Coach," they said.

I think they even meant it.

Their reaction came with the territory. There's a segment out there that can be vicious, and I got a feel for that right away. They didn't care if I was being a good guy or if I was trying to soak up atmosphere that would allow me to better share with recruits what it was like to play for Notre Dame. All they wanted me to do was win and beat the point spread while I was at it. I never looked at a point spread before a game. Never in my life. But I could always tell when we had beaten it.

When we won and people were pounding me on the back and yelling, "Great game! Great game!" we'd beaten the spread. When we won and they said, "It was a good win," I knew we hadn't beaten the spread. Believe it or not, there are people who bet on Notre Dame games. I can understand it. It's part of the thrill, of the fun. I think those people seldom recognize the many facets of the game that can affect not only the outcome but also the point spread. If they did, if they thought about how one ill player, one fumble, one gust of wind or one fast-moving rain storm could change everything, they might keep their money in their pockets.

No coach can guarantee a winner. All he can do is recruit as if his life depended on the outcome of the games—and, professionally, it does.

If I was a good recruiter, and I'd say recruiting was one of my strengths at Notre Dame, it was because I believed so strongly in what we were doing at the University and what it had to offer young men. I worked hard at it. I was on the road all the time, as much as the NCAA allowed. Some head coaches don't do that. It was for me more joy than work. Sometimes I closed the deal. Sometimes I just opened the door.

I loved meeting the families of young men. I tried to put people at ease when I walked in. I'd pat them on the back, start laughing and kidding around. Some coaches don't do that. They're all business. Aloof. Unapproachable. That's not me. I went into homes as much for parents to get to know me as for me to get to know them and to see their son in a family situation, how he reacted. In those circumstances, I could tell if I wanted to bring this young man to Notre Dame to become a part of our larger family.

Once, I was in a northern metropolitan city recruiting an excellent running back who was being sought by several schools in the Big Ten and Big Eight conferences. (That was before the Big

Ten had 11 teams and the Big Eight became the Big 12.) This young man had visited Notre Dame and in those days we were allowed to offer a player a university letter of intent. It was not binding, but it showed that we were committed to the player and would hold a scholarship for him to formally accept on national letter of intent day.

When we walked into this player's second-floor duplex, the stereo was blasting. His mother seemed quite sweet, but I couldn't hear her and she couldn't hear me as we tried to talk. I didn't want to tell her son to turn off the stereo. I didn't think it was my place to do that. Nor did I want to turn off the kid to me and Notre Dame. In these circumstances, you're left groping for the right thing to do. I got up and walked over to the stereo.

It was the biggest stereo I had seen. It must have been 10 feet long. Jet planes don't make as much noise.

"What a stereo," I said. "Do you care if I take a look at it?"

"No, go ahead," the player said.

"Explain some of these things on it to me," I said.

I thought I might get him to show me how the volume worked and either turn it down or off. I was standing on the player's left and his mom was on his right. She reached over to turn off the stereo, because she realized we couldn't talk. As she started to push the button, her son shoved her.

"Don't touch that," he said. "That belongs to me."

I didn't think. I just reacted. I gave the young man a forearm to the rib cage.

"Don't talk to your mother like that," I told him.

It was an uncomfortable situation. When we sat down—by now the stereo was off—I asked if he had the Notre Dame scholarship papers we had given him.

"Yeah," he said.

"Have you signed them?"

"No."

"Can I see them?"

He left the room to get them and when he returned I looked to see if he had signed them. He hadn't.

"I don't want to embarrass your mother," I told the player, "but I can't condone the way you've treated her after what she has done for you in your life. If that's all the respect you have for her, you won't fit in with our family. I'm rescinding your scholarship offer."

As we walked out, I apologized to his mother and told her I hoped her son would learn a lesson. I knew another school would be happy to have him, and one was. He started as a freshman—but, eventually, ended up in jail. He didn't belong at Notre Dame.

Allen Pinkett did. I knew that for the same reason I knew this player should go somewhere where character did not matter. I saw the character we wanted in the way Allen treated his mother.

Greg Blache and I had gone to visit Allen in Sterling, Virginia, and Mrs. Pinkett had just gotten home from work. She drove a bus for the school district. Though Mr. Pinkett was at work, a person could sense just by walking into this house that this was the home of a real family, of people whose feelings for one another ran deep.

Allen had visited the Notre Dame campus and had reduced his list of schools to two: Notre Dame and North Carolina. We knew how much we wanted Allen before this visit. He was a two-time Virginia all-state running back who belonged to the National Honor Society because of his 3.5 grade point average. So we talked for an hour or so and with each passing minute I became more and more convinced that this was my kind of guy. Smart. Caring. But tough on the field.

Then Allen did something that set him apart from many other young men. He asked if he could be excused for a couple of minutes.

"May I speak with my mom?" he said.

"Of course, Allen," I said.

I didn't know what was happening. He asked his mother if she'd go into the other room with him. They were gone about five minutes. All Greg and I could do was sit and talk and wait.

When Allen returned, he said: "I'm coming to Notre Dame."

What he had done was take his mother into his bedroom and tell her what he wanted to do and ask for her approval. Right then, I knew we had a winner. Any time a young man takes his family into consideration, placing its needs above his own wants, you know you have a team player.

We got not only a great football player but also a wonderful person, and to this day, Allen remains one of the all-time quality people I've coached. My only regret is that my situation as his coach distracted the media from Allen Pinkett and other deserving players.

"You wished," assistant athletic director John Heisler says today, "that people in the media would have come in and done features about our team, our players, about an Allen Pinkett who was having tremendous seasons and probably didn't get some of the attention he deserved because so much of the focus ended up being on what was going on with Notre Dame and Gerry. It eclipsed such issues as: Should Allen Pinkett be a Heisman Trophy candidate or an All-American? Allen accomplished a heck of a lot, but sometimes it was lost."

John is right. But, I'll tell you this: The kind of player and person Allen Pinkett was never was lost on me or anyone who knew him.

Mothers and sons bond in such intricate and interesting ways that sometimes it was difficult not to feel as if you, as a coach, were coming between them. For mothers, recruiting was a time of letting go.

When Greg Blache and I were in Virginia visiting Eric Dorsey in McLean, I had to confront not only a player concerned about his mother's feelings but also one who had a unique relationship with her because of the saddest of circumstances.

Eric's father had been a policeman in Washington, D.C. He was killed in the line of duty when Eric was just two years old. So Mrs. Dorsey, who was a business executive, had raised Eric alone. She was on Eric's mind when we met at a bowling center in McLean, where he was participating in a physical education class.

I like to bowl, but I'm not very good. Of course, if I did only the things I'm good at, I wouldn't be too busy. I wouldn't play golf. Some people would say I'd never have coached college football. But on this day, I had a plan. I asked Eric's teacher if he cared if I bowled a little with the class. I got along well with high school teachers. They liked me because I liked and respected them. Heck, I'd been one of them for 23 years.

The teacher said to roll on. So I challenged Eric, something I did often with recruits.

"OK, Eric," I said, "we'll make a deal. Two balls. You knock down more pins than I do and you can go to school anywhere you want. I knock down more than you do and you have to come to Notre Dame."

"Coach," Eric said, laughing, "that's a deal."

He must have seen me bowl before.

I got up on the approach and threw the ugliest ball you've ever seen. The split I produced looked like the uprights in an end zone. One pin was sticking up on each side of the lane. The 7-10.

But hey, I've watched TV bowling. I've listened to Nelson Burton, Jr. I know what to do. I tried to slide the ball down the right side of the lane, nick the 10-pin and slip it over into the 7. The only slip was mine. I hadn't bothered to put on bowling shoes. In my socks, I went down and so did the ball. Down into the gutter.

Eric walked up to the approach and didn't even need to throw two balls. He got eight with his first. Ties go to the recruit. His classmates laughed and cheered.

"Well, Coach," Eric said. "I don't have to come to Notre Dame."

Not so fast, Mr. Bowling.

I asked the proprietor if we could use his office to talk. He said sure. There was just one problem. It was raining and there was a leak in the roof in the office. As I told Eric what a great place Notre Dame is for everyone but coaches who want to learn to bowl, Eric watched these raindrops fall from the ceiling.

Plop. Plop. Plop.

I thought: I'm not getting anywhere. I was wrong. Eric was listening carefully. Finally, he looked straight at me.

"Coach," he said, "I don't think I can play at Notre Dame. I'm not good enough."

Not good enough? I chuckled.

"Eric, do you think I'm going to fly 1,000 miles to come to see you if I don't think you're good enough to play for Notre Dame? Eric, you have the potential to be a great one. Better than that, you're a good person. That excites me even more."

"You know, Coach, I'd come to Notre Dame, but my mom wants me to stay close to home. She's raised me. My younger brother and I are the only family she has. But if my mom said I could come, I would."

"Eric, what's your mom's phone number?"

I got on the phone and asked Mrs. Dorsey if I could come to see her. She said yes. I told Eric I'd talk to him soon. Greg and I drove to Mrs. Dorsey's office, which was an impressive place. She had an important job. She was smart. But more important, she loved Eric. I sat, and we talked.

"North Carolina and Virginia are really close and Notre Dame is 1,000 miles away," she explained, coming right to the point.

"You're right, Mrs. Dorsey," I agreed, "but I'm going to tell you something about college football. You won't see Eric any more at Virginia than you will at Notre Dame. The only difference is it is easier to go to the games at North Carolina or Virginia than it is to come to South Bend. But as far as seeing Eric, his weekends for almost the whole year will be taken up and he won't be home that much. There is another thing: We're on television and you'll be able to see Eric a lot that way."

I complimented her for the wonderful job she has done raising her son, and I meant it. This was not just some recruiting line.

"Eric is a gentleman, first class," I told Mrs. Dorsey. "To me, that is more important than his football skills, which I think are going to make him an outstanding player. I love Eric as a person and as a player.

"The decision you have to make is this: Your son is going to be away from home, period. I can't make this decision for you, but where you feel the head coach, the coaching staff and the atmosphere is going to be most conducive to carrying on what you've tried to teach Eric at home is where he should go to school. And you have to make that decision."

"Well," Mrs. Dorsey said, "that's Notre Dame. I want him to be with you."

"That's great. Will you call him?"

She did. Eric played four years for us, graduated and played defensive tackle for the New York Giants. As great a football player as Eric turned out to be, I had been right: He was an even better person.

So many more players respect what their fathers and mothers have done for them than behave in the way the one player did who thought his stereo was more important than his mom. One of these respectful players was Ed Badinghaus, who played guard for me at the University of Akron.

When I was recruiting Eddie from Cincinnati Oak Hills High School, his mother had told me that none of the family had ever graduated from college and that she would love to have her Eddie become the first to get his degree.

"As long as Ed meets me halfway," I told Mrs. Badinghaus, "I guarantee he'll graduate."

During his junior season, however, Mrs. Badinghaus became ill with cancer. Eddie was starting at center at that time and doing a good job. We needed him. But some things are more important than football. So during a week that we didn't have a game, I told him to forget about practice and sent him home to be with his mother. We had two or three games left in the season. During the week her son was home, Mrs. Badinghaus said she wanted Eddie to come back to Akron to finish his season. I didn't think that was a good idea. Losing your mother while you're winning games is not my idea of a proper trade-off.

"Eddie," I told him when he called, "I think you ought to stay there. You don't know how long your mother is going to live."

Mrs. Badinghaus wouldn't hear of this. She told Eddie to go back to school, that she'd live until he came home after the season.

So Eddie came back and played the last two or three games. Then he left school early and returned home. His father and sisters were working, and his mother needed him. That January during a recruiting trip to Cincinnati, I went to see Eddie. When I walked in, I found this 6-foot-5, 270-pound giant washing dishes in the kitchen. I talked to Eddie for a while and then went upstairs to visit Mrs. Badinghaus, who was on her deathbed. Eddie came up and Mrs. Badinghaus said she had something important she wanted to say.

"There is one thing I want to tell you before I die," she said.

"What's that, Mrs. Badinghaus?" I asked.

"Would you promise me that Eddie will graduate?"

"Mrs. Badinghaus, you have my promise. You can go to God knowing it will happen."

I left there with tears in my eyes. Here's this mother on her deathbed and all she can think about is how much she wants her son to get his degree.

Eddie graduated the following year and now has a great job with Roadway Express. Anytime he would slip a little in his grades or miss a class or encounter some roadblock, I'd call him into my office.

"Eddie," I'd remind him, "do you remember you and me sitting with your mother as she was on her deathbed? What did we promise her?"

"Yeah, I know, Coach."

"You loved your mom, didn't you?"

"More than anything."

"Well then, we've got one thing to get done."

"We'll get it done, Coach."

When I saw Ed after he graduated, I told him: "There's only one person happier than you and me and she's in heaven."

As much as I love mothers, it takes more than winning their hearts to be a good recruiter. A great recruiter, assistant coach or head coach, has to have the personality to communicate with anybody. He has to be organized. He has to be persistent, without being obnoxious. He has to be sincere. And finally, and most important, he has to be able to analyze talent before recruiting it. If a coach can't evaluate talent correctly—and we all miss sometimes—he will sell the wrong players on his university. They will be dissatisfied, and he'll soon be unemployed.

I fired one of the best organizers I've ever met as a coach, and I can't say it often enough: I made a big, big mistake. Tom Backhus played for me at Moeller. He became Ohio State's captain. He coached at Wisconsin and at the Air Force Academy, where he was offensive coordinator. He was a great young man but didn't get along with some of the other coaches on our first staff and I listened to the wrong people. I sent him packing when I should have sent some other guys. I failed because I didn't remember one of the qualities I value most: loyalty. I should have been loyal to one of my own, because I know he was loyal to me. Every player he recruited during his one season with me started and played for us for at least two years. Because I didn't listen to my heart, he didn't get to see that happen. He left coaching and moved back to Colorado where he went into real estate and now owns a dude ranch. I've told Tom that he was one of the bigger mistakes I made in coaching. I've apologized more than once. But how do you make up for changing a person's life as I changed his?

Tom should have been there the day that Greg Blache and I were recruiting Eric Dorsey. He deserved to experience what Greg did that day. I had been recruiting in Texas and flew back to South Bend on the plane of an alumnus to pick up Greg. I called from the plane to the airport in South Bend to ask if we could get some shrimp and cocktail sauce delivered to the plane when we landed. We were taking off for Virginia right away and it was Friday. I know it's OK for Catholics to eat meat on Fridays now, but I still don't do it. So we flew to Washington, eating shrimp, drinking Diet Coke and talking recruiting strategy.

When we touched down at the airport, Walt Connelly, who was a top-notch Washington lawyer and has since moved to Detroit, but remains a dedicated Notre Dame fan, met us to take us to McLean to see Eric and then to Sterling, Virginia, to meet with Allen Pinkett. Notre Dame men would meet us all around the country in their cars and take us where we needed to go. It helped us immeasurably, and it made them a part of the football program. On this trip, Walt pulled up in a white limousine that stretched into next week. I've never been so embarrassed in all my life. I mean, would you want to pull up to a high school in a stretch limousine? They probably thought I was a non-traditional student who got the day for the prom wrong.

Greg and I climbed into the back with Walt. The limo had a TV, bar, anything you wanted. And I don't even drink.

"Walt," I said, "I really appreciate you doing this. But don't ever pick me up in a stretch limo again. I'm just a football coach. I'm not the President of the United States. (That was Ronald Reagan, who had better years than I did.)

"I know you mean well and I really appreciate your loyalty and friendship. But I'm really uncomfortable. It just isn't me."

Greg couldn't contain himself.

"Walt! Coach!" he almost shouted, "I'm going to tell you something. I'm going to make a phone call to my buddies in New Orleans tonight. I'm going to tell them I flew on a private jet today. I had shrimp cocktail. I got off the plane and a stretch limousine met me. My buddies think I'm a coach at Notre Dame. When I tell them this, they'll think I'm selling dope instead of coaching football at Notre Dame."

We all broke up.

"Hey," Greg said, "this is living."

And it was.

Sometimes, though, the living wasn't easy.

When we were recruiting Tim Brown in Dallas, we planned very carefully how to use our three official visits most effectively. Jay Robinson, Brian Boulac and Joe Yonto had a battle plan that would have made Gen. Colin Powell proud. Jay went to Tim's high school, Woodrow Wilson, one day and I came flying in that night. Jay got Tim's transcripts, met his coach, and then we met at Tim's house that night so I could get to know Tim and his parents. A couple of weeks later Tim visited Notre Dame. In the meantime, we were in touch with his brother, whom Tim admired. We saved our final two visits for the day before national signing day and the day itself. We never broke a rule, not even in telephoning Timmy. We were battling three other schools from the Southwest Conference and the Big Eight. It wasn't easy. Texas was new and tough recruiting territory for Notre Dame. Jay Robinson found out how tough.

When Jay and Timmy talked in the high school the day before national letter day, Timmy told him he was going to tell his principal that he had made his decision. He was coming to Notre

Dame.That evening,Timmy was supposed to meet Jay at his house. Jay had taken a tape of "Wake Up the Echoes." Timmy didn't show for the show.When Jay called to tell me what was happening, I told him that he should stay another half hour but not make a nuisance of himself.The Browns had other young children. I suggested he leave his hotel phone number and ask the Browns to call when Tim came in. I got a call an hour later. Still no Tim.

Jay returned to his hotel. He called me again at 11 p.m., upset.

Jeez, I thought, we'd lost Tim Brown.

"Coach," Jay said, "I just got an anonymous phone call and the person told me that if I didn't get out of the state of Texas by midnight, they were going to do me bodily harm."

"Jay," I said, "go downstairs, see the manager, get another room.Tell the manager to call the police and tell them you were threatened. Don't worry. Just call me back when you get your new room. Give me that room number. Tell the hotel to put through only two callers: the Browns and me.Then call the Browns and tell them your new room number."

He did all of this and then called me again.

"Tim still isn't home and the Browns just got a phone call. The person said that if Timmy left the state of Texas, the Browns' house would be burned down."

Nice, huh?

I called Mrs. Brown.

"Don't worry about that," I told her. "It isn't going to happen."

Easy for me to say. I was in South Bend. I was not receiving threats.

I told Mrs. Brown that we had called the police and that we'd go to the newspapers if we had to. I asked her to tell anyone who called that Notre Dame was going to make this public if they received any more calls. She agreed.

At midnight, my phone rang again. It was Jay. Timmy had finally returned home.

Jay had asked where he had been and Tim said that when he told his principal, who operated the clock at SMU football games, that he had chosen Notre Dame, the principal took him for a ride to SMU.They kept him there five or six hours trying to convince him to change his mind.

He didn't.

This required a new plan. I told Jay to be outside of Timmy's house at 5 a.m. the next day. Wait and watch.

"Don't go to the door before 8," I said. "That's when we're allowed to sign Timmy. If another coach shows up and goes to the door, you go with him and make sure he doesn't try to sign that young man until 8 a.m. Have Tim call me after he signs with us."

No one showed up the next morning except Jay and he signed Timmy at 8:01 a.m. When Timmy called I said: "You're never going to regret choosing Notre Dame."

Four years later, Tim Brown won the Heisman Trophy and SMU had been placed on probation, its football program put in mothballs by the NCAA for recruiting violations. It took courage but Tim Brown and his family withstood the pressure and it paid off for him.

In order to recruit players such as Tim Brown in Texas and others nationwide, a coach needed a fast plane and a relentless nature. These things, or magic. Once upon a time, the UCLA staff thought I did it with mirrors.

Ron Hudson, whom we'd hired from UCLA, told the Notre Dame staff that once the Bruins staff argued about me in one of its meetings. One of its coaches saw me in Texas on the same day that another of the UCLA coaches swore he saw me in Northern California. It seemed unlikely that people were going around wearing Gerry Faust masks. So what the heck was going on here? they asked.

Like all staffs, UCLA was trying to figure out who their competition was for certain players.

"We know Faust is interested in this player in Texas," one of them said. "He was there."

"No he wasn't," argued another. "He was in San Francisco, talking to another player. I know. I saw him."

"Look," said the first coach, "I know who Faust is, and he was in Texas that day."

"Well," said the second coach, "I know who he is, too, and he wasn't in Texas. He was in San Francisco."

Actually, I was in both places. I had a private jet and we flew from Texas to California so I could see both players within hours of each other.

I never minded the travel. It went with the territory. That's not to say it wasn't scary at times. Once, I was with my pilot, Bill Corbett, in Joliet, Illinois, on a recruiting trip when an ice storm struck. I had to get back to South Bend, but we'd left the plane outside and ice had formed on the wings. The small airport where we were moored lacked de-icing equipment. We couldn't fly without removing the ice from the wings. I probably could have melted the ice with my hot air, but we moved the plane into a hangar to warm it and melt the ice. It was a good idea, but it wasn't working. That's when we took to brooms. We whacked the wings with the broom handles to knock off the ice. That worked. Except for one thing. We punched a hole in one of the wings.

"That won't hurt," Bill said.

I didn't know whether to believe him or not. Since Bill was going to be in the plane, too, I figured he wasn't kidding me. And he wasn't. We flew back to South Bend on a wing, a prayer and a hole.

I learned to listen to Bill Corbett, to trust his judgment and not to try to tell him how to fly his airplane. It wasn't an easy lesson for me. On one occasion we were flying from South Bend to Ashtabula, Ohio, which is east of Cleveland. Fog had closed the small airport near Lake Erie that would have put us down close to the place where I was to speak.

"I can't land," Bill said. "We'll have to go back to Cleveland and drive over."

"Jeez, Bill," I said, "that's 70 miles. I don't want to drive all the way over there, speak and then have to drive back and fly home."

What I wanted didn't cut through the fog. We contacted Bill McCartney, a Notre Dame supporter for whom I had agreed to give the speech, and he met us in Cleveland.

On the drive to Ashtabula, I was steaming. I didn't say anything, but I wasn't happy. It wasn't my finest moment. I spoke to the all-star sports banquet, got back into the car and returned to Cleveland, thinking all the way about the 2 1/2 hours that we had wasted while driving.

Bill got us safely back to South Bend, and when I got up early the next morning and grabbed the paper, I couldn't believe the headline on the sports page. Memphis State coach Rex Dockery had been killed the night before in an airplane crash. They tried to land in the fog.

When I saw Bill Corbett that day, I said: "Bill, don't you ever, ever let me talk you out of doing what you know is best."

Boy, did I learn a lesson.

Not every coach likes flying in small, private planes, even if he has a pilot as good and trusted as Bill Corbett. George Kelly, our linebacker coach, and I were in Peoria, Illinois, on a recruiting trip and on the return to South Bend, the left engine of the plane quit.

I was sitting in the co-pilot's seat next to Bill, and George was in one of the two seats behind us. We were 60 miles from South Bend and at an altitude from which we could see the airport.

"We can make it fine on one engine," Bill reassured us. "But fasten your shoulder belts."

I hooked mine into position. Bill had his on. I told George to put his shoulder belt on. He said there wasn't one. Only the belt that went across his lap.

"OK, George," I said, "take off your glasses and put your head between your knees and keep it there until we land."

Bill, who is truly a great pilot, brought us down as smoothly as he would have with two engines instead of one. When we pulled over to the fixed-base operation area to park the plane, I climbed out, followed by Bill and, finally, George, who hadn't said a word for 20 minutes. When George set foot on the runway, the words poured out.

"Coach," George said, "you can fire me, but I'll never get in a private airplane again. I'll quit first."

"George," Bill said, "there wasn't any problem."

"You may think there was no problem, but I value my life."

From then on, George Kelly's recruiting was grounded or limited to commercial flights.

As threatened as George felt in that circumstance, I'm glad he wasn't with Don Dorini and me in Florida on a recruiting trip that almost ended in disaster. Don, a Notre Dame alumnus, was flying me from a recruiting visit in Fort Lauderdale to another in Sarasota. As with Bill, I was in the co-pilot's seat. The day was beautiful. We had the plane zeroed in on the course set in our flight plan, flying with the aid of radar. All of a sudden, we dropped like a rock. I had had my eyes closed and opened them just in time to see another plane miss us by a margin so small I don't like to think about it.

If both pilots had dived when they saw each other, there would have been a great coaching job open. Don got on the radio and suggested to the air traffic controller that he do things to himself that I don't believe are physically possible. The controller should have known that both planes were at the same altitude. He should have warned us. When we landed, Don said he'd probably end up with his license suspended for upbraiding the controller as he had, using language laced with words I don't use but which I understood under the circumstances.

"Don," I said, "you won't be suspended. I'll go to court if they do that to you. I saw that plane. I saw what happened. It's lucky we both didn't go to heaven."

Despite such incidents, general aviation is a boon to recruiting. I learned that on the first recruiting trip I ever took for Notre Dame. From Cincinnati, where I had been trying to get things squared away to launch my new life as a college coach, we flew to Morehead, Kentucky, to pick up Tom Lichtenberg, my new offensive coordinator and old friend. We met Lichty at this little airport and flew to Pittsburgh, landing at Monroeville Airport, which is on a mountaintop. I was excited, but not by the airport on a mountain. I was going to talk with Bill Fralic, as good an offensive lineman as there was in high school football.

From there, we flew to Warren, Ohio, where Bill Mayo, another big offensive lineman from Dalton, Georgia, was visiting, with his parents, during the Thanksgiving holiday weekend. Two visits. Two linemen bigger than the Monroeville Airport mountain. But that was only the beginning. We went on to Chillicothe, Ohio, to talk with Garin Varis, a great tight end. We spent an hour at each stop and took off. Our final stop was in Chattanooga, Tennessee, to visit with Tom Taylor.

One day, four visits, four players who became All-Americans. None of them at Notre Dame. We lost Fralic to Pittsburgh, which had been recruiting him, it seemed, from the time he was in diapers. He loved his family and wanted to stay close to home. Bill Fralic told me the toughest thing he ever had to do was tell me no. Notre Dame would have been his second choice. We lost Varis to Stanford because of its track program. We lost Mayo to Tennessee because he wanted to be close enough to home that his parents could see him play. We lost Taylor to UCLA because he wanted to become an actor.

People tell me how easy it is to recruit for Notre Dame. I tell them they should have flown with me for just that one day. My son, Gerry, did fly with me, but not for just one day. He made trips with me frequently. Because I was gone from home so many evenings and weekends, I tried to do something special with each of my children during the times we were together. I'd take my daughter, Julie, to dinner. Just the two of us. We'd talk and share the days that we had missed. With son Steve, it was our Sunday ritual of going to Mass together and then to McDonald's before I had to go to the office and begin preparation for the next opponent. It may seem like too small a moment to matter, but it did matter, believe me. With son Gerry, recruiting was the bond. I'd let him travel with me —as long as he could do his homework on the way.

On one occasion as we winged our way from South Bend to Kirkwood, Missouri, to visit Alvin Miller, Gerry was studying biology. Later it would seem to me that he must have been studying psychology.

When we got to the Millers' home, Bill Corbett, the Notre Dame graduate who flew off of aircraft carriers as a Navy pilot, young Gerry and I were sitting in the living room talking to Alvin and his parents when suddenly Gerry and Alvin began talking to each other. This upset me, but I tried to keep my cool.

As I was trying to give Alvin my pitch, he got up with my boy and they went into Alvin's room. Then I was really upset. Bill knows it, but he keeps quiet. Bill knows me as well as anyone. He should. During my five years at Notre Dame, I think I spent more time with him than I did with my wife. I know: Unlucky Bill. Lucky Marlene.

Anyway, I turned my concentration to Mr. and Mrs. Miller. They are nice people. Critical in the recruiting process. But they weren't wide receiver Alvin, *Parade* magazine's All-America Player of the Year. No matter how much parents like a coach, the young man who is making a life decision is the bottom line.

Twenty minutes ticked by. Slowly. I'm talking, calmly, but burning on the inside, thinking: Wait until I get that son of mine on the plane. I'm going to strangle him for this. Gerry was in the ninth or 10th grade at the time and there was a good chance he wasn't going make it to the 11th grade because of this night. I was so mad I can't even believe it.

When Alvin and Gerry came back into the living room, Gerry announced: "Dad, Alvin just committed to Notre Dame."

In that instant, my anger vanished and my mouth dropped open.

Looking at Alvin's scrapbook in his bedroom, my son had convinced Alvin to come to Notre Dame. Suddenly, I put my arm around the boy I was ready to strangle. Believe me, I was thanking him.

Alvin's parents were proud and happy, but neither of them was the proudest, happiest parent in that room that night. All the way back to South Bend, I kept telling young Gerry that he was my ace recruiter.

"According to the national press," Father Joyce says, "it was Gerry who was a sensational recruiter. Right away, he was the best recruiter in the country as far as the ratings services were concerned.

"Of course, that backfires if you bring all-stars in and then you lose six games. People say: Well, who's fault is it? So it's a double-edged sword. It really is. But for the first two or three years, Gerry's recruiting classes were rated very high."

Sensitive or suicidal recruiter, I always was happy to have any help I could get in finding and recruiting players. I took young Gerry to Missouri to spend some time with him and he recruited this wonderful player with whom he would form the closest of bonds in the next four years. Most of the time, however, it was the Notre Dame birddogs who helped our recruiting most. No longer permitted under NCAA rules, the birddog system that Brian Boulac had in place when I arrived was a wonder to behold. These were people around the country, some alumni, some subway alumni, some members of Notre Dame clubs, who loved to go to watch high school football games and spot talent, people who were willing to pick up our coaches at the airports and drive us to the homes of recruits, guys who would save us time by collecting game films from the high schools and do anything else that would help.

When a school recruits nationwide, as Notre Dame does, this system can save not only time but also money. Don't misunderstand. This wasn't one of those sleazy, big-bucks-in-fat-envelope, sugar-daddy deals. We did it right. Once a year, we had the birddogs come to South Bend at their own expense. We'd give them food, lodging and conduct a two-day seminar on rules and regulations. All they got out of it was a Notre Dame coaching shirt and the feeling, which was accurate, that they were contributing something important to Notre Dame football.

We had to send a coaching shirt to Jim Kennedy, the best of our birddogs. Bedridden for 19 years, Jim made calls from his home in Philadelphia to players, high school coaches or anyone else we asked. If it hadn't been for Jim Kennedy, our recruiting would have been less successful than it was. I had made him my administrative aide to help him pass the time. As it turned out, he helped us more than we helped him. Jim eventually overcame the illness that had put him in bed and now works for Billy O'Leary's Funeral Home in Philadelphia. I owe him a lot.

To my knowledge, neither Jim nor any of the other birddogs ever broke a rule, which speaks volumes about their character. I wish I could say the same about the character of some of the coaches against whom we recruited.

Two or three weeks after my son, Gerry, had locked up Alvin Miller, Alvin telephoned me. He said that an assistant coach from a major school in the Midwest had been on his doorstep for a week. He would sit in his car outside the Miller house and wouldn't leave. Alvin had told him that he was committed to Notre Dame and intended to honor his commitment.

"Is there anything you can do?" Alvin asked me.

I asked where I could reach him and told Alvin I would call him back.

Then I called the home of the head coach from this school. The coach's wife answered.

"This is Gerry Faust," I said. "Is Coach there?"

"Yes," she said, "but he's on another telephone line."

"Well, this is my phone number. You tell Coach to call me back in the next five minutes. If he doesn't, I'll be calling the NCAA."

Two minutes later my phone rang. Surprise, surprise. It was the coach.

"What are you doing threatening my wife?" he screamed.

"Wait a minute, Coach," I said. "Do you want to listen? Or do you want me to call the NCAA now? I don't think it's your wife who should feel threatened."

He decided he wanted to listen.

"Coach," I said, "one of your assistants has been sitting outside of Alvin Miller's door for a week. Alvin just called and said he doesn't want him there. He's tired of it. I'd appreciate it if you'd get the guy out of there. If he's not gone in an hour, maybe the NCAA will be able to get him out of there."

I called Alvin and told him that the coach outside had an hour to leave and asked him to call to let me know what happened. A half hour later, Alvin called and said the coach had left. He never came back. I don't know if the head coach knew the assistant was putting an unwanted full-court press on Alvin Miller, but it didn't matter. It was his responsibility.

You can't control every action of your assistant coaches when they are recruiting. What you can do is tell them what we told our staffs at both Notre Dame and the University of Akron. We'd meet and go over the rules and their nuances. Coaches will make mistakes. They'll misunderstand or misinterpret a rule. I've done it. I can forgive those mistakes. What I cannot forgive is making a mistake between right and wrong.

"If you break any of the rules," I told every staff I ever had, "you're done. You can look for another job."

To my knowledge, no one did. I meant what I said, and they knew it.

Sonny Spielman found out the same thing. Sonny was an assistant coach at legendary Massillon High School. I'd known Sonny for years. Once, when I was coaching at Moeller, he'd gotten in touch to ask if I could send him two Moeller T-shirts for his sons. I did. One of those boys was Chris Spielman, who turned out to be one of the greatest high school linebackers ever. He was so good they put him on a Wheaties box.

When Mike Stock and I were recruiting Chris, we went to visit him at Massillon High, which, I was shocked to find, was more like a dungeon than a school. Here was this great football program and this second-rate educational facility. It wasn't right and the people in Massillon knew it. They've since built a wonderful school for their children, one that matches Paul Brown Tiger Stadium in stature.

Mike had hoped we'd have the opportunity to talk to Chris alone. No such luck. Sonny, who was a junior high school teacher as well as assistant high school football coach, was there, and he had a clipboard.

"I've got a bunch of questions to ask you," he said.

"OK, go ahead," I said.

He studied his clipboard, then began.

"How many season tickets do players get?"

"Four," I told him. "Just what the NCAA allows."

"Is there any chance to get more?"

"Nope. You'll be lucky to get four. The stadium is sold out. The only thing you can do is have Chris talk to the other players. If they aren't using their tickets, they can sometimes help out one another."

"How about a parking pass?"

"Nope. We don't give out parking passes. You can buy them."

I don't remember all the questions. There were about 20. I do remember I said no about 10 times. Sonny didn't like my answers, and Chris, even though he is Catholic, wouldn't even visit Notre Dame. He went to Ohio State, where he became an All-American and then, of course, went on to a Pro Bowl career in the National Football League.

That was not, however, the worst of the auditions staged by a prospective player's parents. While parents may mean well, these dog-and-pony coach shows can get out of hand and should remind everyone that we are talking about a college education for a young man 18 or 19 years old, not about a Hollywood audition. Is it any wonder that athletes sometimes lose their perspective and come to think they are more important than they are?

After Ray Huckestein from Pittsburgh North Allegheny High School had visited Notre Dame, he told us that he wasn't interested. We backed off. That was our policy. We didn't camp, unwanted, on doorsteps. A week later, though, we got a call from Ray's father who told us that Ray had reconsidered. He still would choose among five schools: Stanford, Pitt, Penn State, Ohio State and Notre Dame. He'd make his decision on the following Tuesday night. Ray's father invited us to come talk with Ray and set a time. We said we would be there.

I went to Pittsburgh with another of our coaches. Unbeknownst to us, Pitt, Penn State and Ohio State coaches also had been invited. The Huckesteins had just given all of us different times. We ended up waiting at a local restaurant, and who was there but Joe Paterno and one of his Penn State assistant coaches. They asked what we were doing there, and we told them.

"What are you doing here?" I asked Joe.

"Same thing," he said. "This is the part of college coaching that gets awfully ugly."

"Boy, I agree with you. The parents get involved. They take over. I know they want to do what's best for their son, but they are putting him under a lot of pressure with us going in one after the other."

It was like a wake or a wedding. I can't figure out which. The family formed the receiving line and we went through. Pitt first. Ohio State second. Us third. Penn State fourth. Walking up to the door of the house, I passed Ohio State coach Earle Bruce.

"This is unbelievable," Earle said.

"Tell me, Coach," I said. "And Paterno is coming in after us."

"He is?"

"Yeah, I just saw him in the restaurant."

We went in. Did our half hour. Left. On our way out, here comes Paterno on his way in.

"Isn't this ridiculous?" he said.

"Coach, this is what it's come to. This is what we have to do."

I just started laughing. Then Joe started laughing. But guess who had the last laugh? Stanford. The only school not there that night but the school Ray wanted to go to all along. His parents had been trying to convince him to stay closer to home. Hoping we could help them. I can't blame them for that. We tried.

Waiting in line at a restaurant to see a recruit, I can tell you, is infinitely preferable to waiting in your car in the driveway on what must have been the coldest night in Iowa history. At least it was the coldest night I ever spent in my life. I'd gone with an assistant coach to visit the home of Milt Jackson, a wonderful wide receiver from Fairfield, Iowa. We had a 9 p.m. appointment to meet Mr. and Mrs. Jackson, whom I had not met before. We flew into Ottumwa, Iowa, and drove to Fairfield only to find at Milt's home coaches from Iowa State, one of the three schools he was considering.

We waited in the car for 10 minutes, 20 minutes, 30 minutes. The Iowa State guys did not leave. We were freezing and I believe to this day the Iowa State coaches knew we were out there and were just stalling to make us suffer and to reduce the time we would have with the Jacksons, who were such kind people that they didn't know how to tell the coaches in the house to leave.

It was 9:50 p.m. when Iowa State left and we got out of the car and headed for the door. I knew Mr. Jackson had to get up at 5 a.m. to get to work.

"We're going to stay five minutes," I told the assistant coach.

When the Jacksons had greeted us and welcomed us into their home, I told them: "You know, it's 5 minutes until 10. I just came to meet you, Mr. and Mrs. Jackson. You have a great son, but I'm not going to stay tonight. I know you've got to get up early to go work, Mr. Jackson. It's not fair to you to make you sit up and listen to me talk about Notre Dame. We have a quality university. I think it speaks for itself.

"I'll be up front. If your son comes to Notre Dame, I'll look out for him. I think the world of him as a person and as a football player. If he works hard, I'll guarantee you that he'll graduate from one of America's great universities. Now, I'm leaving."

I hugged Mrs. Jackson and shook Mr. Jackson's hand. You could see the relief on their faces. They were worn out.

"Coach," Mr. Jackson said, "we're sorry. We couldn't get them out of the house."

"That's all right, Mr. Jackson. They were just trying to sell their program. We don't have to sell ours."

We were there five minutes. We wanted Milt in the worst way, and I had no idea what Milt would do. But we had done our homework: We knew his dad had to be at work early and that his mom was a teacher who also had to be at school early.

The other guys overstayed their welcome. We stayed five minutes and got Milt, who called a week later and committed to us. In recruiting, you have to sense how you'd feel in a situation.

If recruiting can depend on a spur-of-the-moment decision based on an understanding of people's situations, it also can come down to a lifelong relationship. That's how I was able to locate Daron Alcorn, a punter and placekicker who won more than one game for me and became our first player at the University of Akron to be drafted by an NFL team.

We needed a great combination kicker, and I have a buddy, Ray Pelfry, who owns a kicking camp in Sparks, Nevada. Ray and I go back to the '60s and my first year at Moeller High School. Because we were a new school and starting with freshmen, we couldn't begin football until September. So I went back to Dayton and volunteered to help Ray at Roosevelt High School in the inner city. I knew if I was going to coach a long time that I would be working with many inner-city athletes. I wanted to understand these young men, to get to know them and to see how a great communicator such as Ray worked with them. I not only learned a lot but I also became close with Ray. Who would know that 30 years later, he would give me the name of a kicker? The Good Lord has done a lot of good things to help me.

When Ray sent me the tape on Daron Alcorn from Mountain View High School in Vancouver, Washington, I called Daron right away and offered him a scholarship. Akron wasn't like Notre Dame. We did not recruit nationally. Our budget wouldn't allow it. But we could target certain players. Daron came to Akron for a visit and liked the University. So I went to Washington to meet his parents, his coaches, his teachers. His father worked at a Christian radio station but also was a minister. We got along great, and Daron chose Akron over Washington State of the Pac-10.

If I didn't know how much of a recruiting coup this was, I discovered quickly. On his first kick as a freshman, he made a 47-yard field goal off the grass at Virginia Tech. I knew then that we had a winner. In a game against Toledo, he kicked a 56-yarder with six seconds remaining for the victory. He did those things consistently and punted the same way. Though he hasn't made it in the NFL, I have always felt that Daron had more potential than John Carney, who played for us at Notre Dame and who is a great kicker for the San Diego Chargers. Daron just needs a break—like the one I got when Ray Pelfry gave me his name.

Daron Alcorn may have been a gift from a friend, but he was not the easiest recruit I ever had. It wasn't even one of my own players from Moeller. It was Mike Golic. Mike, who became a great outside linebacker for the Irish, stood out on a list of must-get recruits that Brian Boulac gave me when I took over as coach. I took the list home to Cincinnati with me for Thanksgiving and immediately began making calls. One was to Mike, a senior at Cleveland St. Joseph.

Mike's brother, Greg, was an offensive tackle at Notre Dame at the time, and, of course, Bob Golic had been an All-America middle linebacker for Notre Dame. So when I told Mike that it was Gerry Faust and that I was calling to offer him a scholarship, I didn't have to say anything else.

"I'm coming," Mike said. "I don't even need to visit. I've been there many times to see my brothers play."

"Mike," I said, "that's great."

I talked to his parents and told them I wouldn't be coming to see them during the normal recruiting period since Mike already knew what he wanted from a college and Notre Dame had it. I said I'd stop by after recruiting season. Everyone said that would be fine.

"I really want to play for Notre Dame and you," Mike said.

That was it.

Even my own players at Moeller who came to Notre Dame that first year—Mark Brooks, Mike Larkin and Mike Lane—visited other schools first.

Like Mike Golic, I knew Notre Dame was right for me. That's why I never considered leaving Moeller for a college assistant coaching job elsewhere or even for another head coaching job on the college level. I had been approached by two universities and had turned them down. In my heart I was holding out for Notre Dame. That's what Stan Smagala did, too.

When Lou Holtz succeeded me at Notre Dame, he found himself facing a commitment I had made. That was to Stan Smagala from Burbank, Illinois, which is near Chicago. We committed early only to the players we felt were the surest of the sure to make it on the level Notre Dame plays. That was Stan.

Lou, however, disagreed. He told Stan and his parents as much but promised to honor the scholarship offer anyway. Lou and I would talk every three or four weeks, and he told me the same thing about Stan.

"Lou," I said, "I think Stan is pretty darn good. But you have to make that judgment. I appreciate that you'll honor the scholarship offer, but I want to try to recruit him for Akron."

"That's fine," Lou said.

So I called Stan. Not every coach has the chance to offer a young man two scholarships. I did. I told Stan that I wanted him to come to Akron with me and I had no reservations about his ability. That went without saying, since I thought he could play at Notre Dame's level. Stan came to Akron for a visit, and I went into his home. I'd become true friends with his parents, who had decided they didn't want Stan to go to Notre Dame if Lou Holtz didn't really want him. Stan's dad had played football and knew if the coaching staff lacks confidence in a player, he won't play. He also knew Stan wouldn't be happy if he didn't play. He loved football too much.

When I got to Stan's home one evening, we headed for the kitchen. It seems I'm always sitting at the kitchen table when I talk to people. It becomes a comfort zone. We can relax, put our arms on the table. People usually have food out. We can nibble and talk. I'm a relaxed recruiter, and I want others to feel relaxed. The Smagalas, however, were apprehensive.

"Coach," they told me, "do a great job tonight. We want Stan to come with you."

I tried. I told Stan how much a football program moving from Division I-AA to I-A needed players of his caliber. How much he could do for Akron. How much we wanted him and that he was the type of player who could play right away. I didn't promise players that they would start, but in this instance Stan's talent dictated that he would play from the outset. As I was getting ready to leave, I asked Stan when he was going to make up his mind.

"I'm going to make up my mind Saturday," he said. It was Tuesday.

"Who's it between, Stan?"

"Akron and Notre Dame. But, Coach, I've always dreamed of going to Notre Dame."

I looked Stan in the eye.

"Stan, if you've always dreamt of going to Notre Dame, then you go live your dream. You go to Notre Dame. If it doesn't work out, I'll always have a scholarship for you at the University of Akron."

His parents almost died when I said that.

But I understood how Stan felt. Notre Dame had been my dream, too. I couldn't have gone to Akron first. I had to try the dream. He had to do what was in his heart.

A year later, Lou Holtz called me. We still talk regularly.

"Boy," he said, "you were right and I was wrong. This Smagala is one heckuva football player."

Stan started for Lou for three years at right cornerback, including on the 1988 national championship team. Recruiting is a calculated risk no matter how good the player is. There always are circumstances—injury, academics, homesickness, early maturation as a player—that cause him to be less a player on the college level than the recruiters had projected. But I was glad I was right about Stan. Glad for him. Glad for Lou. But especially glad for Notre Dame. I never brought the school I loved a national championship, but I left Lou some of the talent that he molded into a national champion. Besides Stan, who was in the 1985 recruiting class, the 1984 group was filled with major contributors: Darrell "Flash" Gordon, LB; Wes Pritchett, LB; Tim Brown, SE; Andy Heck, OT; Mark Green, TB; Ned Bolcar, LB; D'Juan Francisco, CB; George Streeter, SS; Ray Dumas, WR; Tom Gorman, OG; Cedric Figaro, LB; and Frank Stams, DE.

When it came to recruiting Stams, I sometimes couldn't tell whether we had the inside track that we should have had or not. Some Notre Dame fans will remember Frank as the All-American that Gerry Faust played out of position. That's not what I'll remember, except in the context of recruiting. Frank was a much sought-after running back and linebacker from Akron St. Vincent-St. Mary High School. The advantage we had with Frank was guys such as the late Eddy Niam and Dick Pitts. Eddy had been a birddog for Ara Parseghian, with whom he had grown up in Akron. Dick Pitts was

Frank's Godfather, a former great fullback at St. Vincent and Kent State University and owner of Green Hills Golf Course just outside of Akron. They really knew Frank.

The first time I got to know Eddy and Dick was when Mike Stock, who was recruiting Frank, asked if Eddy and Dick wanted to ride up to a Notre Dame game with Frank Sr. and Frank Jr. Eddy and Dick were close friends of Frank Sr., and Mike Stock knew everyone because he was from Barberton, which borders on Akron. As it turned out, Frank Sr. couldn't make the trip and so Frank Jr. came up with Eddy and Dick. When I saw Frank that day I asked if he had had a good trip to South Bend.

"No," Frank said. "I had to drive all the way. Those guys wanted to sit and talk."

Great, I thought. So I pulled Eddy and Dick aside and said: "Hey, we really want to get this kid. You guys drive. He's just 18. He shouldn't have to drive all that way."

They really listened. I found out just a couple of years ago that Eddy and Dick made Frank drive all the way home, too. Those guys were pistols.

When I flew in to Akron Fulton Airport to see Frank and his family, Eddy Niam met me in his big Lincoln. At least it wasn't a limo. Eddy owned a restaurant called Niam's. It's still in the family. Great place. It's stuffed with Notre Dame memorabilia, and Eddy made something called the Pigskin Sandwich, an oval-shaped hamburger. Eddy knew I loved them. So he had a couple in the car that I ate as we drove over to St. Vincent-St. Mary.

After I'd met Frank's principal and some other people, I went to the classroom where Frank was studying Algebra II. I talked to all the students for a few minutes and then asked Frank's teacher, who loved Notre Dame, if I could stand in for her for a few minutes. I guess Marlene was right about me wanting to dominate the room, but I was just having some fun. Learning should be fun.

I started writing a formula on the chalk board.

"Is that right?" I asked the class.

"Yeah," came the answer in unison.

"And this?"

"Yeah."

By now, the class is cheering, and I explained I had taught Algebra I at Moeller and how much math would help them to discipline their minds. When I left the classroom, a coach from another school was waiting in the hall. Eddy and Dick Pitts had told me that this coach was at St. V-M every day, which was illegal. So I confronted him: "Coach," I said, "you're breaking the rules right and left and I'm going to call your head coach. You live by the rules like the rest of us or suffer the consequences."

I didn't make the call. I hoped I wouldn't have to because Frank would commit to Notre Dame. That night when I went to the Stams' house, Eddy Niam was driving me. He's like a brother to Frank Sr., and when we got there he started to get out of the car.

"Eddy," I said, "you can't go in the house with me."

"What do you mean?" he said.

"I can't take you in. It's a rule."

"I grew up with these guys."

"Eddy, I don't care. I can't take you in. It'd be a violation."

I went into the house and didn't even tell them that Eddy was out in the car. We were talking. Time flew, and and I was thinking that Frank Sr. wanted to be recruited more than Frank Jr. He's just a wonderful guy, a vice principal who loves his son so much. It was that evening that I promised Frank Jr. he could play fullback. That's what he wanted. And he WAS a good fullback. He wasn't a great one, but good enough to play at Notre Dame's level.

"I'll let you play fullback, because that's what you want," I told him, "but you'd be a better linebacker."

Lou Holtz moved him to defensive end, which is a move we were going to talk to Frank about making if we had had the record to stay at Notre Dame. Maybe we'd have been better with Frank at defensive end. Maybe the record would have been better. But I'm not sorry I played Frank at fullback. That's the commitment I made and that's the commitment I kept. I think football should be fun, and for Frank, it was fun to play fullback.

We shook hands and the Stams family asked why I didn't stay longer.

"No," I said, "I've got Eddy Niam out in the car."

I pronounced it Nay-em.

"Who?" Frank Sr. said.

"Eddy Nay-em. N-i-a-m."

"That's Nigh-am. Why isn't he in the house?"

"He isn't allowed to come in."

"Why? He's like a brother."

"I know, but the NCAA says I can't bring him in."

"You made him wait outside for an hour?"

"Yeah."

They came outside with me and everyone is laughing about Eddy having to wait out there.

"Boy," Frank Sr. said, "is this guy by the book!"

"Yeah," Eddy said, "he wouldn't let me come in. If he had, I'd have had Frank sewed up by now."

The NCAA rules could be infuriating. Later, while recruiting Frank, I was invited to speak at a St. Vincent-St. Mary banquet. All I could do is say hello to Frank and tell him I wasn't allowed to talk to him any further. Same with Mr. and Mrs. Stams. It was stupid, but it was the rule and I wasn't going to break it.

The Sunday after Frank Stams visited Ohio State, he committed to us. Notre Dame got a great player, and I got some great friends in Eddy Niam, Dick Pitts and the Stams family. I wouldn't realize until a few years later how important they would become in my life. Regardless, what I cherish most about the recruiting experience are the people I met, some of whom I came to truly love.

As awkward as it was to keep Eddy Niam waiting outside the Stams' house, it was hardly my most awkward moment in recruiting.

When I was at Akron, one of the few distant states we recruited regularly was Florida. One season I was in the state to recruit the son of a family that worked in agriculture, picking oranges and other fruits and vegetables. They were hard-working people but didn't make much money and lived in a home that was spartan but clean. In Florida's near-tropical climate, a person can have a house that looks like a surgical suite and still have roaches. Down there, roaches are called Palmetto bugs. They're the size of B-29s and fly faster. They're scarier than Southern Cal.

As this player, his mother and I sat in their living room and discussed the University of Akron, I noticed some chicken in a skillet on the table in the kitchen. It smelled great and looked better. Col. Sanders would have been envious. I was on a diet, but anytime you go into a home and the family asks if you'd like something to eat, you eat. If you don't, the family may consider it an insult. This time, however, there were a number of problems and all of them were crawling on the chicken.

Holy mackerel—or, holy chicken!—I thought. Palmetto bugs!

"Would you like some chicken, Coach?" the player's mother asked.

My mind was whirring, my stomach churning.

"You know," I said, "I do love chicken but I'm on a diet. If you don't mind if I take off the skin, which is where all the calories are, I'd love to have some chicken."

"That would be fine," the mother said.

I figured by removing the skin, I was removing the part the Palmetto bugs had been running over, tap dancing on and doing no telling what else. The chicken was good—provided you didn't do too much thinking, chewing and swallowing at the same time. The best part was we got the player.

If what I put in my mouth almost got me in trouble, what came out of it had me worried in an entirely different circumstance. While recruiting our second class at Notre Dame, I visited California to talk with Rick DiBernardo, who was a tremendous linebacker at Huntington Beach High School.

When I arrived, Jack Snow, Notre Dame's All-America end in 1964, met me at the Los Angeles International Airport. Jack, of course, went on to fame with the Los Angeles Rams and as the father of J.T., San Francisco Giants' first baseman. As we were driving to Huntington Beach, which takes about an hour, Jack and I were talking and it became obvious to both of us that I couldn't pronounce DiBernardo.

I'm like that. I mangle words and names.

"OK, Coach," Jack kept saying, "how do you pronounce Rick's last name?"

"DeBartolo. No. He owns the 49ers and malls. Ah, Diba...Diba...Diba."

I just kept stuttering and sputtering, splattering that name the way a windshield splatters a bug when the bug hits it. It was ugly and about to become embarrassing.

As we were walking up the sidewalk to the house, Jack says one last time: "How do you pronounce the name?"

I butchered it again. I just couldn't get it. As we were knocking on the door, I'm telling Jack: "Man, this is going to be terrible. I just can't pronounce the name."

Then, as I was about to ask Jack the first name of Rick's father so I could call him by that name, the front door opened and Rick's dad was standing there, greeting us.

"Hey, Mr. DiBernardo!" I said. "How ya doin'?"

Jack almost fainted. He had been telling me all the way to the house that I was never going to get it right. Then Mr. DiBernardo opened the door and I nailed it the first time and every time after that.

When we left an hour and a half later and were back in Jack's car, Jack couldn't stop laughing.

"I can't believe it," he said. "Mr. DiBernardo opens the door and you get it right."

"When the pressure's on, Jack, you gotta come through."

Though I had done just that, I still thought we were going to lose Rick. The weekend he came to visit South Bend, it was 20 degrees below zero. Those were the days when we could pick up a player at the Chicago airport and fly him to South Bend. So Bill Corbett met Rick in Chicago and introduced himself. All the while, he's thinking: It's 20 below. This kid's from California. We don't have a snowball's chance in you know where with this guy.

But on the plane, Rick said to Bill: "Man, I love flying in this plane, and I really love this weather." Bill said he was thinking: I hate this weather. But what he said to Rick was: "Yeah, isn't this weather great!"

Rick committed to us that weekend.

As many rules as the NCAA has about recruiting, some situations defy even its edicts. That's when a person must fall back on his own standards of conduct. He has to know what is right and what is not. Admittedly, my standards aren't for everyone.

When we were recruiting quarterback John Paye from Atherton High School near Palo Alto, California, Ron Hudson and I flew into the San Jose airport to meet with John's mother, who was a Stanford University professor. John and his dad already had visited Notre Dame and liked it. So we had a shot at John.

As we were sitting in an airport restaurant talking to Mrs. Paye, Ron excused himself to go to make a telephone call. I felt embarrassed. Some men wouldn't be, but I was. Mrs. Paye, besides being intelligent, is blonde and attractive. There I was alone with her and I begin to worry that people would think it was a rendezvous of some sort. I'm recognizable. People know my wife, Marlene, is a brunette. So I was uncomfortable. I was talking to her about her son and Notre Dame. I was just recruiting, but it still didn't feel right. And it probably showed.

Not only did we lose John—he started for three years at Stanford—but I was embarrassed. When Ron came back I told him not to put me in that position again. It wasn't just about me, either. When we got back to Notre Dame, I told all the coaches that any time we were recruiting and we were talking to a mother and the father was not present, either in a public place or a private one, I wanted them with me. I wouldn't leave them, either. Maybe it sounds silly and naive. But it's a safeguard—for everyone.

Once, recruiting got even more awkward than it was with Mrs. Paye.

When I was coaching Akron, we were trying to recruit a kicker at an Arizona junior college to replace Daron Alcorn. This young man was from the Midwest, and we thought that might help attract him back to the area. So an assistant coach and I went to Arizona to see him. We were recruiting several players in Arizona and visiting all of them. We finished at another stop early and went on to the kicker's apartment. We knocked, but no one answered. We knocked again. Still no answer. Then, just as we were leaving, the door opened.

"Coach, I'm here," the young man said.

"We're early," I said. "We can come back."

"Naw, come on in."

He had a one-bedroom apartment, with a living room and kitchen. The bathroom was right off the kitchen and near the bedroom. So as I walked back to use the bathroom, I couldn't help but see a girl in bed. I don't think she had any clothes on.

I went on to the bathroom. I didn't know what to do. This guy was single. I don't want to preach or impose my moral values on others, but if a player will have a girl in his room in Arizona, he might do the same thing in Akron, and there is always the potential for trouble, and the person who is responsible is the head coach. I stayed in the bathroom longer than I would have otherwise, hoping the girl would have time to get dressed. When I heard her voice, I figured it was OK to come out.

She was sitting at the kitchen table with the kicker and my assistant coach as if nothing happened. But it had. I knew it. She knew it. And I was embarrassed again. The kicker introduced me to the girl. She seemed very nice. I told myself to stay out of it. But when we were leaving, the kicker said he would walk us to our car.

"Do your Mom and Dad know you're doing this?" I asked when we were outside.

"No," the young man said.

"Well, I can't condone it, and I don't know if your parents would, either. You have a lot of potential. You're an excellent student. But there are ways to date girls and ways not to do it. I don't know what you were doing, but it doesn't look good when I walk into the apartment and there is a girl in your bed with no clothes on. It doesn't leave a good impression. You'd have been better off if you had had us come back. You should use more common sense."

We had offered the Arizona kicker a scholarship, but he turned us down. I think we both knew why. We really needed that kicker. But I needed my self-respect even more. That's the rule I tried to follow, whether I was recruiting or coaching. It isn't in the NCAA rules book anywhere. You can't tuck it into your hip pocket and look it up. You have to carry that rule in your heart.

5

■ It's Not the Man, ■
It's the Position

Every Notre Dame football coach should drop by a hat shop once in a while and ask a sane hatter to measure his head. It's easy for it to grow bigger than it should be— even if he wins only a few more games than he loses, as I did.

The Notre Dame coach's mantra should be: It's not the man, it's the position.

It's not the man, it's the position.

It's not the man, it's the position.

People didn't want to meet Gerry Faust. They wanted to meet the Notre Dame football coach. And once you're the Notre Dame football coach, you're always the Notre Dame football coach.

I knew Ara Parseghian was. And why not? He won game after game after game, not to mention national championships. I know Lou Holtz will be a Notre Dame football coach forever. But me?

I couldn't see myself as Notre Dame coach emeritus. Not with my record (30-26-1). But Dan Devine told me it would happen to me, too. I didn't believe him. That's for the winners. I tried to bring honor to Notre Dame, even if I brought it less glory than I had hoped. Dan was in a different position. He won the 1977 national championship. If he received criticism, it was for not being as accessible as I was. Truth is, though, national championships rank higher than accessibility in most memories.

"Gerry," Dan told me at one point, "I've been out of coaching for three years now and I've found out something. Everywhere I go, Notre Dame people come up to me."

He seemed surprised. It was as if he were more approachable as the *former* Notre Dame coach, more accepted and respected, than when he had the job.

"Once you're the Notre Dame coach," Dan said, "you'll always be the Notre Dame coach."

For my own selfish gratification, I thought it would be nice if this were to prove true. But all I knew for sure at the time Dan told me this was that everyone viewed the Notre Dame football coach in a different way from other coaches. They put him on a pedestal. They expected more of him, certainly more than they had expected of the Moeller High School coach.

Lying just beneath the surface of this good-as-gold treatment are the expectations. When a man becomes Notre Dame's football coach, the expectations grow, even if he doesn't. On the outside, a man may appear to the world a greater success than he was before he became the Notre Dame coach, but on the inside, he is still the same guy, with the same faults, the same doubts, the same fears.

When I became the Notre Dame coach, I didn't consider myself to be famous or important. Those descriptions, I thought, applied to such men as Father Hesburgh and Father Joyce. Father Joyce had been a multi-dimensional leader not only on the Notre Dame campus but also nationally. In athletics, he was a national legend, in the NCAA and as one of the founders of the College Football Association (CFA). As for Father Hesburgh, he had served on so many national panels and committees and had received so many honorary degrees that it boggled the mind of a simple football coach who was lucky to have even three degrees to his name: bachelor's, master's and 98.6.

Early on, however, I came to understand that it was not always apparent to others whom they should consider important and whom they shouldn't. On one instructive, embarrassing occasion, Bill Corbett had flown me to Chicago where I was to catch a flight for the West Coast to recruit. I walked up to the ticket counter and presented my ticket. We had a rule at Notre Dame that we were to purchase coach-class tickets. I got my seat assignment. No fuss. No problems.

Then I got to the gate.

The person collecting the tickets recognized me, which was not unusual. My picture was often in newspapers and magazines and on television.

"How are you, Coach Faust?" the man asked.

"I'm fine," I said.

"We're really glad to have you at Notre Dame."

"Well, thanks. But I promise you, I'm happier to be at Notre Dame than you are to have me there. I really love the University."

The man smiled. I could tell he was thinking.

"Coach," he said, "we have some empty seats. I'm going to bump you up to first class."

"Thank you," I said, "but that's not necessary."

"No," he said, "I'm going to bump you up. It's no problem. I want to do it."

I didn't want to seem ungrateful or to hurt his feelings. So I said OK. Deep down, I was happy about it. It's a long flight to the West Coast—3 1/2 hours—and I knew I would be more comfortable in first class.

So there I was, sitting up there in the lap of luxury, drinking my tomato juice, stretched out, getting some work done when 10 or 15 minutes after takeoff one of the flight attendants stops at my seat and asks: "Aren't you Gerry Faust, the coach at Notre Dame?"

Notice, she didn't say: Aren't you Gerry Faust, that bright, handsome, clever guy who just happens to be the coach at Notre Dame?

I said: "Yes, ma'am, I am."

"Well," she said, "there's another person from Notre Dame in the rear section. He's a priest."

I thought it might be one of the many priests whom I had met since becoming coach. I asked her if she knew the priest's name.

"Yes," she said, "it's Father Hesburgh."

Oh no, I thought. You've got to be kidding. There I was, sitting in first class and Father Hesburgh was in coach and telling the flight attendant to come up and tell me hello. I got up and walked back to face the music. I didn't think it would be the Hallelujah Chorus.

"Hey, Father," I said. "It's great to see you. This guy at the gate recognized me when I was boarding and bumped me up to first class. You're welcome to sit up there. I'll take your seat."

"No, Coach," Father Hesburgh said, "you sit up there. But the thing that bothers me is that you've been at Notre Dame less than a year and I've been there more than 30 years and that guy puts you in first class and I'm sitting in coach."

He was kidding, but I really felt rotten.

"Father," I pleaded, "the seat is yours."

"No," he said. "You stay up there."

From that moment on, even though I knew Father Hesburgh was not really upset by the fact I had received an upgraded seat, the flight was ruined for me. My boss, this man whom I respected so much, was flying coach while I was in first class. I felt like two cents. No, make that one cent. I knew it was the position of Notre Dame football coach that the airline representative had upgraded, that he had wanted to do something nice for the man who happened to hold that position. But it was Gerry Faust who was sitting in the seat and, right then, it felt awfully hot to the man on it.

If Notre Dame football coaches in general and Gerry Faust in particular were on the hot seat, it was all Rockne's fault.

As people with even a casual interest in Notre Dame know, Knute Rockne was a student at the University, a chemist by training and football coach by choice. In Rockne, Notre Dame created a new faith—he converted to Catholicism—and he in turn created a deeper faith in and love for Notre Dame football. When he took over the football team in 1918 and started winning, people began to pay attention to this small, Catholic university that was knocking off the giants of college football. Here was David taking on Goliath, but with an early-day twist: Notre Dame was David. That sounds odd now, but with victory after victory, the school gained an East Coast following, particularly among Irish immigrants. The East Coast media was forced to pay attention to the little school from South Bend. First, Grantland Rice began writing about Notre Dame and, later, Red Smith. Rockne was beating the great Army teams in the East and eventually traveling to the West Coast to whip USC. The football not only was good but was also doing good. They say six or eight dorms on campus were built with proceeds from Rockne football. I like that. That's what football should do—contribute toward making a university great off the field as well as on it.

During Rockne's days my dad, Fuzzy, was an assistant coach at Cathedral Latin High School in Cleveland. My dad had played at Cathedral Latin and returned there from the University of Dayton to begin his coaching career. Everyone wanted Rockne as a speaker in those days. He was both eloquent and fiery, and while my dad was at Cathedral Latin, Rockne did come to speak at a football banquet, because he was recruiting a Cathedral Latin player. My dad, this obscure assistant high school coach, met the great Rockne the night he spoke. Three years later, after my dad had become head coach at Dayton Chaminade, he once again found himself at a function with Rockne, this time in Dayton.

Rockne walked right up to my dad and said: "Fuzzy, it's great to see you."

He had remembered my dad from three years before, and my dad never forgot that. From that moment on, he was a Rockne man. My dad used to talk about Rockne all the time. Talk to anyone in my dad's generation about football coaches and Rockne was the first name that came from their lips.

Rockne was different from other Notre Dame coaches. He was *the* Notre Dame football coach. In his case, it was the man, not the position, that mattered.

I think it was because I heard my dad talk so much and so glowingly about Rockne and Notre Dame that I became a Notre Dame fan and eventually the coach. I hope Rockne understood that the day I stood in the middle of the Stadium, looking to the heavens and talking to him like some crackpot. I mean, it *was* his fault I was there.

In the latter part of my tenure at Notre Dame, Ara Parseghian, who, as I've said previously, was kind, helpful and supportive, nevertheless made a statement about being Notre Dame football coach that upset me. He said that no one should be hired to coach Notre Dame unless he had 12 or 13 years of college head coaching experience. Now I wonder to whom Ara could have been referring?

After I cooled down, and as I looked back on it, not only did I understand the point Ara was making but I also think he was dead right. It troubled me at the time, because I thought of Ara as a good friend and this seemed as if it were an unnecessary slap at me. The job is difficult enough without your friends cuffing you around, too. So why would he say that?

Deep down, I knew. He said it because it was the truth. From Day One, Ara was honest with me. Much of what he told me came true, but it wasn't until I had coached at Akron for six or seven years that I truly appreciated what Ara had been saying that upset me at the time. By then, I had 11 or 12 years of experience and the problems we were experiencing at Akron weren't the consequence of my naivete but the result of other unique obstacles in the transition from Division I-AA to I-A football. What I had come to realize by then is that I knew so much more than I had during my first years at Notre Dame. I thought I had become a pretty dog-gone good college coach—my .500 record notwithstanding—and I finally realized that Ara wasn't taking a swipe at me. He was just saying that the Notre Dame position is unique and so demanding that without 11 to 13 years of experience, a coach may well be doomed to failure.

I'm glad he didn't put it to me that way when I first went to visit him after I'd been hired. If he had, I might have seen the future and it isn't something a person should see. I mean, do you want to know when at least a part of you is going to die?

What Ara said, in essence, is that the job is impossible. I was too naive to hear that. What he said was that people were seldom happy with a win—unless you weren't supposed to win, which is an oxymoron, because you are *always* supposed to win. They expect you to win. They expect you to recruit great players. They expect Notre Dame to have the No. 1 recruiting class each year. You can't do anything that isn't already expected from the man in that position.

The demands on the Notre Dame coach to be here, there and everywhere at the same time are unrelenting. Everyone's cause is an important one. So you stretch yourself. Father Joyce warned me. He said that I could turn down requests for my time and the University would support me. There are, after all, only 30 hours in a day. The irony is, the University asked me to do any number of things for it and that, too, added to the load. I did them, of course, because I truly wanted to do them. Anything to help. That was my motto.

When big donors came to campus, I met with them. When Bill Simon, former Secretary of the Treasury, visited, Notre Dame wanted me to entertain him. That was no problem. I knew and liked Bill. It was a pleasure. But it did take time.

In the middle of the 1983 season we had just beaten USC and were scheduled to play Navy the next week. Father Hesburgh and Father Joyce were going to Washington, D.C., to have dinner with President and Mrs. Reagan on Sunday night and they wanted Marlene and me to accompany them.

I told Father Joyce and Father Hesburgh that I'd rather stay home and prepare for the Navy game. Sunday was the staff's most intense night of preparation, the night that kicked off the week, in the right or wrong way. They said I ought to go. When Father Hesburgh and Father Joyce say you ought to go, you go.

We were flying from South Bend to Washington on a private jet and Father Joyce and Father Hesburgh had dug out of the Notre Dame vault a copy of the film "Knute Rockne All-American" in which President Reagan played George Gipp. They were going to present it to him that night. You talk about the mystique of Notre Dame and the power of the position of football coach: This was it.

I was a big fan of President Reagan, and now I was going to meet him and have dinner with him, along with a number of others. I couldn't think of a greater honor.

When we arrived, we had to go to the back entrance of the White House, where I saw for the first time the care exercised by the Secret Service. If these guys had been protecting my quarterbacks, they might never have been sacked. There was a Secret Service person about every 100 feet. Even on the White House lawn.

In the rear of the White House, we had to wait for a half hour. I swear it was so they could check us out with hidden cameras. It was a pretty upstanding group: Merlin Olsen, Joe Theismann, the publisher of *Sports Illustrated*. What it was, I think, was sports night at the White House.

When we went upstairs for a cocktail hour, there was a reception line in which Marlene and I met President and Mrs. Reagan. A photographer took our photo with the Reagans and President Reagan signed it and mailed it to me. I have it on my wall at home today. It's one of my prized possessions. It also reminds me what a picture or an autograph can mean to someone. It's one of the reasons I never turn down someone who wants an autograph. I'm not in President Reagan's league, but there's no accounting for taste.

Speaking of which, our Presidential dinner was much the same as on the sports-banquet circuit—chicken. It was good, but economical. I want everyone to know that Gerry Faust wasted no tax dollars. They must have spent the money on the china. I was really impressed with it. Remember the flap about Nancy Reagan and the china? Well, when you're sitting there eating off a plate with the presidential seal on it, that becomes more memorable than the food. But I know I would never have been eating dinner with the President of the United States if I hadn't been the Notre Dame football coach. Come on. They didn't invite me to these events when I was coaching Moeller High School or the University of Akron. Maybe they didn't know a person doesn't get elected president unless he carries Ohio.

A hostess told us where to sit. The men sat at two or three tables. The women at two or three others. Guess where I sat? One seat from President Reagan. Father Hesburgh, me, Merlin Olsen, a minister from Atlanta and the president. President Reagan, I discovered, loves to talk about football. So most of the night he talked to me. I didn't know what to do. Here's my boss, Father Hesburgh, one of the more famous and important men in the country, and the president wants to talk to me. I thought I was back in the first-class seats. It made me very uncomfortable.

It wasn't because I was talking with the president, the man who can call for the real bomb. President Reagan isn't intimidating in that way, and I wouldn't know enough to be intimidated if he were. Besides, I love to talk football—or most anything else for that matter. I'll talk football with anyone. White House custodian or White House proprietor. Doesn't matter.

The problem was, I didn't think it was my place to control the conversation. Later, it struck me. I wasn't controlling the conversation at all. The Notre Dame football coach was. No one wanted to hear what Gerry Faust had to say, but everyone wanted to hear from the Notre Dame football coach. I just happened to be the man in that position.

After dinner, at which Father Hesburgh and Father Joyce had presented President Reagan with the film, we adjourned to the White House movie theater. We had seats behind President Reagan and Mrs. Reagan, who sat in the front row, eating popcorn, having a soft drink and watching a movie, just like ordinary Americans out for a Sunday evening. There was, of course, a plot twist. The Ronald Reagan, who would stop the film now and then to tell us about the filming of a scene, was an actor who had risen to President, and I was a high school coach who had dreamed an equally big dream and had had it come true as Notre Dame coach. We may have been ordinary men, but the positions in which we found ourselves were extraordinary indeed.

To return to South Bend, we had to receive special permission to fly out of National Airport after 10 p.m. They don't give such permission to the Notre Dame football coach or even the president of the University. They do, however, give it to the White House chief of staff when he telephones on behalf of the President. Once again, position matters.

A late-night flight from Washington to South Bend might seem as if it would be a burden. It was just the opposite. Father Hesburgh made it a joy. He talked us home, and it was wonderful beyond words. Seldom does a person have the opportunity to simply sit and listen to the important pieces a man like Father Hesburgh can cut out of his life story and embroider for his listeners. He told us about the time when President Carter arranged for him to undergo a portion of the astronauts' training. Father Hesburgh had served so well and so generously on so many commissions and panels that addressed the important issues of the day—desegregation, equal rights and others—that President Carter asked what he could do for Father Hesburgh in return.

Father Hesburgh said he had done many different things. One summer when I was at Notre Dame, he served as chaplain on a French cargo ship for two months so he could improve his French. Now, he wanted a different adventure: to fly in the SR71 supersonic reconnaissance plane similar to the U-2 made famous when the Russians captured pilot Gary Powers over their territory. To do this, however, a person had to go through some of the astronauts' training, because the SR71 flew at such an incredibly high altitude. Father Hesburgh was given a two-day crash course—oops, poor choice of words—in astronaut training and then went up in the SR71. He said it was the most amazing experience.

As Father Hesburgh talked, I sat and listened, enthralled. The difference between Father Hesburgh and me was obvious. In his case, it was the man, not the position. Father Hesburgh was fascinating. He would have been fascinating if he had been something other than Notre Dame's president.

I found Father Joyce to be much the same. His door was always open to me and I often took advantage of it. I enjoyed going to his office just to talk.

"Gerry," Father Joyce says, "liked to come over every month or so. I always enjoyed our visits, but he didn't have to do that. I never expected any reports from him. I think he just wanted to brief me on what was happening. He was always so optimistic, which is just his nature. When Ara Parseghian was coach for all those years I would make the trips with the team and sit by him on the plane. I'd get the chance to chat with him about how he felt things were going. I did that with Gerry as well. But that was in addition to our other visits."

I can't speak for the relationship that other Notre Dame coaches have had with Father Hesburgh and Father Joyce, but I feel I had a special one, and it is among the things I cherish most from my Notre Dame years.

When I was flying out of Washington, D.C., on a recruiting trip I'd made to see Eric Metcalf in a nearby Virginia suburb, my position presented me with the opportunity to meet another President. I got to the airport at 10:30 on this particular night and was walking to the fixed-base operations area when I saw a cluster of men wearing conservative suits and little plugs in their ears. Those tiny devices always are a tipoff to Secret Service personnel. I asked them if the President was there. They said no, President Reagan was not there, but that former President Carter was.

I'd never met President Carter, but I had tremendous respect for the kind of man he is, the work he does with Habitat for Humanity, his ability to serve as a mediator in conflicts. A person has to respect the humanity he shows in the way he lives his life, especially since he left the White House.

The Secret Service men got on their two-way radios and then told me that if I would wait five minutes, President Carter and Rosalyn would be coming to the area and that he'd like to meet me. I spent a half hour with President and Mrs. Carter, and you'll never meet two nicer people. I talked about recruiting and he told me to stay out of Georgia. I had to admit to him that I'd already pirated Wes Pritchett away from his home state. President Carter said that was OK, but don't come back and get anyone else, that the rest of Georgia's outstanding players were required to go to Georgia or Georgia Tech. We really hit it off.

A few years ago, President Carter was in South Bend at the same time that a close friend of our family, Dru Cash, was there. Dru went to St. Joseph High School in South Bend with my sons and eventually wound up working for Indiana Sen. Richard Lugar. Dru happened to be with Father Hesburgh when President Carter was, and President Carter asked how I was doing. This was at least eight years after we had met, yet he remembered. That meant a lot to me. It reminded me, in fact, of Knute Rockne remembering my father when he encountered him a second time.

Meeting everyone from presidents to entertainers, such as Wayne Newton and Don Rickles, came with the position. Anyone who is or had been Notre Dame coach could have done it.

One of the truly interesting men I had the good fortune to meet in this manner was Gene Kilroy, who is a casino host in Las Vegas. Marlene and I and friends, Sandy and Dorothy Cundari, had gone to Vegas on vacation and were at an Italian restaurant in the Golden Nugget one night when Gene Kilroy came up to our table while I was away. He asked Marlene if I was Gerry Faust, the former Notre Dame coach. She said I was.

Gene had been Muhammad Ali's business manager, setting him up for life with $300,000 a year. Gene is still close to Ali. In fact, he's the person who first gave the Atlanta Olympics Committee the idea of having Ali light the torch at the '96 opening ceremony. Gene was a man who knew people. That night he wanted to know the former coach of Notre Dame and has since become a very close friend. He bought our dinner, and said he wanted to introduce us to Don Rickles. He got us front-row seats for Don's show and said we'd go backstage afterward to meet Don.

Don Rickles always has been one of my favorite comedians, and he loves football. As the show was about to begin, I told Sandy and Dorothy: "Watch Rickles nail me." That's the price of being down front. It was a packed house and Don just ripped on people, and who could be easier to rip on than me for what I had done at Notre Dame? So I was waiting.

Nothing happened. Don got to the end of his show and I turned to Marlene and said: "Thank God." I laughed through the entire show and it wasn't even at myself. Then Don came out for an encore. I should have known. He saved me for dessert.

I had hardly gotten the words out, bragging about how I had made it through unscathed, when Don went to work on me. I can't say what he said, but it wasn't about Notre Dame. I'll give you the context. I'm the coach at this point at the university in the Rubber City. He put it on me, all right. It was funny, but he would never have taken off on an Akron topic if I hadn't been at Notre Dame first. Fact is, we wouldn't have had those front-row seats.

I always tried to remember that as much as I enjoyed the fruits of the position, that it carried tremendous responsibilities. For better or worse, some people put meeting the Notre Dame football coach in the same category as I placed meeting Presidents Carter and Reagan.

When I first returned to the Notre Dame campus after going to Cincinnati to take care of matters left undone at Moeller, one of the fellows at the Notre Dame laundry asked if I would just walk through and say hello. It was during this visit with the people who do the students' laundry that I got my first inkling of how much the Notre Dame football coach means to people. I spent an hour. I

walked through the entire operation, shaking hands, talking to
people. It wasn't Gerry Faust whom they wanted to meet, it was
the new Notre Dame football coach. It was a big, big thing to them,
and after I'd done that I realized that I should go to other places on
campus. To the fire house. To where the telephone operators work.
To all these similar places. To this day when I call Notre Dame,
those operators recognize my voice. Of course, that could be because my voice sounds like someone just dumped a load of gravel
down a chute leading into the telephone line.

The visits didn't end with the University staff. They only began there. One of the students at Notre Dame when I arrived was
Paul Kollman. He's a priest now in the Holy Cross Order, the order
that runs the University. But in those days, Father Kollman was just
Paul. He'd been one of the trainers of the Moeller football team and
he served in the same capacity at Notre Dame. As close as we are,
I can't bring myself to call him Paul anymore. He's Father Kollman,
and in that capacity he helped to celebrate the Mass at my daughter Julie's wedding.

At Notre Dame when Father Kollman was a student, he lived
in Morrissey Hall. You have to understand about the dorm system.
It's unique. There is great rivalry among the dorms, which have
these big, beautiful chapels and intramural athletic programs that
are as serious as intercollegiate athletics at other schools. If a person tells someone from Notre Dame that he lived in a certain dorm
and that it is the best and most famous on campus, he's likely to get
an argument. I was in all of them and to me, they were equally
amazing. Each time I visited, I was moved by the depth of feeling of
the residents for one another and the University.

We were allowed 30 scholarships in those days and we'd di-
vide each recruiting class into two players per dorm. The first year,
each player lived with another player. After that, they could pick
anyone they wanted as their roommate. Unlike on some campuses,
Notre Dame athletes are integrated into the dorms. They are students just like everyone else.

Well, Father Kollman, when he was still Paul, asked if I'd come
over and speak to the residents of his dorm. I said sure. I hadn't a
clue what I was getting into. He invited me to come at 8 one night
in March after our first recruiting season. When I walked up to
Morrissey Hall, I could hardly get through the door. The dorm was
jammed. I think students had come from the surrounding dorms.
They had to form a human funnel that sort of propelled me along

and into the chapel. The bodies were wall to wall. When I was in the middle of all of them, this chant suddenly went up:

"He's a man...Who's a man?...He's a Notre Dame man!"

Then they began chanting: Geeeeerrrrrrree. Geeeeerrrrrrree. Geeeeerrrrrrree. It was enough to make a grown football coach cry. When I finally got up to speak, I went on for a half hour, caught up in the emotion of the moment. Everyone in the place was going bonkers. It was like a pep rally, with one obvious exception. It was March.

Then the phone calls began to come. One after another. Dillon Hall. Alumni Hall. All the halls began calling. Going to the dorms became a practice. I was the first coach, at least in modern times, to go into the dorms to talk. I even went to the girls' dorms. I didn't just talk, either. I listened. It became another way to become close to the Notre Dame students, and what is Notre Dame, if not its students?

This kind of fervor was new to me. I had been a high school coach for 23 years. I'd had great success. I'd been the focus of attention. But if ever I got to feeling too important or self-satisfied, there was always a moment around the corner to remind me who and what I was. We'd win a state championship or a mythical national championship at Moeller one day and that same night I'd be mopping the floors with the managers, picking up the towels and turning out the lights. The next morning I'd be out there with my players picking up the trash left from the victory celebration the night before. You don't lose those habits overnight. When I went through the Notre Dame locker room, I'd still pick up towels and turn off the lights, do whatever needed to be done.

One day athletic director Gene Corrigan cornered me and said: "Gerry, I don't know how to tell you this."

"What is it, Mr. C? Just go ahead."

"There's something you've got to learn. You're the Notre Dame football coach, Gerry. You're not a manager. You've got to quit picking up towels and turning off lights."

"But, Mr. Corrigan, I've done it for 23 years. I was responsible for those things, for everything. I still feel responsible. You don't break a habit like that overnight."

"I understand, Gerry," Mr. Corrigan said, "but that's not the job of the Notre Dame football coach. The Notre Dame football coach, like all our major head coaches, has to have an air about him. He has to be above those things. So you just walk through the locker room and leave the picking up of towels to others."

I knew what Mr. C. was trying to tell me. I had seen how other great coaches carried themselves. Woody Hayes. Bear Bryant. When I visited Bear one year at Alabama, I didn't see him pick up a single towel. He didn't turn out the locker room lights. In fact, when he walked into the locker room, a silence fell over it. A dead silence.

As we walked to the practice field, he would put his arm around me and we'd head up to his tower and everyone in front of us would get out of the way. It reminded me of Moses parting the Red Sea. Me, I'd put my arm around a guy and there the similarity would end. People would come running up to me, clamoring, laughing, shouting: Coach! Coach! And I wouldn't have had it any other way. But not Bear Bryant.

He had a door that led from his office to a room where the coaches held their daily staff meetings. His assistant coaches would come in by way of another door. They'd be laughing and yukking it up until Bear's door opened, then the room would fall as silent as the locker room when he walked in. You could hear the assistant coaches breathing. In that room were some excellent assistants who would go on to achieve fame of their own, guys like Pat Dye. But they shut up, too. Everyone shut up. It was the same in the hallways. More Red-Sea partings. No one spoke to Bear unless Bear spoke first.

When I went to lunch in Alabama's football cafeteria with a couple of the assistant coaches, I saw Bear sitting over by himself at a table. He was reading the *Wall Street Journal*. I asked the coaches why they didn't go over and sit with him.

"No way," they said. "He doesn't want to sit with us, and we want a little time of our own, too."

They loved him and respected him. But they also feared him. That was the way it was.

Nobody feared Gerry Faust, and that hurt me as a college coach. When I picked up the towels and turned off the lights and did all the other ordinary things that people do, it made me just like any player, like any other guy. And, I was. There wasn't any job too low for me. No job I wouldn't pitch in to help get done. That was me. I couldn't do it any other way. I understood what Mr. C was saying to me, and I got better at leaving some things to others. But I never completely lost the feeling that I was just another guy.

In the years to come, Mr. Corrigan would return to this issue and to similar ones. He even wrote a list of things I should do and things I should avoid if I didn't want to become a part of Notre Dame history sooner than I expected. When Mr. C had an opinion, he offered it. He was direct. But he tried to help his coaches. He was the kind of person I liked, even when I disagreed or couldn't change without turning myself into someone I didn't want to be. The person I wanted to be was the first Notre Dame coach to put together a team of football staff members and to play Bookstore Basketball, which is the largest intramural basketball program in the country, as far as I know. If there's a larger one, count my team out. We might win more than a game and then we old guys would really be in trouble.

Bookstore Basketball, which attracted more than 600 teams when I was playing, started on the outdoor baskets behind the Notre Dame Bookstore. Today, there are outdoor baskets all around the campus. One of the reasons I loved this tournament is that it's a little like football. They play the final outdoors behind the Joyce Center and tipoff comes, rain or shine. They set up bleachers and draw 4,000 to 5,000 people. Not that my team knew anything about the final. What I did know was that Bookstore Basketball was a big deal, and if it was a big deal at Notre Dame, the football staff ought to be involved. So we put together a team. Our team included Jim Higgins and Brian Boulac, Tom Lichtenberg and Greg Blache, Steve Orsini, a former player who was ticket and promotions manager, and me. OK, we weren't the Bulls of the '90s or Celtics of the '60s. But we were a draw.

For our first game they put us on the Bookstore court where the tournament started. There were people everywhere; must have been 3,000 to 4,000. At least it seemed like that many to someone in serious danger of making a fool of himself. The ones with the best view were sitting on top of the bookstore.

We entered the tournament for the same reason I went to the dorms to speak. To know the students. To let the students know us. That's the only kind of air I want to have about me. If there's Air Jordan, then that's Air Faust. We made only one mistake. We won a game. We were expecting to be beaten in the first round of the tournament—hoping to be beaten. We weren't in good shape.

We lasted two rounds, which allowed us to meet even more students and made the tournament a success from my point of view. After that first year, teams bid to play us. They didn't want just to beat Gerry Faust. They wanted to beat the Notre Dame football coach.

"That may be true," says assistant athletic director John Heisler, "but I think Gerry's relationship with the students and everyone else endeared him personally to the Notre Dame community."

One of those communities was inhabited by the retired nuns who lived in the convent at Saint Mary's College across the street from Notre Dame. There were 120 to 130 nuns living there and these religious older women loved their Notre Dame football. They'd watch the games on a large television in one of the common rooms, off of which was a chapel. The nuns told me that when the games got tight no one would say anything but one by one they would all go into the chapel to pray.

When I visited these nuns one day, one of them told me: "Coach, you have us going to that chapel more than any coach who has ever been at Notre Dame."

I started laughing. I could just see myself stomping around on the sidelines when things were going wrong while these nuns walked quietly from the TV room to the chapel.

"Maybe, Sister," I said, "that's why the Good Lord put me here. He wants you in church more often."

"But, Coach," she said, "do you have to send us to the chapel that often?"

Talk about pressure on the Notre Dame coach! Even retired nuns give you heck. No rulers needed. Their caring was sweet.

The pressure comes more subtly at times. When I was at Moeller I often gave speeches to businesses, even ones as large as IBM. I tied Moeller High School football to business by showing, including in photographic slides, what kids went through to become successful players. There's a common denominator. It's called hard work.

Not long after I became Notre Dame coach I went to California with Marlene to make an unpaid speech in San Francisco and one in Pasadena, for which I was paid. In Pasadena, I was one of two motivational speakers on the program. I hadn't been at Notre Dame long enough to change my speech. I still used Moeller and the same slide presentation. On this occasion it wouldn't have mattered what I said or what props I had brought.

The other person on the program was an older man who was as great a speaker as I've ever heard. He spoke first and as I listened, I wanted him to go on all night. So, I'm sure, did everyone else in the room. For the first and only time, I had reservations about how good a job I could do following on the heels of this man's tongue. And I didn't do very well. When I got home from California, I called Ken Schneider, my attorney, who also booked my speeches. I told him how concerned I was about my performance and that I wouldn't do any more events where I did not speak first. That was my one rule.

I've long since abandoned that rule. I don't care when I speak now. But I was a rookie back then. I didn't have the confidence that what was in my heart would come out of my mouth in the way I felt it. I wasn't the Moeller High School coach anymore. When I spoke, paid or unpaid, the audience expected more. I was the same man, but not in the same position.

I had a position to uphold now. *The* position. I was Notre Dame's coach.

6

■ THE FIRST SEASON ■

 In the dark, a place I found myself on more than one occasion during the 1981 season at Notre Dame, I heard the drumbeat that would, during my lowest moments, lift me and keep me pounding forward. It was a thudding reminder of why God had opened the door for me to this special place.

It was two nights before the Louisiana State game, which would turn out so well. The moment already was magic. After our meeting with the team in the Athletic and Convocation Center, I walked across campus to the Grotto to pray. The night was warm, the air scented with the beginning of fall, a night for walking and listening.

The Notre Dame campus forms a cross, with the dorms located along the apexes. At the end of one arm of the cross stands the Rockne Memorial, at the other end the Hesburgh Library. At the top of the cross is the Golden Dome. At the bottom, the circle off which the Morris Inn is located.

Even before I heard the drumbeat, another sound broke the silence of the night as I walked back across campus toward the Athletic and Convocation Center and my car. What I heard sounded as if it were a name.

"Emil."

It came from first one window and then another, leaping like flames from dorm to dorm.

"Emil."

Just that one word. That name.

The shouts carried an unmistakable conviction, a plaintiveness of tone. I didn't understand until the next day, when I talked with Brian Boulac, the meaning and significance of the name.

Emil was Dean Emil Hoffman, who guided Notre Dame freshmen through the rigors of the Freshmen Year of Studies on their ways to the more specific work of their majors. Dean Hoffman also taught chemistry and each Friday morning, without fail, he would give his students a quiz. It had become a tradition for freshmen, on the night before Dean Hoffman's quizzes, to open their windows as they studied and to cry out his name.

Cries of deference, of anguish, of learning.

It was uniquely Notre Dame, and so was the drumbeat.

The Band of the Fighting Irish was coming off the practice field behind the Stadium, moving, four abreast, in the growing darkness. Up the walk they came, heading toward Washington Hall, the band complex, which is near the Golden Dome. There must have been 150 band members, maybe 200. It was too dark to count, but I could hear the fall of their feet, quick-stepping to that drumbeat.

Ka-boom. Ka-boom. Ka-boom.

It froze me in fascination in the center of the campus. It was the first Thursday night of five years of Thursday nights that I would spend with the band in this place. At this moment, though, I didn't know what was about to happen. I was simply mesmerized by the ka-booming cadence. If our offense could move with the relentlessness of the band, I knew we would be all right.

Then it happened.

The band reached the point at which the arms of the cross intersect and suddenly the Victory March erupted into the night. It sent chills up and down my spine and made me wish that every Notre Dame fan—and those people who don't like Notre Dame—could witness this. The chills turned to goosebumps. Tears were coming down my face. Here was Notre Dame, defined in a single moment: spirit, athletics, academics in a setting of serenity watched over by the Blessed Mother.

No one knew, but I never missed another Thursday night. I was always there when the drumbeat began, foretelling a moment of sound and fury that always became a great victory for the human spirit. I quietly shared this with a couple of people, including a friend named Craig Leaver who came to visit from Cincinnati.

Craig had been in an automobile accident and was paralyzed from the neck down. A Notre Dame fan, he and a friend of his, Joe

Reinhart, contacted me and asked if I could get them tickets to a game. I said I could. In fact, they'd be my personal guests provided they would do one thing for me. They would have to take Friday off work or school or whatever and get to South Bend by 7 o'clock Thursday night.

"Otherwise," I told them, "no tickets."

I'm as subtle as an avalanche. But it worked. They arrived on a Thursday evening and I told them they were going to witness a moment few Notre Dame fans have the opportunity to experience.

"Tell me afterwards," I said, "how it makes you feel."

I knew Craig and his friend, Joe, because one of my former players at Moeller, Nick Haverkos, had befriended Craig. It was dark when we reached the center of campus, but you could hear the drumbeat and see the light shining off the Golden Dome.

Then the band appeared. And, as always, at the moment it arrived at the center of the cross, it burst into the Notre Dame Victory March. The looks on the faces of those guys said more than they ever could have with words. I didn't have to explain anything to them. I didn't have to share how I felt. They knew.

Craig's situation would have tested anyone's resolve. I think, however, that he left the campus that night with a greater sense of serenity and peace, a feeling that God's love would guide him through the destiny that was his.

Craig came to other games, both at Notre Dame and Akron, and not long ago I spoke at a Catholic Men's Conference in Cincinnati where I saw him. We've become fast friends, and I'm glad he is the only person with whom I ever shared Thursday night.

The darkness that I experienced on those special nights created in me the exact opposite feeling that I had going into the LSU game. The Thursday-night darkness was warm and comforting. The darkness that LSU left us in by having played a game the week before was cold and foreboding.

Though LSU had lost to Alabama, I still worried about playing a team with a game's experience when we had none. This was a first for me. In high school, we would have had two or three scrimmages against other teams in which to learn how our new and untested players performed under fire. In the pros, they play four preseason games—for the money and to come to the conclusions with which they make their squad reductions. Colleges have nothing except an intrasquad spring game which lacks tested-by-fire intensity.

More than once during my college coaching tenure I advocated to the coaching association and to the NCAA that the rules be altered to permit a spring game against another school. Not only would it prove beneficial in personnel decisions, but also in deepening a team's financial base and that of the NCAA. What I proposed was a game from which one third of the proceeds would go to each of the two schools and the other third to the NCAA. So it would be a controlled, useful situation in which the competitiveness didn't get out of hand, each team would be required to play its first unit in the first quarter, its second team in the second quarter and its third unit in the third quarter. In the fourth quarter, the teams could play whomever they wanted and do as they wished.

On the college level, there is no preview. That's tough. It's even tougher when the other team has already played a game. Even working together as a new coaching staff would have been easier if we had had something more than an intrasquad spring game behind us. We tried to simulate game conditions in the spring, with some coaches in the press box and others on the field. But it's not the same. Compounding the team's lack of experience was my own. Had I had more college coaching experience I might not have made some of the changes I made in the offense in the spring, in positions players played or who would be our quarterback.

The first mistake I made, and one I would still be hearing about two years later, was dumping Dan Devine's offense. Instead of putting in a new offense, I should have simply added more passing and changed some formations and plays. What I failed to appreciate was that Dan and his staff had recruited players because of their ability to play certain positions in the Devine offense. It leaned more to power than to speed. The multiple offense we installed combined speed with power and a good deal of shifting from a full-house backfield in order to create misalignments by the defense.

In a harsh 1983 overview of my first three years as coach at Notre Dame, *Chicago Sun-Times* sportswriter Phil Hersh focused much of the criticism on mistakes made during that first season. Players from that team who had graduated had come to much the same conclusion I had: I was less than perfect.

"He thought he was so good," starting offensive tackle Phil Pozderac told Hersh, "that he was going to teach us a whole new system in the off-season to beat teams that had known their system for four years."

While I might not put it quite like Phil did, he was right. I thought these players were capable of learning a new system and they were. We had 20 days of spring practice spread out over a 30-day period. We tried to be especially aware of the demands of some of the high-powered academic programs the athletes were in and particularly avoided Tuesday or Thursday practices. Those were lab days at Notre Dame, and labs came before football. I mean, they even had labs in the business school.

The spring and preseason practices were our labs, and I may have overdone the mad-scientist-experimenting-with-his-new-elements bit. Rockne was the chemist, not me. Two of the experiments that I would regret were moving Tony Hunter from split end to wingback—his best position was tight end—and switching Tom Thayer from tackle to guard, even though Thayer started at guard for the Chicago Bears for years.

"The year (Coach Faust) came to Notre Dame," Thayer complained to Hersh, "we should have won the national championship. He made too many changes, and there seemed no real reason for a lot of them. It eroded our confidence."

Coming off a 9-2-1 season and with eight starters returning on both offense and defense, our record should have been significantly better than it turned out. And yet, after we moved the ball up and down the field against LSU, no one was complaining about the new offense and the position changes or who was quarterbacking. It is when things fall apart that it becomes natural to search for the reasons and an understanding of what happened.

Tom Thayer had one answer. I tinkered too much. Sometimes you have to make changes because of injury. Sometimes you just want to get another good player into the lineup, and so moving an experienced player seems like the right thing to do. But as I look back, I've come to the conclusion that on the college level a coach should move as few players as possible if they have been performing successfully.

"As far as player criticism," says former associate athletic director Roger Valdiserri, "Dan Devine went through the same thing. But we've had very, very little of that at Notre Dame. I don't know what causes it. Losing. Disappointment. Whatever it is, it's not a happy thing to go through.

"Most of the criticism came from three disgruntled players who had problems with Gerry, but they were players who would have had problems with any coach."

Criticism comes with the job. All of us want to succeed. That's why we still try so hard to figure out what went wrong.

"It isn't easy to do," says Father Joyce.

"I know there are times," Brian Boulac says, "when I relive those days, trying to come to a conclusion. When Gerry came to Notre Dame, I wanted him to be successful. A lot of people wanted him to be successful. It just didn't turn out that way.

"One thing I wish is that he could have made a decision on the quarterback that first year. We just couldn't settle on a quarterback early. I think that had a lot to do with the way that and subsequent seasons progressed. I find it hard to believe that Blair Kiel was the focal point of Gerry Faust's career at Notre Dame, but he may have been."

It is hard for me to believe, too. I'm not sure that I do believe it. Going into that first game against LSU, we hadn't made a decision on whom we should start at quarterback. Blair Kiel, a sophomore, was the returning starter. Tim Koegel, having received an additional year of eligibility after a neck injury ended his season early in 1980, was a fifth-year senior. What put me in a difficult position, besides judging them in practice, was the fact that Tim had been my quarterback at Moeller and the Ohio player of the year. It wasn't that I liked Timmy and didn't like Blair. I wanted to play the best quarterback, the one who would give us the best chance to win. I just wasn't sure which quarterback that was. Blair had taken the team to the Sugar Bowl as a freshman, but I knew Timmy and trusted him. He was level-headed on the field and threw better than Blair. There was no question in my mind or anyone else's that Blair was the better athlete. It was my first big decision and I blew it more by not making it than by choosing the wrong quarterback.

We discussed the quarterbacks at length in staff meetings. Some of the coaches liked Blair. Some liked Tim. I know Brian Boulac remembers it differently.

"At the time," Boulac says, "it was hard to envision why Gerry was having so much difficulty making up his mind. To most of the staff, it was clear that Blair should be the quarterback."

Choosing a quarterback, the on-field leader of a team, the young man who is an extension of his coach, can be difficult under the best of circumstances. This time, it was even more difficult than that.

"Tim," Boulac says, "was a constant figure for Gerry, someone he had had success with, so much success that he felt he knew what Tim could do. There were times Gerry would come into meetings and say: 'Well, Tim had a great day.' And most of the offensive staff would say: 'Yeah, but Coach, Blair did this and this and this.' Gerry had a hard time putting his finger on what he really wanted the quarterback to be able to do."

Tim's only problem, I thought, was his speed. Blair couldn't throw as well as Tim, but he had great speed. It was hard to separate them and without the benefit of a true spring game or preseason scrimmages against another team, it was all the more difficult. Blair had a strong arm and, as time went on, became a better passer. A lot better. Tim had touch. He was really good at picking out secondary receivers. It was a tough decision. We really wanted to make it based on the first game.

Let me reiterate: I wanted the best quarterback to play. I didn't care if it was Tim or Blair. I know Blair probably thinks that I tried to come to the conclusion that the best quarterback was Tim, and I can't deny that Tim was like a son to me. Some of the coaches suggested that the easiest and best decision was to choose Blair. He had, after all, quarterbacked the team successfully as a freshman. Choosing him would provide continuity. I didn't feel that continuity was the criterion on which a decision should be made or that it would be fair to Tim or to the team.

We started Blair against LSU but alternated the quarterbacks, and that clarified nothing. They both played well. Blair threw a 7-yard pass to Larry Moriarty for the opening touchdown, but Timmy completed 6 of his 7 throws for more yards (101 to Blair's 29). He also connected with Dave Condeni for our last touchdown.

Tim had the better game but not to the point that you could make a final decision—and one should have been made. Even if it was wrong.

"It became a real focal point," Boulac says. "The staff had made the point of saying: 'Coach, name our quarterback. We can't juggle back and forth all the time. If there is a difference—and we feel there is—then we should name our quarterback.' He was hesitant to name Tim and eventually named Blair to start. Then the alternating threw it back into a tizzy. I know Gerry wanted to make a decision. He was just unable to live with it."

In the afterglow of the LSU game, an immediate decision on quarterback didn't loom quite so large. I knew we had to settle on one person. But it still wasn't clear, at least in my mind, whom that should be. There had been so many other distractions during the week of the first game. At Notre Dame the head coach is deluged with requests for tickets, many from people who have helped the University and who deserve them. You can't tell these people no.

It seemed as if everyone had my private phone number. My friends and supporters from Moeller all wanted to see how the dream would begin. For 21 years I had begged and borrowed from so many people to help Moeller football. Now I had something that these people wanted: Notre Dame football tickets. But even I didn't have enough. It wasn't as if they were gifts, either. These friends were buying them. But we couldn't even find enough tickets for them to buy.

Poor Jan. My secretary, Jan Blazi, also had a hard time telling my friends no. So we had to really scrounge for tickets. I think people might be afraid, or at least reluctant, to call Bear Bryant for tickets, but with me, they just called. That was my image. Ol' Ger. Everyone's friend. And—that's what I wanted to be. Most of the successful college coaches I know create an image of fear or, at least, a wall of aloofness. I didn't want that. I wouldn't do it differently if I were coaching today. I would not change. People mean too much to me.

The people who meant the most—my family, including my mother and father—were at my home after the game. First we had attended a reception at St. Joseph's Bank and Trust in South Bend. I co-hosted it with Gene Corrigan. Dan Devine had held these events himself, but I thought that we were a family and that Mr. Corrigan should be the co-host and invite people. I'd invite people. He'd invite people. It was a happy and exciting time, both at the reception and at home. What it was not was unusual. As happy as everyone was, they were used to winning. Winning was not unusual. We had won 72 of our last 73 games at Moeller. I certainly took the LSU win in stride. What I found more unusual and, of course, difficult was the losing. And my family felt the losing even more than I did. We had been living in a dream world and were about to be rudely awakened.

I felt responsible for ending their dream, though I knew no one could win on the collegiate level as we had won at Moeller. There are too many good teams with too many good players and all of them seemed to be on the Notre Dame schedule. So many things were different. When you are coaching high school players, you have a shared responsibility with parents. When practice or games end, a coach doesn't have to worry until the next school day. The parents are responsible. That's not the case in college. The coach is responsible. It's odd in one sense: these young men have entered a phase of their lives in which they are testing their wings, trying out their values, taking on more responsibility. Yet if anything goes wrong, it's the coach's fault.

Even though the coach cannot control some of the things that happen away from the field, if you are the Notre Dame coach —or any college coach—the players you've recruited are your responsibility 24 hours a day, 365 days a year. Any action or reaction of theirs reflects on the university. The many positive and selfless acts of these young men bring credit to themselves and credibility to the university. The negatives, on the other hand, carry a tremendous burden.

The first time someone gets into a fight or some other conflict, everyone comes to the coach and asks why. Why did it happen? What kind of person did you recruit? Why did you bring this kind of person to Notre Dame? Shouldn't you have known ahead of time what would happen? What people should understand is that student-athletes are people, and people make mistakes. As coach, you try to recruit not only the right kind of athlete but also the right kind of person. It's the reason I insisted on seeing a young man in his home environment, at school and in as many other circumstances as possible. But good people can do bad and stupid things. At Notre Dame. At any school. It's just that at Notre Dame the consequences are nationwide, because that is Notre Dame's constituency—the nation.

I used to hear that the three toughest jobs in America were: President of the United States, mayor of New York and football coach of Notre Dame. I laughed at that—until I became coach at Notre Dame.

There was one night of the week I didn't have to worry about the players. That was Friday nights before home games. The top 50 players and some of the assistant coaches stayed in the seminary. Getting sleep in the dorms on a football weekend at Notre Dame would have been almost as impossible as I found it to get to a major bowl game. So we went to the quiet and serenity of the seminary. There, we didn't have to do what I'd done at Moeller when we went on the road for state playoff games. In those days, I'd sit up in the hallway reading until 3 or 4 o'clock in the morning to make sure no one was sneaking out to go to visit the local library or some other point of interest. At the seminary, no one was going anywhere. It was isolated.

Speaking of isolation, I wish we had had a little more of it in Ann Arbor, Michigan, the night before our second game and the first on the road. Joe O'Brien, one of our assistant athletic directors in 1981, was the master of arrangements on the road. Over the years Joe and I became close. I developed a great respect for his decisions. On this first trip, though, things went wrong through no fault of Joe's. He had asked the hotel where we were staying to separate our players from the other guests. We wanted to keep them away from the football-weekend celebrants and the noise they would make. The hotel personnel promised this would be done, but it wasn't. So it was a noisy night. The other guests were there for a good time and couldn't care less who was in the next room. It was an inconvenience, not a disaster. The disaster would occur the next day during the game.

If a single personnel decision, in this case Blair Kiel and the quarterback position, set the course of my Notre Dame career, and I'm skeptical about that, then one play may have been even more important: a fake field goal. In this instance, the two situations were woven so tightly they might as well have been one.

After stopping a 74-yard Michigan drive and forcing a field goal that the Wolverines missed, we put together a mirror drive that led to no points. Then we came back at them again, using both quarterbacks, but with Tim Koegel getting considerably more time than Blair Kiel.

We took the ball from our 16-yard line to the Michigan four, where we faced fourth and goal. I had been calling the plays. I did it against LSU; I was doing it against Michigan. It seemed natural, It's what I had done at Moeller. I'd tried it during spring practice and decided I would continue to do so at Notre Dame. The difference was preparation. High school defensive coaches are limited as to the time they have to prepare for you. College defensive coaches, on the other hand, are limited only by the number of hours in the day and their endurance and willingness to use them. They don't have to teach algebra or English. I quickly learned that at Notre Dame there were both more distractions on and off the field for a head coach who calls the offensive plays. Lou Holtz did it, and did it well. But he had the kind of college coaching experience that Ara Parseghian indicated was a prerequisite for success at Notre

Dame. Me? Well, I had press conferences and a hundred other things that I never had had to find time for before.

I didn't think it mattered—not until the fake field goal.

During our week of preparation for Michigan, offensive coordinator Tom Lichtenberg noticed on the game film of Michigan and Wisconsin that on field goals and extra points Michigan covered receivers man-to-man and sent a hard rush at the kicker. When Tom analyzed this, he concluded correctly that the fake field goal was a play that would take advantage of Michigan's hell-bent-for-the-kicker rush, if the circumstances were right.

On the four-yard line they were perfect.

I made the call quickly. I don't remember asking for input from the staff. There was no time. If you delay in that situation, the defense senses a fake and prepares to react. So I sent Harry Oliver onto the field to fake the kick and Dave Condeni to hold the ball.

Dave, a split end, was one of nine former Moeller players on our squad. Like Tim Koegel, I knew from experience what Dave could do in the clutch. He had great hands. But, to be honest, that isn't the reason he was holding. Dave Condeni was holding because I had been unable to make up my mind as to whether Tim Koegel or Blair Kiel should be our quarterback. Had I chosen one as *the* starter, I would have had the other one holding for placements. That puts not only a person with good hands and nerves in the holder's position but also a player who can jump up from the kneeling position and throw the ball effectively on either a fake field goal or a placement gone bad. Neither Tim nor Blair was on the field. They were on the sideline with me.

As the ball was snapped, Tony Hunter went in motion behind the line of scrimmage from his position on the right wing. The tight end on the left side of the line and the wingback on the same side ran crossing patterns downfield and took with them the two defenders in man-to-man coverage on the left side of the secondary. As the ball was snapped, Tony drifted into the left flat. He was all alone, an easy target at the four-yard line.

The risk, of course, was that there were too few defenders to block against the rush, particularly on the left side. Dave rolled in that direction and ran into trouble. He is 6-feet tall and while he could throw, he was not the passer either the 6-foot-1 Blair Kiel or the 6-foot-4 Tim Koegel would have been in that situation.

With the rush in his face, Dave Condeni had to lob the ball to get it over the linemen. It floated toward Tony, too high and too slow.Tony leaped to make an incredible catch. As he landed, however, he was off balance and fell four yards from what would have been the first touchdown of the game and a tremendous confidence-builder for players and coach alike.

Instead, we got no points, and the momentum shifted on the next series when Michigan quarterback Steve Smith and Anthony Carter teamed up on a 71-yard touchdown pass play. At halftime we were down 7-0 instead of up 20-0, as we had been against LSU. What's more, we had failed by gambling on a play that would be labeled by media and fans alike as a high school play. It wasn't a high school play, but the observation dovetailed with what Bo Schembechler had been saying all week: that we ran a high school offense. He had prepared his team by studying films of Moeller games. He had lost to Wisconsin the week before and with that loss went the No. 1 ranking in the nation that had been Michigan's. He wasn't too happy or about to lose to some guy running a high school offense.

The fact is, our offense did have many elements that Moeller had used successfully. I'd gotten many of those by observing college offenses and attending clinics at which college coaches explained the ways in which they attacked defenses. The offense wasn't the problem. The play wasn't the problem. I was the problem. And I knew it.

"I still remember running off the field after that LSU game, his first game," says All-America linebacker Bob Crable. "I remember the pep rally. The excitement. How the fans were. And how things changed from there to the next week at Michigan. Taking his offense from Moeller into a big-time setting like Notre Dame, I look back on that and I question it."

I was so upset about the failure of the fake field goal and the fact that we weren't moving the ball as we had against LSU that I decided it would be best if Tom and the offensive staff called the plays. It was a mistake that grew from a mistake (to not have a quarterback as the holder) that grew from still another mistake (failure to settle on a quarterback). Normally on fourth and four, I would go for the field goal, particularly early on in a game. But I had been sure the fake would work.

Michigan dominated the second half, winning 25-7, and afterward the questions came at me from every direction about the failed fake field goal. I didn't attempt to defend it or to shift the blame to Tom. It's his job to suggest plays. It's my job to decide if we follow those suggestions. Tom's suggestion was an excellent one. I just said it was my decision. It was wrong. It didn't work. I left it at that.

But inside, I couldn't leave it at that. I was devastated. I felt sorry for myself. How could I put us in such a vulnerable position? Why hadn't it worked as smoothly as such decisions always seemed to work at Moeller? A thousand questions spun through my head. The bottom line: I wasn't used to losing. In two games at Notre Dame, I had equaled my previous number of losses in six seasons. That one loss, to Cincinnati Princeton, took me a year to get over. I took the Princeton game film home every week. I was determined it wouldn't happen again. And it didn't. We beat Princeton 32-7 the next season. We had that team down pat. College is different. There isn't time to dwell on defeat. Not even a Notre Dame can cruise through its subsequent opponent while its coach wallows in self-pity. At the college level, a coach has to learn from the loss, then forget about it and move on.

I couldn't.

My reaction, I think, affected the players. I was so bitterly disappointed by the loss, so hurt, that I think it deepened their hurt. Usually, unless a conference championship, national championship or a major bowl berth is at stake, college players make an overnight emotional recovery following a loss. I made it more difficult for such instant healing to occur. I found out soon enough that losing one game in college happens. In fact, losing three games or more in a season happens to 85 percent of the teams playing college football each year. You have to go on. You have to be resilient. I wasn't. I couldn't be. I didn't call up from myself the very quality that I sought to bring out in our players. And that hurt our preparation for Purdue, our third opponent.

"There were times," says assistant athletic director Brian Boulac, "when you could see that our preparation may not have been as thorough as it should have been. Gerry was intrigued because he knew these Notre Dame athletes were better than those he had at Moeller. I think he felt that it would be the same kind of progression he had made at Moeller, not realizing that everybody we played against had the same kind of people."

If I didn't realize this, I realized it when we let Purdue beat us with a 12-play, 80-yard drive on which they scored with 19 seconds to play and topped it off with a two-point conversion. We lost 15-14 when all we had to do was to prevent them from scoring in the last three minutes. I can't even blame the loss on the shenanigans of the Boilermakers. I wish I could have.

There is a story, which could be apocryphal, but is funny and telling nevertheless. It addresses the competitiveness of the game. For Purdue, Notre Dame is *the* game. For Notre Dame, it's not. Supposedly one year, a Purdue assistant coach donned priest's garb and sneaked into a Notre Dame practice. A number of priests show up to watch practice each day and a coach doesn't necessarily know every priest on campus. So it's possible someone could have sneaked in. Allegedly this guy was there in his Roman collar, taking mental notes. There wasn't even a bolt of lightning from on high. Unbelievable.

After the Purdue game, I was in tears again, but they were not tears of joy as they had been previously. I remember the stories describing me as looking as if I had lost my best friend. Losing to Michigan and then another game on the road right after that got to me. I was at Notre Dame, living my dream, wanting so badly to win for the University, and two weeks in a row, we lost. This time with 19 seconds to play. Purdue not only scored on a 7-yard pass from Scott Campbell to Steve Bryant but it also threw the same pass from a different formation and we didn't stop the conversion. It was almost too much to bear, but I realized from the Michigan game that no one was going to feel sorry for me and that I had to stop feeling sorry for myself. I was learning, even if it wasn't fast enough to satisfy me or anyone else.

On the bus ride home from West Lafayette, I did something that I regret to this day. It haunts me still because it ran counter to everything I believe. It was another lesson, but it was worse than any other because it was gained at the expense of a player, something no coach should allow to happen.

Here's what happened: Mark Zavagnin, our weakside linebacker, had in his hands what appeared to be the interception that would have halted the final drive by Purdue. He dropped the ball. So on the bus, rather than being understanding and supportive and remembering that there are so many plays in a game that make up the outcome and not just one play loses a game, I went back to where Mark was sitting and told him that if he had intercepted the ball, we'd have won. I never should have done that. That made him feel like two cents. He knew the situation. What he should have gotten from me was comfort and support. Instead, without malicious intent, I ripped his heart out. I was stupid and thoughtless.

My frustration was showing. He took what I said the wrong way— as anyone would have—and he never again had any respect for me.

I don't blame him. I didn't deserve his respect.

Mark was among the players who talked to the *Sun-Times'* Phil Hersh, telling him: "Not once at St. Rita (a high school in the Chicago suburb of Evergreen Park) was a player ever blamed for losing a game."

No Notre Dame player should have been blamed, either. It may be no solace to Mark, even today, but from my mistake with him I was reminded ever after to put my arm around the player and give him the encouragement he deserved when he needed it most. It was a painful lesson. This wasn't supposed to be part of the dream.

When I was at my lowest after the Purdue loss, Father Hesburgh did for me what I should have done for Mark Zavagnin. He sat down the day we lost and wrote a short note to me that was long on feeling and short on blame. It said:

"Dear Gerry—Don't get discouraged. Out of adversity comes character, courage, new resolve and, in the end, victory."

This time, I bounced back. I didn't allow yesterday to color tomorrow. And Mike Read, who is from New Orleans and a member of the Notre Dame Alumni Board, helped me in a way different from, but just as important as Father Hesburgh's. Before our game against Michigan State, Mike presented me with an honorary membership from Notre Dame. The alumni also wrote me a letter of support and gave me a Notre Dame ring. I couldn't believe it. I had been at Notre Dame for three games and had lost two of them, and Notre Dame people were treating me like this. I never took that ring off until I had to leave Notre Dame. It meant the world to me and the sentiment and generosity that prompted it meant even more.

We didn't score much in the second half against Michigan State—just 3 points—but we didn't have to. We took control of the game 14-0 in the first quarter, added a 38-yard Harry Oliver field goal five seconds before halftime and played defense the rest of the way. It was a victory, but not a turning point.

We thought we could move the ball against Florida State when the Seminoles showed up at Notre Dame Stadium the following Saturday. Everyone else had. Although it had just beaten Nebraska and Ohio State on the road, Florida State had done it more with offense than defense. So what happened? It was 3-3 at the half. We had our chances to win, failed to take advantage of them and suddenly I had proved I could coach Notre Dame to losses at home as well as on the road, losing 19-13 after Florida State intercepted a pass in the fourth quarter. Worse, USC loomed on the horizon for "The Game."

We had an extra week to prepare for USC and during that time I sat down with the player who was like a son to me, Tim Koegel, and told him that Blair Kiel was my No. 1 quarterback. When I made the decision, a couple of our coaches told me that they thought it was the right one for the team and that by removing my personal feelings from it, I had come to the correct conclusion. I had never thought that my feelings were that tangled up in the quarterback decision, but I may not have recognized it if they were. When I told Tim, he was disappointed but he understood. He remains one of the greatest young men I've ever coached.

The irony, of course, occurred against USC. With Blair quarterbacking, we scored only 7 points, despite the fact that Phil Carter outrushed (161 yards to 147) the marvelous Marcus Allen, who would win the Heisman Trophy. In all, we outgained USC, 312-264. In addition to inserting Blair as the starter, we moved Tony Hunter from wingback to split end because both Dave Condeni and Mike Boushka had suffered season-ending leg injuries. Tony immediately proved I had had him in the wrong position. He caught five passes for 76 yards.

We had a chance to take the lead in the first half, but Harry Oliver missed the first of two field goals, one with the line of scrimmage at the two-yard line and the other with it at the one. It wasn't Harry's fault. We had to kick from the hash marks and hadn't practiced such short field goals from such sharp angles. Harry had played for me at Moeller, and I had talked Dan Devine into giving him a scholarship. He repaid both of us that first year by kicking a 51-yard field goal into the wind to beat Michigan. Dan telephoned me the following Monday.

"Boy," Dan said, "am I glad you talked me into taking Harry Oliver."

Harry helped Dan Devine win but couldn't help me in the USC game no matter how hard he tried. Makes a man wonder. The greatest wonder, though, was what had happened to our offense. After the enticing start against LSU, it had become obvious that there were big problems, and not even inserting Blair Kiel as the quarterback had solved them. We had scored 7, 14, 13 and 7 points in four of the last five games and lost four times. We closed practices and made changes. Usually closed practices are not closed to the media. When we said these would be, John Fineran, who covered Notre Dame for the *South Bend Tribune*, got upset. In a way, I couldn't blame him. He had a job a do, just as we had a job to do. Sometimes those jobs conflicted. If a coach can avoid such conflict as often as possible, he will find he is better off. Fights with the media are mostly ones a coach can't win and almost always are avoidable.

I talked with John and *Tribune* sports columnist Bill Moor and explained to them what we were doing and why, that we were changing our offense from a multiple-set to the I. Tony Hunter would move to tight end, where he could be shifted outside when the situation warranted, and we would run with a tailback and two wide receivers. We didn't change our terminology or throw out all our plays. We were careful and positive about the changes and it breathed new life into the team. But the media were ready to strangle me. After a day of closed practice, I told all the media they were welcome at practice if they would agree not to write about the changes. Most reasonable people can understand and accept that a coach making such changes does not want to announce it to the world and to his opponent, in this case Navy. I think my rapport with the media has been good, because I've tried to be open with them. Shut the media out with no explanation and they'll go after the reason like starving wolves after raw meat.

Despite those moments of tension, the changes worked. We shut out Navy and scored 38 points, which was not as easy as it may have seemed. The players the service academies put on the field may be outmanned, but they would never be outfought or quit. These are our future leaders, the men who will stand sentinel duty for this country. Football is the easiest part of their day. So you may beat Navy, but it will make you work to do it.

The following week against Georgia Tech, the Yellow Jackets took a 3-0 lead, but that was their only moment. Not only did we continue to score—35 points—with our revised, rejuvenated offense, but also on defense Bob Crable led an effort that was suffocating. His 13 tackles left him only three shy of Bob Golic's Notre Dame career record. If that wasn't enough, he intercepted a pass as well.

"I never realized until that season," Crable says, "the importance of experience and chemistry."

Crabes and I both made this discovery but in different ways. I had moved defensive line coach Joe Yonto to an administrative assistant's job and inserted Bill Meyers into Yonto's former job.

"When I looked at Joe Yonto," Crable says, "I thought he was not open-minded enough, not with it. I thought he was not modern enough because he had been with Ara for all those years. But Joe Yonto might have been the experience that the staff was missing. Hindsight is always 20-20, but in hindsight I can see in Joe Yonto someone who had a tremendous amount of knowledge in Notre Dame football over 20 years. But, quite honestly, when Bill was made the line coach I remember thinking that this would be good. He was a rah-rah, go-get-'em, stick-it-in-their-ear, technique-oriented guy. I thought: 'Wow, this will be great.'

"Now I ask: 'What didn't Bill have that Joe Yonto did?' The answer is: three things. He didn't have Scott Zettek. He didn't have John Hankerd. And he didn't have Donnie Kidd. Those guys were great defensive linemen. They were the guys who made me look good by keeping the blockers off me so I could make tackles. We had a lot of players back on defense, but sometimes it's not the number of players who return but who doesn't. When I look honestly at the staff that Gerry brought in, I thought it was a good staff."

After we defeated Air Force 35-7, scoring three times in the last 12 minutes in a high-altitude game at Colorado Springs, there should not have been any question about the team's conditioning. Bob Crable set the record for the most career tackles, a record he still holds at 521. Moreover, Tim Koegel came off the bench late in the game when Blair Kiel was struggling, and breathed life into the offense. But the next week at Penn State, we lost after the Nittany Lions scored with 3:48 to play. Because of this loss, the last-second loss to Purdue, and winning fourth-quarter TDs by Florida State and USC, critics suggested we didn't have our players in good enough shape. The media took up that cry. It was wrong. The mistake I made began in preseason practice. I worked the team too much rather than not enough. I took the players' legs away from them by demanding too much of them. I did not realize the college game at 60 minutes, not 48 as in high school, was compounded by the physical challenge of stronger opposing players. That can be doubly draining. I never made the mistake again.

It wasn't just the media and fans who pointed out my mistakes. My son, Gerry, spent the Penn State game with me on the sideline. It was a great game for a spectator, but no one in the Faust family could be classified that simply. They were involved not only with their heads and hearts, but also by blood. They felt my pain and I felt theirs.

After Penn State drove 82 yards to take a 24-21 lead with 3:48 to play, we responded with a drive of our own that reached the Penn State 40-yard line before stalling at fourth and six. More than two minutes remained. Decision time. I sent the punt team onto the field. After we had punted, young Gerry began screaming at me.

"Dad," he shouted, "you shouldn't have punted. You should have gone for it."

Now my son is on my back, too, I thought. It's getting crowded on my back with fans, nuns and sons.

"Gerry," I told him, "there's still time to win."

I wanted to put Penn State deep in its territory. Fourth and six is tough to make. The field goal would have been 57 yards, which was too long. As it turned out, the move worked. We held. They punted. We got the ball back just over midfield.

Gerry comes up to me on the sideline.

"Dad," he said, "that was the greatest move you ever made."

We were filled with hope. We had time to win. But we didn't. The drive ended on the 39-yard line when Blair Kiel's fourth-down pass that was intended for Joe Howard fell incomplete.

Gerry was back at me.

"I told you that you shouldn't have punted," he said.

I almost laughed. Losing wasn't funny, but Gerry's reaction was. It perfectly illustrated how the Fighting Irish fans ride the lows to the highs and back to the lows. They want Notre Dame to win so much, and perhaps we could have won or at least tied in this case if I had kicked a field goal when we were on the Penn State 4-yard line with a 21-17 lead. The reason I chose not to kick the field goal is that they hadn't stopped us all day and a 28-17 lead would have forced them to score two touchdowns, which I didn't think they could do. It was a calculated risk that didn't work.

Joe Paterno understood. He had Todd Blackledge at quarterback and Curt Warner at tailback and yet for much of the 1981 season his team had found it difficult to score when it got inside the 5-yard line. Penn State fans took to booing Joe. I couldn't believe it. Booing Joe Paterno? In Happy Valley? I could hear my future.

After the loss to Penn State, a game to which we had given so much and gotten back too little, we played our worst game of the season in the worst possible situation: If we had won, we would have finished with a winning season instead of with the first losing record at Notre Dame since 1963. We just got whipped. Miami beat us with speed, our problem. I did not recruit enough raw speed, the kind that can make up for mistakes. Besides Miami's speed, it was hot and we withered by halftime.

Jim Kelly became the first of the great quarterbacks who would go on to NFL careers that my teams would face, both those at Akron and Notre Dame. In addition to Kelly, there was Dan Marino (Pitt), Bernie Kosar (Miami), Jim Everett (Purdue), Jim Harbaugh (Michigan), Doug Flutie (Boston College), Eric Wilhelm (Oregon State) and Jeff Blake (East Carolina).

It was a terrible way to end the season, one that made people forget that even though we lost to five Top 20 teams, we had played competitively and often well. My inexperience as a college coach hurt us. Maybe I called the wrong plays at the wrong times. Maybe I could have dealt better with situations, such as choosing a quarterback. Maybe I could have handled losing in a way that didn't rub off on others. But I didn't. With more experience on my part, we could have been 9-2. Later, some people would say, including some players, that I had begun during that first year to lose the respect of the players because of the losing and the way I handled it.

"When young people come to Notre Dame," says athletic director Gene Corrigan, "they come to win a national championship. They've been recruited by all the great football powers in the country. They've seen the beautiful athletic dormitories. They've seen the wonderful training tables. They've seen all the glitz you can see. When they come to Notre Dame, they don't get any of that. So what they really want to do is get on that field and win."

Fail to do that and a Notre Dame coach risks losing respect. While I know that some players had reasons to doubt me or feel bad about the way I had treated them—Blair Kiel and Mark Zavagnin, for example—the majority, I believe, felt differently and recognized I only wanted what was best for Notre Dame and for them.

"The only situation I observed," Bob Crable says, "came as a result of an article that came out in the school newspaper after a loss. It talked about three players having been seen in one of the bars on a Thursday night before a game. It basically said: 'How are you supposed to win when you have one or two starters down there drinking two nights before the game?' It didn't say these players were drunk, but Fuzzy lost it.

"He came into the locker room after he read this and he was ranting and raving. Basically, he said—in that screaming, maybe out-of-control voice he has—how could you do this? This was something near and dear to his heart. If a kid is putting in jeopardy a football game, that is the one thing that will get under his skin. He carried on for what seemed like 15 minutes but was probably 45 seconds. Then he was off in a whirlwind, and we all kind of looked at one another like: What was that?

"There were some guys from that—and I don't think it would be fair to name names—that he lost. They were guys who were playing but whom I didn't view as real good influences on the team anyway.

"I firmly believe that when things are going well and you're winning football games, that people look at moments like this one with Fuzzy and say: 'Yeah, that's great. That's electric. That's enthusiasm.' But as soon as you lose a game or two, it's: 'Put that high-school crap in your bag, pack it and take it back to Cincinnati.' There were some guys on the team like that."

I think most people, including the administration, felt it was a learning year and were willing to accept it as that. I knew it would be a learning year, but it was more of one than I could ever have anticipated. I tell people today that the University of Akron was the toughest coaching job I ever had, but there is one qualifier: No one cared if you lost except a few of the people around Akron and some alumni. It wasn't a national disaster when you lost. It was at Notre Dame.

Father Joyce, though he was closest to the situation having picked me as coach, was able to keep my first season in perspective. He believed college football is bigger than Notre Dame. He felt that no one team should dominate the game. He had told me that more than once. So, quite a while after the season, when the pain of a losing record had been dulled somewhat, I went to Father Joyce's office for a chat.

"Well, Father," I reminded him, "I listened to you."

"About what, Gerry?"

"You said that Notre Dame shouldn't win every game. And we didn't. We were 5-6."

He laughed. I laughed. I even think he was laughing with me.

7

■ THE PHANTOM SEASON ■

No one hailed me when I suggested saying Hail Marys as well as throwing them. Just the opposite. The Hail Mary, from which I've always drawn quiet inspiration, became not only objectionable on the Notre Dame sideline but also made me an object of derision. I didn't mind that so much. What bothered me was the guilt by association that was heaped on the Blessed Mother.

If there were any place in college football where a suggestion that players on the sideline might say a Hail Mary, when during the course of a game tension mounts and the going gets tough, I thought it was a Catholic institution such as Moeller or Notre Dame. It was an old and comforting habit for me.

For years at Moeller, I would say a Hail Mary during a game and tell the players to do the same. We never lost a single game because of prayer—nor do I think we ever won a game due to it.

The whole Hail Mary controversy was blown out of proportion.

Gene Corrigan brought the Hail Mary issue to my attention during the first season, and I tried from then on to keep my Hail Marys to myself and for on-field use in desperate, last-second passing situations. I may still have quietly said a Hail Mary on occasion. But that's me. I put JMJ for Jesus, Mary and Joseph at the top of each letter I write. I say "God bless you" when I end a conversation —and I mean it.

If we had won more games, no one would have suggested that saying Hail Marys was counterproductive. As it was, my critics brought the issue up privately and, eventually, in a public forum.

"I'm Catholic. I go to mass every Sunday," Mark Zavagnin told Phil Hersh for his critical *Chicago Sun-Times* story. "But in the middle of a game, I don't have time to say Hail Mary. I have other things to worry about. And I know the Lord has more things to worry about than whether Notre Dame wins or loses."

Mark was right. I was the person who had to take responsibility for whether Notre Dame won or lost. If you have to call on God to win a game, you're not doing a very good job of coaching or playing. Never, however, did I say Hail Marys when I should have been coaching. And never did I suggest that a player who should have been concentrating on playing do so. At Moeller we encouraged players to pray the Hail Mary as part of their spiritual growth during their formative years. In college, players already have made up their minds about how they're going to live their lives spiritually. So I tried to stop suggesting the Hail Mary, except in more appropriate circumstances such as pre- and post-game locker rooms.

I was not, however, the only Notre Dame coach who took comfort in the power of prayer.

"I can remember," Father James Riehle, team chaplain, says, "Dan Devine coming up to me on the sideline and saying: 'Hey, Father, say a prayer, we're going to throw a long pass.' They threw it and completed it for 70-some yards and Dan said: 'Thanks for the prayer.' The thing is, I never said a prayer.

"It is amazing when we lose a game that someone will come up to me and say: 'I guess you didn't pray hard enough, Father.' As if I had anything to do with it. But this is the mentality of people. I keep saying to them: 'What do we do when we play Boston College? Do you think God's up there flipping a coin to decide which Catholic school to help?' It's absolutely ludicrous.

"To Gerry, telling someone to say a Hail Mary was just something he would say, like 'Tackle hard.' Religion becomes another excuse for why we lose or why we win. What it boils down to is who the players are, how much luck you have. As many times as Gerry said to pray and something didn't happen, it wasn't because they had prayed or hadn't. It just wasn't supposed to happen. That's all there was to it.

"I think we ought to pray to accept God's will in our lives. That's far more important."

It also can be far more difficult, especially when it seems as if God's will may be in conflict with our own. More than anything, I wanted to do well for Notre Dame and that meant producing something better than a 5-6 record. So following the season we redoubled our recruiting efforts and put together a class that included such players as Wally Kleine, Eric Dorsey, Tony Furjanic, Tim Scannell and Milt Jackson. These players and their freshman teammates were highly regarded by those who rank recruiting classes.

Of course, we didn't get every player we wanted. A coach never does.

One of the more interesting misses we had occurred the year before and had the potential to haunt us. We wanted quarterback Sean Salisbury who lived near San Diego and was a Mormon. Religion may have no place on the college football sideline, according to some, but there is no denying the factor it can play in recruiting.

Sean, who was also a great basketball player, had visited Notre Dame, and later, I went to California to see Sean, his family, relatives and church officials. The question was whether the bishop of his Mormon Church would allow Sean to attend a Catholic university. There must have been 20 people at Sean's house when I arrived, the men in the living room, the women in the kitchen. I sat down in the living room with the bishop, which in the Mormon Church is similar to an elder in the Baptist Church.

"Coach," he said, "you know Sean is a devout Mormon and that we're quite conservative. We don't know about the idea of Sean going to a Catholic university."

"I think that's an excellent subject and a real concern," I told the bishop. "Being a Catholic, if my sons wanted to go to Southern Methodist University or to Baylor, I would have second thoughts. You know, Bishop, I bet you're a great Brigham Young fan."

"How'd you know that?"

"It's pretty simple. You're a Mormon and BYU is a Mormon university. You also live in California where many of BYU's players and students come from. So I'm sure you follow them. They had a great team this year."

"They sure did," the bishop said.

"Well," I continued, "two of the reasons were BYU's wide receiver and quarterback. They were outstanding."

"They sure were."

"And they're both Catholic. Jim McMahon was the quarterback. And, by golly, if BYU can win with a Catholic at quarterback, then Notre Dame should have the opportunity to win with a Mormon at quarterback."

"Coach," the bishop said, "that's a great scenario. I don't have any problem with Sean going to Notre Dame when you put it like that."

We agreed that I would visit Sean the next day at his high school, meet his principal, counselor and coaches. After Sean's basketball practice was over, I went down to the court and asked his coach if I could shoot around with Sean and the other players. I was meeting and kidding around with his teammates and watching Sean shoot. He was a jump-shooter and a good one. He was cocky and had a right to be. He was a really good-looking athlete. What I wanted to see, though, was the range of his jump shot.

When I had that figured out, I did something similar to what I had tried with bowling and Eric Dorsey. I made Sean a deal he couldn't refuse.

"I'll tell you what, Sean," I said. "I'll shoot baskets with you and if I win, you come to Notre Dame. If I lose, you can go to any school you want."

"Coach," Sean said, "that's a deal. Where do you want to shoot from?"

"Out there," I said, pointing to a spot well beyond where Sean was comfortable shooting his jump shot. "You shoot first."

Airball.

I had him. I'm an old one-handed set-shooter. It isn't pretty, but it gives me range. I shot and hit the backboard. Sean tried again. This time he got the ball to the backboard. I shot. The ball hit the rim. Third shot. Sean bounced his off the backboard and I swished mine. The place went crazy. The basketball coaches were laughing. The kids were laughing. You should have seen Sean's face. It just dropped. I went right over and shook hands with him.

"Welcome to Notre Dame," I said.

It didn't work. Sean went to USC, where our shootouts would become the real thing. Prior to the USC-Notre Dame showdown on the final Saturday of the season, the 1982 Fighting Irish would prove that a high school coach's offense can be effective and that even the best team in the country could be beaten. Our journey carried us from thoughts of a national championship to feelings of despair and no bowl game. In other words, just your normal season during the Gerry Faust era.

The season began like a sweet refrain. Before each summer camp, we would gather the team at the Grotto to pray, not for victory but for the opportunity to represent Notre Dame well. The prayer we shared before the '82 season went like this:

"Notre Dame Our Mother—We, the 1982 Notre Dame football team, would ask for your intercession to help us represent the University of Notre Dame as mature Christian people. We also ask that you watch over all of us so that no serious injuries occur to us or to our families this year. Thanks for giving us the opportunity to represent the University of Notre Dame as student-athletes."

And, it went without saying, as coaches. In trying to represent the University well by winning, the purpose of our presence at Notre Dame could have become obscured. The only good thing about night games in college football is that is gives you a chance to think about such things—and about everything else under the sun and moon.

In order to be on national television, a decision I endorsed, we had decided to turn our season opener against Michigan into the first night game ever played at Notre Dame. The television network brought in portable lights, and then we waited from sun-up to well past sun-down to play the coach who a year before had said we had a high school offense and said he'd never lose to such a pipsqueak popgun of an attack.

In high school, school activities fill the day prior to a game. In Saturday-afternoon college football, there never was too long to wait before going to work. Saturday nights were different. It took forever to get to kickoff. The days lasted six weeks. On Saturdays when we played at nights, we held meetings. People who say college football does not necessarily prepare a young man for the business world should have followed our schedule prior to a Saturday-night game. It was just like business. We would hold meetings just to hold meetings. They may have been useless, but they prevented idle minds from drifting from the subject.

In addition, at Notre Dame, we set aside time for players to see their families on game weekend. Many families came from great distances. Parents and children needed to and deserved to see one another. I would also try to spend time with parents, to talk with them about their sons and the progress they were making, academically and athletically. I went out of my way to talk with them. I'd call them when something good happened to their sons or if I was concerned about one of them. They weren't able to see every practice or check on their sons after each practice as they had been when the players were in high school. So I tried to keep both an open door and open dialogue. One of the hardest things was to explain to parents and to help a young man to accept why he was not playing.

I would sit and talk with players and parents alike and remind them of the priorities of college: First and foremost was the education they were receiving. But even if a player recognizes that Notre Dame recruits other players as good as or better than he is, no one enjoys facing the fact he won't be playing. I should know. I almost quit the University of Dayton football team for that very reason.

During my junior season, the coaches switched me from quarterback to tight end and linebacker. It was 1956 and we were in Columbus at our preseason camp. It wasn't as if the switch allowed me to go from backup quarterback to starting tight end or linebacker. It didn't. I didn't know anything about playing tight end or linebacker, and I wasn't getting any better. Every day my teammates were kicking the crap out of me. After 10 days of that, I said: That's it. I'm quitting.

I called my dad from the kitchen of the dining hall where we ate. I told him I had had enough, that I was going to quit. He said: "Son, that's your decision. But once you quit something, you'll quit other things the rest of your life. I'd rather see you stick it out this year and then if you don't want to play your senior year, that's up to you. You have to make the decision."

I'll never forget his words.

"If you decide to quit," he went on, "you know you are on your own to pay for your education. I can't help you. I'm a Catholic high school teacher. I don't have the money. Right now, your schooling is paid for by playing football. But you make your own decision. I'll still love you no matter what you decide."

When we hung up, I was still thinking of quitting. I went to Stan Zajdel, who coached the position I was playing.

"Coach," I told him, "I'm thinking of hanging it up."

He was eating supper. He leaned back in his chair with a sad and surprised look on his face.

"Gerry," he said, "you're the last person on this team I thought would ever come to me and say he was quitting."

That hit home with me.

"You know," he said, "you've made it through 10 days of practice here at camp. There are only nine to go. Why don't you stick it out?"

I decided Stan was right, and so was my dad. I didn't want to begin a pattern of quitting. The fact I didn't would become obvious as my seasons at Notre Dame unfolded. For better or worse, I don't quit. There's dignity in effort. So I don't believe in quitting, even if things don't work out as well for me as they did at Dayton.

Our No. 1 quarterback got hurt early on and one of his backups also suffered an injury. The coaches moved me back to quarterback, which I had played all through high school for my dad, and I became the starter.

Not long ago I wrote Stan Zajdel a letter. I thanked him for sticking with me and convincing me to stick with him and the team. It changed my life. I never would have made it to Notre Dame if I had quit that night. So every time a player in high school or college came to me and said he was quitting, I always shared with him what I had been through and how it turned out for me. I felt I owed that to my players. I also believed I could understand better than the coaches who always had been the top players on their teams how a player who wasn't doing as well as he had hoped might feel. I spent my time on the bench. I understand that frustration.

It was another sort of frustration that I felt from the result of our 1981 performance at Michigan, the fake field goal and its ramifications and the condescending attitude of Bo Schembechler, who said he would never lose to a high school coach. I never brought it up, though. I just told our players that they might want to remember the thumping we had taken on national television the year before. Now we were at a similar moment. National TV. Michigan. We had almost everyone back from the previous season, and we had another opportunity to show that we were a better football team than the audience saw that day in 1981. They got the message. Boy, how they got it!

The game was electrifying. Not even a terrible quirk of fate could keep us from victory. But it did make me say to myself: Don't tell me we're going to lose again. It happened with 7:38 to play in the fourth quarter. Michigan quarterback Steve Smith, throwing from our 39, found freshman Gilvanni Johnson at the 25. As Johnson caught the ball, Stacey Toran and Dave Duerson sandwiched him with such hard hits that Johnson should have felt like a piece of pressed meat. The ball popped out of Johnson's hands and came to rest on Toran's shoulder. Instead of falling harmlessly to the ground, however, it was snatched off Toran's shoulder by Michigan's Rick

Rogers, who ran in for a touchdown. Believe it or not, I was speechless.

Unlike those first-season games that got away from us in the fourth quarter, we held on to this one for a 23-17 victory, with Duerson picking off a pass with about two minutes to play. As I had the year before, when I was the person suffering my first loss as a college head coach, I ran across the field to shake Bo Schembechler's hand. Guess what? No Bo.

He had stormed to the Michigan locker room. I guess losing to a high school coach was more than he could take. I could understand why he was upset. I like Bo. He's a dynamic person and a great competitor. But I can say I never ran off without shaking the other coach's hand. That isn't the way they taught us to do it in high school. Maybe that's why Bo won more games than I did. Maybe his will to win was so strong and his hatred for losing so great that it carried over to his players. Maybe that kind of demeanor makes the difference. Maybe I had it all wrong.

For once, we did what we were supposed to do the following week: Beat Purdue. Though we went to a quick 14-0 lead, it wouldn't be that simple or easy. Not with Purdue. By halftime, the Boilermakers had fought their way into a 14-14 tie. Scott Campbell was throwing the ball all over Notre Dame Stadium, usually to someone in a Purdue jersey. Meanwhile, we relied on the running game we had established in Week One, with Larry Moriarty going over 100 yards for the second game in a row and Phil Carter, whose usual relief, Greg Bell, had been sidelined with a fractured right tibia in the second quarter, getting a game-high 154 yards on 27 carries. The 28 points we scored in a 28-14 victory would look like an offensive bonanza the following week when, despite leading 11-0 at halftime at Michigan State, we hadn't scored a touchdown.

On the way to our locker room at halftime, a Notre Dame fan decided to take exception to an offense that produced just three field goals and a defense that added a safety. The gentleman, drink —and I don't mean soft—in hand, approached me as I was running off the field and introduced himself as a Notre Dame alumnus. Paul Harvey, not the radio commentator but the former captain on the South Bend police force who served as my gameday escort, usually could keep such conversationalists at a distance, but this man had managed to sneak through. That isn't easy.

Paul, who also owned two McDonald's franchises, played point guard for John Wooden's South Bend Washington High School basketball team before Coach Wooden got famous at UCLA and Paul grew into the size of an offensive lineman, for which I was always grateful. I mean, I wouldn't want some point guard protecting me. Paul did more than that, though. As a black man, he served as a great influence on our minority student-athletes. They loved him. They had to stand in line. I loved him, too. He became like a brother to me, and we remain close friends.

On the sidelines, Paul would pull me back off the field when I got so engrossed in the game that I wandered into an area I wasn't allowed. This time, however, it was the Notre Dame alumnus who had wriggled his way into no-fan's land. And he was lacing me. He said he had had two sons attend Notre Dame, not to mention being a graduate himself.

"So, Coach," he demanded, "when are you going to get this offense going?"

I tried to ignore this. It wasn't my first encounter with an alumnus, but it was the first I'd experienced *during* a game.

"I'm sick and tired of these field goals," he said.

"Look at the scoreboard," I reminded him. "It's 11-0. I'm very happy with that at Michigan State."

"Well, I'm not," he said. "I'm not a bit happy. You'd better get it going in the second half."

With that, he turned and headed back for the stands. I didn't say anything. I was just going to let it and the guy go. Then, all of a sudden, I thought: That's wrong. He shouldn't do something like this. So I grabbed the guy.

"You're going into the locker room with me," I told him, "and you're going to talk to the players at halftime. You're going to tell them what they're doing wrong and how disappointed in them you are."

This startled him. He began stammering: "No," he said. "No."

"You're going," I said.

I hauled him into the locker room with us. Paul Harvey was about to die he wanted so badly to burst out laughing. I pointed to a spot in the room.

"Sit there," I ordered.

With his drink in his hand, he sat on the floor, knees up, head between his knees. He was shaking his head.

"When we're through," I said, pointing to the coaches, "you can tell the team what it has been doing wrong."

He didn't know what was going on. The coaches moved to the chalk boards and were working with their players. They were Xing and Oing and this guy didn't have a clue. It was a foreign language to him. Half covers here. Aiming blocks to the outside pad and slipping to a linebacker there. Taking the outside course and looking for the first man inside. It's terminology. To most of the public it doesn't make sense. To the player, it's simple. The more this guy with the drink heard, the more shaken he became.

Then, just before we went back onto the field, I slipped over to him and told him he didn't have to say anything.

"Oh, Coach," he said. "Thanks. I don't know what I'd have said. I apologize."

He probably didn't like the second half, either. It was a great defensive battle. Mark Zavagnin returned an interception 16 yards and recovered a fumble, and Chris Brown swiped two passes. Even more impressive, we held the Spartans to 19 yards rushing and improved our nation-leading defense against the rush in an 11-3 victory.

The interesting thing about this incident is that the man with the drink became one of my biggest supporters. His name was Charles Kitz. He was from Highland Park, Michigan, and he worked for Chrysler. He even wrote a letter to the editor in one of the Detroit newspapers defending me. Every time he came to campus, he'd stop by to see me and he was among those who wanted me to stay when it was time for me to go.

This man was one of the people that my friend Mike Leep talks about.

"People who knew Gerry Faust away from the public spotlight," Mike says, "really accepted him. He did so much community work that nobody knew about. If anybody needed anything, Gerry would be there, trying to help."

I got to know Mike because he supplied our coaches with cars from one of his auto dealerships in South Bend. He was our car coach. But more than that, he became a friend.

"The community as a whole," Mike Leep says, "thought Gerry was a savior when he first came to town and that we possibly would never lose another game. This town doesn't expect a winner — it demands it. When that didn't happen, there was a lot of animosity from a lot of people.

"But anybody who knew the man personally was behind him. He's the kind of man you love to follow, to be a part of. Just watching him win was the good part of life."

Maybe I should have invited all of the Notre Dame fans to the locker room at halftime. In a sense, though, that was what I was trying to do by being accessible. I wanted people to know me and not just because it might turn critics into friends. I wanted them to understand that college football is a complex set of circumstances in which equally complex people find themselves. Sometimes, a coach can do things right and still have it turn out wrong in terms of victories.

There was, however, nothing wrong during the first four games of 1982. We completed a 4-0 run with a come-from-behind 16-14 victory over 17th-ranked Miami, as Mike Johnston kicked two fourth-quarter field goals, the last a 32-yarder with 11 seconds to play. This game reversed our previous trend of losing to fourth-quarter comebacks. Though we weren't scoring an excessive number of points, Blair Kiel was playing well, Moriarty and Carter were a potent one-two running punch and the defense remained spectacular. Miami got 67 yards rushing.

Though we were playing well and with a confidence we had not previously experienced, we prepared as hard and carefully for 1-2-1 Arizona as we would have if the Wildcats had also been unbeaten. We took a 10-0 lead in the first quarter and I couldn't help but think that this might silence some of our critics and give us some breathing room. Max Zendejas kicked two field goals for Arizona in the third quarter, but Mike Johnston added a 43-yarder for us at the beginning of the fourth quarter. All we had to do was hang on. We didn't.

Our offense went into the tank. The running game was stymied and Blair Kiel, though completing 13 of 21, threw three interceptions and managed only 80 yards. Even so, it took a 48-yard Zendejas field goal at the gun to win.

Why do such games slip away? There are so many reasons and no reason. We had four turnovers to Arizona's one. We gave it opportunities to stay in a game that should have been ours. Great teams—and coaches—don't let that happen. I discovered quickly in college football that the difference between winning and losing is, as often as not, turnovers. Embed in the minds of your players the cost of turnovers and you'll win. I didn't get that done. Again, maybe it was a lack of fear. I'll bet Bo Schembechler's players and Bear Bryant's feared the consequences if they committed a turnover.

Also, notice that some great coaches do not gamble in their play-calling when they're having a bad day against an opponent they should beat. And we should have beaten Arizona. Such coaches become conservative. It's boring, but they stay employed. Maybe I should have been more boring.

At Oregon the following week, we played for a 13-13 tie in another game we should have won. Again, we generated too little offense. Kiel struggled and finally in the third quarter I inserted sophomore Ken Karcher. We needed a spark, but it was a difficult decision. The last thing I wanted was to recreate a quarterback controversy or to undermine Blair. But we needed help. Ken had his moments, completing a 53-yard bootleg pass to Joe Howard that took us to the Oregon 31, but then a 15-yard holding penalty and a Karcher fumble cost us the ball. I went back to Kiel in the final 1:24 of the game, and we drove 55 yards to the Oregon 18 before stalling on three incompletions.

Decision time.

Chances of making a first down at the 8-yard line or a touchdown were 1-in-100. We had 11 seconds. If we kicked the field goal and tied the game we're 4-1-1. If we win the remainder of our games, and I'm thinking about how well we have played in the first four, we could be 9-1-1. That might put us in the national championship picture, which is the only picture a Notre Dame coach has to look at as an independent with a history of such achievement. I know that may sound silly when you're facing a field goal to tie Oregon, but that's exactly what ran through my mind. So Mike Johnston kicked a 35-yarder, and I don't regret it.

Of course, I was criticized for the decision. The next week we beat Navy 27-10 at Giants Stadium to move to 5-1-1, and I was criticized for playing Navy. Why do we do it? We beat them all the time. Well, we play Navy because it's tradition. Notre Dame plays the service academies. We play Air Force. No one asks why we play Air Force after it beats us. Except me.

The first Saturday in November we had the opportunity to prove the value of the tie at Oregon: We were playing No. 1-ranked Pitt in Pittsburgh. We didn't know how we were going to stop the Panthers. They had Dan Marino at quarterback and a line that included future NFL stars Bill Fralic and Jimbo Covert to give the future Pro Football Hall of Famer time to throw to excellent receivers such as Dwight Collins and Julius Dawkins. We concluded we weren't going to stop Marino. He was *that* good. So we decided

to take away the deep pass. If Marino was going to throw successfully, he was going to throw short.

That decided, the question became how to attack Pitt's defense. We noted two points: They played a lot of man-to-man coverage and had trouble covering backs running pass routes out of the
backfield. In addition, their free safety, Thomas Flynn, reacted quickly
to stop the run. Maybe too quickly for his own good.

As if Pitt weren't a difficult enough assignment in itself, one
of our biggest supporters, Frank Fuhrer, lives there. Not only is he a
generous, civic-minded man who loves Notre Dame but he also is a
man of principle who will tell you how it is. Coach a lousy game,
Frank will tell you. Misread a potential recruit, Frank will tell you.

The Friday night before the Pitt game, Frank and I went to
watch a high school player we were interested in.

"The kid can't play for Notre Dame," Frank said.

"Frank," I said, "that kid is a heckuva player."

"He can't play," Frank said flatly.

The kid was big and quick. We recruited him but he didn't
come to Notre Dame. He went to another top school—and never
played during an injury-plagued career.

In his straightforward way, Frank told me what was what, including what we had to do the following day against Pitt.

"Gerry," Frank said, "you've got to win this game. The whole
town has been on my back, all those Pittsburgh fans. They know I
love Notre Dame. If I've gotten five calls, I've gotten 50, and all of
them are telling how this high school coach at Notre Dame can't
coach. I got so mad at these people I told them: 'Put up or shut up.'
I've got a lot of money on this game. You have to win so I can live in
this community."

"Frank," I said, "we're going to give it our all, but they are truly
the No. 1 team in the country."

So now I not only have to worry about Pitt but also about
disappointing Frank. It isn't the money. Frank can afford his losses.
It's the pride. And he was defending me, the high school coach,
with his wagers.

After we warmed up the next day and headed for our locker
room in Pitt Stadium, there waiting for us by the locker room door
was Keith Penrod in his wheelchair. Keith was a man of about 30
who lived in South Bend. His whole life was Notre Dame football.
He was born with a handicap that made it difficult for him to speak.
He talked out of the side of his mouth and when he got excited

and talked fast he could be difficult to understand. The players understood Keith, though. They loved him. Before the season-opening Michigan game, we had gotten him a new wheelchair on which we put a leprechaun and a sign proclaiming: "Penrod...Notre Dame's No. 1 Fan." Keith can walk some, but when he does he has to lean on the wheelchair for support. He also leaned on us. Linebacker coach George Kelly looked out for him and became his godfather when he converted to Catholicism, and Bob Crable also became extremely close to him. Keith would come to practice each day with a motorized cart on which he had a horn that played the Notre Dame Victory March. He'd start playing his horn and the players would go wild. I think the players looked upon Keith and thought: There go I but for the grace of God.

Keith was always welcome with our team but he had told no one he was coming to Pittsburgh. When the players saw him sitting there in his wheelchair with this big smile on his face, they went bonkers.

"Keith," I said, "how did you get here?"

"I took a Greyhound bus," he said.

"Well," I said, "you're not taking any bus home. You're flying with us. Now you come into the locker room."

If seeing Keith Penrod and knowing the effort he had made to get to Pittsburgh to be with us weren't enough, I had laid in some pregame fuel for the players' fire. I'd asked Roger Valdiserri and John Heisler to research all the No. 1 teams that Notre Dame had upset throughout its history. I knew there had been several. They came up with seven from the various ratings services.

After our prayer, I went down that list, ticking off the games: Northwestern in 1936. Texas in the '70 Cotton Bowl. Alabama in the '73 Sugar Bowl.

"Today," I told the team, "we're playing the No. 1 team in the country in its stadium. It's November 6, 1982, and you're going to go down in the annals of Notre Dame history as the eighth team with a great upset of a No. 1 team. You are about to carry on a Notre Dame tradition."

These weren't just words.

Our game plan worked perfectly, if a little late. Keeping Marino's receivers in front of us, we did not allow a touchdown pass despite giving up 314 yards. Then in the fourth quarter, we used the flea-flicker to take advantage of their free safety. The irony is, Pitt's starting free safety, Thomas Flynn, had been injured, but the play worked anyway because his replacement played the same aggressive, come-up-fast-to-stop-the-run game.

The first time we had the ball in the last quarter, Blair Kiel handed off to tailback Phil Carter and the safety took the bait. As he rushed to the line of scrimmage, Joe Howard streaked past him and Carter turned and pitched the ball to Kiel. Blair threw 54 yards to Howard, who scored untouched.

Marino wasn't finished, but cornerback Chris Brown knocked down one key pass and then our other cornerback, John Mosley, recovered a fumble. Meanwhile, freshman Allen Pinkett was having his second consecutive 100-yard game—this one 112 yards on 10 carries—including touchdown runs of 76 and 7 yards in the fourth quarter.

Before we took our fourth-quarter lead, some guy in the stands who was sitting behind Marlene and our kids had been taking great pleasure in berating me. Finally, Marlene had had enough. She got up, walked back six rows to where the man was seated and confronted him.

"Those are the coach's children down there," she said, "and if you don't keep your so-and-so mouth shut, I'm going to come up here and hit you. You're going to be the most embarrassed man in this stadium, because I'm coming after you. I don't care what you think of their dad, but you can keep it to yourself with them sitting down there."

Marlene wasn't kidding, either.

I had told her many times that she couldn't react this way and if she was going to do so, she should avoid the situation. Father Riehle, who provided great comfort and counsel not only to me but also to my family, had told her the same thing.

"They did have some choice," Father Riehle says. "They didn't have to go to the games. Ara Parseghian's wife used to go out to the mall during games. Nobody knew her there. But Marlene would go and sit and listen to all that abuse.

"I'm sure she did it because she wanted to give her moral support to Gerry, but to take that abuse had to be awful. People are ruthless. Beth Holtz told me the same thing. She told me that one time she turned around to somebody and said: 'What is that you want me to tell my husband?' The guy shut up."

Marlene's loudmouth heckler shut up, too, and after we had won 31-16, she got a measure of revenge when the man came down to Marlene and asked for her autograph.

"I told that SOB I'd never give him an autograph," Marlene says. "Then I walked away. He was a fair-weather fan."

Someone might have accused Frank Fuhrer of being the same thing when he didn't show up at the game. But they'd have been wrong. When I saw Frank wasn't around afterward, I called him at home.

"Frank," I said, "why weren't you at the game?"

"Ger," he said, "I was so nervous and I had so many people I would have had to face if we lost that I didn't want to go. In fact, I had to turn off the radio three or four times during the game. I couldn't stand to listen."

I had to laugh. I've felt on more than one occasion as if I wanted to cover my eyes and not watch.

"I'll tell you what," Frank said. "I won a lot of money; the University is getting a check. I'm just going to enjoy collecting it and donating it to Notre Dame. Gerry, this was one of the greatest days I'll spend in my life. Now I can live in this town and tell those sons-of-guns that I only have one thing to say to them: 'Where's my money?'"

The locker room was a scene I'll never forget. I gave one of the game balls to Keith Penrod and the players went crazy. And you should have seen Keith. Of all the things I've done, I probably got more from the look on his face when he received that game ball than anything else. He still has that ball from one of Notre Dame's greatest victories.

"It was by far," Father Joyce says, "Gerry's greatest victory. That was the high point—but nobody knew it at the time."

When we arrived back in South Bend, there were 10,000 to 15,000 people waiting for us on Notre Dame Avenue as we rolled up in three buses. It took us longer to travel the one mile to the circle on campus than it had to drive from the airport to the campus.

I was standing in the front seat of the bus and people were pounding on the outside. When we stopped, they climbed on top of the bus. They were cheering. The street was jammed. They were singing the Notre Dame Victory March. Here, in this great moment, I look up and see the light shining on the Blessed Mother and the Golden Dome and as Yogi Berra used to say: It's deja vu all over again.

I spoke at the impromptu pep rally that broke out when we got out of our buses and were swallowed up by the cheering crowd.

We are 6-1-1 and the glow of victory over the No. 1 team in the nation was like a bonfire. I asked the students to just remember it and recreate it the next week when we would play host to Penn State. That's the problem when you play the kind of schedules Notre Dame does. In 1982 it was rated 13th most difficult in the country, which means it is a road that comes with few smooth stretches and many bumps.

Bumps and bruises, as it turned out. What I didn't know as I was fanning the flame of victory that we had lit was that quarterback Blair Kiel had a bruised shoulder.

During the following week we sent Blair to Indianapolis to see a specialist in that kind of injury. The doctor couldn't find anything significantly wrong, but Blair couldn't lift his arm or move his shoulder. The specialist said Blair could play if he could tolerate the pain, that the injury would do no lasting damage to the shoulder. The results of the tests and the exam, however, were inconclusive.

There is a school of thought in college football that if a player can't suffer permanent damage it is OK to shoot him with Novocaine or some other painkiller and let him play. This happens more frequently when the player is being paid and what he is doing is his job, not just his sport. I've always held to the philosophy that a college player is in school to get an education—and I don't mean in pain. So even if the player were willing to have an injury numbed in order to play, I wouldn't allow it. I wanted to win. We all wanted to win. But not that way. Blair received no painkillers and tried to play. He handed off the ball a few times and couldn't do it. So Ken Karcher took over. It put Ken in a difficult spot because Blair had been on a hot streak. We led at the half 14-13 but just couldn't sustain our offense and lost 24-14.

One week glory, the next week pain. Blair Kiel wasn't the only person feeling it.

We took a 6-2-1 record into our game at Air Force, a team Notre Dame had beaten in 11 previous games. This would not, however, be the typical Notre Dame-Air Force game in any sense. From the outset, there were complicating factors beyond the loss of Blair Kiel. Bowl bids were due to be extended the weekend of the Air Force game in Colorado Springs, and we had received word that the Fiesta Bowl wanted us. That excited the players and me. A number of them had been to the Sugar Bowl two years before and they relished the atmosphere surrounding a major bowl game. And, of course, it excited me doubly. Not only was the Fiesta Bowl invitation one to covet, but it also signified we were making progress. Obviously, I needed to send that message after a 5-6 season.

There was a catch. The Fiesta Bowl wanted a commitment before the Air Force game because it was afraid that the Orange Bowl or Cotton Bowl would come after us if we were 7-2-1. Father Joyce refused to make such a commitment, which is something a person, including the coach, must understand about Notre Dame. Some years, Notre Dame didn't go to a bowl game when it was 9-2. As the seasons have passed, it has relaxed that policy somewhat but it still is an administrative decision rather than one made by the coaches.

The Fiesta Bowl said it would not wait. So hasta la vista, Fiesta Bowl. The Bluebonnet Bowl, on the other hand, said it would take us after the Air Force game, and Father Joyce told the Bluebonnet officials that we'd entertain such a bid if we beat Air Force.

The players heard about these bowl maneuverings and they weren't thrilled. Father Joyce met with the seniors to explain the decision. I had no problem with it. I knew who ran what. I'd have gone happily to any bowl. But the players had other ideas. Remember, a number of them had been to the Sugar Bowl. They conveyed to the assistant coaches their disappointment. They made it clear: They didn't want to go to the Bluebonnet Bowl whether they beat Air Force or not. They needn't have worried.

We lost.

I don't blame the loss on bowl machinations. I blame it on myself. I obviously didn't say the right words to help the players past their disappointment. I explained that when they came to Notre Dame they had come to a university unlike any other. It does things in a special way. It won't always be what the players want, but it will be what the University believes is best. I told them that in the years to come they'd see how much such a special place such as Notre Dame had benefited their lives. They couldn't see it that Saturday in Falcon Stadium, though. That wasn't Father Joyce's fault and it wasn't Father Hesburgh's fault. It was my obligation to have the team ready to play. I should have gotten the players mad at me with a series of tough practices and made them forget the bowl decision. I should have done something that I didn't do, but I didn't know what it should be.

Walk-on senior quarterback Jim O'Hara started and threw the ball well enough (14-for-23 for 216 yards) but our running game was inadequate and Air Force's wishbone offense baffled us. On paper, right there in black and white, we were better than Air Force. But when they got the ball on the field and we didn't stop them, it frustrated us and before we knew it, we were behind 17-0. With that went the bowl game that the players didn't want anyway.

Three weeks earlier we had beaten Pittsburgh and looked as if we not only could be in the major-bowl picture but also the National Championship hunt. At the very least, we had a chance to end up with a great year, as good as 9-1-1. Now, we had to play USC on the West Coast on Thanksgiving weekend and 7-3-1 is the best we could do. Worse, when I got to my Tuesday press conference, I learned that John Robinson was going to leave USC, that this would be his last game. In the Notre Dame-USC game, no coach wants the other team to have the added incentive of playing for a victory in its coach's last game. Yet here it was.

After flying home from Colorado on Saturday night, having been shot down by Air Force, we turned around and flew back to the West Coast on Wednesday. It was a quick turn-around, with classes ending Wednesday, but Jack Snow and other West Coast alumni made Thanksgiving memorable for us by inviting our players to share Thanksgiving with them in their homes. That's what makes Notre Dame and its people so special. They never forget and never stop caring. The players loved it. And the families, which played host to two or three players each, got to meet some fine young men who knew how to represent their university off the field as well as on it.

During our free time we wanted the players to relax and enjoy themselves. Some of the players went to the beach, and a couple of them, including offensive linemen Tom Doerger and Jay Underwood, went fishing. They caught a baby shark and brought it back to where we were staying and put it in bed with one of the sleeping players. It was the funniest thing. Afterward the players were telling the coaches and everyone was breaking up. It relaxed the entire team and set the tone for the way we would play on Saturday. Loose.

The USC game came down to one controversial play. With Blair Kiel again at quarterback, we played confidently and well and had a 13-3 lead late in the third quarter. During the week, John Robinson had had some fun with his team, beginning a "Win One for the Fat Guy" campaign, and in the third quarter, the Trojans became serious about getting that done for their coach.

It was USC quarterback Scott Tinsley rather than young Sean Salisbury, with whom I'd shot baskets, who was pinpointing passes into our defensive secondary with success. Before the game, I'd walked over to Sean as he warmed up and tugged on his jersey.

"Hey, Sean," I said, "I hope you pass the way you shoot, because if you do, we're going to win."

He got the biggest kick out of that, but I was right. When Sean did become the quarterback, we would beat his Trojans three times. This, unfortunately, wasn't one of those days.

When Michael Harper scored on a 5-yard run for USC with 1:55 to play in the third quarter, everybody was asking themselves: Michael who? He hadn't even been on USC's two-deep personnel chart. But these things happen when you're a school known as Tailback U. They can come at you from nowhere.

Still leading 13-10, we responded, driving to the USC 14-yard line. On fourth down, we sent placekicker Mike Johnston onto the field. Three points, however, wasn't what we needed. We still would have lost to a Trojan touchdown. So—fake field goal. This time, I did have a quarterback—Ken Karcher—holding. His pass was just beyond the reach of Mark Brooks in the end zone. It was the right call, and it didn't beat us. The officiating crew beat us.

I know how that sounds. Like sour grapes. But sometimes, officials do make incorrect decisions and this one was a mind-bender. USC got the ball with 1:50 to play. The scoring summary will always say that USC took the ball 51 yards. It didn't. USC took it 50 and dropped it.

A pass interference penalty called by the split officiating crew —some of the officials were from the Big Ten Conference, some from the Pac-10—put the ball on the 1-yard line. Michael Harper took a deep handoff and a flying leap toward the end zone. Before Harper became airborne, Tinsley had trouble getting him the ball. It hit Harper's knee and Kevin Griffith, our defensive end, came up with it, as Harper completed his dive toward the goal line.

If this had been Olympic diving, maybe Harper should have gotten a score of 7.0. It wasn't. In football, a diver needs the ball to score. Harper didn't have it. The linesman on the side of the field where Harper made his dive, a Pac-10 official, signaled touchdown. The Big Ten umpire, however, waved it off and indicated it was Notre Dame's ball. As our players were running off the field, Kevin with the ball in his hands, the officials conferred. Then the referee —yep, Pac-10—raised his arms.

Touchdown.

I went bananas. I may also have gone apricots, apples and a few other fruits. In the press box, from which the view is better than on the sideline, our assistant coaches also went crazy. It didn't do any good, of course. We had 48 seconds. We also didn't score. The difference is, we lost and I was livid. I ran into Father Joyce after the game, and he tried to calm me down.

"The officials screwed us, Father," I said.

"Now, Gerry," he reminded me, "you can't say anything publicly on that."

"I know," I said.

Well, the statute of limitations has expired.

In the dressing room, I found a team that was emotionally crushed. I told the players I couldn't have been prouder of a team and that as far as I was concerned, they had won. We would have run out the clock after Kevin's fumble recovery and would have had Notre Dame's first win at USC in 14 years. That ate at me.

While I may not have been able to say anything publicly about the officiating mistake, I decided I could not keep my mouth totally shut. What I did was a no-no. I mean, a big no-no.

I grabbed Roger Valdiserri and told him that he was going with me to the officials' locker room. Coaches don't do this. I probably shouldn't have, but I felt that strongly about the situation. The officials were shocked when I walked in.

"Men," I said, "I'm not here to yell or to bad-mouth you. But you did an injustice to a football team that worked awfully hard. That was a fumble. The ball was recovered on the 2-yard line and you didn't have the guts to make the right call. I'd appreciate it if you'd go in and explain that to our team. I can't. I don't know what to tell them. I'm sorry for interrupting. I just wanted you to realize what you had done."

Then I went to the USC locker room and congratulated the Trojans on a great comeback victory and for not letting Coach Robinson's career end with a loss. When I got back to our locker room, the officials had not been there to offer an explanation.

We're still waiting for them.

The next morning in the *Los Angeles Times* there appeared a photo that showed Michael Harper in the air over the goal line on his dive for the winning touchdown. Guess what else the photo showed?

Harper didn't have the ball.

I promised myself right then that it wasn't the last time our players would see that photo of The Phantom Touchdown.

Today, the photo seems a symbolic summation: That touchdown wasn't the season's only haunting moment. There were other phantoms, other things that seemed so clearly real after a 4-0 start and a victory over No. 1 Pitt and then were gone. The Phantom National Championship. The Phantom Bowl Game. Even, some people were beginning to believe, the Phantom Golden Dream.

8

■ BOWLING WE WILL GO ■

 Going bowling never created so much con-
troversy at Notre Dame as it did in 1983,
and, of course, I was smack-dab in the
middle of it. I had some company, too: A
fine gentleman named A.F. "Bud" Dudley,
Notre Dame alumnus and executive director of the Liberty Bowl in Memphis.

If it hadn't been for Bud and me, Father Joyce might never
have committed to go to the Liberty Bowl, only to have the decision called into question when we lost the last three games of the
regular season and finished with a 6-5 record.

These bowl situations usually had been more clear-cut.

"We used to be able to hold off until the end of the season,"
Father Joyce says. "All the bowls would have to sit back and wait for
us."

I changed that.

Because we weren't winning as often or with the consistency
that Notre Dame was accustomed to or wanted, we placed Father
Joyce and Gene Corrigan in a difficult position.

"What I did," Father Joyce says, "I did largely out of charity to
Gerry. It was his third year. It was his only chance to be in a bowl
game. It was obvious that we weren't going to go to a major bowl."

No one, me included, likes to feel as if they require charity.
That isn't the way I looked at this situation. What I saw, what I
wanted to believe, was that I had brought to Notre Dame football
enough good things that Father Joyce and others wanted to see me
succeed and would do whatever was necessary to help me. Maybe
that blinded me to a reality that others, including my wife, began to
see sometime during our third season.

"Everyone has adversity in their lives," Marlene says. "It's the way you react that matters. I spent a great deal of time at the Grotto. I lit many, many candles and sat down there, praying. But in the third year, after all those prayers, I realized that this probably wasn't where God wanted us to be. If He had wanted us there, something would have happened. We lost games that we never should have lost."

Many Notre Dame fans agreed with Marlene. They just differed with her on the reason why we lost.

"It was dumb stuff, mistakes, things that had nothing to do with Gerry's coaching," Marlene says. "I finally concluded that there was just something going on that we had no control over."

That didn't seem to be the case when we opened the season with a 52-6 win at Purdue in the most adverse weather conditions. After a cool preseason, it turned hot. It was 95 degrees. We had no control over that, but we overcame the circumstance of our environment. In fact, we had begun overcoming difficult circumstances the night before.

Purdue wasn't a thorn in our side. It was an entire rose bush. On Friday the team stayed in a hotel outside of Lafayette. During the night, people outside, yelling and screaming, woke me. I wasn't worried about my sleep, but I was concerned about the players. So I went down to Col. Jack Stephens' room. Col. Stephens, who had retired as commanding officer of the Army ROTC at the University, had been an assistant and then associate athletic director but had just retired from the latter post. He continued to work on special projects for the University and one of them was keeping life in order for us on these road trips.

Col. Stephens was a man of stature. I don't mean height. He wasn't tall. I mean in the way he carried and conducted himself. He had a bark bigger than his bite, but on a night like this when we needed his bark, it was there.

It was about 11 p.m. when I knocked on his hotel room door. He answered it in a long nightshirt and a sleeping cap. You should have seen him. I almost fell down right there in the hallway and rolled around, I was laughing so hard. I never thought I'd see a full colonel in a get-up like that. I'd gotten him up from a sound sleep. I was upset about the noise, but the sight of Col. Stephens cooled me down.

"Colonel," I said, "there are people outside making noise. Will you take care of it?"

"Yes sir," he said, "it'll be done right away."

I went back to my room, and I'll be dog-gone if it didn't get quiet. I don't know if Col. Stephens wore his nightshirt and cap outside and scared the rowdies to death, but I sure appreciated our one-man rapid response. Maybe he put his "bird" colonel insignia on the shoulders of his nightshirt before confronting the noise-makers. Whatever he did, it worked.

That was just the beginning of our problems at Purdue that weekend. Though Purdue built a new, air-conditioned locker room at Ross-Ade Stadium for the visiting team before I left Notre Dame, it wasn't in place in 1983. The visitors' quarters in those days were typical of the old-fashioned inhospitality in vogue during the '40s and '50s. Schools made the visiting team's locker room a place of turmoil. There was little space to dress. No place for meetings. No way to communicate. And it was hot. We set up fans, blowing over blocks of ice. Even that didn't work. Finally, I had our two air-conditioned buses moved into the stadium next to the locker room and we used one for offense and the other for defense. It was an old high-school trick. So who says high-school coaching experience can't prove valuable in college? I was used to solving these problems and they didn't upset me. Of course, when we built a 31-0 lead by halftime, there wasn't much that could upset me.

Our biggest problem was not having enough managers to get water to the players on the sideline and field. I recruited my sons, Gerry and Steve, and some of their buddies out of the stands. That worked. Everything worked. Blair Kiel threw only 14 times but completed 9 for 166 yards, including a 9-yarder to Greg Bell for our first touchdown. Bell (11 carries for 45 yards) was back from a season-ending broken ankle the year before against Purdue. Sophomore Allen Pinkett (15-115) picked up where he had left off in 1982 and freshman Hiawatha Francisco from Cincinnati Moeller (9-81) gave us even more depth. We gained more than 500 yards.

Once again our recruiting class had been one of the nation's best. One of the players who would get some time at linebacker as a freshman and become a three-year starter was Robert Banks. His is a lesson not only about Notre Dame's expectations but also the opportunities of which young men can sometimes prove themselves worthy.

Robert, who was from Hampton, Virginia, was one of the most sought-after players in the country, a 6-foot-5, 230-pound linebacker. His transcript had all the right courses to get into Notre Dame, including three years of math. He had good scores on the college-entrance exams but, for some reason, his high school grade-point average was not what it had to be for automatic admission to Notre Dame.

I had never met Robert until I visited his high school with one of our assistant coaches, Greg Blache. We had to wait until class was over, and when Robert Banks walked out of the classroom the first thing I noticed wasn't how big he was or how clean-cut he looked but that he was carrying a briefcase. We went into an office and when he had to get some information out of the briefcase for me, he opened it and I got a glimpse inside. He had his books, papers and pencils neatly organized and you could tell that here was a young man who was serious about his studies. I said to myself: This guy can make it at Notre Dame. If he is doing this on the high school level, he's mature and has his priorities straight.

We offered him a scholarship. When I returned to Notre Dame, the admissions personnel informed me that they didn't know if they were going to accept Robert. I told them the story about Robert's briefcase and about the feeling I had that this was a young man who would make the most of his opportunity to attend Notre Dame. Admissions said it would get back to me.

Two weeks later I learned that they had decided to accept Robert Banks, and the next day I ran into Father Hesburgh on campus.

"What about this guy from Hampton, Virginia?" Father Hesburgh asked.

"You mean Robert Banks?" I said.

"That's the name. I hear a lot of good things about him."

"Father," I said, "he is a great young man."

Then I told Father Hesburgh the story about the briefcase and what it told me about Robert.

"Those are the kind of kids we need around here," Father Hesburgh said. "Kids who are dedicated to their studies in high school. I know a lot about this young man. A lot of people have told me about him. I hear he's a great athlete, too."

"Yeah," I agreed. "He is, Father."

"I heard he got accepted."

Then Father Hesburgh put his finger, gently, in the center of my chest.

"Better graduate," Father Hesburgh told me. "If he doesn't, you're going to be looking for a job."

"Father," I said, "he'll graduate."

And Robert did.

In fact, Notre Dame was the first team in the College Football Association to graduate 100 percent of an entering class, my next-to-last group of recruits, which graduated in 1988 and won the national championship. No matter which measurements a person uses—CFA, NCAA or Notre Dame's—our football players graduated. Scholarship football players who were freshmen in our first four classes and stayed for four years had a 100 percent graduation rate, and in the class that entered in 1985, 23 of 24 (95.83 percent) who stayed graduated.

Another great beginning to a season turned to ashes when we outplayed but didn't outscore Michigan State. Spartan punter/kicker Ralf Mojsiejenko had a superb game, averaging 48.8 yards on nine punts. Every time we held Michigan State in its own territory, he'd boom the ball out of there, and we'd face another long drive. It weakened our will. Four turnovers (three interceptions and one lost fumble) hurt us as well. This became one of the 15 games we lost by eight or fewer points during my five seasons. In contrast, we won only eight such close games. Why? If I had found the answer, I might still be coaching at the University I love with all my heart.

"It got to the point," says Brian Boulac, who moved to an assistant athletic director's job after the 1983 season, "that the players would question a lot of things. In a good football program, you can't have a team questioning the decisions of the head coach. He may make a bad decision, but you don't question those decisions. Our players did.

"For Gerry to have been successful, I think he would have had to rely on other people around him to help him be successful. I don't think he was capable of allowing people to help him."

While I don't agree totally with Brian—I let the defensive coaches have virtually free reign—I may have tried too hard to find my own solutions to our offensive problems.

"There were a lot of times we thought we were going to come out of the doldrums," Boulac says. "But Gerry couldn't just wait for something to evolve. He'd force the issue so many times."

When we went to Miami in the third game and couldn't move the ball, we took Blair Kiel out and inserted Steve Beuerlein, who was a freshman. He showed some promise (13 for 23 and 145 yards), but Bernie Kosar, the quarterback I said wasn't good enough to play at Notre Dame, showed much more than promise. He was 22 for 33 for 215 yards and one touchdown and he ran the Hurricanes like the national champions they would become. It wasn't a disgrace to lose, but we shouldn't have been shut out, 20-0. Maybe that was what Gene Corrigan was trying to say when he was quoted in some East Coast papers before our game at Colorado. Though I know he wanted me to succeed, Mr. C sounded less than convinced I would, less than supportive. I think these were the first of the serious rumblings concerning the job I was doing.

"I think in some ways," says assistant athletic director John Heisler, "that Gene was trying to get the message to Gerry that regardless of what Gerry was telling everybody, things weren't going quite as well as we would have liked.

"Sometimes Gerry was so prone to look at things through rose-colored glasses that you wondered whether he understood that there were still some things we had not figured out."

I understood. But just when a person might think drastic changes were in order, we would go on a run of victories and the doubts and questions would recede, if only for the moment.

When I got calls from friends who had read what Mr. Corrigan said in the newspapers, it left me feeling as if my legs had been chopped out from under me. That's not the way I'd do it if I were ever an athletic director. If I were in that position, I would support my coach to the hilt publicly. If I had problems with his performance I would call him into my office and tell him exactly what those problems were and what he had to do to address them.

I think that was the problem. Mr. C didn't know exactly why things weren't falling into place any more than any of the rest of us. So I didn't say anything to him about his comments. I didn't feel that was my place. My place was to produce victories and then there would be nothing more to say.

We started Steve Beuerlein against Colorado. He was 18 years old. He didn't know what I knew, which was that he should be nervous. He played well, and with Allen Pinkett running like a tornado (18 carries for 132 yards), we won 27-3. If there was a point at which I totally lost Blair Kiel, this was it. Steve started the remaining games, except for the Liberty Bowl. I understand how Blair felt. The way it had begun between us, with one of my former Moeller players competing with him, and now one of my recruits being given the starting job, it must have seemed very personal. It wasn't, but I don't know if I would have believed that, either, had I been in Blair's position.

"Blair," Brian Boulac says, "probably had the most frustrating three years of any quarterback in the history of Notre Dame."

I wouldn't dispute that. Certainly Blair had the most frustrating three years that a good quarterback should be forced to endure. As a staff, we felt our future should be in Steve Beuerlein's hands, and on the way home from Colorado that future was looking bright until someone who was visiting the cockpit overheard one of the scores coming in on the pilot's radio.

South Carolina had beaten USC. And when I say "beaten," I'm being polite. Flogged is more like it. This SC had done a 38-14 number on the SC which is our Big Game opponent. The game was in Columbia, S.C., where we had to play the following week. After hearing that, I couldn't relax and enjoy the Colorado victory. All I could think of was 38-14.

It may seem odd, but sometimes the men who have the most intense rivalry treat each other with the most respect. So it is with the Notre Dame and USC coaches. We go at each other with everything we have. But we also can talk. When we asked the USC coaches what had happened, they said one problem was the noise. Playing in Williams-Brice Stadium at South Carolina is like playing in a horror chamber of sounds. The Trojans couldn't hear when they tried to change plays at the line of scrimmage. If the fans weren't loud enough, the Carolina band played every time the USC offense had the ball and kept playing as it prepared to snap it. That's against the rules.

We had to shut up that crowd.

Southerners are a hospitable, talkative bunch. Everyone wanted to talk to me on the Friday night before the game. When we went to the stadium to work out under the lights, I had to go over early with the South Carolina sports information folks to do some live TV spots. Jimmy Johnson, not the one with the immovable hair but our defensive coordinator, brought the team over. We worked out and as our players were dressing, some of our coaches and I accepted an invitation from the South Carolina coaches to tour their facilities, which were tremendous.

I got delayed in the weight room and by the time I got out to our buses for the ride back to the motel, the buses were gone. I couldn't believe they'd left me. Maybe it was a hint. In any case, I was fuming. The only person left in the stadium was the South

Carolina equipment manager, who took pity on the stranded Yankee and hauled my tired old bones back to the hotel.

When I walked in, my coaches were sitting in the lobby with sheepish expressions on their faces.They didn't know where I had been, but when they saw me they knew I was mad.The steam coming out of my ears was probably the hint they needed.

"Coach," one of them said, "we just realized that we didn't know if you had a way back."

"You know what," I said, "I didn't."

Then we all laughed about it. But I'm thinking: Oh no. It's not going to be another one of *those* weekends, is it?

It wasn't.

Before the game, I told the players that the only way they could win was to take the noise out of the crowd. And the only way they could take the noise out of the crowd was to score early and often.Which we did.

We jumped to a 13-0 first-quarter lead with two Mike Johnston field goals and a 26-yard touchdown pass from Steve Beuerlein to Chris Smith. Meanwhile, the defense was playing with fire in its eyes and gut, especially Mike Golic, who had 11 tackles and drove South Carolina quarterback Allen Mitchell crazy.Mitchell completed just 4 of 14 passes. If that weren't enough, we also got help from the officials.

I had telephoned the Big Ten Conference office, which provided half the officiating crew for the game. I told Big Ten officials what had happened to USC. So when the Carolina band began to play, the umpire, who was from the Big Ten, stopped the game until the band stopped. I'll give him credit. He never backed down. He enforced the rule, which was easier said than done in that environment.

Allen Pinkett not only had another 100-yard rushing performance but he also caught two passes, including a 59-yarder for a second-quarter touchdown on our way to a 30-6 victory. You'd never have known seventh-ranked South Carolina was the undefeated team.

The next week, we played Army at the Meadowlands, and when we were holding our Friday workout there, a nice thing happened, the kind of thing that makes you forget about the problems you sometimes encounter with other coaches. Bill Parcells, a man for whom I have the utmost respect, was coaching the New York Giants at that time.While our players loosened up, we talked.

"Coach," he said, "I'm going to tell you something that not many people know about this stadium."

"What's that?"

"The wind is different," he explained. "If you look at the top of the stadium and see a flag blowing in one direction, the wind on the field will be blowing in the opposite direction."

I'd have never figured that out until it was too late. On artificial turf, which the Meadowlands has, a person can't pluck a few blades of grass out of the ground, toss them in the air and get a reading on the wind. And there isn't always a hotdog wrapper floating around when you need one for that purpose. So that was really nice of Bill Parcells. He didn't have to bother to tell me, but he did.

We found Eastern hospitality equally warm on a trip into New York City to visit Wall Street, Central Park, St. Patrick's Cathedral and Radio City Music Hall. There was just one exception. That was Barry Manilow. He happened to be in New York, preparing for a concert when we encountered him at Radio City Music Hall. On these trips, I always tried to arrange for our players to see the cities where we played and to tour the campuses of the universities to get a feel for whom they were playing. Some of the players hadn't traveled much. So this was another part of their educations.

When I saw Barry Manilow on stage practicing, I told the team that I'd ask if he would come down and talk to them. Everyone was excited about the prospect. You have to understand how I am. I go into a place as if I own it. Some people think it's being friendly, which is my intention. Others consider it pushy. But I figure if my door is open to people, theirs is open to me. Right? I've always been that way.

I walked up onto the stage and was stopped by a couple of guys who asked where I was going.

"I'm going over to talk to Barry Manilow," I told them.

"No, you're not," they explained.

"I'm Gerry Faust," I said. "The football coach at Notre Dame."

"Coach," they said, "Barry Manilow doesn't talk with *anybody* when he's rehearsing."

"I'm sorry. I can understand that. I know when we're preparing for a game, I don't want anyone talking to the players during practice. So I do understand. But would you do me a favor? Would you go over and tell Mr. Manilow that I have the Notre Dame football team here and ask if he'd come and talk to the players when he's finished?"

"Sure," the guy said, "I'll do that."

The guy went over to Barry Manilow, who stopped playing. They spoke. Then the guy came back to where I was standing on the other side of the stage.

"Barry's not interested," he said.

I thanked the man, but I was so upset I could have eaten the legs right off Mr. Manilow's piano stool. Here's a guy in the public eye, like I am. He's making a lot more money than I make and he won't take the opportunity to give some student-athletes two minutes of his time so they can feel they've gotten to know him? Unbelievable!

I never told the players that this guy wasn't interested in them. I just said he was in the middle of his concert preparation and couldn't take the time. I didn't bad-mouth him. But I guarantee you, we don't have any Barry Manilow tapes or CDs in my home.

Not much bothered us, wind or otherwise, against Army. We pitched a 42-0 shutout in our fourth consecutive game on the road. Even though he was a freshman, Steve Beuerlein wasn't making mistakes and that created confidence in him among his coaches and teammates alike. We used 64 of 69 players, including four quarterbacks. In our last three games we had allowed only nine points and were on the greatest roll in my three seasons at Notre Dame, and just in time. USC was coming to South Bend.

During our week of preparation I gave the players something to think about, a reminder of our 1982 visit to the West Coast. The Phantom Touchdown photo. I turned Michael Harper into a pin-up. He was in every player's locker. Flying through the air. Over the goal line. Without the ball. But that wasn't the only psychological trick I had up my sleeve.

We had to beat USC. You always look ahead to a season in its totality and pick out its critical junctures. The must-win games. USC was one. It was my third season. We hadn't beaten USC. In fact, Notre Dame had beaten the Trojans only twice in the last 10 seasons. It was time. Past time.

So before the season began, I called Gene O'Neil aside. Gene was our equipment man and a marvelous person. I was blessed not only at Notre Dame but also at Akron to have quality, loyal people in this key position. At Akron, it was Kevin O'Connor. Another Irishman. Both guys would do anything they could to help the coaches and players. What I asked Gene was if he could pull off again something Dan Devine had done six years earlier.

"I'd like to have green jerseys for Southern Cal," I told Gene. "And I don't want anybody to know. Not the assistant coaches. Not the athletic director. Nobody. Once one person knows, it'll get out."

It's too delicious a secret to keep.

"I have to tell the guy from Champion knitwear," Gene said, "but this guy will keep it quiet."

"Good," I said. "And there's something else."

"What is it, Gerry?"

"In the green jersey, I want a blue stripe. This is Our Lady's University and Her color is blue. I don't think we should forget that for even one special game."

"They could do that," Gene said. "They could put the blue on the sleeve between two golden stripes."

It was perfect. I guess I wasn't the only one who thought so.

At my Tuesday press conference, which was usually attended by 8 to 10 writers and electronic media people, with another 15 to 20 participating through a conference call, what was the first thing one of the writers wanted to know?

"Would you go to the green jersey since you haven't beaten Southern Cal?"

The guy had been doing his homework. It worked for Dan Devine. After losing his first two games to USC, the Fighting Irish came out wearing the green and won 49-19. Still, I was shocked by the question. I will not go so far as to say that writers are smart. But this was in the neighborhood.

Since I don't lie, the answer to this question became problematic. Say the wrong thing and it could come back to haunt me personally. Blow the surprise and it could come back to haunt the team on the scoreboard.

"You know," I finally said, "this is Our Lady's University and as long as I'm the coach here there will always be blue in the jersey."

That's it. I didn't say we would always wear blue jerseys. I just said there would be blue in the jersey and left it at that. No one picked up on it.

Practices went well. The gameday roll we had been on carried over, and those Phantom TD blowups got everyone's attention in our practice locker room in the Athletic and Convocation Center.

The trap was set.

We went out to warm up in our usual home blue jerseys. I couldn't wait for pregame drills to end. No one knew a thing. The managers didn't know something was up until Gene O'Neil brought in sealed boxes while the players were on the field. He told the managers to open the boxes and hang the jerseys in the lockers. Then, he watched. When the managers opened the boxes, they went crazy. As they were putting the jerseys in the lockers, they were screaming: Get Southern Cal! Go Irish! Right then, Gene knew this was going to work.

I'm usually the last guy back up the tunnel and into the locker room before a game. But this time, I was the first. I wanted to see the players' reactions. A coach can't anticipate the game's most exciting moments. He can have a feeling about something like this, though. When Father Riehle walked into the locker room and saw the green jerseys, he walked up to me and gave me a little punch.

"Way to go," he said.

Then, his eyes glistening, he went to meet the players and to bless each one as he came up the tunnel. After Father blessed the first player, the player took about 10 steps and was in the locker room. No reaction.

I'm thinking: "Aw, jeez."

Then I realized that he hadn't seen his jersey yet. He was intent on the game to come. When it hit him, he froze. Then he started jumping up and down and yelling and running around the locker room. Father Riehle was trying to bless the players but he couldn't. They were bursting into the locker room. It was like a child coming downstairs on Christmas morning to find the perfect gift under the tree.

The coaches didn't know what the noise was. Then they saw the jerseys.

"Why didn't you tell us?" they said.

It was a wonderful, crazy madhouse. Coaches always are asked to describe the turning point of a game. This USC game turned right there in that locker room. I knew it and went looking for Gene O'Neil.

"Thanks, Gene," I said.

"Coach," he said, "it was a privilege."

The players wanted to get onto that field and into the middle of USC. For most games, we walk out at the same time as our opponent. Not this time. I told the players that we were coming out last

—even if we got penalized for delaying the game. I wanted USC on that field and to see a sea of green coming at it.

We sent our captains out in their blue jerseys for the coin toss. Then we gathered in the tunnel and the people on the edge of the tunnel who could look back into it, saw just before we came onto the field that we were wearing the green. They started screaming. The rest of the people in the Stadium couldn't see us.

Then they did.

As we came out of the tunnel, the place erupted. It was the loudest moment I'd ever experienced. And here's USC, just like the picture I had seen from six years before to the day. Coaches and players were stunned. Just stunned.

Sean Salisbury, now USC's starting quarterback, threw for only 34 yards. That was 25 fewer than tailback Allen Pinkett, who completed a 59-yard pass to tight end Mark Bavaro to set up our first touchdown. When we practiced the play during the week, it hadn't worked well. But in the green jersey, Pinkett was transformed into Paul Hornung. His 20-yard throw hit Mark in stride and Mark took it to the USC 21-yard line. Allen, who gained 122 yards on 21 carries, scored the first of his three touchdowns, this one from the 11-yard line.

Emotion lifted us and created something that lasted. Harper finally scored in the third quarter, the first touchdown our defense had allowed in seven quarters, but we never were in danger of running out of gas in the 27-6 victory. Using something like the green jersey works once in a while, but you can't do it all the time. It would be like a jockey whipping a dead horse and thinking the color of his silks made a difference.

When I met with the media after the game, the person who had asked me on Tuesday about the green jersey was hot on the trail of an apparent lie.

"Gerry Faust," he said, "you didn't tell the truth."

"What do you mean I didn't tell the truth?"

"You said you'd wear blue jerseys."

I must have looked as if I'd died and gone to heaven, as Father Joyce predicted I would some day.

"Look at your notes," I said.

He didn't understand.

"I said we'd always have blue *in* the jersey."

Then I turned to one of our players in the interview room.

"Look at this player," I told the writer. "See that blue stripe on his sleeve?"

The writer hit himself in the forehead.

"I told you that I'd never lie to you guys."

Everyone laughed. It was a happy moment. We'd beaten USC —finally.

Navy might not have scored a touchdown in our fifth consecutive victory if Allen Pinkett hadn't fumbled on our 15-yard line. Allen said afterward he played sloppily. Even so, he set a Notre Dame record with his fifth 100-yard game in a row, this effort for 121 yards on 29 carries. In addition, he scored twice and caught three passes. I can live with that kind of sloppy.

The victory marked the first time we had won five games in a row since I had become coach. That fact and our 6-2 record were forgotten in a blink of an eye as the rest of the season unfolded.

Maybe I wasn't introspective enough. Maybe I didn't reflect on why bad things happen to coaches who try to be good on and off the field. I don't know. We just put every ounce of energy we had into coaching each week. If I was taking the short view, others were taking the long one. The media, for instance.

They kept bringing up that we had not been a winning team at the end of our seasons. The players are human. They read that and wonder if perhaps the media are right. They start to doubt they will win and it becomes a self-fulfilling prophesy. The writers need something to write about. They look at it as if they are addressing a problem. A coach looks at it as if they are creating one. Maybe I'm too sensitive. But if the writers were so smart, why didn't they have an explanation for what happened?

"We didn't fulfill Gerry's expectations or ours," John Heisler says. "And people were always trying to figure out why. One of them was a writer from the *New York Times* named Pete Alfano. He wouldn't be at Notre Dame every week, but he was somebody we all got to know.

"We used to kid him, because at about the same time every year he would come out to see us. It'd be the middle of the season. He'd want to do an update. It was like the movie: "Same Time Next Year."

Pete Alfano had company. The regular writers as well as those from the national media would be drawn back to South Bend to see how I was doing. Again, it wasn't Gerry Faust. It was the position. And, in my case, the former position: How's that high school guy doing in the biggest job in college football?

"We used to kid Pete," Heisler says, "that we should just make a standing reservation for him at the Morris Inn on campus for the middle of October, because, one way or the other, Pete would be motivated to come see us. Sometimes it was because Gerry had won a couple of big games. Sometimes it was because he'd lost a couple. We'd always be on the verge of getting it done but then we'd lose a game. Or two games."

Or three.

It began with Pittsburgh and it began at home, which made it worse. We didn't play particularly well, certainly not with the fire we had had against USC. Pitt, on the other hand, had not forgotten what we had done to it when it was No. 1 the year before. With Steve Beuerlein struggling, I finally inserted Blair Kiel and he really did a nice job. His 9-for-16 performance for 134 yards and a touchdown toss of nine yards to Allen Pinkett served as a reminder of his individual frustration at my decision to turn the team over to a freshman. The team's frustration—and mine—was just beginning.

It is one thing to lose a game. It is another thing to then let two more get away that were won and should have stayed won. It was during our 34-30 loss at Penn State and Air Force's 23-22 victory at Notre Dame Stadium that Gene Corrigan may have quit believing in me as a college coach.

"I always felt," Gene Corrigan says, "that there were some key games that Gerry needed to win to keep the kids on his side. Basically, when you don't win, they stop listening to you. I don't care who you are."

If that's true, Mr. C had in mind not just the final two games at the end of my third season but others as well.

"The Penn State game (21-24) in the first year," Gene Corrigan says, "Southern Cal in Year Two. Those were games where the doubts began to spring up. We lost them at the end. We had the worst things happen. It was as if Gerry was snake-bit. You look at some of those Penn State games and you say: My God, he lost two of them on the last play of the game. And in both instances we had outplayed the other team."

This Penn State game may have been one of the best offensive college games ever played. There were 64 points scored. Close to 1,000 yards in total offense. Allen Pinkett ran for 217 yards and four touchdowns. Steve Beuerlein completed 14 of 20 passes for

257 yards. But on the last play of the first half, after we had managed the clock well, I called a quarterback sneak and Steve didn't get the yard. I could say that Allen might have been a better choice, but when I called his number in the fourth quarter on third and one from our 17-yard line with a minute to play, we missed a block and Allen didn't get the first down, either.

Snake-bit? Maybe.

Then, following the stop against Allen, the punt was poor and Penn State had the ball on the 50.

Snake-bit? Where's the tourniquet?

Still, we should have stopped Doug Stang from putting a 36-yard pass right down the throat of our defense to tight end Dean DiMidio. Stang scored from eight yards out with 19 seconds to play.

That loss complicated not only my life but also the lives of Gene Corrigan and Father Joyce. Bud Dudley, the Notre Dame alumnus and executive director of the Liberty Bowl, had always wanted to bring his alma mater to Memphis. And it always had been out of the question. If Notre Dame were good enough to go to a bowl, it attracted the big bowls. If it weren't good enough to go to a big bowl, it had a habit of just saying no.

But this was the 25th anniversary Liberty Bowl and, despite our two losses in a row which had turned a nice 6-2 season into a struggling 6-4, Father Joyce and Mr. C told Bud Dudley before the Air Force game that we'd come play Boston College and its great quarterback, Doug Flutie, the 1984 Heisman Trophy winner. He could call it the Catholic Bowl.

"There were two factors that made me decide to go to the Liberty Bowl," Father Joyce explains. "Bud Dudley is a Notre Dame guy. He was president of our national alumni association at one time. So I wanted to do it for Bud. It also gave us the possibility of doing something for Gerry. He badly wanted to go to a bowl.

"So we said: OK, we'll go—and lived to regret it."

Thank me for that.

Again, trailing Air Force, this time 10-0, I asked Blair Kiel to save us and he very nearly did. With a 9-yard pass to Milt Jackson in the third quarter, we took a 16-10 lead and then expanded it to 22-10 when Blair connected with Joe Howard on a 67-yard touchdown. Despite the fact we let Air Force score twice in the fourth quarter for a 23-22 lead, we still had this game won with Mike Johnston lining up for a 31-yard field goal with four seconds on the clock.

Mike got the ball off, but Air Force's Chris Funk, who was blocked as he leaped into the air, twisted his body sideways and got a hand on the ball. The kick looked as if it would have been true and long enough. Instead, it proved to be Funk's second blocked field goal of the game. It was another loss to Air Force and a true spoiler of a season that once again had turned from promise to ashes. At least the perfect person blocked it. I could see the headlines: Funk puts Faust in funk!

After I had congratulated Air Force coach Ken Hatfield, I passed Gene Corrigan on my way to the locker room. He looked worse than I felt—if that was possible. He didn't know what to say. He still doesn't.

"You can always second guess," Corrigan says. "I thought we played very well against a good Penn State team, but when we lost to Air Force because a guy blocks a chip-shot field goal ... I don't know what to say."

In the locker room, Mr. Corrigan sat with Father Joyce. Neither one knew what to do or say. Finally, Mr. C came over and talked to me.

"Gerry," he said, "we made this commitment to the Liberty Bowl and I don't think we can get out of it."

I told him I would support anything he decided. If we go, we'll get ready and play well. If we don't go, I'll understand. Father Joyce decided that Notre Dame had to honor its commitment. But he took some flak, especially from one of our major contributors.

"We didn't lose him as a benefactor," Father Joyce says, "but this fellow was really mad. He's an Irishman with a fiery temper, a charming man to be around on most occasions. But he was highly critical of me and of Notre Dame for going to that bowl. Highly critical to a lot of people and to us. To me. To Father Hesburgh. So I went up and sat down with him at the University Club in Chicago to talk about it. I don't think I changed his mind."

At the same time Father Joyce was facing our angry benefactor, I was responding to rumors that I would resign before the Liberty Bowl. I told everyone who asked that I wasn't a quitter, that I had two years remaining on my 5-year contract and I intended to fulfill them and to be at Notre Dame even longer than that. None of this bothered me. What bothered me was the look of hurt on Father Joyce's face after the Air Force game and the Phil Hersh story that appeared in the *Chicago Sun-Times* after that loss. Of all the stories ever written, that was probably the most devastating. Not

only did Hersh quote five of my players who had come to the conclusion that I was not a good coach and, in some cases, not even a
good man, which hurt most, but he also attacked my family. He
suggested that my sons had told players they didn't care enough
about winning and that I allowed my teen-age son to sit in on some
team meetings.

Hersh quoted Mark Bavaro as saying:"He'd make comments
like,'This football team is a family, we have no one from outside the
family,' then his kid would be at team meetings with his feet up on
the seat in front of him."

My sons, Steve and Gerry, did sit in on some meetings. What I
guess the players may not have understood is that they are family.
Any coach's children sacrifice. They give up their fathers for much
of the year. It's why I encouraged coaches to involve their children,
to have them help us in small ways. It's why I set the example in
doing this.

After Hersh's story appeared, three of the players told me
they had not said the things they were quoted as saying. It was nice
of them to say, but it wasn't the issue. Some of their points were
valid. I've said and I'll repeat it: I hurt Mark Zavagnin in that first
season, even though I hadn't meant to do so. And I could understand why Blair Kiel didn't consider me his favorite person. I never
said a word to Blair. He had contributed too much to Notre Dame
for me to do that. What I did, and the staff supported this, was to
name Blair the starter for the Liberty Bowl. He deserved it as a
senior, and he had done everything he could to rescue us against
Air Force.

Despite the controversy surrounding our trip to the Liberty
Bowl, we prepared well and made a change that caught Boston
College by surprise. We switched from an I offensive formation to
the split backfield, a move that would lead to 100-yard games by
both Allen Pinkett and fullback Chris Smith.

It would prove to be an entertaining game but the best single
entertainer the team encountered that season may not have been
Barry Manilow, practicing in New York, or even Elvis Presley, the
late king of Memphis. It might have been Jay Underwood, one of
our juniors. Some of the enjoyable and memorable experiences
involving bowl games occur when the players meet one another
and socialize three or four days before the game. They come to
know and respect one another in a way that is impossible when a
university just goes into a city to play a regular-season game. In

Jay's case, the Boston College players were in for a treat. After dinner one night before the game, players from each team were asked to perform. Jay stole the show with his Elvis impersonation. He had The King down. The mannerisms. The singing. All of it. We had seen Jay do this before, but the Liberty Bowl people were amazed, and this was Elvis' town. It was as if in all those stories about where Elvis might be hiding, they had never thought of the one place he could be really anonymous—the Notre Dame offensive line, where Jay moved from defense as a junior.

It was moments such as the one Jay created that convinced me the number of bowl games should never be reduced or sacrificed for college football playoffs. The bowls bring people together. If there are 19 bowls, they make 38 teams feel like winners. I'm all for a one- or two-game playoff after the bowls. But don't eliminate this wonderful educational experience for 38 teams. I know it was an education for me.

I received another education from an unlikely source, a young woman who would later become embroiled in a controversy concerning nude photos and would have to resign her title as Miss America. When we met, however, Vanessa Williams was young, beautiful and just beginning her career. She was 19 and spoke at one of the Liberty Bowl events. Something she said made me think.

"I hope you'll buy my records and that you'll follow me and support me," she told the audience.

I thought at the time that I would never get up and ask people to support me or to buy what I was selling. But as I look back on it, she was just trying to get started, much as I was in college coaching. In that process, she was appealing to people to become her fans. I see now that is little different from me standing up at a pep rally and asking fans to come to the stadium to cheer us on. When I matured as a coach and put it into the proper perspective, I understood that we all are just trying to win support and there is little difference between Vanessa Williams and me. And, of course, there is now one other bond: We both had to give up our biggest prize.

Any sacrifices I've made seem small when compared to those Sister Henry Sussa had made over the years. When I was at Moeller, the Dominican nuns staffed St. Gertrude's, which was one of 12 elementary schools that fed Moeller. One year, Sister Henry was about to be forced to drop football because she didn't have enough boys who wanted to play. She called and told me the situation and said she didn't want to drop football. I suggested she call St. Colombians, which was 10 miles away. It was a parish without football. They combined forces. It was good for them and for Moeller. I kept a parish that played football and added one that didn't. Sister Henry and I became friends in the process.

By the time I had been at Notre Dame for three years, Sister Henry had returned to the order's mother house in Nashville. She had cancer. During a visit to Nashville, I went unannounced to visit her. The nuns who love Notre Dame became really excited that I was there and Sister Assumpta Long, the provincial and a friend of mine, said she was glad I had come, because Sister Henry was on her deathbed.

They took me into the chapel and then to the third-floor infirmary, where I spent 10 minutes with Sister Henry. When we were coming down the steps from the infirmary, Sister Assumpta said: "Coach, you don't know what this means to Sister Henry. She has talked about you ever since you were at Moeller High School. She said you were her favorite coach and one of her favorite people. We're going to pray for you to beat Boston College, even though it's another Catholic school."

"Sister," I said, "would you like to have the nuns come to the game? If you can come to Memphis, you'll be my guests."

Twenty to 30 nuns did come to the Liberty Bowl and with the help of another person, I bought their tickets. It was a cold, icy night and after the game the nuns in their black-and-white habits came down to see me. I always called them the Penguin Nuns, and I told them this had been the perfect night for them. None of us was feeling the cold, though, because we had upset Boston College, 19-18, in a game I consider one of the six or seven best victories I had at Notre Dame.

If sitting outside Milt Jackson's house in Fairfield, Iowa, waiting for the Iowa State coaches to leave was the coldest night I ever spent recruiting, this was the coldest night I ever spent coaching. How cold was it?

"Well," Father Joyce says, "it was such a cold, cold night that up in the press box where I was watching the game with Speaker of the House Tip O'Neil, we had to use vodka and gin to keep the windows from fogging up. It didn't help very much. As soon as we cleaned them off, they just fogged up again. The alcohol didn't really help us clean them but the cold did keep us from drinking much."

Too bad. This would have been a game to toast rather than to drown your sorrows after watching it.

"It was a marvelous game," Father Joyce says. "A great game on a terrible night. I didn't regret my decision to come much then."

My father never knew how cold it was. He was recovering from surgery, so he had not been able to come to Memphis. My brother, Fred, and sister, Marilee, and her husband, Ken, played host to Dad and Mom for the game in Cincinnati because no Dayton station was carrying it. I called them after the game and Fred got on the phone and said: "Gerry, I've never seen Dad drink more wine during a game. He was half plowed when the game was over. The pressure was on him too."

So that's the bottom line: My coaching drove my dad to drink.

My father wasn't the only less-than-impartial observer of the Liberty Bowl. When I stopped to talk to the television reporter as I was leaving the field at halftime, Bill Simon, the former Secretary of the Treasury, was there. I'd played host to him at Notre Dame and we had become friends. We'd talked at length about the pain that can accompany being in the public eye—especially for the families. He said he'd never run for public office again for just that reason. We were standing there talking and I had my arm around him. The TV guys were going to talk to him right after me because Bill was a trustee at Boston College.

"Bill," I said, "it's just great to see you here."

"Well, Ger," he said, "even though I'm a trustee at Boston College, I'm really rooting for you."

Somehow, that exchange got on television. He laughed about that later. Bill loved Boston College, but I was a friend and I needed a win. Guess who helped me get it? Blair Kiel.

Blair had a great game. In 12-degree temperatures with the wind chill at zero, he completed 11 of 19 passes for 151 yards and one touchdown, a 13-yarder to Alvin Miller. It wasn't easy, though. Right before the half ended with us leading, 19-12, Doug Flutie missed connecting for a touchdown with receiver Brian Brennan by less than a foot. Brennan, whom one of my Moeller teams had played against when he was the quarterback at Brother Rice High School, did catch a 17-yard TD pass and made me tremendously nervous when Boston College had the ball during the final minutes. No one will ever forget Flutie's Hail Mary (oops, I'm not supposed to mention that) to beat Miami the following season.

Afterward, for only the second time in my career, some of the players lifted me on their shoulders and carried me to the center of field to shake hands with Boston College coach Jack Bicknell. It was wonderful and one answer to the Hersh article and the criticism that the University, and Father Joyce, in particular, received for accepting the Liberty Bowl invitation.

"It was most unfortunate," Bud Dudley wrote to me later, "that all of us received so much undue criticism, but I think in the final analysis your victory over Boston College vindicated all of this.

"I am somewhat amused by the silence of the critics after a 6-4-1 UCLA team won so handily in the Rose Bowl, a 6-4-1 Oklahoma State team won the Bluebonnet Bowl, a 6-4-1 Kentucky team came so close to winning in the Hall of Fame Bowl, and a 6-5 Ole Miss team came so close to winning in the Independence Bowl. All of this just proves to me that you really can't put too much faith in the won-and-lost columns when it comes to a bowl game."

Winning solves 99 percent of your problems, and because I remained convinced that I could win at Notre Dame, I did not pursue a serious feeler that came my way from the University of Cincinnati at about this time. Mike Gottfried had moved to Kansas and a mutual friend of athletic director Mike McGee and mine, Barry Scholak, called to see if I wanted the job.

"We could have gone back to the city I love," Marlene says, "and I felt Gerry could have won there. Everybody loved him. He would have recruited all the top-notch local players and filled the stands with people who wanted to see them."

I said no.

"Gerry wanted to finish his years at Notre Dame," Marlene says. "He was the optimist. I was the pessimist."

9

■ THE COMEBACK TEAM ■

 In the isolation of the Canadian wilderness, as far from big-time college football as a person could get, Father James Riehle helped me to face the truth that is self-evident to every Notre Dame football coach.

You have to win.

Sounds straightforward enough. But the enormity of the demand can, at some point, leave any Notre Dame football coach shaken.

Before I had gone off in June 1984 on a vacation so unusual and so unlike me that it became a standing joke at Notre Dame, Father Joyce had visited me in my office. When he closed the door, I knew the visit was serious. The bottom line of the conversation reminded me of my one-line, five-year contract. Simple. Unvarnished. To the point.

"Gerry," Father Joyce said, "you know we've got to start winning more."

What could I say?

"Father," I replied, "you're dead right."

And I could have added—"And I'm dead gone if I don't."

"We love you here," Father Joyce said. "We just have to win more. A lot of people are starting to question our decision to hire you."

"Father," I said, "I understand and know where you're coming from. I really feel for you and Father Hesburgh. I know I've caused turmoil by not winning more games."

There is an odd juxtaposition of emphasis at Notre Dame. Nowhere do the leaders of a university place winning and athletics more properly in perspective. Yet nowhere is there more pressure on the coach to win. The difference from some universities is that at Notre Dame a coach is given every chance to succeed. If he hangs himself, it's because he was given plenty of rope.

"I think we're the only college in the country," Father Joyce says today, "that hasn't gotten rid of a coach or bought out his contract. They've even done it at Stanford. They've done it at every college I know of. After a couple of years if a coach hasn't been successful, they get rid of him. They're ruthless."

The only ruthlessness at Notre Dame comes from outside pressures, but even those can be overblown. For instance, I don't think my failure to win enough games, or take the team to a major bowl or win 10 games or rack up another national title affected the generosity with which donors responded to the University.

"They used to ask during Joe Kuharich's time whether lack of success on the football field affected contributions," Father Joyce says. "Usually contributions doubled or tripled. The football had nothing to do with that. It just meant we were becoming more sophisticated in our fund raising. We were putting on campaigns. Donations had no relationship that we could see—and Father Hesburgh would testify to this—to football wins or losses.

"People who really give us big money don't give it for the football successes. They give it because of what they think Notre Dame is. Football has brought a lot of benefactors to us. But they don't give money because of football."

Winning football attracts a following and mediocre football does not. As I went off to Canada with my sons, Gerry and Steve, Bill Corbett and Father Riehle on a fishing trip arranged by Spike Sullivan of Tulsa, Oklahoma, the mediocrity of our record weighed heavily on me. Not only that, I didn't know whether or not I could stand this trip. I'd never fished in my life. I hated fishing. My kids loved it, though. So I wanted to take them.

Bill Corbett flew us into International Falls, Minnesota, where we rented a car and drove to a nearby lake. There, we boarded a pontoon plane and flew into Canada to meet Spike, his sons and grandsons. Back home at Notre Dame, they were placing bets that I wouldn't last a day fishing from a canoe and would come bolting out of the Canadian woods like a bull moose.

I didn't bolt. But on the first day, with Father Joyce's words freshly imprinted on my mind, I asked Father Riehle, whom I dearly love, if he would take a walk with me. I told him everything, that I knew all along I had to win, that it wasn't enough to fit in and win friends for the University. I was supposed to win games.

What bothered me was that Father Joyce had been forced to tell me I had to win more. I didn't want to hear that. I already knew it. But I knew Father Joyce had to tell me. He was both my boss and my friend, and he had been up front on everything. If I sound confused, it's because I was. Every person wants the continued support of those he admires and when he knows he doesn't deserve it, it can be devastating.

"Gerry," Father Riehle said, "you have to understand where they're coming from."

"I do, Father," I said. "Completely."

"This is part of the game," Father Riehle said. "There isn't anyone who would rather see you stay at Notre Dame forever more than I would. And it's not only because we get along and are friends but also because you belong at Notre Dame."

I guess before I could find peace with the fact that no matter how much people loved and respected me as a person, it wouldn't keep me at Notre Dame, I had to talk it over in this way with someone whom I knew was 100 percent on my side.

"But," Father Riehle said, bluntly, "black's black and white's white. You have to win."

That conversation opened me to some of the best days of my life. We'd have Mass, go fishing, come back to the lodge and play cards. Watching my boys catch fish left and right amazed me. It wasn't fair to the fish. I wished victories were as easy to reel in. The trip meant the world to me and I'll be forever grateful to the Sullivan family for making it possible. I went to Canada with a problem and came home with another reminder of what's important: family and friends.

Even so, I never told Marlene about Father Joyce's visit to my office or about my heartfelt conversation with Father Riehle. No need to worry her any more than she already was. Week One of the 1984 season, unfortunately, heaped worry upon worries.

We were supposed to play Purdue at Notre Dame Stadium, but an unusual set of circumstances prompted us to move the game to Indianapolis for the dedication of the Hoosier Dome. A good friend, the late Bob Welch, had been involved in getting the Hoosier Dome built and in luring the Colts to Indianapolis after he tried to buy an NFL team. When that didn't work out, he wanted to bring Notre Dame to the Dome to play.

I had met Bob my first week at Notre Dame. We were both staying at the Morris Inn on campus. I knew he was a big supporter of football. So I went to his room, knocked on the door and introduced myself. We became great friends. Any time I needed a jet for recruiting, Bob would offer one from his company, R.V. Welch Investments. The previous recruiting season, Bob had been there for me when I really needed him.

I had received a call from a coach at an inner city high school in Miami. In fact, he was near Carol City, where rioting and other civil disturbances had caused such heartache for many people. It was a tough area for young men to grow up and there was this one athlete there whom we really liked. He had visited the Notre Dame campus before this call occurred and liked the University.

"Coach," the high school coach said, "if you can get down here today, you can get this young man."

"But, Coach," I told him, "I have no way to get there."

"Well," he said, "this young man is going to make a decision and I want him to go to Notre Dame. It will be a great place for him. He doesn't have anything, and it will put him on the right track. Can't you get down here?"

"Let me call you back," I said.

I called Bob Welch and told him the story.

"Can I borrow your jet?" I asked.

"Sure," Bob said, "I'll have the pilots pick you up in an hour."

Ron Dallas, a Notre Dame graduate, Fort Lauderdale attorney and one of the birddogs who helped us with recruiting, met me at the airport in Miami and drove me to the high school. When we got there, the young man was nowhere to be found and no one knew where he had gone.

"Coach," his coach told me, "he just took off. I'm really sorry."

I said that I couldn't hold up the return of the private jet any longer and left. As we were driving to the airport, we stopped at a stoplight and in the car that pulled up beside us was the young man for whom we had been looking. He was in the passenger seat and another boy was driving.

"Hey," I yelled out the window at him, "I was just at your high school to see you. Where were you?"

"Take a right," the player told the driver. "Let's get out of here."

There was nothing I could do but fly home to Notre Dame, fuming. When I landed, I telephoned the high school coach.

Check the passing form! I'm five years old. It's 1940, and I have on a "C" sweater, the "C" for Chaminade, the Dayton high school team coached by my father.

Still a great passer, huh? I weighed only 155 pounds as a Chaminade senior.

Notice the snappy stripes on the sleeves of my University of Dayton jersey. It's 1958, and I'm a senior and still a quarterback.

The Golden Dream years are a long way off, but in 1971 at Moeller High School I already knew the most dear part of the dream—my family. With me are my sons Gerry III, left, and Steve.

The boys, Steve, left, and Gerry III may have grown some by 1981, but they still lean on their ol' Dad.

Good help can be hard to find. That's why when it turned out to be a hot day in Purdue's Ross-Ade Stadium in 1983, my sons, Steve (second from left) and Gerry III (right), and their friend Jaque Joubert (center) volunteered to serve as waterboys. As they watch the action, Coach Jim Higgins (left) and Neil Maune (behind Gerry) keep them company until they are called to action.

Julie Marie helped to surprise Marlene and me with a 30th anniversary party in the spring of 1994.

My mother Alma with me in Akron at a family gathering in November of 1992. If my father inspired me on the field, my mother always put my well-being at the top of her priority list. *(Photo by Mickey Stefanik)*

One of my inspirations, first as a player and then as a coach, was my Dad, Fuzzy. He not only taught me how to play football but also about tough love. Here we share a moment during the 1983 Notre Dame football season.

The family and Father Ken Sommer, S.M., a former all-state center for my Dad at Dayton Chaminade, helped my parents celebrate their 50th anniversary. Left to right: Dad (Fuzzy), my brother Fred, Mom (Alma), Father Sommer, my wife Marlene, me, my sister Marilee, and her husband Ken Oberhue.

In June 1996 we gained not only a daughter-in-law but also a second doctor of veterinary medicine. Both Steve and his bride, Pij (Patricia) are graduates of the Ohio State School of Veterinary Medicine. From left: son Gerry III, Marlene, Steve, Pij, the father of the groom, daughter Julie Marie and her husband, Steve Buzzi.

Three generations on Marlene's side of the family: Marlene, mother Angela Agruso and daughter Julie Marie. This is in 1992.

This happy bunch helped Marlene and the old Coach celebrate our 30th anniversary in April 1994. From left, Laurie Faust, my brother Fred's wife; Marlene; Fred; Aunt Stella Eiben, my mother's sister and the only living sibling of my mother or father; the happy bridegroom 30 years later; my sister Marilee, and her husband Ken Oberheu.

Bet you can't tell who won more games as Notre Dame football coach from this photo. Lou Holtz and I share a laugh during a golf outing at Fairlawn Country Club in Akron in 1993. *(Photo by Jeff Glidden, Kent State University)*

On the first football Friday or Saturday in 37 years that I hadn't coached, my friend Dick Pitts, owner of Green Hills Golf Course (center) and my former assistant head coach at Akron, Bob Junko, were at the Akron-Eastern

Michigan game to keep me smiling. Bob is now the defensive line coach at the University of Pittsburgh. *(Photo by John Ashley, University of Akron)*

My friends Frank Eck and Anne Ray (left) get together with once and future Notre Dame head coaches. This is at the 1995 spring game. Bob Davie, with his wife, Joanne, was defensive coordinator at the time but has since succeeded Lou Holtz as head coach. *(Photo courtesy of Frank Eck)*

Phil Gigliotti coached quarterbacks and running backs for 16 of my 18 varsity seasons at Moeller High School. He also lived with me in the House of the Eight Bachelors.

Brother Larry Eveslage, S.M., and I in 1993 at a fundraiser at Cincinnati Purcell Marian High School. Brother Eveslage gave me my start as a head coach at Moeller High School.

The Rev. Lawrence Krusling, principal at Moeller during many of my years, was more like a brother and partner than a boss. We returned to Moeller in 1993 for a gathering at which this photo was taken.

This is the moment I had dreamed of—being introduced as Notre Dame football coach. With me as I address the media in November 1980, from left: retiring Notre Dame Coach Dan Devine; the Rev. Edmund P. Joyce, Notre Dame executive vice president; athletic director Gene Corrigan, and former athletic director Moose Krause. *(Photo courtesy of Notre Dame sports information)*

I call this the "Joy of Victory." Offensive coordinator Tom Lichtenberg and I celebrate a happy moment during a victory in 1982. With us is flanker Joe Howard. *(Photo by the Rev. F. Thomas Lallak, courtesy Notre Dame sports information)*

And this is the "Agony of Defeat." *(Photo courtesy of Notre Dame sports information)*

Before the first night game ever played at Notre Dame, Paul Harvey, my friend and former captain of the South Bend police force, escorts me onto the field and past our excited fans. We beat Michigan that night, 23-17. *(Photo courtesy of Notre Dame sports information)*

Phil Carter and I have a lot to laugh about in the spring of 1981. Hey, I hadn't lost a game yet. *(Photo courtesy of Notre Dame sports information)*

Bob Crable and I spent a lot of days and nights talking like this. Before he became an All-America linebacker and captain at Notre Dame, he had been both for me at Moeller High School in Cincinnati. Now he teaches and coaches at Moeller. *(Photo courtesy of Notre Dame sports information)*

Allen Pinkett deserved all the hugs I could give him for what he brought to our football team: Character, courage and a generosity of spirit that made him not only a delight to coach but also to know as a person.

Fist raised and floating on air, I run toward a tunnel of the Los Angeles Coliseum where a number of Notre Dame fans await to celebrate in 1984 Notre Dame's first victory at USC in 16 years. It was rainy and cold, but I was glowing and warm.

This is the Gerry Jig. It's a dance step I invented to celebrate our victories at the University of Akron. It proved popular, though seldom danced.

The Rev. Theodore M. Hesburgh, Notre Dame president, and I get together with Notre Dame students in the spring of 1984.

The Rev. Edmund P. Joyce, Notre Dame executive vice president, speaks at the 1985 Notre Dame football banquet with kindness and regard for my contributions to the University. I had just resigned as coach and did not know what the future held.

Marlene and I met the Meyos, Marie and Ray, at left, during the Notre Dame years and that friendship only grew when we moved to Akron, where Ray is president and chief operating officer of R&R International Inc.

Now this is the way to watch Notre Dame football—in the stands with old friends, including, from left: Jake O'Connor, Pat White, Jeanette O'Connor and Jan Blazi, the secretary who brought order and friendship to my life during my Notre Dame years. This is at the Notre Dame-Washington game in 1996.

The Rev. James Riehle, who was both football team chaplain and guiding light for me during the Notre Dame years, came to Canton, Ohio, for a Pro Football Hall of Fame luncheon with speaker Moose Krause, former Notre Dame athletic director. Guess who showed up to see Moose and Father Riehle.

At Akron I meet this bunch at Eddy Niam's restaurant. We call ourselves the Saturday Morning Breakfast Club, and we talk football. In the front row, from left: Bob Bruno, Norm Singleton, Joe Petracca and Joe LaRose. Back row: Bill Doria, Pat DeAndrea, Bill Greenzalis, Ron Tedeschi, Bruce Romeo and the coach.

New York Yankees owner George Steinbrenner (left) spoke at the University of Akron Football Kickoff banquet in 1993. With us is Karl Benson, then the commissioner of the Mid-American Conference and now commissioner of the Western Athletic Conference.

It isn't all about football. Friends are even more important. Two of our best friends are Sandy and Dorothy Cundari. We met because I coached Notre Dame and, like so many others, they remained our friends after I had left the University.

When we go on vacations and do other things together, I like to introduce Frank D'Andrea (center) as my accountant and Ken Schneider as my attorney. More important, they are great friends. We especially like to get together at Ted Gregory's Montgomery Inn in Cincinnati. Ted cooks the best ribs in America.

I suited up for the Rev. Edmund P. Joyce's retirement as Notre Dame's executive vice president in the spring of 1987. I'm the handsome one on the left. The others are Art Decio, Jerry Hammes, Digger Phelps, Professor Tom Bergin, Father Joyce and Lou Holtz.

My favorite place on the Notre Dame campus wasn't Notre Dame Stadium. It was the Grotto, where I found peace. The Grotto is a replica of the one at Lourdes, France, where I'm kneeling in the foreground to pray.

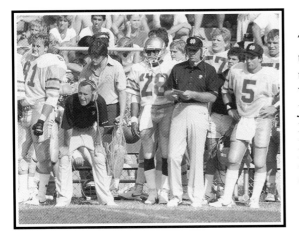

Tension can bring a person to his knees—or at least to the hands-on-knees position. With me on the sideline are Jay Underwood (81), Greg Bell (28), Coach Mal Moore, Mike Johnston (behind Mal), Dave Butler (57), Blair Kiel (5) and Tom Doeger.

"Irish make dream real for Faust" story by Enos Pennington, *Cincinnati Post*.

Irish make dream real for Faust

By Enos Pennington
Post Staff Reporter

SOUTH BEND, Ind.—Gerry Faust, who began dreaming about coaching Notre Dame football in the fifth grade, accepted the biggest challenge of his coaching life today by taking the job of his dreams.

The Rev. Edmund P. Joyce, executive vice president of Notre Dame, described Faust as an immensely successful coach who is capable of repeating his high school success at the college level.

"But I can't believe that any coach, including a Rockne or the archangel, can win 71 of 78 games like Faust has," Father Joyce said today at a press conference announcing Faust as the new Notre Dame football coach.

ACTUALLY, FAUST has won 70 of his last 71 games (not 71 of 78) in a phenomenal coaching career at Moeller High School.

Faust revealed that he had met with Father Joyce on Nov. 9 in Indianapolis to discuss the Notre Dame job but was given no official word that he had been chosen until 3 p.m. Monday.

"The hardest decision I've ever made in my life was when I left Moeller High School yesterday," Faust said. "It was very difficult for me to turn onto I-74 and head for South Bend. It took a heckuva place to come to for me to give up Moeller after putting 21 years of my life into it."

DAN DEVINE, the outgoing Notre Dame coach who announced his retirement on Labor Day, appeared at today's press conference with Faust and said the two men had been close

"Gerry is the type of individual I would like my son to play for," said Devine. "In coaching, that's the greatest compliment you can pay a person."

Faust said no decision had been made on which of the Notre Dame coaches will stay.

"I will interview every one of them personally," said Faust. "They have done very well this

coaches. There are a couple of people I have in mind who are excellent people, excellent coaches."

However, Faust said his Notre Dame staff will primarily come from the college ranks.

FAUST EXPECTS to get immediately involved with recruiting but will not be involved with

year, I plan to talk to each one and then let them know as soon as possible."

FAUST HINTED that he may take some of his present Moeller assistant coaches with him to Notre Dame.

"But I don't want to hurt Moeller High School," said Faust. "I have to go back, talk to my

the football team until Devine retires.

"I did not get a chance to tell my players I had the job before leaving school," Faust said. "But the first thing I did when I got here was to call some of them and I offered scholarships to three of my players if their grades are good."

At left is Notre Dame pilot Bill Corbett, and the Notre Dame airplane. I spent many hours in this plane recruiting and attending speaking engagements.

Our Bookstore
Basketball team in
1981 wasn't very
good but it was
pretty. From left,
Coach Greg Blache,
Coach Tom
Lictenberg, the
gunner Gerry Faust,
ticket manager and
former Notre Dame
defensive back Steve Orsini, Coach Brian Boulac and Coach Jim Higgins.

Jim Kennedy, an unofficial
telephone recruiter for us in the
early '80s when he was
bedridden in Philadelphia, visits
Notre Dame in 1984. People like
Jim would do anything we asked
to help the football program.

A man must be well groomed.
So Morris Roberts, my barber
from Cincinnati, would visit me
at Notre Dame and cut my hair.
Sharp-looking, aren't I?

Coach Stan Zajdel joins me
before the University of Akron's
game at the U.S. Military
Academy at West Point in 1992.
Coach Zajdel, as a University of
Dayton assistant coach, talked
me out of quitting the team.
(Photo by Dick Baratieri)

Father Joyce, whom I join here at his retirement party in the spring of 1987, gave me the chance to live my Golden Dream.

As my University of Akron players lift me to their shoulders after the final victory of my coaching career, my daughter, Julie Marie (lower right), rushes onto the field to greet and congratulate me.

"Coach," I told him, "it just cost a Notre Dame alumnus between $5,000 and $7,000 to fly me down there because you told me that we could get this kid. I understand you can't shackle the young man, but in the future don't call me unless you're sure. I know your motives were good, and I appreciate that. I've been through the same thing as a high school coach. But please, just don't call unless you're sure."

On national letter of intent signing day, this coach called again and said the young man had changed his mind and wanted to come to Notre Dame. I asked if he had signed with anyone else and his coach said that he had signed with a small school. It was a national letter of intent that the NCAA honored. So we couldn't sign him.

"Why does he want to come to Notre Dame now?" I asked the coach. "He didn't want to four weeks ago."

"I'll tell you the truth," the coach said. "I called the kid in and chewed him out for making me look foolish. And he said: 'Coach, the other coach gave me $500 to sign. I needed the money.' "

"You mean you let the kid go somewhere else for $500 when he could have gone to Notre Dame on a scholarship worth $60,000, a scholarship that would have put him on the right path for the rest of his life?"

"Coach," he said, "you've never lived in the ghetto. You've never been without money. To him, $500 is what $10,000 is to you."

"Coach," I said, "I'd never thought of it that way."

It's a sad story and a sadder commentary on the differences between the haves and have-nots of our society. Bob Welch had tried to help. It wasn't the first or last time. I owed him. Bob asked Father Joyce about moving our Purdue game to the Hoosier Dome and Father Joyce had no objections. So Bob called me. I said sure. I didn't even hesitate. Looking back, it was the right thing but not the smart thing to do.

Maybe it's wishful thinking, but I believe if we had played at home, we would have beaten Purdue instead of losing, 23-21, while committing five turnovers (three interceptions and two fumbles). Although the crowd (60,672) was predominately a Notre Dame crowd, there is just something about the routine of staying in the seminary before the game, of being on your own campus, of not traveling, that makes playing at home seem a little easier.

In my situation I couldn't afford generosity that led to losses, but the decision of where the game was played did not become the post-game issue. My coaching did. At least the media were consistent. The lightning rod of the criticism became my decision to open the game with freshman Timmy Brown as our kick returner. He was just getting into his return to begin the game, and his career, when he made a cut. In changing direction, the ball glanced off his protruding hip pad and popped loose. Purdue strong safety Corey Cooper grabbed it at the 12-yard line and four plays later Mike Rendina kicked a 31-yard field goal. This was the same Mike Rendina who had kicked two field goals to help Florida State beat us, 19-13, in 1981. What did this guy do, transfer to get another shot at me? It wasn't too funny and neither were the media questions as to why I had started a freshman as our kick returner. My answer was simple and direct.

"He was the best guy to bring it back," I said.

In practice that summer we knew in the first couple of days that with the burst of speed Timmy had and with his ability to change direction, he was a special talent. You didn't have to be a coach to see it. He stood out that much.

"He's an outstanding kick returner and an outstanding player and he'll stay at that spot," I said. "This wasn't his fault."

The irony, of course, is that three years later Timmy Brown would win the Heisman Trophy and his victory would in large part have to do with his kickoff returns. I guess he was OK after all. At that point, the media, like everyone, including us, were looking at anything that moved and breathed to determine why we weren't winning. I didn't have a problem with that. But the side effect is that players came in for unwarranted criticism.

The year before, when we beat Navy, tailback Napoleon McCallum fumbled three times and the fumbles contributed to our victory. Napoleon, who was truly a great football player, got hit so hard on two of the fumbles that no one could have hung onto the ball. In the postgame press conference Napoleon was in the front of the room in his Midshipman's uniform and the press was beating him up one side and down the other. I was standing in the back, awaiting my turn, when finally it reached the point I couldn't listen to this any more. I waved at the Naval Academy sports information director, and he got the gist of what I was trying to tell him: Get out of there. So he said they had a plane to catch and would have to leave.

When I got before the media, I had a question for them: "How can you get on a guy like that? He's a role model for every young person in America. The caliber of athlete he is, going to the Naval

Academy to serve his country, going through the regimentation he does each week in addition to football, and you're criticizing him? You know as well as I do that two of those three fumbles were caused by tremendous defensive plays. You ought to be ashamed."

And we ought to have been ashamed of our first half the following week at Michigan State. We fumbled, threw interceptions, missed tackles and let the Spartans waltz to a 17-0 lead. I was waiting for my Detroit friend, a fresh drink in hand, to come strolling out of the stands, go into the locker room with us and this time, tell us what was wrong. He or anyone else could have told us. It was one word: Mistakes.

We rallied for a 24-20 victory on balanced offense and a more aggressive second-half defense, led by linebacker Rick DiBernardo, who had come back earlier than anyone expected from a broken wrist in spring practice. You can bet I knew how to pronounce his name now. As a junior, he lent stability to a defense that included eight sophomore starters.

Though we could do no wrong in a 55-14 victory over Colorado the next week, the moment proved an ambivalent one. As glad as we were not only to win but also to play well, all of us empathized with what Colorado had gone through in the days leading up to the game. The Buffs' tight end, Ed Reinhart, had suffered a head injury the previous week at Oregon and remained in a coma in an Oregon hospital. I had called Colorado coach Bill McCartney on Monday to see how Reinhart was and checked again a couple of times during the week. We played our younger players most of the second half, wanting not to take advantage of this difficult situation.

It's odd, but all these years later, Bill McCartney and I are both heavily involved in movements intended to inspire men to live up to their responsibilities as husbands and fathers. Bill left football, despite tremendous success that included a national championship, to devote his time to Promise Keepers, a Christian men's group, and I'm a part of a similar Catholic organization called Answer the Call.

I became involved because of Father Ken Sommer, a priest who was the captain on my dad's 1945 football team. Father Sommer celebrated the Mass on my parents' 50th wedding anniversary and at the burial of both my mother and father. I have to be honest. I didn't want to get into another organization and did so only because of Father Sommer. I spoke at Answer the Call's first two conferences in Cincinnati. As happens so often, I've found myself getting far more than I'm giving and now participate joyfully and without a shred of hesitation or feeling of obligation. Our goal is to put 80,000 men in Notre Dame Stadium in the year 2000. Lou Holtz spoke at our 1997 conference. I'll always remember the first conference. A minister who was our guest speaker came up to me and said: "Bill McCartney wanted to thank you again for not running up the score on him. He still remembers."

So do I. Those, in fact, are the moments I'll remember over all others, the ones when a coach is able to do his job but with heart and generosity.

Going into Faurot Field at Columbia, Missouri, to play the University of Missouri has much the same appeal as playing at South Carolina. None. I mean, they're tough places to play. The fans are, to put it politely, demonstrative. If that weren't enough, just before we go to the locker room prior to the game, Roger Valdiserri came up to me and said:"Gerry, I can't substantiate this, but I think Missouri is going to come out in its gold jerseys."

They were wearing black. They always wore black at home. They hadn't worn gold jerseys since Don Faurot put them on his great teams 30 years before. Seems as if someone was saying: Turnabout is fair play.

I had a decision to make. Do I tell our players? What if Missouri didn't come out in gold jerseys? That could prove a distraction to us. How do I handle this?

I talked to a couple of our coaches and decided to gamble and tell the players that it looked as if Missouri would come out in gold jerseys, hoping to do to us what we had done to USC when we wore green the season before.

"Men," I said in my pregame address to the team, "this is a tough place to play but if anybody can do it, you can. If you can come from 17-0 behind at Michigan State, you can win here today. But it's going to be tougher for one reason. They're going to come out in gold jerseys. They're going to do to us the same thing we did to USC a year ago. The difference is: They're not Notre Dame. They're Missouri. And putting on a gold jersey doesn't have the emotional impact that putting on the green does at Notre Dame.

"So when they come out and the place goes wild, you dig down in your hearts a little deeper, you dig down and prove to them that even though they haven't worn gold jerseys in 30 years, wearing them today isn't going to help."

When the Missouri captains came out in black jerseys, I thought: "Uh oh." All I could do was hope that they were doing the same thing we had done when we sent our captains out in blue jerseys to meet USC. It wasn't two minutes until the place erupted in a roar as Missouri came out in its gold jerseys. I was happier to see gold than a prospector in old California.

Because of the decision to tell the team and prepare it for this emotional moment, the players weren't fazed. Steve Beuerlein threw to Reggie Ward on a 74-yard touchdown play in the second quarter. That gave us a 10-2 lead and we held on, as John Carney kicked three field goals. If anything, our 16-14 victory was proof that the wearing of the gold is not the wearin' of the green. How else do you explain Missouri senior placekicker Brad Burditt missing from the 39-yard yard line with seven seconds to play? Burditt had never before missed inside the 40.

We got on our charter airplane with a 3-1 record and should have been 4-0. All was right with the world but not the airplane. It was kaput. We had to sit on it for two hours before another plane could be flown in from Kansas City. But I'll tell you what: It is a lot easier sitting for two hours after you've won a game like that than it is to make a two-hour bus trip from State College, Pennsylvania, to Harrisburg after a last-second loss to Penn State.

Unfortunately, the plane problem was an omen. The wheels were about to come off our season. And who was it who would loosen the first lug nut? None other than the quarterback who threw like a stork standing on one leg and moved with all the swiftness of an overloaded B-29. That's right: Bernie Kosar.

Back for his third and final season—I mean, the guy was smart enough to graduate in three years—Kosar just took us apart after we had managed a 10-7 halftime lead against Miami. Every time Kosar completed a pass, I would think of telling Tom Lichtenberg that Bernie couldn't play on Notre Dame's level. I was right in a way. He played above our level. He completed 20 of 29 passes for 205 yards and two touchdowns and had taken the Hurricanes to the national championship in 1983.

The thing that I didn't see, the thing so many of the coaching masters also missed, including Joe Paterno, was that side-arming Bernie Kosar throws with his head, not his arm.

There is another game played with the head and arm called squash. I wasn't very good at it, either. I knew this because each Friday at noon Father Dave Porterfield, who serves as liaison between admissions and football, would come to my office ready for our standing squash match. We would play three games to 15 and I never, but never, beat Father Porterfield.

On this particular Friday, it was different.

He walked into my office with his shorts on and his squash racquet in hand. He also had a letter with him.

We had been recruiting this excellent running back from the western part of the United States. He had good grades. He had come to visit the campus. We thought we were in good shape with him until this Friday when Father Porterfield showed up. Admissions always gave us a letter explaining why it was rejecting an applicant. It was for us to file in case questions occurred. This letter was about the running back we wanted to sign. Father Porterfield handed it to me.

"Who is it?" I asked.

Father Porterfield told me.

"Why him?" I said.

Father Porterfield explained that on this student-athlete's transcript a counselor had written one sentence. It said the young man was a trouble-maker. I couldn't believe it. This wasn't the player I had come to know.

"Are we taking one person's word for this?" I asked. "Why don't we check with some other people?"

"No," Father Porterfield said. "That isn't the way we do it. He's rejected."

I was hot. You could have fried an egg on my forehead. We went on to our squash game and for the first time I beat Father Porterfield. I didn't beat him once. I beat him all three games. He couldn't believe it.

"I'm never bringing another rejection letter over here on a day we play squash," Father Porterfield said.

We laughed about it. I knew there was nothing I could do but accept the decision. That's Notre Dame. At least I beat Father Porterfield on the squash court. That's more than I could do with Air Force on the football field.

During my five years at Notre Dame, Air Force was at its football zenith. But that didn't explain this loss. This Air Force team had the least talent of any we faced. It shouldn't have mattered that Steve Beuerlein was hurt and we had to play Scott Grooms at quarterback. We outweighed Air Force 40 pounds a man. We should have been able to run the ball down its throat. Instead, it was the

Air Force wishbone that ran as if it were all alone on the field. Air Force outrushed us 371 yards to 90 and beat us 21-7. As we were coming off the field, the Notre Dame fans booed us. Or maybe it was just me. It was the only time this ever happened.

I tore into the team with a full-throated croak. I told the players that anyone who didn't want to play football—and they hadn't bothered playing on this day—didn't have to show up on Monday. I warned them it was going to be the toughest week they'd ever spent at Notre Dame. South Carolina was coming to South Bend, and when it did, it wasn't going to find this kind of Notre Dame team waiting for it.

"This was *not* Notre Dame football," I sputtered. Then I walked out.

Monday at practice, we hit. Tuesday, we hit. Wednesday, we hit. Thursday, we hit. Every player showed up. Every player did his job. It was a no-nonsense week. If the players weren't sick of giving this kind of performance, I was sick of getting it. Period.

On Friday, my parents arrived, as did Dorothy and Sandy Cundari. They knew and cared deeply about one another, having met on a tour of Europe in 1983. I was the nominal tour leader, which meant that I got to bring my family for serving as a drawing card for those who wanted to visit Europe and get to know the Notre Dame football coach simultaneously. It was great. Dorothy and Sandy became like brother and sister to Marlene and me. They're Notre Dame subway alumni from Detroit. We became such close friends that we've gone on vacations together for the last 13 years. We go to Las Vegas. Eat out. Take in the shows. Have a great time.

That weekend, Sandy and Dad came to practice while Mom and Dorothy sat in the car and talked. After practice, as we were walking off the field, I had my arm around Sandy when he reached into his pocket and said: "Here."

He handed me a rabbit's foot.

"Dorothy and I want you to have this," Sandy said. "Put it in your pocket during games."

This was nice. But I had already tried Ara Parseghian's three buckeyes. They were given to him as lucky charms and he left them at Notre Dame. They should have worked as well for me as for Ara, right? We're both from Ohio, the Buckeye State. I put them in my pocket. Nothing.

I also carried a rosary in my pocket. I'd clutch it in my hand and in a tight situation say a little prayer to myself.

"Sandy," I said, gently, "what am I going to do with a rabbit's foot? I have my buckeyes. I have my rosary. I've been over to Notre Dame Stadium to talk to Rockne as if we were holding a football seance. Digger Phelps told me it would work. So I tried it before the Air Force game. It didn't work. What the heck is a rabbit's foot going to do for me?"

"Look, Gerry," Sandy said, "this is a special rabbit's foot."

"It is?"

"It really is. When I was wildcatting as an oilman, Dorothy gave me this rabbit's foot. I was going to Crockett County, Texas, to drill some oil wells and she gave me the rabbit's foot."

"And?"

"Gerry, we hit 102 straight wells."

"You better give me that rabbit's foot."

I put it in my pocket, right next to the buckeyes and the rosary. Hey, when you've just lost to Air Force for the third straight time, you'll try anything. Now, we were playing a team that was 6-0, ranked 11th in the nation and would become one of the seven teams on our 1984 schedule to advance to bowl games. We played great, especially for three quarters. Unfortunately, the game lasted four quarters. South Carolina scored 22 points in the final period. Another el foldo, right? Not quite.

In fact, we had plays such as the one made by Hiawatha Francisco, who had moved from tailback to the defensive backfield this season. He intercepted a pass with South Carolina fourth and two on our 8-yard line. Pass interference canceled the interception and South Carolina scored two plays later. Then, with a withering rush underway, we let quarterback Mike Hold escape and scramble 33 yards for a touchdown. Then we gave them a final touchdown when the foot of blocker Larry Williams came up and hit the ball and caused fullback Chris Smith to fumble.

After I helped set Larry up with his lovely future wife, you wouldn't think this would happen. But it did. As we were leaving the field, two of our big offensive linemen were in front of me and one of them said to the other: "What do we have to do to win?"

I said to myself: "Boy, do they have the right question." The problem is, I didn't have the answer. I told the team that although I had just tied the wrong kind of record for a Notre Dame coach—three consecutive losses at home—I was as proud of them as I had ever been of any team after any victory. Then I made a prediction:

"You have four tough games left: Navy, LSU and USC on the road and Penn State at home. Three of those four teams are in the Top 20. LSU is No. 6 and we have to play in Baton Rouge, fondly known as Death Valley, home of the live Tiger and the world's largest outdoor cocktail party. But if we play the way we played against South Carolina, we'll win the next four games. I'm glad they're tough games. It will turn us into one of the great comeback teams in Notre Dame history."

Some teams wouldn't have known how to take such optimism in the wake of three consecutive losses. But our players knew exactly how to react. They thought I was nuts.

Sandy and Dorothy Cundari were at the house when I got back from taping my coach's show. When I saw Sandy, I reached into my pocket, pulled out his rabbit's foot and handed it back to him.

"No, Coach," Sandy said, "keep it."

"Sandy," I told him, "that thing hit 102 straight oil wells. It's worn out. It isn't going to win any football games."

We laugh about that to this day.

As if preparing to go to sixth-ranked LSU isn't challenging enough, I discovered that *Sports Illustrated* wanted to come to South Bend and then to follow us to LSU to do a story. Roger Valdiserri broke the news to me, which I took with my usual graciousness.

"Do I have to, Roger?" I whined. "I don't have time this week."

He said I had to, and that Kenny Moore, the distance runner who was on the U.S. team at the Mexico City Olympics, would be the writer. When Kenny came into my office on Monday, I was startled by what he said.

"Coach," Kenny Moore told me, "I want you to win. I'm a great fan of yours. You've been through a lot of tough things, and I understand that as a runner."

He put me at ease by saying that and we had a great week together. I know writers are supposed to be impartial, but it's nice that even if their work reflects that impartiality, they still, in their heart, might be pulling for you.

We didn't spend the entire week discussing football, which also was a relief. When I invited Kenny and *Sports Illustrated* photographer Heinz Kluetmeier to the house for supper on Wednesday night, we talked for three hours about their trip to Hawaii in search of a rare bird. It was really interesting to hear about how

Heinz climbed trees and waited for his chance to photograph this bird.

When we got to LSU, it was too hot even for tropical birds. It was over 90 on the thermometer and the humidity stood at 98 percent, that is if anything can stand in such an oppressive atmosphere. It was so hot and wet, they wouldn't let us practice on LSU's field on Friday night. The next morning I woke up and couldn't even breathe, because the humidity was so suffocating. I told the coaching staff that we were going to play every player and substitute according to a schedule, regardless of the score.

If the weather wasn't enough to cope with, I expected to be greeted at the visitors' locker room in Tiger Stadium by none other than the live, roaring tiger. I mean, it *roars*. It scares the bejabbers out of you. I asked our trainer at our pregame meal to take one of the steaks and lace the meat with a non-harmful tranquilizer.

"You mean it, Coach?" he said.

"Yeah," I said. "Go ahead. As long as it won't hurt the tiger."

I was going to tell the team that we'd shut up one tiger and now it was time to shut up another. The problem was, it was too hot and rainy even for the tiger. They didn't bring him out. In his stead, however, as many as 1,000 LSU fans greeted our buses and formed a gauntlet of humanity for us to walk through from the buses to the dressing room.

It was hotter than heck—heck is the place you go if you're not a good person— and I was dripping with sweat in my shirt and tie. What's more, the fans forced us to scrunch up as we walked in order to get through the gauntlet. More than a few of them had begun the cocktail hour in the morning. And now they were screaming:

"Tiger Bait! Tiger Bait! Tiger Bait!"

They were trying everything to intimidate us. Instead, it got the competitive sap flowing. By the time I reached the locker room I was so fired up that I was hitting each player as he came in the door and doing my own screaming.

"Tiger Bait, Hell!" I said.

And I don't cuss. I really don't. But there it was. A single, comparatively mild cuss word stunned the players. They'd never heard me say hell. They started laughing and it really cranked their engines. We dominated the unbeaten, sixth-ranked team in the country. You couldn't tell the 3-4 team even with a program. Using both a one-back set as well as a two-back formation, we controlled the ball on the ground, with Allen Pinkett carrying an unbelievable 40 times for 162 yards, mostly behind a line utilizing two tight ends. Meanwhile, linebacker Mike Larkin and strong safety Joe Johnson were keeping the pressure on LSU quarterback Jeff Wickersham. Only a last-second 50-yard Hail Mary (sorry, I said it again) allowed LSU to make the score as respectable as it was at 30-22.

As the game ended, Heinz Kluetmeier came running up to me and gave me a big hug, proving that if you're quick enough you can hug a hugger before a hugger hugs you.

"Coach," Heinz said, "I've been taking sports photos for years and you are the first guy I've ever rooted for."

That was a kind and generous thing to say, an admission that Heinz didn't have to make. In any case, I became one of the few college coaches to make the cover of *Sports Illustrated* and I'll be forever glad I did. Not for myself. That's the cover, with its "I'm Gonna Make It" theme, that Brad Arling, my young friend from Cincinnati, seized on and used as his own inspiration to fight his way back to a productive life after his head injury.

In Kenny Moore's story, which did not give me a free pass to stand beside Rockne, Leahy and Parseghian, Larry Williams captured in a nutshell Notre Dame and what it means to play and coach football there. "At other schools," Larry said, "hope springs eternal. Here, *demand* springs eternal."

Where there are demands, there also can be great rewards— and bumper stickers such as the ones that began popping up during the three-game losing streak at home. The sticker said:

Oust Faust.

Hey, at least it rhymed.

I knew there would be an emotional letdown after the only Irish victory in Death Valley, but I didn't think it would include trailing Navy 17-7 in Giants Stadium with four minutes to play. With the time remaining, we created a comeback within our comeback. Four tough games. Four tough minutes. In both, we proved resilient.

Steve Beuerlein drove us 83 yards in 1:45, completing three consecutive passes of 29, 15 and 15 yards to sure-handed freshman Tim Brown. Allen Pinkett, who gained 165 yards on 37 carries, went the final yard with 2:17 to play and we added a two-point conversion. We didn't use a single timeout on the nine-play drive. Now, Navy needed one first down to win. It didn't get it.

With the ball on our 18-yard line, we had one minute. It was just enough time. Beuerlein's 29-yard completion to Pinkett on a reverse screen put us on the Navy 26-yard line, and Steve stopped the clock by throwing out of bounds with 18 seconds to play. As we debated whether to send John Carney in to kick the field goal —he had missed one from 50 yards and this one would be 44—or run one more play, we ate up too much of the 25-second clock but still got the kick away in time. John made the winning field goal with 14 seconds on the game clock.

There were two ways to look at this game: One was that if we hadn't committed six turnovers, including throwing four interceptions, we wouldn't have needed to stage such a great comeback. The other was to simply appreciate the comeback. I think the response of most people was that we shouldn't have been in the situation to need the comeback. But I can tell you that the players and coaches thought the comeback was unbelievable and will remember that 18-17 victory for the rest of their lives. Different people, different perspectives.

Against Penn State we solved the turnover problem and almost every other problem anyone might have thought we had. We didn't just win. We played our way back into bowl contention with a 44-7 victory, at that time the third worst defeat a Joe Paterno team had ever suffered. I was just glad that Penn State officials didn't take too seriously Joe's loss to a high-school coach and fire him.

We generated 543 yards of offense and allowed Penn State just 169. We scored on our first five possessions. We did everything right and with a 31-7 halftime lead, I began playing the younger players. I just wanted to win, not rub it in. Of course, someone watching might have thought otherwise when our reserve quarterback Scott Grooms changed the play at the line of scrimmage in the final minute and threw a pass. I'd been running the ball up the middle, running out the clock, and Scott heaves one. I went bonkers. Fortunately, time ran out so that I could go looking for Scott on the field.

"Why did you do that, Scott?" I demanded. "We called a running play."

"Coach," he said, "if they come out in this defensive front..."

"You're right," I said.

Scott had changed the play to the one he was supposed to against the defensive alignment Penn State was in. He'd just done as we had coached him to do all week. I should have reminded him before he went into the game of the circumstances: We didn't need to throw.

"Do me a favor, Scott," I said. "Come with me and tell Coach Paterno what happened."

Scott did, and Joe was gracious about it.

If there were victories to cause a person to have a celebratory drink, this was one. Some people, however, don't know when to say no, and think their designated driver is a club in their golf bag. Of course, there also are those fans who drink after Notre Dame losses to drown their sorrow.

After one of our losses earlier in the season I was driving Marlene home from a post-game party at St. Joseph's Bank and Trust before going on to tape my coach's show. We came upon a car on U.S. 31 that was weaving from one side of the road to the other. This guy was a real broken-field driver.

"Those guys are drunk," I told Marlene. "Now I'm going to get blamed for driving people besides my dad to drink."

When we got to a stoplight, I told Marlene to scoot over and drive, that I was going to get out and go over to the car and try to talk the men into getting off the road.

"Gerry, don't," Marlene said. "Those guys might shoot you."

That would be a rather strong reaction to a loss, even for a Notre Dame fan. Besides, they were too drunk to remember my record. I decided the potential benefit was worth the risk. When I got to their car, the driver was slumped over the wheel dead drunk and the other guy was just as bad off.

"Sir," I said to the driver, "let me drive your car and park it for you. You're in no condition to drive. I'll get you home, and I won't call the police."

The guy agreed. So we drove over to a side street near the Notre Dame campus. I took the keys and then asked at a store if I could use their phone. I called the police and told them it was Gerry Faust and that I had made a promise to two guys who are drunk. (No, not that I'd win more games.) I explained that I promised I would get them home. The problem was, I had to be at my coach's show and I didn't have time to drive them myself. They lived about 15 miles away.

"I promised I wouldn't call the police," I told the officer. "So unless you promise me you'll take them home and not charge them, I can't tell you where they are."

The police said they'd come, take them home and not arrest the men. When the officer arrived, he thanked me for doing what I had done. I wasn't trying to be a hero. I just kept seeing my children being on the road with these guys. So I stopped them.

If I had done what I would have liked to have done before the USC game, the fans at the Los Angeles Coliseum might have thought they'd had one drink too many, too. Notre Dame hadn't beaten USC on the West Coast in 16 years, unless a person wanted to discount the Phantom Touchdown. On Monday prior to the game, I got a call from a Notre Dame fan on the West Coast.

"Coach," he said, "I've got a great idea."

"What's that?"

"You know how Ara hated that white horse the USC Trojan rides? How the white horse leads the team onto the field? And how every time USC scores and the rider and horse circle the field, it drove Ara crazy? Why don't you get four horses and dress four people up like the Four Horsemen and have them lead the Notre Dame team out onto the field."

"You know," I said, "that's a great idea."

I called a couple of people on the West Coast to see if anybody involved with Notre Dame had a horse farm and if they'd do this. Everyone thought it was a great idea. Then I had second thoughts.

"Jeez," I said to myself, "if I go out there with the Four Horsemen in a little one-upmanship of the Trojan horse and we lose, I'll be the laughing stock of the country." If I had been more secure in my position and we had been winning more, I'd have done it, and it would be a Notre Dame legend to this day. But I backed off.

The team didn't back off, though. We played unbelievably well given the circumstances. The Coliseum was a quagmire. USC fumbled eight times and lost six of them. We held on to the ball, fumbling only twice and recovering both of those. Those mistakes by the Rose Bowl-bound Trojans offset their statistical advantage.

After two second-quarter touchdowns—an 11-yard Steve Beuerlein-to-Tim Brown pass and a 3-yard Allen Pinkett run—John Carney locked up the 19-7 victory and his title as Notre Dame's most accurate kicker for a season (17 of 19 for .895) in a most unusual way. The first of his two 45-yard field goals came after holder Mike Viracola bobbled the snap, forcing John to stop after taking two of his usual three steps to the ball. After Viracola regained control of the ball and set it up for the kick, the composed Carney took just one step and still made the field goal.

That had us all dancing the hula in the dressing room, and you have not lived until you see a 300-pound lineman doing the hula to celebrate being invited to Hawaii to play Southern Methodist University in the Aloha Bowl. Between hulas, the players were hoisting me onto their shoulders like a rag doll. It was a sight.

Sunday morning, as was our custom when we played at USC, we attended Mass, a communion breakfast and went to Disneyland before returning to South Bend. After getting a team picture taken in front of Disneyland—is that Mickey Mouse or Coach Gerry Faust in the picture?—I saw Father Joyce standing off to one side and I asked him what he was going to do.

"I'm just going to walk around a little," Father Joyce said.

"Father," I said, "you come with me. I've taken my kids to Disney World in Florida three times. I know all the great rides."

So we went on Space Mountain, riding around in the dark in these little carts, having a ball. To Pirates of the Caribbean. To It's a Small World and to the submarine ride. Father Joyce seemed surprised by how he felt.

"You know, Gerry," he said, "that was fun. In every person, there's some child. This was great."

I thought Father saw something at Disneyland that we sometimes forget: How to enjoy the child that's in all of us. As we grow up, we put a shield up and won't often let that childlike enjoyment come through. You don't have to do that. If I had any success at Notre Dame, it was because I never put a shield up. You got what you saw. All of it. All of me. I was on the greatest ride of my life for five years and though it had as many ups and downs as a roller coaster, I wasn't going to pretend I didn't enjoy it.

After the Liberty Bowl in cold Memphis, the Aloha Bowl brought a different problem. We didn't have to worry about snow and ice but about the players getting sunburned by spending too much time on the beach. We told them we wanted them to have a good time but limited them to an hour and a half, twice a day, in the sun.

As nice as the sun and surf were, they aren't what I'll remember. We took the team to Pearl Harbor and the Arizona, one of the ships that was sunk when the Japanese attacked. One of my friends from the Moeller days, the Rev. James D. Pfannenstiel, head of the chaplains for the Navy's submarine operations, helped me set up the Pearl Harbor tour.

Each evening they play taps and take down the flag at the Arizona. It's a moving experience, looking into the bay and seeing the hull of the ship on which so many men lost their lives and knowing that they remain buried there at sea. When the flag was folded, the color guard handed it to the Rev. Pfannenstiel, a Methodist minister. He had served in the submarine corps with Father Joseph O'Donnell, assistant fleet chaplain for the Pacific Fleet. The Rev. Pfannenstiel and Father O'Donnell presented me with the flag, and it remains one of my most cherished possessions.

The 27-20 Aloha Bowl was a great one for spectators, and we could have won had Steve Beuerlein's pass not sailed over the head of Milt Jackson who was alone in the end zone with 23 seconds to play. The worst part, both for the team's sake and my own, is that all some people would remember was this loss to a team that was about to have its program closed down for recruiting violations. If we had won we would have been 8-4, with five straight victories, three of them against teams ranked among the top 15. That's how the 1984 team deserves to be remembered, as The Great Comeback Team.

During this 7-5 season, my attorney, Ken Schneider, called to say that a search committee which was working on filling the University of Cincinnati athletic director's job wanted to talk to me. So after the season I drove to Cincinnati. In Ken's office in suburban Montgomery, I met with some of the members of the search committee. After the meeting, I told them that I wasn't interested in replacing Mike McGee, who had left to become athletic director at USC. I wanted to stay at Notre Dame.

This was a more formal inquiry than the one I'd received the year before concerning returning to Cincinnati as the university's football coach but in both instances, I was not offered the job. Had I been and had I not been at Notre Dame, I'd have taken the jobs. I like Cincinnati and the university. It was the timing and the circumstances that caused me not to be interested. I still hadn't thought about giving up on The Golden Dream that for me was Notre Dame, the only school for which I would have left Moeller.

Sooner than I realized, within days in fact, I would be forced to think about doing the one thing I learned not to do—quit.

10

■ LEAVING OR STAYING? ■

Choices fill our days and make them interesting. Some, because we make them. Some, because we avoid them. And some, because we never expected to be confronted with them. A career choice was the furthest thing from my mind when I bounded into my monthly meeting with Father Joyce after the 1984 season.

I thought we'd review the season, shoot the bull, talk about the future. We did. But the conversation quickly took an unexpected turn. I knew my long-term future did not include Notre Dame unless we won big—and I mean B-I-G—in the fifth and final season of my contract. But Father Joyce focused on my immediate future.

"I wanted to be perfectly frank with Gerry," Father Joyce says today.

And he was.

He told me that he and Father Hesburgh were continuing to take flak from alumni and Notre Dame supporters about the football program and the flak was coming in more heavily and with greater frequency. As a result, he and Father Hesburgh found themselves having to spend time addressing my situation and Notre Dame football that should have been devoted to other University matters.

"Gerry," Father Joyce said, "you have a fifth year on your contract if you want it. If you don't, we'd be willing to honor the money."

As odd as it might sound to those who don't know Notre Dame and Father Joyce, I was convinced that he was thinking as much about my welfare as he was about that of Notre Dame.

"I wasn't trying to twist Gerry's arm," Father Joyce says, looking back on that conversation. "I just felt sorry for him. If things continued as they were, we would not renew his contact at the end of the fifth year. I thought it might be easier for him to get a good position elsewhere if he resigned now rather than as his contract was running out at the end of an unsuccessful fifth year.

"I thought he ought to seriously consider this. Not that I would have been too happy if he had left. We really do love him here."

Father Joyce suggested that I weigh this option and ask for the opinions of my closest friends and advisors.

"No matter how optimistic you are," Father Joyce said, "the possibility that your contract will be renewed doesn't look bright."

So here was an option—leave early, taking, if you will, a golden parachute out of The Golden Dream. Because it was presented by this man I trusted and respected, I didn't automatically reject it. I talked to my family and called three people with different but insightful perspectives. I chose people whom I knew could give the question cold-eyed scrutiny without being cold-hearted. But it had to start with the family, because those persons, like Father Joyce and Father Hesburgh, were taking the flak for my failures. Maybe I was wrong to want to use every last minute I had to make the dream come true. Maybe this was the time to find a situation where a coach who had taken his team to consecutive bowl games would be seen as an asset rather than a liability.

I told Father Joyce that I would base my decision on two things: What was best for my family and what was best for the Notre Dame family. I didn't want to hurt, or to see others hurt, either family.

From incidents such as the one in Pittsburgh when Marlene told the heckler to take a long walk to a hot place, I knew how criticism of me affected my wife. She would call offending writers and broadcasters after they had written or spoken something about me that she considered unfair, and she would read them the riot act. I told her not to make these calls, that they would only aggravate the situation, but as long as there was a telephone, it was there to strike back as far as Marlene was concerned.

The criticism also bothered my daughter, Julie, and son, Steve. At Saint Mary's College and St. Joseph High School, they found it impossible to avoid the hurtful remarks that others made about their father. By this time, my oldest son, Gerry, was a sophomore at the University of Dayton. Even a state removed from South Bend, he became the most obvious example of how the family can become embroiled in the coach's troubles and take the brunt of them.

Gerry was working as a bartender at one of the bars near the University of Dayton. The job helped pay his way through school. One night, some guy in the bar was drunk and began saying things about me that no son would want to hear said about his father.

"That's my Dad," Gerry finally told the man. "I don't want to hear any more of that."

The guy refused to shut up. So Gerry jumped over the bar and punched him. The police came and took Gerry out to their car. When he explained what had happened, they released him. But that's how bad it got: The son fighting his father's fights.

Despite this, the family, to a person, wanted me to stay the fifth season and try to make it work. They said that after four years, they were more convinced than ever that I was the kind of person who belonged at Notre Dame, and, of course, they knew it was the one place this side of heaven I wanted to be.

I also worried about how this affected my parents and other family members. On one occasion, a friend from Cincinnati was staying with Marlene, who had had surgery, and I took the kids to Arizona to see Marlene's father. From there, we went on to Nevada and California on vacation.

Marlene's father, Vic Agruso, had retired to Sun City near Phoenix after years in the concrete business in Cincinnati. He was a great businessman. Meticulous. And just a tough, tough guy. That's why it shocked me when we walked into his house and found hanging on the wall a gallery of pictures of me at Notre Dame. He wasn't the kind of guy who would put up such a display.

"Jeez, Pop," I said, "you've got all these pictures of me. That surprises me."

"Yeah," he growled, "and they're coming down unless you start winning. You're embarrassing the heck out of me."

I laughed, but I knew he meant it.

Before we continued our trip, I went to church one morning and Vic asked if he could go with me. He had drifted away from the church. So I was happy he wanted to accompany me.

After Mass when I'm on the road, I like to thank the priests and to tell them I'm Gerry Faust from Notre Dame. It connects them to the University. This particular priest knew me. He had retired to Sun City from Columbus but had followed Moeller football when he was in Ohio. I told him my father-in-law was waiting for me in front of the church and asked if he would take the time to meet Vic and perhaps befriend him.

"Sure," the priest said. "I'd be happy to do that."

So I introduced them and Vic and the priest exchanged telephone numbers and talked for about 10 minutes. When we got in the car, my father-in-law started chewing me out.

"I knew you'd do that," he said. "I knew you wanted that guy to get me squared away."

He was mad, or appeared to be. Two years later, when my father-in-law was dying of cancer, that same priest was there with him. He had become Vic's friend and my father-in-law came back to the church on his deathbed. It never would have happened it he hadn't asked if he could go to church with me that morning. I'm glad he asked. I think he wanted help in finding his way back to the church.

In a different way I needed and wanted help in finding the right path to take concerning Notre Dame. I wanted to stay. I wanted another chance to do what we had done during the last four games of the 1984 regular season. I believed with all my heart that we could play that way for an entire season. But I'm the optimist. I needed realists. So I called Dr. Ken Oberheu, my brother-in-law who is a heart surgeon in Dayton; George Castrucci, who was the executive vice president of Taft Broadcasting in Cincinnati and later the president of Great American Broadcasting Company; and Frank Sullivan, a Notre Dame trustee who was president of Mutual Benefit Life, one of the largest insurance companies on the East Coast.

I chose these men carefully and because I didn't know what answers they would give me. I could have called my friend and attorney Ken Schneider, but I knew Ken would tell me to stick it out, partly because he believed that was the right thing to do and partly because he knew that was what I wanted to hear.

Despite the fact Ken Oberheu is married to my sister, Marilee, I knew he could look at my situation with the objectivity he brings to his work as one of the better heart surgeons in the country. He's level-headed. Detailed. Pragmatic. He never jumps to judgments. He thinks situations through. I expected he and the others would tell me to quit, to move on to another coaching job or to another phase of my life. I knew that Ken could bring himself to tell me. He is used to telling people what they don't want to hear and doing it in a way that cushions the blow.

Ken told me to stay with it. He said I belonged at Notre Dame and that I was doing more good for more people than could be measured by my wins and losses (25-20-1 at that point). Ken, who is a Lutheran, told me that by example I had done more good for the University than any coach in the last 25 years, that I had done everything except go 9-2 or win a national championship.

I explained to Ken and George and Frank, who, as a trustee, didn't need the explanation, that the football coach at Notre Dame has to win and it doesn't matter how much good he does in other ways. If he loses, he becomes part of Notre Dame history, not legend.

"Stay," Ken said.

George Castrucci brought to the question the ability to make tough personnel decisions based on what a company needs rather than on his friendship with a person. He looks at the pluses and minuses. An honors graduate of Xavier University with a business degree, George told me a person has to look at debits and credits.

"You haven't hurt them," George told me. "The University has too much to gain if you win and too much to lose if you resign. You are one of the few people in this country who people can look up to and say: 'There's a man who lives by his principles.'

"Stay."

In a way, Frank Sullivan came from a football family. His brother, Billy, once owned the New England Patriots. I didn't have to tell Frank what was required of a Notre Dame football coach. Frank was close to Father Joyce and had been around the University a long time. Frank had seen a lot. When he was going to the University, he served as Frank Leahy's personal secretary. Later, he became Leahy's administrative assistant. Frank had always stopped in to visit me when he was on campus and had always been straight with me. He knew my problems, my strengths, my weaknesses. Equally important, he knew the sentiment among the trustees.

"Stay," he said. "Stick with it."

Frank told me to take my feelings to Father Hesburgh and share them. So I called Father Hesburgh and told him that I had talked to Father Joyce and that I needed to talk to him. I went to his office about 10 o'clock one night and we talked until midnight. I told him to whom I had spoken and why and what they'd said. To me, it confirmed that I had to see my dream through, even if it turned out less than golden. I thought I could do this without hurting Notre Dame, the one thing I had sworn never to do.

"Gerry," Father Hesburgh said, "I don't have any problem with your decision. I feel it's an honest one and I support it 100 percent. You have a five-year contract here, and I want to see you win."

Not everyone, of course, supported my decision to stay. Athletic Director Gene Corrigan thought it was wrong and said so one night in January or February when he walked across the sixth fairway of Knollwood Country Club from his house to mine.

Father Hesburgh or Father Joyce had told Mr. Corrigan of my decision to stay for the fifth year, and he was upset.

"Gerry," Mr. C. told me, "you ought to step down."

"No," I said, "I'm not going to do that."

It got loud and emotional after that, and Mr. Corrigan left in a fury. Marlene had been upstairs when the conversation turned into shouting. She came down just as Mr. C left and asked what was wrong. I told her.

"He shouldn't get upset like that," she said.

"Marlene," I said, "if I were the AD, I'd have done the same thing. We haven't won the way you have to win at Notre Dame and he is responsible for that as athletic director."

The bottom line was Mr. Corrigan didn't feel I was getting the job done.

"I wanted him to consider resigning," Corrigan says. "So I went over to talk to him about it. I told Gerry I did not see any way we were going to win in that fifth year of his contract.

"Football is a tough game. You almost need to be a little cold-blooded. I don't think Gerry is. I don't think it's in his nature. I've always felt there were some key games that he lost that he needed to have won to keep the kids on his side. Basically when you don't win, they stop listening to you. I don't care who you are.

"My point to Gerry was that I didn't want him to have that program go down so far that people would despise him for it, because he's a good person. He came from a high school and had this enormous change. I just felt like it was going to be another year wasted."

Mr. Corrigan expressed his reservations about my coaching in a handwritten note that he brought by my office after our conversation. To me that was the sign of an excellent athletic director. I wasn't going to go away. So he listed the reasons he thought I hadn't been successful and what he thought I should do to overcome them. I didn't agree with all 12 of his points, but I think they showed he was willing to do whatever he could to, as he put it in his note, help me survive.

The "C" Paper is worth reviewing even today:

1. "Organize your thoughts and prepare meticulously for every meeting with the team. Don't be vague and repetitious— lengthy off-the-cuff talks work against you."

I agree. Sometimes I am repetitious, and even to this day I seldom put much on paper before I speak. Maybe a word or two. I do have a reason for that, though, and I think it's a good one. I've found that when I speak from the heart it comes out with more honesty and people listen. People hear and respond to sincerity as often as they do to well-organized, pretty words.

2. "Put yourself in the background where possible. Let assistants or (Joe) Yonto or (Brian) Boulac handle announcements, formations, getting the team ready to go on the field. The same holds true for pep rallies. Let the players, assistants, ex-players do the talking."

Another good point. When I was at Moeller, I ran the pep rallies. I'd speak and get other speakers involved. It was a difficult habit for me to break. I tried. I'd see Johnny Lujack at a pep rally and call him up onto the stage. A need to run everything had nothing to do with this. It was a unique situation. I was a high school coach coming to a major college, to the premier football job in the country. I wanted the players to be the focal point, but from the day I arrived I wore the bullseye whether I wanted to or not. I couldn't escape the limelight. I tried. Mr. C. probably thought I didn't try hard enough. I disagreed. I was the lightning rod. There was no way to divert the heat.

3. "Make your discipline more evident. It must be firm, fair and equal to all."

I don't think equal discipline is fair. For one thing, when you are dealing with college athletes, it's a dictatorship and in each case, you have to handle it based on the person's experience and background and the circumstances surrounding the incident. Sometimes discipline helped players grow. Other times, discipline stunted their growth. I looked for the best in the young men. That may have made it seem as if I wasn't tough enough.

Here's an example: Rob Finnegan was late for the plane on one Notre Dame trip. I waited. Why? I didn't know if he had a good reason for his tardiness. It turned out he didn't. But he was a third-string center. It's easy to make an example out of young men who aren't going to play anyway. It's more difficult to take the time to assess a situation and then mete out punishment that also lends itself to improving the person, in this case physically by running laps.

At Akron, we had a similar situation to Finnegan's. Jeff Sweitzer was late for the bus on an out-of-town trip. I asked the other players where Jeff was, and they said he had been arrested. If I had left, instead of trying to find out what had happened, not only would we have been without our starting quarterback against Virginia Tech, but also a young man would have been done an injustice. As it turned out, someone in Pittsburgh who Jeff knew mailed him stolen merchandise. The sender had addressed the package incorrectly. The package fell into the hands of the postal inspectors. Jeff Sweitzer knew nothing about the stolen items. But he had been arrested and taken to jail. After an hour of sorting this out, Jeff was released.

4. *"Keep your devout Catholic faith as a personal thing. There is enough religion here to take care of the players—and it would let Father Riehle do his job easier."*

I don't remember Father Riehle ever saying anything to indicate this was a problem. In fact, Father Riehle seemed to appreciate the depth of my faith and where I tried to place the emphasis.

"I have heard him so many times talk to parents and young people about the priesthood," Father Riehle says. "That's one of the big problems in vocations: The parents do not want their kids to become priests and nuns. Whether the kids do or do not is up to them, but it should be important. I think there is a real attitude in this country against becoming a priest. You can do anything you want, but don't become a priest. That's the theme. I think it's too bad."

I think it's too bad, too. That's why religion is part of my everyday life, including when I coached. I speak out. If I think a young person might be interested or seem as if he would be especially suited for the priesthood, I go up to kids and say to them: "Why don't you think about becoming a priest?" My son, Gerry, has decided to enter a trial program in preparation for the seminary, a decision that is one of the joys of my life. None of this emphasis is new or should have come as a surprise to anyone at Notre Dame. As Denny Dressman wrote in his book *Gerry Faust: Notre Dame's Man in Motion*: "Say a Hail Mary was an order given to everyone on the Moeller sideline on every play of importance for 20 years."

5. *"Stay out of the players' lives as much as possible off the field. You have people who can handle a lot of problems for you (Yonto, Boulac, Roger Valdiserri and me)."*

I think what Mr. Corrigan was saying is that his concept of a successful head football coach would be one who had an air about himself like Bear Bryant. But you know, as tough a guy as Woody Hayes was, he was like me. I know, because he coached many of my players and would call me if he had a problem with one of them or if they had a problem with which he thought I could help. I think head coaches should get involved in one way or another. If a young man comes to me, what choice do I have? I would send him to someone else if I thought I couldn't handle the problem, but if I can help and I don't, what does having an open-door policy mean? Let me offer an example:

Mark Bavaro came to me at the end of his junior year and said: "Coach, I just want to let you know that I'm leaving." There were about eight days of spring football remaining.

"Mark," I said, "why are you leaving?"

"Coach, you're not going to talk me out of it. I just want to go back home. I'm not happy. I want to live on the East Coast so I can be close to my family. I'm tired of football. I just don't want to be here anymore."

"Why don't you come to my office and we'll talk about it?"

"Coach," Mark said, "you're not going to change my mind."

"Mark," I said, "I'm not going to try to change your mind. (And I really wasn't trying to change it. I looked out my office window and there was his car and everything was packed. He was gone. At least he was kind enough to come in and tell me instead of just taking off. That was the kind of person he was. He was an up-front person. So I told him the story about my coach Stan Zajdel helping me.)

"I would not feel comfortable, Mark, if I didn't tell you what I thought the pros and cons of your decision are. A coach did that for me when I felt the way you do and it changed my life forever. If you graduate from Notre Dame, you are going to have a degree that really means something. You are a bright young man and you're doing well in school. If I were you, I'd play my senior year. You only have eight days of spring practice and the fall left. There's a good chance that you'll be drafted by an NFL team. I think you're a great prospect. You are one of the toughest young men I've ever coached.

"You also have a lot of friends here: Jay Underwood. Mike Gann. They're close friends and you'll miss them. But you do what you think is best. I just wanted to present these points to you. And there is one last thing you have to think about and that is what you're going to do when you get home. Are you going to go to school? What if next fall you miss football and want to play?"

Mark had listened patiently and thoughtfully.

"Coach," he said, "I'm staying."

He shook my hand. I hugged him. He stayed and was a fourth-round draft choice who became an All-Pro with the New York Giants, played on Super Bowl champion teams and graduated from Notre Dame. Should I have not interfered? Should I have just let him get into his car? Should I have sent him to his position coach or to a priest? I'd been through it. I knew how he felt. A coach who refused to stay out of my life changed my life. Sorry, but I wanted to be the kind of coach Stan Zajdel was.

6. *"Show confidence when it is easy to panic. Part of being in charge is appearing that you are."*

I think I had an inner confidence. I never questioned it. The only pressure I felt was in telling myself I had to win this game or that game because I wanted so badly to be at Notre Dame for the rest of my life. On the sideline my mannerisms might have led someone to the conclusion that panic had set in. It hadn't. I'm emotional. Always have been. But I learned long ago how to rant and rave and still think about what needs to be done next. There are all kinds of coaches. A Schnellenberger, an Osborne, a Walsh, a LaVell Edwards is subdued on the sideline. A Schembechler or a Hayes was emotional. A Joe Paterno is a 'tweener. On that continuum, place me toward the emotional end, with Woody Hayes.

7. *"Don't praise victory too highly. Suggest you not give out game balls until after the film is graded ..."*

From the Moeller days on, I always gave out game balls after games, but they went to supporters and others who deserved special recognition. I agree that it is best to wait until you've studied film of the game to award game balls to players. Otherwise, someone may be overlooked. But supporters have to be recognized in the joy of the moment. That's what they'll remember when they look at that ball. The euphoria. Everyone I gave a game ball at Notre Dame and most who got one at Akron wouldn't give them up for anything. It's a prized possession. I know the two game balls my Akron staff gave me—one following a 31-0 victory over Cincinnati and another when we beat Eastern Michigan 27-9 for our first Mid-American Conference victory—have great meaning for me.

8. "Forget words like great, super, fabulous, outstanding, etc. Try using not bad, pretty good, pretty darn good."

I speak in hyperbole. I admit it. Some words pop up too often —like someone is a "class" person. I don't use the word unless I mean it, but when you overuse a word, you devalue it. Lou Holtz was the master of "pretty good," of turning an attack dog into an underdog. Of course, he did it so often that I'm not sure people believed him. That's the other end of the vocabulary spectrum. I get wound up. I'm optimistic. I raise expectations rather than lower them. The danger is that you can't meet those expectations you've raised.

9. "Share the spotlight—for four years you have been almost the only figure in Notre Dame football. It's not your fault, but it should be the players who get most of the recognition."

See Point No. 2. I agree completely. But there was nothing I could do. And I tried. To the media, I would bring up the players, the other coaches. The story they wanted almost always was mine. I couldn't tell them what story was most interesting. The only thing I could have done was to reduce access to me. The reason I didn't is that I felt the media had a job to do just as I did. I wouldn't have wanted restrictions placed on my ability to do my job. Why should I place restrictions on theirs?

10. "Stay away from making statements that end up sounding like promises. One game at a time. One day at a time."

That's my run-away optimism again. But specifically, I was criticized from Day One for saying that we would win the national championship. I didn't say that. What I did say to our players was that our goal was to win the national championship in that first year. They told others, instead of keeping it in house as I would have preferred. It was passed on in a different context. You set lofty goals in-house that you don't necessarily announce to the world. That's what I did. And at Notre Dame, if the goal is not to win the national championship then the goal is too low. It doesn't matter if it's stated or unstated. It's there. Conference championships and other intermediate goals don't exist at Notre Dame.

11. "Take time before making decisions. Let some things sit overnight to see how they look when time is not a critical issue.... Be reflective. Be analytical."

I guess Mr. C thought I had a problem. I didn't think so. I learned decision making from a master, Father Krusling at Moeller. When he could, he would sit on a decision he didn't want to make, and sometimes if he waited long enough, he wouldn't have to make it. It would work itself out. I tried to listen to everyone before I made the decision. The coaches told me I was a better communicator than other head coaches they had worked with. Guess my communication fell short with Mr. Corrigan.

12. "Remember, unlike high school, these players—the great majority—are not looking for a father figure or a friend. They want you to teach them how to win and they will respect you if you do that."

There's no question that that is what players want on the college level. That's why I tell high school coaches who have aspirations of going on to college coaching that they can do more good on the high-school level. If I hadn't gone to Notre Dame, if there hadn't been the dream, I would have stayed at Moeller for the rest of my life because of that influence you have on young lives. I felt I did good. I felt I helped more young men with their lives because they were at a more impressionable age and would listen. In college, the young men already have determined what they are going to do and how they are going to do it. But I still tried to help young people when I could.

I don't know if I would have stayed in college coaching if I couldn't at least try to help people. If that was a problem at Notre Dame, one of the things I wasn't good at or was wrong about, I'm still glad I did it my way. That's why I got into coaching in the first place. I wanted to help young people, not just win games.

If I had won more games and still had been able to help a few people, it would have been a great marriage between Notre Dame and me. In the final analysis, I think it is more important to win lives than games. Isn't that a teacher's or coach's No. 1 objective? Or are we as educators taking the wrong approach to our mission?

I don't think my approach was wrong. That's why I can look into the mirror today and not flinch. I didn't win as many games as I wanted, but I hope that I had a lot of wins that weren't reflected on the scoreboard.

Among the reasons I wanted to take every opportunity permitted me to continue my association with Notre Dame was Frank Eck and the many people like him. Frank owns Advanced Drainage Systems (ADS) in Columbus. He was the person I turned to on Sunday, July 21, 1985, when I got a call from my brother-in-law, Ken Oberheu, telling me that my dad's appendix had burst while he was vacationing at Kiawah Island in South Carolina.

The year before Dad had gone through triple-bypass heart surgery. Frank had offered one of his two company planes, which had oxygen, to fly my father back from Milwaukee after the surgery. My brother-in-law got the best surgeons to perform the operation because he couldn't do it. He loved my dad so much and had become so close to him that he thought it best if someone less personally involved performed the surgery.

I thought of Frank in this emergency in which Ken said my dad had to be flown back to Dayton immediately. I telephoned Frank at 10 a.m. that Sunday and 15 minutes later the plane was on its way to Kiawah. It was my dad who was dying, but Frank responded as if it were his own father. As the ADS plane flew dad from South Carolina to Dayton, Bill Corbett was flying me from South Bend to Dayton. I met Dad's plane. He could hardly walk. They rushed him to Miami Valley Hospital for surgery. All I could do was pray.

When Dad reached the hospital, Dr. Chang Kang was there to greet him. He had become my dad's anesthetist and his presence was comforting to both my dad and me. As soon as Dad saw Dr. Kang, a smile crossed Dad's face, and I knew he was in good hands with Ken and Dr. Kang. Still, I thought a few prayers couldn't hurt.

For a while I prayed in the non-denominational chapel at the hospital, but then I drove over to the University of Dayton chapel because it has a shrine to the Blessed Mother and I needed to be near Her and ask Her to hear my prayers for my dad. When I finished my prayers and returned to the hospital, the doctors told me my dad was going to live. I called Frank Eck.

"What you've just done for me, Frank, I can never repay," I told him. "You've just saved my dad's life."

My dad and mom were the two most important people in my life besides Marlene and the children. The decision that I had had to make about whether to give up a final shot at Notre Dame or to stay and try again was important. But this was more important. This was life and death, and it was a Notre Dame man who came through for me and helped to give my dad six more years with us.

That's the greatness of Notre Dame. When one of the family is in trouble, the other members of the family do everything in their power to help. How could I voluntarily leave a place which produces such a depth of feeling for others?

11

■ SAYING GOODBYE TO ■
THE GOLDEN DREAM

My definition of a cockeyed optimist is a football coach who, in the last year of his contract, after four less-than-satisfactory seasons, builds a new home and moves into it the week before his team opens its season at Michigan.

It was supposed to be our dream home. Instead, it became the end-of-the-dream home. Bad game plan, huh?

We took the chance of having Jack Hickey build us a 5,000-square foot, stand-alone home that was part of a condominium concept because I still believed that we would find a way to win enough games for my Notre Dame coaching career to continue. It wasn't just a Faust fantasy. To turn it into reality all we had to do was to win eight games, one more than my previous season high of seven. We had to play well and consistently. And any losses that occurred could not come at the hands of teams we should beat. A tall order, yes. But not impossible.

"It would have been interesting if Gerry had had a 9-2 season that fifth year," Father Joyce says, looking back on this moment. "You can speculate on what would have happened then. We might have kept him. Maybe even at 8-3. It depends on whom you lose to and how."

I had some personal goodwill in the bank. I just needed to deposit more victories. There was no limit to the number of people who wanted to help me.

One of them, Professor Jim Carberry, of the chemical engineering department, came to my office one day and asked if he could meet with me. The professor was something of a legend, having coached one of the intramural tackle football teams. Football was taken so seriously, even on the intramural level, that Coach Carberry had been banned for a season for some infraction. He was still thinking in Xs and Os, however, so he closed the door to my office, sat down and took out a diagrammed play. He explained the blocking schemes. The whole works. It might have been a great intramural play, but it wasn't one that was going to work on the intercollegiate level.

He was in my office a half hour, and I took his play in the spirit that it was offered. He was sincere and wanted to help. I thanked him. The professor was not the only person who thought he could coach. There was, for instance, Butch.

Every year at Christmas time, some of the coaches would play a basketball game with the students at the Logan Center, a facility for the mentally handicapped located on the edge of the Notre Dame campus. Digger Phelps always asked me to play and I would. Among our opponents each year would be Butch and his buddy, Dome, who was bald, not golden. They were in their mid-30s. They played pretty well and would always "beat" us when the fourth quarter rolled around. Then, during the Christmas party, they'd give us a hard time about how we had played.

Well, one year, Digger decided to let Butch sit with him on the bench of one of Notre Dame's basketball games. We were playing Providence, which wasn't playing well at the time. We were a 15-point favorite. Digger had on his snappy suit. Butch had on his snappy suit. Digger had his green carnation in his lapel. Butch had his green carnation in his lapel.

Just before halftime, we were ahead by only two points, and Butch was getting mad. He thought he was coaching the team. The players all knew Butch from our basketball games with Logan Center. They liked him and liked him being with them on the sideline. But I'm not so sure they liked Butch's halftime speech.

Digger got to the dressing room after Butch and the players. When Digger walked in, he found Butch chewing them out. He's telling them that he's the coach for this game and they're playing terribly. Digger cracked up. But Butch was serious.

During the second half, they still were not playing well, and after a Providence player intercepted a pass and went in to score, Butch stood up and tried to call time out. That was enough for Digger.

"Now, Butch," he said, "you go sit down."

Digger assigned one of his assistants to make sure Butch didn't do any more coaching and we managed to win by two points. After the game, Butch was so proud that we all had to smile. He thought his coaching had made the difference.

Now, if Butch's coaching made Digger better, it might save me. Right? So during one game when we were leading comfortably and were relaxed on the sidelines, I heard this voice: "Geeerrrreeeee. Geeerrrreeeee."

I turned around. It was Butch.

"Can I come down to the sideline?" he asked, standing at the gate to the stands. At one game each year, some of the Notre Dame students gave up their tickets so the Logan Center students could watch us play. Other Notre Dame students accompanied the Logan students to the game.

In that spirit, I thought: What the heck? It's the fourth quarter. We're winning. Why not?

"Butch," I shouted, "you can come down, but you *can't* call any timeouts."

"I won't, Coach. I won't," Butch promised. And he kept his promise.

I came across another bit of coaching advice in an unusual way. I was visiting a person I knew who was experiencing some psychological problems. He was recovering in the psych ward of Memorial Hospital in South Bend, which is the kind of place that you can't just stroll into and out of. You have to be buzzed in and checked out. Because they have televisions in the ward, many of the patients enjoyed watching Notre Dame football and many of them knew me.

As I was leaving, I had to wait for an attendant to let me out, and a man came up and tapped me on the shoulder and told me his name.

"I'm a patient here," he said.

"Is everything going well?" I asked.

"Yes," he said. "And I'm an MIT graduate."

"That's quite an accomplishment," I told him.

"Yes, I'm a math major, and I've been watching your quarterback. If you use this formula (he rattled off something that sounded impressive to me), he'll throw the ball well and you'll complete more passes."

"Thanks a lot," I said. "I really appreciate it."

"No, thank you," he replied.

After I'd gotten out the door, I said to myself: Not only are people from around the campus and throughout the country trying to help me coach, but I've also got a guy in a mental ward trying to help me. Everyone cared and often at a very emotional level.

Maybe I should have written down the patient's formula. We could have used it.

Our strategy, if not our season, changed on the opening kickoff of the second half at Michigan. We had built a 9-3 lead on three John Carney field goals and were about to spring a surprise on the Wolverines that we hoped would make our offense more productive. We had predetermined that we'd wait until the second half and then switch from the I formation to a split backfield, forcing Michigan to adjust on the fly. With Steve Beuerlein at quarterback and Allen Pinkett and Alonzo Jefferson at the split-back spots, we were going to run and throw to the backs coming out of the backfield.

It was similar to what we had used successfully against Boston College in the Liberty Bowl. It took advantage of Alonzo Jefferson, a junior from Cardinal Newman High School in West Palm Beach, Florida, who had an unbelievable burst of speed, much like Pinkett. In fact, they were built alike. Both of them fireplugs, Alonzo a little smaller. Both were very strong runners, with big legs. I felt good about our scheme.

Then, on the kickoff, the ball took a nose dive in the wind. In scrambling to field it, Alonzo took a blow to the knee. He fumbled, and Dieter Heren recovered for Michigan. Three plays and 14 yards later, Michigan had a touchdown.

We lost the lead. Worse, we lost Alonzo, a player we had been counting on. We had to change our strategy; all in a matter of a split second.

We were still in the game, though. We even took a 12-10 lead, though we obviously were having problems in the offensive line. It permitted six sacks. The final blow, though, was a roughing-the-passer call against Wally Kleine on a third-and-seven incompletion from our 26-yard line. Wally tried to avoid Michigan quarterback Jim Harbaugh but couldn't. They got a second chance and took advantage of it.

Back in South Bend, Marlene was watching the nationally televised game in our new house, which we had, in part, because of an unusual set of circumstances.

"What happened," Marlene says, "is a friend of mine in real estate was hunting for a house for some people from Chicago, and they saw ours and asked about it. They didn't want to build their own. So my friend asked if we'd consider selling. We decided if we could get the price we wanted, we would sell and rent a free-standing condo from Jack Hickey.

"Then Gerry thought:'Maybe we should build one. We don't want people to get the idea we're leaving.' It was our dream home. I put a lot of time and effort into it and went $25,000 over my budget. It was a large house on a small amount of land on a golf course. It would have been a great retirement home."

I wasn't ready to retire just yet. I was only 50.

"So I'm watching the Michigan game," Marlene says, "and I thought: That's it. This house is history."

When I walked in the door, Marlene hit me with it:"So now I have to put *this* house up for sale."

"I was just devastated by that loss," she says.

It wasn't the way to begin the season. But I wasn't ready to put up the For Sale sign just yet.

We decided to try something different against Michigan State and, if it didn't affect the outcome of the game, it at least proved interesting. We inserted the entire No. 2 offensive unit into the game in the second quarter. We had decided after the Michigan game that the second offensive line deserved to play. Unlike defensive substitutions, a man here and a man there on offense tends to disrupt the continuity of a unit. So we put the whole bunch in, including sophomore quarterback Terry Andrysiak. I would like to announce that this innovation turned around the game. It didn't. Tim Brown did. He broke a 7-7 halftime tie with a 93-yard touchdown return on the second-half kickoff and we went on to a 27-10 victory. No one asked any more why Tim Brown returned kicks. In fact, in the NFL, playing for Oakland, he has returned more punts than any player in history.

It would be several weeks before I would become convinced that enough was enough, but to be honest, our season and my career all but ended during the next two weeks on the road. I don't have to tell you where we traveled, do I?

Purdue and Air Force.

I cannot explain what happened to us when we played these teams. We knew we were a better team, but nothing I said or did changed the fact we didn't play that way. Our losses were mental, not physical. Purdue's future NFL quarterback Jim Everett threw for 368 yards and three touchdowns in a 35-17 victory. We couldn't even beat them when we had 12 men on the field, which happened on a couple of occasions. That's poor coaching. Pure and simple.

Lee Corso, with whom I had been friends for many years, was in West Lafayette for the game, and afterwards he took time to talk with Marlene and tell her what his family had gone through when he was coaching at Indiana. It made her feel better to know that she and the kids were not alone in suffering with the coach/husband/father whom they loved.

As fate would have it, Father Hesburgh, who usually did not attend our away games, flew to the Air Force Academy with us because he had a meeting with Air Force officials. I wished he hadn't been in Colorado Springs to see this. Looking back, as Father Joyce pointed out, it isn't simply how many games you lose, but to whom and how the losses occur.

This was our fourth loss in a row to Air Force and resulted from—does this sound familiar?—a blocked field goal. This time, linebacker Terry Maki blocked John Carney's 37-yard attempt and A.J. Scott scooped up the ball and took it 77 yards for a touchdown. One player blocked to the outside on the field goal, another player blocked to the inside. Maki went between them and we were dead.

How bad was it?

Well, we had driven from our 41-yard line to the Air Force 2-yard line. Allen Pinkett, who had 142 yards on 31 carries, moved the ball with the help of fullback Frank Stams, the Akron St.Vincent-St. Mary player whom I had promised the opportunity to play running back. On first down from the two, Pinkett lost a yard. On second down, Pinkett, carrying, and Stams, blocking, went right on a sweep. The problem was, everyone else went left. Minus six. From the 9-yard line Steve Beuerlein dropped back to pass and threw the ball away to avoid being sacked. Sorry. Intentional grounding.

So instead of locking up a victory with a touchdown, we were kicking from the 27-yard line. Then, we didn't block correctly for the field goal.

In addition to our own errors, two players, backup guard Mike Perrino and starting guard John Askin, had become ill the night before with a gastrointestinal disorder. On the 2-yard line of that fateful failed drive, Perrino came running off the field ill and Askin, who replaced him, heard the right play but the wrong direction when he rushed onto the field and asked Steve Beuerlein at the line of scrimmage what the call was. He pulled and went one way. The other guard pulled and went the other way. They collided. So it didn't really matter which way Pinkett and Stams went. The blockers had blocked themselves. It sounds like a play the Three Stooges might have run if they were coaches. But it wasn't funny.

It was difficult enough to lose, but to lose doing dumb things was unforgivable. That may have been why at the airport waiting for our charter flight I had to field a call from a Chicago writer who had heard that I resigned after the game. Maybe he figured that I had to have resigned given that performance. I told him that his information was incorrect, but I knew that what had happened the last two weeks reflected on one person and only one. Me. It was a long plane ride home.

We won the next four games, all in Notre Dame Stadium, starting with 6-0, 19th-ranked Army (24-10), then USC (37-3), Navy (41-17) and Ole Miss (37-14). But, frankly, the victories could not erase the losses to Purdue and Air Force. I even got criticized for the manner in which we beat USC for the third year in a row—four if you don't count USC's Phantom Touchdown.

Though I recognized that the use of psychological ploys, such as the wearin' of the green, could be overdone, I had ordered green jerseys with a blue stripe on the sleeve again. Everyone was asking in the week before the game if we'd wear our green jerseys and I told them we would come out in the blue. Which we did.

We switched at halftime. The problem was, we already were leading, 27-0.

"Coach," Gene O'Neill said, "do you want to put the jerseys on?"

"Gene," I said, "I know we have a big lead, but this is a big game. I don't think we want to gamble. Let's do it."

I remembered watching Ara Parseghian's team take a similar lead over USC only to lose 55-24. We couldn't afford a second-half letdown. If I had any hope of remaining as coach, and I clung to a sliver of it like a shipwrecked man clinging to a wooden plank in the ocean, we could not lose to USC.

The jerseys did not generate the same euphoria they had two years earlier, but the players were excited and proud to wear them and played the second half in a way that reflected as much.

After the game, the media seized on the jersey switch and wanted to know if I was trying to rub it in on USC. I explained my concern, based on history, about a USC comeback. I don't think the answer satisfied them. It was as honest as I could be without dwelling on my precarious position as coach, which I would not do.

Questioning the coach, whether in the interview room or from the stands, has become more America's pastime than baseball. Sometimes, however, those posing the questions lack some of the facts, which is what happened during our Ole Miss victory.

The outcome never was in doubt but as I ran off the field at halftime, one fan in particular was taking me to task in language that even sailors don't use. What upset this gentleman was that we had been leading 17-0 with 10 seconds to go in the first half and were in position to score again when I called Steve Beuerlein to the sideline.

"Steve," I said, "we have time for two plays. We're going for the touchdown on the first one with a play-action pass. If the receiver isn't open, throw the ball into the stands. Just throw it away. We'll kick the field goal and go in 20-0."

We wanted the touchdown, because it would psychologically bury the Rebels. As the play-action pass unfolded, Steve spotted an open receiver. His opening didn't last. The Mississippi defense closed on the receiver, but Steve tried to squeeze a throw in anyway. It was intercepted.

I was not a happy coach and told Steve as much. But I also recognized why it happened. Steve Beuerlein is a competitor. He was trying to make the killer play. I understood. The guy in the stands didn't. He said I couldn't coach and did it without using a word of more than four letters. He didn't know that the player had done exactly the opposite of what he had been told to do.

Paul Harvey, friend and guardian, was running off the field with me and heard what the fan thought of me.

"These people are something else," Paul said.

"Paul, just ignore it. We know we were doing the right thing."

After the game the same guy was yelling: "Way to go, Coach. Great win."

"Paul," I said, "do you want to have some fun?"

"Sure."

So I went over to the guy and I shook his hand.

"What did you think of the team today?" I asked.

"Boy," he said, "they played well."

"They did, didn't they? That second half, we really took charge."

"You sure did."

"Well, thanks for your support."

"Coach, keep it going."

He never knew that I knew he had been the one cussing me up one side and down the other only two quarters earlier.

"I can't believe it," Paul said. "We must have beaten the point spread."

We could not, however, beat top-ranked Penn State, which did not need the advantage that its groundskeepers created for the Nittany Lions by taking the tarp off the field early in the morning during a rain storm. Joe O'Brien had contacted Penn State officials and arranged for the tarp to be left on until an hour before game time. We'd done the same thing the week before when Ole Miss coach Billy Brewer and I agreed that the teams deserved to play on a Notre Dame field in as good a condition as possible.

Because that was our expectation at Penn State as well, we left the motel an hour later than usual and had planned an abbreviated pregame warmup. As the players suited up, I walked out into the rain and asked the custodians when the tarp had been removed. Someone had sabotaged us.

When Joe Paterno came over to talk before the game, he acted as if nothing was wrong.

"You've really got it rolling," he told me. "Hang in there. You're going to be OK."

Right, with the help of my friends in the coaching fraternity.

"Coach," I said, "I'm really upset."

"What's wrong?"

"We contacted your people last night and had an agreement the tarp wasn't going to come up until an hour before the game and I know it has been off since 10 this morning."

"I can't control the groundskeepers," he said.

"Coach, you control the president of the university. Don't tell me you can't control the groundskeepers."

The field hurt Allen Pinkett, whose game depends on his ability to make quick cuts. He was limited to 61 yards on 12 carries. The field did not explain how poorly we played or how efficiently one of my former quarterbacks at Moeller, John Shaffer, went about beating us, 36-6. We had tried to recruit John to come to Notre Dame, but Steve Beuerlein committed to us first and we had been up front with John and told him that we were only going to take one quarterback in that recruiting class.

In the final home game against 17th-ranked Louisiana State, we nursed a 7-3 lead to the end of the fourth quarter before falling behind 10-7. A fumble recovery by senior tackle Eric Dorsey, who stripped the ball from LSU running back Dalton Hilliard with 1:50 remaining, gave us one last chance on the Tigers' 36-yard line.

On the first play, Beuerlein threw a perfect pass to Tim Brown. Tim was in full stride when the ball came in, right on his numbers. Uncharacteristically, Tim bobbled the ball and LSU strong safety Steve Rehage grabbed it and our hopes away.

As I was shaking hands with LSU coach Bill Arnsparger after the game, one of our assistants came running up to me and asked if I could come to the locker room right away.

"Tim Brown is really shaken up," he said. "I can't calm him down. He blames himself for the loss."

"This wasn't Tim's fault," I said. "There were so many different points at which we could have won. I'll talk to him."

When I got to the locker room, I found Tim in a corner, tears streaming down his face. This was one of the moments when I thought back to the lesson that Mark Zavagnin had taught me in my first season. Because I had unintentionally said the wrong thing to Mark when he dropped the chance for an interception and victory against Purdue, I would never say the wrong thing again to a player in these circumstances. I knew what Timmy needed.

I put my arm around him and told him he had played one heck of a game, which he had. He had run 18 yards for our touchdown and caught three passes.

"Tim," I said, "that dropped pass had nothing to do with winning and losing this game. It should have been won in the first half. We had a chance to put it away and didn't.

"I can name six or seven decisions that we coaches made that weren't good decisions and contributed to our loss. I don't want you to worry about this. You're a great football player who gives 100 percent, and I'm proud of you."

As I walked away from Tim, I knew for the first time that I had to walk away from Notre Dame. In that moment, I made up my mind to do something I had known might become necessary but had not given a second's thought.

Tim Brown's pain made me realize that it was time for me to face my own pain rather than let the players suffer in this way. They were pressing to win because of all the pressure on me. The media never let up. The players knew each game was a must-win situation. They weren't playing as well as they were capable of playing because of the turmoil. I think they had so much empathy for my situation that they took my pressure upon themselves.

At the post-game press conference, I never so much as hinted at what I had decided I had to do. The media, of course, asked me about my future, and I told them I wasn't concerned about that at the moment. I only wanted to think about our final game at Miami and ending the season with a win. We were 5-5, our worst record since Year One. The circle was complete and it formed a noose around my dream, now worn and tarnished gold.

When I got home, I sat down with Marlene and the children, including Gerry, who was visiting from the University of Dayton, and told them I had made a decision.

"It's best," I said, "if I step down as coach. It's best for the University. Best for you. Best for me. And best for the players."

I told them that I had a way in which I wanted to handle this and that they could not say anything to anyone until I talked to some people and told those at Notre Dame who had to know. They understood.

"But if you're stepping down," Marlene said, "then I want you to get out of coaching. You've coached the greatest high school in the country. You've coached the greatest university in the country. Now, why don't you go into business and make some money? You can't duplicate those places or those experiences."

Before her last word was out, the kids, in unison, objected: "No, Mom, Dad belongs in coaching."

That's how I felt, too. I love working with young people and perhaps my own children sensed that. Then, too, there was the feeling that I had not accomplished the things I set out to accomplish. I had let Notre Dame down. I couldn't do anything about the shortcomings that caused my failure at Notre Dame. But I could take all I had learned and apply it in another situation and make a fresh start.

"All right," Marlene conceded, recognizing a steamroller when one was staring her in the face. "But if you're going to stay in coaching, I want to be a part of the decision about the next place we go."

"Fair enough," I said.

Once again I found myself in need of advice. I called two people who had the pulse of the most important people at Notre Dame, Dr. Bill Sexton, University vice president in charge of development, and Art Decio, one of three fellows on the Board of Trustees, its highest honor.

I had become close to Bill Sexton, who was one of the top five men at the University. He knew what the biggest donors to Notre Dame thought and felt. When I told him that I was thinking about resigning in the next few days, he surprised me.

"Coach," he said, "you shouldn't do it. You should talk to Father Hesburgh and ask him for another year. I really feel he'll give it to you."

That was nice to hear, but I wasn't sure I wanted to put Father Hesburgh in that position. Nor could I get the tear-stained face of Timmy Brown out of my mind.

When I talked to Art Decio, he said something I'll never forget:

"Gerry," he said, "that's a decision that you have to make. You and you alone. Notre Dame will survive without you and Notre Dame will survive with you. But the decision has to come from you and not from your friends."

I thought that was real wisdom. What I knew was that I didn't want Notre Dame to merely survive. I wanted it to flourish, to be respected in every way and if I couldn't contribute to that respect, it was time to leave.

"When Gerry talked to me and asked how he should handle it," Decio says today, "I told him that he had exactly the right way: He was going to see Father Hesburgh and Father Joyce before they had to do something.

"But I'll tell you this: Gerry Faust wasn't bad for the University. He wouldn't be bad for anybody. He is a unique individual. I'm talking about the person. He's genuine. A very simple man. A God-fearing man from his toes to his nose. He truly likes and loves everyone, as we're supposed to do as Christians.

"I think if you threw a bucket of garbage in his face, he'd wipe his face off and hug you. You have to love a guy like that— separate from the football field."

That, of course, had become the issue. I might be a good person, a Notre Dame man, off the football field, but could I help a team win when it was on the field? Though I still believed with all my heart that I could, the record suggested otherwise, and it was difficult to argue with the record.

"When you get to know Gerry Faust," Art Decio says, "you have to like and love Gerry Faust. It would be hard for me to understand how anyone could not. A person like that, associated with Notre Dame in any capacity, would have to be an asset. Notre Dame is a special place. Yes, it is a fine academic institution. One of the tops in the country. *U.S. News & World Report* says that. But you can go to other places among the top-25 rated universities and get a good technical education. What makes Notre Dame special are the values, the Catholic character of the place, its ecumenical nature. We have Protestant theologians, Jewish theologians. Not just the big 'C' Catholics. And, in my opinion, Gerry is an example of that. How could anyone say that Gerry Faust, with his values, didn't add to Notre Dame? He did.

"Unfortunately, in the materialistic world we live in today, Notre Dame fans—and Notre Dame has a lot of fans who are subway alumni—judge those great Notre Dame football teams by wins and losses."

And I failed that judgment.

I told Art: "I'm going to Father Hesburgh and Father Joyce and tell them my decision, and then I'll let you know."

On Monday morning, I called Father Hesburgh only to learn that he was at a nuclear disarmament meeting in Maryland. His secretary, Helen Hosinski, gave me the phone number, which I tried all day Monday without success. I kept trying. I thought Father Hesburgh, as president of the University, should be the first person I told.

Finally, I reached him Tuesday morning in his hotel room at 8 o'clock.

"Father," I said, "this is Gerry."

"Gerry, call me back. I'm in the middle of Mass."

He was saying Mass in his room. So I called back in 15 minutes. It wasn't an easy wait.

"Father," I said, when I reached him, "I'm going to step down as football coach. I wanted you to be the first to know. I think this is best for the University. I think it's best for me. And I think it's best for the football program."

"Gerry," Father Hesburgh said, "you have my blessing."

"Father, please don't tell anybody. I want to tell Father Joyce myself."

"Gerry, I'll see you when I get back to campus."

One person down. It was only the beginning.

I knew that Father Joyce usually said Mass before going to his office about 10 a.m. and then worked until as late as midnight. So after my call to Father Hesburgh, I headed for the Administration Building. I had called Pat Roth, Father Joyce's secretary, and she said Father Joyce would be in. I told her I was coming over to see him.

As I drove through a fog to Father Joyce's office beneath the Golden Dome, the gray day seemed like fate to me. I pulled into the parking lot behind the Administration Building, got out of my car and looked up. I couldn't see the Blessed Mother or the Golden Dome. It was 10 in the morning. The day Notre Dame announced that I would replace Dan Devine as Notre Dame coach, the sun had glittered off that Golden Dome as if the symbol of my golden dream. That first day of spring practice, the sun again had been shining through the wind and the cold, creating in my heart the glow that those in love feel.

Now, the sun was gone.

On the second floor of the Administration Building, I walked into Father Joyce's anteroom and asked if I could see him for a few minutes.

"Sure," he said.

We went into his office and sat down.

"Father," I said, "I'm going to step down. I feel it's best for Notre Dame if you get a new football coach."

Father Joyce got up and said:

"Gerry, I was hoping you would do this."

It meant that he didn't have to call me in and tell me what I knew: It was over.

"Father," I said, "I told you when I took this job that I'd never hurt Notre Dame. I want to thank you for giving me this great opportunity. I talked to Father Hesburgh this morning. I felt that as president of the University, he should be the first to know."

"I agree with that, Gerry," Father Joyce said.

"But Father," I continued, "I wanted to tell you personally rather than having it come from Father Hesburgh, and I'd appreciate it if you wouldn't say anything to Mr. Corrigan. I'm going over to talk to him as soon as I tell my staff."

We talked for about 10 minutes more, and I told Father Joyce that if the rumors I had been hearing were true and he planned to hire George Welsh, the coach at Virginia, that he was getting an outstanding person. Father Joyce didn't say anything. He just gave me a quizzical look.

I thought: Maybe that's just a rumor. But from my experience, I thought it was safe to conclude that Father Joyce had begun planning to replace me after the season turned sour with the losses to Purdue and Air Force, that from that point on there might have been some preliminary work done, a feeling-out period, a checking for interest in the job if I were to leave. Notre Dame always had a list of people.

"I wanted badly to see him succeed," Father Joyce says. "We just felt sorry for Gerry. We can suffer losing football games for a certain period of time but when things weren't getting better, it became obvious that after his five years we weren't going to renew his contract. Everybody would have thought we were crazy.

"You're either successful or you aren't, and we couldn't call the shots for him, get other assistant coaches or anything else. He had to live and die on his record. But every year, Gerry was optimistic. So every year we kept hoping that he was right, that they would finally do something good and have a fine record. It never happened."

I think it was difficult for both Father Joyce and me in that room, as we confronted the truth of my unrewarded optimism. But as sad as I sensed Father Joyce was, I know there was a sense of relief. He didn't have to fire me.

When we had gotten through the part that made me want to cry, the admission that it would be better for Notre Dame if I left, I had to make two requests of Father Joyce, one professional, the other personal.

I asked that the assistant coaches' children who were attending Notre Dame be allowed to complete their educations, which at that time the University paid for, and I requested that the assistants be sent to the coaches' national convention to look for jobs and that if they didn't find any that they be paid until July.

"That's no problem," Father Joyce said.

I didn't think it would be. Notre Dame has a conscience. As for the personal favor, I knew it fell in a category above and beyond Notre Dame's obligation. I had to ask. It was important.

"Father," I said, "I have a son, Steve, who's a senior in high school and has been accepted by Notre Dame. With this change, I'm not going to have the money to send him to school here, but both Marlene and I would like for one of our children to graduate from the University."

I knew I was asking a lot, that Steve be treated as the son of a man who was still coaching at Notre Dame, that he be allowed to continue the dream, if in a different way.

"I'll have to talk to Father Hesburgh about Steve," Father Joyce said.

When I gathered my assistants, I was able to deliver the good news for their children along with the bad for them. I was moving fast. I told them I had 45 minutes before my regular Tuesday press conference at which I would announce my resignation and that first I had to go see Mr. Corrigan and tell him. I thanked them for their great efforts at Notre Dame and asked one last thing.

"I'd appreciate it," I told them, "if you'd give the rest of the week to the players here. I know you're going to be looking for jobs, but three or four days aren't going to make any difference. Let's put an effort into preparing for Miami. I'd like to see the se-niors go out in style. They deserve it."

I had decided not to say anything directly to the players about my resignation. I would come to regret this decision, but I didn't know that then. It was, after all, the first time I'd ever quit. My hope was that I could make their final week of the season and, for the seniors, of their college careers, as normal as possible. I should have known better. Once again, my decision and its consequences would overtake and overshadow all other issues.

John Heisler was the associate sports information director in those days and ran the press conferences. I hadn't told him that the first thing I was going to say wouldn't be about Miami but about my decision to step down. He says that someone pulled him aside a few minutes before the press conference began and told him what was about to happen, but it didn't look as if anyone had. When I said I was resigning, his jaw dropped to his shoe tops.

"Gene Corrigan did grab me literally 15 minutes before this was going to happen so I wouldn't be blindsided," Heisler says. "Gerry may have been mulling this over, but this was not some-thing that anybody had expected. Brad Palmer from Channel 7, the ABC affiliate in Chicago, was sitting next to me and just happened to be there that day with no idea this was going to occur. He couldn't believe it. The looks on some of the people's faces were unbeliev-able.

"It shocked the heck out of most everybody in the room. I'll guarantee you. Some of the guys went running to the telephones. That began a week that was pretty bizarre as far as not knowing what was going to come next."

Maybe the person who wasn't surprised was my friend and John's boss, Roger Valdiserri.

"I could see that what was happening was taking its toll on Gerry," Valdiserri says. "When I walked into the locker room after the game before his resignation, he was there with his head in his hands. It was the most disconsolate scene I'd ever seen. I felt so bad for him. At that moment I said to myself: He's going to resign. He was just hurting so bad. Hurting for Notre Dame. It was tough to witness."

When Roger came upon me, I'd just talked with Tim Brown and tried to comfort him, to make him understand that the loss to LSU was not his fault, no matter how it might have seemed. I knew it was over. I knew what I had to do. And Roger was right. It hurt. It hurt more than anything had ever hurt in my life.

I answered the media's questions at the press conference, but I didn't come close to ending them. It was only the beginning of what would become the longest day of my professional life.

"We were getting so many phone calls from people who were caught unaware," says John Heisler, "that as difficult as it was to ask Gerry to go through it again, we had to. The national media were jumping on airplanes and into cars and coming to South Bend. We had every Cincinnati television station coming up for live reports. The rest of the world had a great interest. They wanted to know more, which says something about both Gerry and Notre Dame.

"I could have told them: 'Here's my tape recorder. You can listen to what he said and think that was the end of it. But it wouldn't have been the end."

I understood what John and Roger were facing. I had calls from a couple of the Cincinnati writers—my friend Denny Dressman and Enos Pennington. I felt close to both of them and believed I owed them a personal interview. I knew people in Cincinnati would be interested. But when Roger and John asked if I could do another press conference that Tuesday night, I nearly balked.

"I don't want to, Rog," I said. "I want it to be over with. I already had one press conference."

"Ger," Roger said, "you need to do this."

So I did it.

"Before he did, however," Heisler says, "I walked into his office to check on some of the specifics. I can tell you it was an emotional time for him. There were tears. I'm sure there had been many of them when he was by himself. This just happened to be one of those times when someone was around. But I'll tell you, Gerry was a trouper about this."

I didn't feel like a trouper.

Before meeting the second wave of media, I had to go to practice. Word of my resignation was all over campus but I never said a word to the players. The very people I should have been talking to, I wasn't. I just wanted to get the focus off me and back on the Miami game. It was impossible. I would know this the second time this happened in my coaching career. The focus was going to be on Gerry Faust's last game. There was no dodging it. No shifting it.

When I got to the Monogram Room in the Athletic and Convocation Center for the second press conference, the place was packed. There were as many people there as had been present the day I got the job. Every Chicago television station. All the networks. The writers from the nation's larger papers. They were all there, and I went through it again for them. It was tough. Tougher than in the morning.

I didn't want to leave Notre Dame. I loved the University and everything it stands for, but I knew that this was the right thing to do. Being right doesn't mean not crying. I got through it. Somehow.

"He was disappointed in himself," Father Riehle says, looking back. "I had long, long talks with Gerry and became very close to him. And, if I may use the expression, Gerry hung on the cross here for five years.

"Here's this guy who has had this dream all his life and it finally comes true. It's not his fault. It's something he wanted, but someone else made the appointment. I heard him say: 'I let Notre Dame and my family down.' I heard Lou Holtz say the same thing: 'The only thing I'm concerned about is that I don't let Notre Dame down.'

"Well Notre Dame is so much bigger than any one of us that it's unbelievable. But you can develop that mentality, that hey, I let it down. You're just one person, and I'm absolutely convinced that that Lady up on the Dome watches over us and protects this place.

Just the natural growth of the University, the phenomenal history of it. It's living proof of it. All of us are players in it.

"But in Gerry's case, here was this man who really did hang on the cross because he had this great ambition and it wasn't fulfilled, but I never heard him complain about it. I think he came to understand what life is. That it's not always the way we want it to be. That it's an awful lot of carrying the crosses that come to us, of learning how to handle those. I think that is the reality of Gerry Faust. I think that is what he brought to all of us at Notre Dame, and I have a great respect for the man."

Being at Notre Dame didn't feel like carrying a cross. I took a positive approach. I felt the hard work would pay off. That's why I never thought of stepping down prematurely. I kept waiting for the payoff. I knew it wasn't going to come when I saw Timmy Brown wracked with the burden of defeat in the locker room after the LSU game. Until I saw Timmy in tears, I never thought of resigning, although I knew my days might be numbered. After I saw him and talked to him and put my arm around him, I never had a second thought about the decision. It came to me in an instant but had been years in the making.

As usual, I prepared no statement for that evening press conference. If ever there was a time to speak from the heart, this was it, because my heart was overflowing. I just told the truth about how I felt. Some of the media may have thought I'd been fired. I wasn't. No one ever said: It's over. Though, if I had waited, I'm sure someone would have. If I'd been fired I'd have said so. Akron fired me. No bones about it. It's part of coaching. But I never thought about Notre Dame firing me. Not even when we were losing to Purdue and Air Force. That's how positive a person I am. Positive to a fault, I guess.

When the second press conference had ended, I felt glad I had put myself through it. It had given me the opportunity to say again how much Notre Dame means to me and how grateful I am to have had the opportunity to be the Notre Dame football coach. A dozen years later, that appreciation has only deepened. Of 25 men who have coached Notre Dame, only nine have coached the Irish for more than five seasons. I'm in the five-year club—Jesse Harper (1913-17), Terry Brennan (1954-58) and me (1981-85)—and no one in it won a national championship. On the other hand, among those coaches with more than five seasons, only one, Elmer Layden (1934-40), failed to win a national championship. The others—

Knute Rockne, Frank Leahy, Ara Parseghian, Dan Devine and Lou Holtz—touched football's holy grail.

When I got home, I explained the day, briefly, to Marlene. I just said that it went well and left it at that. Marlene knew how I felt about Notre Dame and its people.

"Even though we didn't win as many games as people wanted us to," Marlene says, "people treated us in a first-class way. On the whole, they remained supportive. The majority of people in South Bend were in our corner because they knew us and liked us as people. But we all felt bad. Notre Dame was used to winning, and we weren't winning in that style.

"Despite everything, I can remember only one person whom we had thought was a friend who just dropped us. This guy used to call me every Sunday night when he knew Gerry wasn't home. He would keep me on the phone for an hour, talking about Notre Dame football and what Gerry should have done, what he didn't do. He did this for five years. After we left Notre Dame, we never heard from him again."

As it turned out, Marlene knew all too well what to expect. She'd known since I walked into our new home after losing the first game of the season to Michigan and she said: "Now we have to sell."

But as much as Marlene knew about football and me, I hoped that she wouldn't guess what was going through my mind that Tuesday night of my resignation. I would have liked to have stayed at Notre Dame in some capacity, but I wasn't going to ask. I felt it best that I leave, best that the new coach have free reign. That created another problem. I didn't have a job.

I had a family to support. I was going to have three children in college. What was I going to do? In that single evening, I came to understand what other people go through when they suddenly find themselves without a job. I'd never faced this. I'd always been in demand. Now, I realized, there might be no demand for me at all.

As disturbing as that might have been to me personally, it was even more worrisome because of my obligations as a parent and as the family breadwinner. There's pride. I hadn't gotten the job done and I knew it. But this was more elemental than that. This was: How could I help my family? I didn't want to worry Marlene and the children, but I was worried. I needed a job.

Oddly, that fact turned into one of the lighter moments of the second press conference. At one point, I announced that if anyone out there was looking for coach, I was available.

"It's easy to contact me," I told the media. "Just call Notre Dame. I need a fresh start."

Everyone laughed. But, hey, a little free national advertising never hurt an out-of-work coach. I repeated my Job-Wanted commercial on national television prior to the Miami game. I don't know whether that affected Notre Dame and caused someone not to ask me to stay in another capacity or not. It didn't matter. It was the right decision to leave, to be out of Lou Holtz's way. I was even more convinced of that a couple of weeks after I had resigned and Lou was at Notre Dame.

I'd gone to Mass at Sacred Heart Church, and Lou and his wife, Beth, were there. After Mass we were talking and a guy walked up to us and told me how sorry he was that I was leaving. I thanked him for his kindness and introduced him to Lou.

"Coach Holtz," the man said, "it's nice to meet you. Now, Coach Faust, can I get a picture with you?"

"Sure," I told him. "But how about getting Coach Holtz in the picture, too? It'd be great. The old coach and the new coach."

"No," Lou said, "he wants just the two of you."

"Get in here," I prodded Lou.

"That would be great," the man said.

So we took the photo together. But it brought out, in a small way, the awkward moments that would have been inevitable if I had remained at Notre Dame. Lou didn't want to impose himself on the situation when the man was asking for a photo with me. On the other hand, I didn't think the new coach should be put in the position of just standing there, watching.

That's how I felt in the hours after I announced my resignation, like a man standing around watching the world go by, not quite a part of it. I was so much luckier than many people who lose their jobs, though. My period of doubt and feeling as if I no longer had an anchor in my professional life was brief.

When I got to my office on the Wednesday morning following my resignation, the first call I received was from William R. Cotter, the president of Colby College in Waterville, Maine. He offered me the head coach's job at Colby, which plays Division III football. I told him that he could not believe what his call meant to me. It was the kindest gesture I could have hoped to have received. It made me realize that there were people who would still want me, who still believed in me as a coach. I knew I would be able to support my family.

I told Dr. Cotter that I didn't know what direction my career was going to take because I was concentrating on getting ready for the final game of the season against Miami but that I would get back to him as soon as I started sorting it out.

Because he made that call, I'll never forget Dr. Cotter. To know that someone wants you is one of the greatest feelings. I've been lucky in that way. Not 15 minutes after Dr. Cotter's call, I received one from Milt Kantor. Whereas Dr. Cotter and I were strangers, Milt and I went way back. We were Dayton guys, Milt a Roosevelt High School graduate who went on to become one of the most brilliant men in the grocery business.

When I was just getting started at Moeller High School in the 1960s, I needed to supplement my income with summer jobs. As many great rewards as there are in working in the Catholic school system, lots of money is not among them. I knew this, of course. My dad had taught all his life in Catholic schools. I accepted it. But I did need to work in the summer to make ends meet. So I called Milt at Rinks Supermarkets and asked if he could hire me.

"Well," Milt said, "I can hire you as a stock boy."

"That's fine, Milt. I'll do anything."

I wasn't the only one who felt this way. Ken Griffey Sr., who played for the Cincinnati Reds, also stocked shelves for Milt during the off-season. It was a different time. I don't believe Ken Griffey Jr., who followed his father into major league baseball, has to seek off-season work in grocery stores. Working for Milt Kantor, however, was no hardship. Just the opposite. It was another opportunity to learn about people.

I worked for a man about 10 years older than I was. He was in charge of the back room where the shipments arrived. One day, we were unloading a truck when I noticed this guy take a case of canned goods and slide it under a table instead of stacking it. I can be naive, but I'm not stupid. I knew what he was doing.

"Hey," I said, quietly, "we work for a good guy, don't we?"

"Yeah," he said. "Milt's the best."

"He's given you a job, and he's given me a job. I'm not going to say anything this time, but you take those canned goods and put them where they belong."

He cussed me out but put the canned goods back. For the next week, I got the crap jobs, things like cleaning maggots out of garbage cans. I never complained. I never said a word to Milt.

Every two weeks when Milt paid us, he would call me over the public address system in the store and ask me to come to his office. It was a ritual. We'd sit and talk football, especially Moeller football, which he loved, and then Milt would give me my paycheck. I'd thank him and go back to work. After the incident with my boss in the back room, however, Milt reached into his pocket and pulled out a hundred dollar bill.

"Here," Milt said, "take this."

"Milt, I can't take that," I said. "You pay me a fair wage."

"No," he said, "I want you to have it. Buy something. Take your kids out."

"Milt, I can't take it. You're a friend and you gave me a job. I don't deserve this money."

"Yeah, you do," Milt said. "You're loyal."

"What do you mean?"

"The guy came up," he said, "and told me the whole story."

"What story?" I asked.

He repeated it just the way it had happened.

"That's true," I said. "I'm glad he told you. That shows that you have a good employee who just made a mistake."

"Yeah," Milt said, "but I think he came up because he thought you were going to say something."

"I told the guy I wouldn't. Do you mind if I say something to him about our conversation?"

"No," Milt said, "go ahead."

So I went to the guy and told him I'd just found out he had gone to Milt. I told him again that I hadn't talked to Milt. From that point on, we were friends, but never like Milt and I were friends. The last thing Milt said to me that summer was: "If you ever need a job, you've got one. You can work for me anytime."

I left and went back to my teaching and coaching and could not have realized that 20 years later I would be without a job and the first person who would call from outside the education community would be Milt Kantor, who now owns Victory Wholesale, the largest food diverter in the country. They buy food on the West Coast, bring it to the Midwest and sell it at lower prices than other companies can.

Milt not only offered me a job but also a salary that, excluding the perks, was higher than the one I was being paid at Notre Dame. I felt great, and I've always remembered that feeling and tried to help as many people as I can when they need to find work.

I bet during the last 15 years I've tried to help 400 to 500 people get jobs and succeeded with perhaps 200. I enjoy doing it, because I remember how I felt when I didn't have a job.

I told Milt that he had always been a great friend and always would be, but I wanted to stay in coaching. It was comforting to know, though, that if that didn't work out, I had another career horizon.

During the week of my resignation and as we were preparing for Miami, I received two or three more calls about jobs. Before I finally made a decision, I had heard from 13 schools and eight of them were ready to put offers on the table. I eliminated some because of their location and size but one that intrigued me and made me certain that I'd find another place in coaching started with a call from Bill Kleine, the father of our defensive tackle, Wally. Bill, the president of Permian Oil in Midland, Texas, said that one of his best friends happened to be the chairman of the Board of Trustees of Rice. His friend wanted to know if I would be interested in becoming Rice's football coach and athletic director. I said I would be. It sounded good. If I had to fire the football coach, he'd still have a job.

It didn't take long for me and everyone else to learn who would have my job at Notre Dame. On Wednesday, the day after I resigned, we were getting ready to leave for Florida. It was Thanksgiving weekend and because there would be no classes the rest of the week, we left early and would complete our preparation in Fort Lauderdale, where George Steinbrenner had generously agreed to let us use the New York Yankees' spring training facility. George Kelly, our linebacker coach, came running down the hallway with the news.

"Coach," he said, "Lou Holtz is the new head coach."

I almost passed out. I really thought it would be George Welsh. That's how much I knew. The question of who knew what and when is an interesting one. There is more than one version of the story. In one way or another, though, they all mesh with my experience of Notre Dame hiring me. Father Joyce approached me with the idea that an opening might exist, depending on Dan Devine and his wife's health. They talked to me more seriously after Dan announced on that preseason NFL game that 1980 would be his last season at Notre Dame. But they offered nothing. They hired me and announced it immediately after Moeller's season ended but before the Irish had played in the Sugar Bowl. It isn't Notre Dame's habit to wait.

Four years after I resigned I asked Lou about the timing of his hiring. Coming so quickly on the heels of my resignation, it made it look as if Lou, who was coaching Minnesota, had been approached before I resigned and was waiting in the wings. It didn't matter. The change was coming, one way or the other, and plans had to be made. Still, I was curious.

One report said that Gene Corrigan had been seen having coffee with Lou before we played Purdue. In which case, Marlene's instinct that the dream was over at Michigan may have been shared by Mr. Corrigan.

Lou, however, told me that he was first contacted on the Tuesday night after I had resigned. Father Joyce told him that if he wanted the job, it was his. He told him what the offer was. He told him what he could and couldn't do at Notre Dame. No negotiating. Here's the offer. Take it or leave it. Father Joyce asked for an answer by noon the next day. I never had any doubt that that was the way Notre Dame approached Lou. But other people had doubts.

The flight to Miami on Wednesday night proved different from any I'd ever taken. Everyone was talking about the new coach. Players. Assistant coaches. Everyone. Rather than relieving the minds of the players, the announcement of Lou seemed to prey on them. They knew Lou was a very successful coach, one of the better ones in college football. They didn't know where they stood, or what this last game might mean in that regard, and I'm sure it concerned them. The assistant coaches, most of whom didn't know Lou well, were wondering whether or not he might consider them for his staff. Everyone had been hit with a one-two punch. First, my resignation. Then, Lou's hiring.

On Thanksgiving we continued the practice of sharing part of the day with Notre Dame alumni. This time, of course, it was the South Florida alumni. Before, it had been those around Los Angeles. The result was the same. It was a great experience. I went with three players—Flash Gordon, Reggie Ward and freshman quarterback Steve Belles from Phoenix—to the home of my friends, Don and Jeannie Dorini. Everyone was so kind to me, and I was upbeat, not down in the dumps, especially after the players with me told me how much they'd miss me. They couldn't know how much I was going to miss all of them.

On Friday, after a light workout at the Yankees' facility, we followed a tradition that I had brought with me from Moeller. Following the final practice of their college careers, the seniors would walk along a line of their teammates, shaking hands, talking about all they had shared. At the end of the line, the assistant coaches wished the seniors good luck and thanked them for what they had given to Notre Dame. Then the seniors came to me, the last man.

I talked to them as a group and then individually. They were a great group: Allen Pinkett, Milt Jackson, Mike Larkin, Tony Furjanic. I could go on and on. This was the hardest part: Perhaps they could have wanted a better coach, but I could never have asked for better players.

Leaving the field, television broadcaster Brent Musburger came over with his son and I talked with them, and then something happened that surprised me. Phil Hersh from the *Chicago Sun-Times* approached me.

"Coach," he said, "I just wanted to wish you the best of luck."

I put my arm around the man who had written the most devastating story of my Notre Dame career and we continued walking.

"Phil," I said, "I appreciate that. I hope everything goes well for you in your life."

"Coach," Phil said, "I've got to talk to you."

"Sure. What is it?"

"Coach," he said, "I really respect you."

That stunned me. Based on what he had written, not only about my coaching but also about the kind of man I am—a heartless hypocrite, according to some of his player sources—I thought he had no respect for me at all.

"You never held that story against me," he continued, "never even said anything to me about it."

"Well, Phil," I said, "since you've brought it up, I'll be up front with you. It was devastating to me. You have to do your job and I have to do mine. I understand that. The problem I had is that I felt there were some half-truths in the story and then I had three of the players you quoted say that what was written didn't come out as they had intended. Regardless, it's over. I've forgotten about it. I don't hold anything against you, and I appreciate that you would say something about it now."

I think we parted as friends.

That Friday I received another phone call from a university, this one from a trustee at Youngstown State University. I think he had caught my second video position-wanted infomercial. I'd tossed it into a Thanksgiving interview with ESPN.

"We've all got a lot to be thankful for," I said on ESPN. "I'm thankful that I had the opportunity to be at Notre Dame for five years. I don't regret it a bit. And by the way, I'm looking for a coaching job. If there is anybody out there listening who's interested in a football coach, just contact me."

Youngstown did.

Remarkably, Youngstown and the others were still interested after the Miami game, which Steve Beuerlein said the players wanted to turn into Win-One-For-The-Gerry. It didn't work out as well as Win-One-For-The-Gipper. Miami blew the game open early and simply outclassed us, 58-7. How classy it was to put 21 points on the scoreboard in the fourth quarter was debatable, according to my friend Father Riehle.

"Don't you go shake that SOB's hand," he said as I prepared to cross the field to congratulate Jimmy Johnson. "He doesn't deserve it."

"I'm going," I said. "It's the Notre Dame way."

And that's what we told our players: Be Notre Dame men. Shake their hands. And they did.

In the locker room after our prayer, I went around to every player and thanked each one and wished him good luck. As I hugged each player, many of them told me how sorry they were they couldn't win my last game. I told them not to worry about it. The ones I felt bad for were the seniors. I figured, given the telephone calls I had received, that I had another day to coach. This could have been their last day of football.

My final post-game press conference proved another surprise. I thought I was going to have to explain the 58-7 beating we'd taken, and I dreaded it. Instead, the media concentrated on whether Miami had needlessly run the score up on us and I ended up defending Jimmy Johnson. They wanted me to say I was upset with Jimmy. I wasn't, and I'm not to this day. I think he's an excellent coach. Would I coach and react as he does? No. But everybody has to live by their own principles.

On Sunday, we attended a communion breakfast that the Notre Dame alumni held for us on Miami Beach. After losing as we did, it wasn't easy to go. I should have known, though, that these Notre

Dame people would do everything possible to make us feel good about ourselves.They even presented me with a plaque of appreciation for my five years as coach.That floored me.They must have had it engraved before the Miami game. But that's the way Notre Dame people are. How many coaches could resign with a record that was not one of the better ones at a university and have an alumni group honor them? Only at Notre Dame. People don't understand how unique it is.

To complete this otherwise disaster of a trip, we had a landing problem. Instead of landing in South Bend, we almost wound up in heaven. It was snowing hard as we neared touch-down on the South Bend runway. About three-quarters of the way down the runway, I turned to Father Riehle and said:"Father, we're not going to make it.We're going off the runway."

I had landed on this runway as many as four or five times a week. I knew every inch of it.

"What?" Father said, turning to me.

As he spoke, the plane lifted off again and we flew on to Chicago where we landed successfully but had to wait for buses and then endure a two-hour ride home. By the time I reached my house, I have to admit that I was about two quarts low on optimism. I hadn't wanted Marlene or any of the children to go to Florida. I thought it would be just too emotionally draining for them. But Marlene had watched the game on TV.

"Gerry," she said,"you've got to look at this.You may be down, but this is what the media feel about you."

She had taped the closing segment to that terrible final loss. It included a moment on the sideline in the fourth quarter. I'd pulled the seniors toward the end of the game and let the young players have some experience. On the sideline I was talking to the seniors and thanking them. I had my arm around Allen Pinkett, who had had such a marvelous career, and was telling him how glad I was that he had come to Notre Dame.

"Coach," he said, "it was a great four years. I just wish we could have done better today."

Then Allen's smile lighted up what otherwise might have been a dark moment. And over it all, the producers of this segment had played a song emotionally appropriate for this farewell.

As I watched it, I started to cry and my spirits began to rise. What was really important to me is not what those who knew best —the players, the people of Notre Dame—thought of me as a coach but how they felt about me as a person. Deep down, any coach feels he's a good coach. But the one thing that you want more than anything, at least I do, is to be respected as a person of integrity and ethics.

On the Monday after Thanksgiving, less than a week after I resigned, I began moving from my office to one in the back of the ACC, near Father Riehle, Col. Stephens and Moose Krause. It felt odd. I was still at Notre Dame, but I was no longer coach.

"I know an awful lot of men," Father Riehle says, "who would not have been able to handle all that Gerry did. There are people here who might say he was a lousy coach but a good man. Based on wins and losses that might be true. Based on what he did with players, that is something entirely different. People say he's a good father, a loving person, a man concerned about others. That's why they respect him.

"I know people who say: 'Who cares about the role model?' Well, I think a role model is so important that it's unbelievable. I don't feel that a kid, because of Gerry's emphasis, thought football was any less important. Anybody who could see Gerry's reaction after a loss would certainly know how important football was to him. I had an opportunity to see a lot of that."

Just because football finishes third to faith and family doesn't mean I don't care. I did. Maybe I cared too much, tried too hard and the pressure I heaped on myself buried not only me but also the players and coaches around me. I don't know. I do know that when I sat down with Lou Holtz and Gene Corrigan and we closed the door and I spent two hours telling Lou what I'd learned about Notre Dame, its people and coaching at the greatest place in the world, I got an unexpected response.

Lou had a lot of questions and they were more thoughtful than mine had been to Dan Devine, reflecting, I think, Lou's vast college experience compared to my dearth of it. I answered from the heart. I held nothing back. I wanted Lou to succeed in a way I had not, because if he did, Notre Dame would be succeeding. For six months, Lou called me every three or four weeks with questions. That cemented our relationship. It made me feel good that he would ask, and maybe the answers helped him in some way. I know Lou helped restore some of my confidence that had been chipped away.

"Gerry," he said, "don't ever second guess yourself as a head coach. You're an excellent coach. Your work ethic. Your coaching. Everything was done right. You just had a lot of bad breaks."

Lou said the one mistake I made, and I would agree with him completely, was in not recruiting enough speed. We weren't quick enough at certain positions to compete against some of the schools we had to play. Miami, for instance.

I should have known that. I had had enough lessons while coaching in high school. When I was at Moeller and we would play Cincinnati Princeton, Princeton would make mistakes but overcome them with speed. We countered that by just hammering them, by not making mistakes. That's how we beat them.

We couldn't win that way at Notre Dame. Just hammering an opponent doesn't work. And even when a college team doesn't commit unforced errors, the opponents are good enough to force a number of mistakes.

In the days and weeks after my resignation, people dropped by to wish me luck, and letters poured in. I received more than 3,500. Some came from the most famous and successful coaches in the country—Bill Walsh of the San Francisco 49ers, Tom Osborne of Nebraska—others from people whom I had never met. There wasn't one negative letter. Perhaps 10 of them suggested they were glad I wouldn't be coaching Notre Dame anymore but that the writer would miss me as a person. The rest were even more supportive, and they meant the world to me. Let me share a few of them in the hope that they reveal what I think is an important truth: Not everyone measures success simply by wins and losses:

Bill Walsh, San Francisco 49ers—"We have chosen a profession that is inherently inequitable and can expect at any time to be victimized in any number of ways. Just wanted to write and remind you, you are one of the finest coaches in the game and have been held in the highest regard by your colleagues."

Vi Furjanic, mother of senior linebacker Tony Furjanic— "Thank you for recruiting Tony and giving him the opportunity to get his education from Notre Dame and to play football also. This is not only the dream/desire of many young men but it sure is *my* dream come true. Coach Faust, we wish you the very best in whatever the future has in store for you. ...You are an asset to whomever you will be with. God has blessed you and I know He will continue to...."

Tom Osborne, Nebraska football coach— "...Just a short note to let you know that I admire very much the positive attitude and genuine Christian demeanor that you have displayed through a good deal of adversity and some rather unfair criticism. I ... want you to know that you certainly have a friend and admirer in me."

Rusty Lisch, former Notre Dame quarterback—"Your love of Our Lord, your devotion to Mary will not wane as He sends you crosses (in whatever form), but will be opportunities to come close to Him and his life of suffering. Coach, you seem to be a very good instrument of what He is asking of us.... Everybody loves a 'winner.' Your spiritual intonations into the football circles are, to some people, great if you win ballgames; if you don't win, your convictions, ideals become an obstacle to winning. Ultimately, God will and does see us in our true worth and certainly judges differently than the passing fickle sentiments of the world."

The Rev. James F. McQuade, Paulist Fathers—"No matter what is said and written, you are a winner! Appreciated your taking the time for lunch with me and some other priests at the Clergy Institute at James Hall during the Fall of 1983."

Ann Landers, syndicated columnist—"We've never met but I know you well through Ted Hesburgh, one of my dearest friends. Although you didn't produce many victories for Notre Dame, you did something more important. You conducted yourself like a gentleman, kept the standards high, never whined, never complained, never passed the buck and always behaved in a way that brought honor to Notre Dame. In my book, you are a winner."

Richard Nixon, former president of the United States—"As a long-time football fan, may I express my admiration and respect for your conduct at Notre Dame. The way you handled your critics was an inspiration to your fellow citizens, young and old....By demonstrating class and poise when losing, you showed you were a winner."

Martin Sheen, actor—"You demonstrated far more courage and strength of character in defeat than any coach has ever shown in victory."

The Rev. Ted Hesburgh, president of Notre Dame—"Everybody has remarked how beautifully the change-over took place and that's the way it should be. You should receive a good deal of credit for this and your own sensitivity in the matter."

Bill Corbett, Notre Dame pilot and friend—"I kept hoping that it was all a bad dream, that our days here in South Bend really were not over, that I was not going to lose one of the best friends that I ever had... We will miss you and your family terribly...(but) please, for all our sakes, go into your new job with the promise that you will be firm with your new charges, that you will discipline them and demand obedience and respect from them. You had the (latter) from the Irish but they took advantage of you too often."

William E. Simon, former Secretary of the Treasury— "I know that your decision must have been a gut-wrenching one for you and my heart and friendship go out to you. I salute you for doing an outstanding job under extraordinarily difficult conditions and I thank you for having been a good friend to me. No matter what changes may take place in your life, and mine, that friendship will be a constant."

Josiah Bunting III, former president, Hampden-Sydney College; current superintendent, Virginia Military Institute— "You're a hell of a guy, and you have my great admiration. Your conduct— your composure—in the face of Miami's reprehensible behavior last Saturday set a standard that I have not seen equaled among members of your profession. You will leave with your players, forever, the memory of grace under pressure by a man whose stature will never wane in their minds."

Wally Kleine, Notre Dame defensive tackle—"I remember growing up in Midland, Texas, always cheering for the Irish, wearing ND T-shirts, bragging about the tradition and just loving Notre Dame. I would lay awake at night and dream of becoming a Notre Dame football player.... I'll never be able to thank you enough for giving me this wonderful opportunity—this chance of lifetime. I've learned a great deal from you, Coach. I've learned to care and to love, to work hard and to face the challenge and, above all, to keep reaching for the stars and to be forever optimistic. I'll admit that there were times when I might have disagreed with one of your decisions or wished that you would have done something differently, but that's only natural. I have always respected what you stand for. You stand for everything a man should be—honest, loving, caring, devoted, hard-working and many more fine qualities. It's too bad that coaches are judged on their win-loss record, because even though that record was not what we would have liked, your record as a man is 100 percent winner. I've been very proud and happy to have been able to spend four years with you. I feel very fortunate in that not only are you my coach, you are my friend forever. I love you."

Robert I. H. Hammerman, chief judge, Circuit Court, Baltimore—"As one who is not a fan of Notre Dame, I have always been a fan of yours and have greatly admired all that you have stood for and taught during your five years at Notre Dame and in the many years before that....You are one of the great people of this country, and I know that wherever you may now go you will continue to impart inspiration and values to American youth and to all of our society."

That was the question, the decision that lay immediately ahead: Where do I go now? I knew what I wanted to do. I wanted to coach. I wanted to prove I could win. But more than anything, I wanted to make a difference, to be to other football players what Wally Kleine said I had been to him. That is, after all, why I became a coach. It is why most coaches do what they do, at least in the beginning, before ambition seizes them and the tradeoffs in priorities begin.

In my most difficult professional moment, strangers and friends alike lifted me with their kind and generous words in the way no victory ever could. This was lasting. Especially Wally's final three words: I love you.

Well, Wally, I love you, too—you and so many others.

12

■ DECISIONS, DECISIONS ■

 Fog changed the course of my career. Not the fog my detractors thought I lived in on gamedays, but a real fog. The sky was pea soup. It prevented Marlene from making a trip that could have altered the next decade of our lives. But even the way it worked out, and with all the problems, I can't complain.

"I think God was trying to tell me something," Marlene says.

It was a crazy, mixed-up time. Different universities calling. Trips to check out the possibilities. It all happened so fast.

In the middle of our search for a new job and home, Marlene was scheduled to visit Marshall University in Huntington, West Virginia. The governor of West Virginia had called her. They were sending a plane. I'd already made one visit to Huntington and even though I had reservations about going to a I-AA program, I felt the chemistry at Marshall was right for success. When Marlene failed to get off the ground, so did any possibility of a move to Marshall.

South Bend was fogged in. The plane couldn't land. Marlene canceled the trip. With that, our destiny was changed, even if we didn't realize it.

"I feel bad about that now," Marlene says. "I think about it all the time. I think Gerry could have won right away at Marshall and gone on to bigger and better things."

Instead, I wound up consumed by the most difficult job of my career.

I began to consider jobs that resulted from my resignation at Notre Dame only after two banquets, one honoring the 1985 Notre

Dame team and another paying tribute to Moose Krause, former Notre Dame athletic director.

Though I was no longer the Irish coach, I asked Mr. Corrigan if I could attend the College Football Hall of Fame Banquet in New York at which Moose was to be honored and Greg Dingens, one of our players, was to receive an academic award. I wanted to be there for Moose, but as so often happens, when a person does something for someone else, it ended up being at least as fulfilling a moment for me. Two incidents occurred that lessened the blow of losing the job that I had lived for all my life.

In addition to Moose Krause, the Hall of Fame was honoring Paul Brown, my old friend from Cincinnati who said something in his speech that reminded me that we had one important thing in common. What Paul Brown said was that the greatest years of his life had not been with the Cleveland Browns, the Cincinnati Bengals or Ohio State University. They had been with the Massillon Tigers.

As I sat and listened to Paul's words and reflected on them, it hit me: Yeah, just like Moeller. The five years I spent at Notre Dame were the greatest of my life. But the 21 I had spent at Moeller allowed me to do the greatest good for the most young people.

The other rewarding moment occurred when longtime sportscaster Chris Schenkel, who was serving as master of ceremonies, introduced the head coaches at the banquet. There were about 50 or 60 coaches present and I was three-quarters of the way down Chris' list. But when he came to my name, Chris said:

"We have in our audience a man I really respect. He just stepped down as head coach at Notre Dame—Gerry Faust."

I stood up. Then, there were other people standing. And there was applause that just kept growing, as if all these coaches and all these presidents of corporations and all the other people in the room were saying: He did it right no matter what the record might indicate. It was a humbling yet rewarding moment, to know that so many people cared.

At Notre Dame's banquet, Father Joyce said he had been a member of the Hall of Fame for 20 years and had attended its banquets for that long and he had never seen anything like the response I had received.

I didn't expect our own banquet to provide the similar reinforcement for the values that I tried to bring to the game. I thought it was going to be my toughest night. I mean, what do you say after a 5-6 season that ends on a 58-7 loss? I should have known better.

We had a packed house and New York Yankees owner George Steinbrenner, with whom I started a friendship that night that endures to this day, gave one of the most inspiring speeches I've ever heard. Much better than mine.

When it came time for him to speak, Father Joyce recited a poem. It was Rudyard Kipling's "If":

If you can keep your head when all about you
     Are losing theirs and blaming it on you;
If you can trust yourself when all men doubt you,
     But make allowance for their doubting too;
If you can wait and not be tired by waiting,
     Or, being lied about, don't deal in lies,
Or, being hated, don't give way to hating,
     And yet don't look too good, nor talk too wise;

If you can dream—and not make dreams you master;
     If you can think—and not make thoughts your aim;
If you can meet with triumph and disaster
     And treat those two impostors just the same;
If you can bear to hear the truth you've spoken
     Twisted by knaves to make a trap for fools,
Or watch the things you gave your life to broken,
     And stoop and build 'em up with wornout tools;

If you can make one heap of all your winnings
     And risk it on one turn of pitch-and-toss,
And lose, and start again at your beginnings
     And never breathe a word about your loss;
If you can force your heart and nerve and sinew
     To serve your turn long after they are gone,
And so hold on when there is nothing in you
     Except the Will which says to them: 'Hold on':

If you can talk with crowds and keep your virtue,
     Or walk with kings—nor lose the common touch;
If neither foes nor loving friends can hurt you;
     If all men count with you, but none too much;
If you can fill the unforgiving minute
     With sixty seconds' worth of distance run—
Yours is the Earth and everything that's in it,
     And—which is more—you'll be a Man, my son!

When Father Joyce finished the recitation, he said: "This is the man.This is Gerry Faust."

I got a lump the size of a baseball in my throat. I could not have been given a greater honor by this man of such distinction. Well, OK. Maybe a contract extension would have been better. The poem wasn't the end of this kindness. John Healy, president of the senior class, presented me with a plaque to thank me for my contributions to the University. Later, in the spring, the student body would give me the Irish Clover Award and Senior Fellowship Award, making me, I think, the only football coach to receive these two awards. What's more, Allen Pinkett's future wife, Joanne, who was an editor of the yearbook, included in the yearbook the Kipling poem and a photo layout of the Grotto and me on the tower from which I got an overview of practice. It's framed and hangs in my office to this day. How can anyone have bad memories of a place and people who treat you like that?

As nice as all this was, I knew I couldn't live in a land of memories. I had to move on, and I had to do it in a way I had not done before. I had to be inclusive in the decision of what happened next. Marlene had to have a say. When I had come to Notre Dame, she had had none. She left the Cincinnati that she loved. She suffered the criticism of her husband as if it were criticism of her. She had earned the right to say no to Marshall when the time came. It wasn't as if it were my only option.

The option that looked the best—at first—was Rice.

I had received a call from the best friend of Wally Kleine's dad, a man who was the chairman of the Rice University Board of Trustees. I'd also gotten a call from another trustee of Rice who was an attorney, and one from a former Rice player who was involved in the hiring process. I told them I was interested and wanted to come to Houston to talk with them.

Before I went, however, Gene Corrigan said he had received a call from Dave Adams, the University of Akron athletic director, who wanted to talk with me. It was the only call about a possible job that had not come directly to me, which was curious. But I always try to return every call I receive, even if they aren't offering me something. I told Mr. Corrigan I would call Dave Adams. In my mind, though, I had settled on Rice. I had already begun to tell other schools that I appreciated their offers but that I wasn't interested. Among those calls was one to Columbia University. I had talked with the Columbia athletic director when I was in New York for the Hall of Fame dinner. It's a wonderful academic institution. That seemed to be my great fortune, that quality universities such as Notre Dame, Rice and Columbia saw value in my approach to life, academics and athletics. But Columbia was a I-AA team, and I wanted to coach at the I-A level.

Before Marlene and I set off to Houston to visit Rice, I called Dave Adams at Akron. He asked if I would be interested in the head football job. The first thing I asked was about the current coach. I had been keeping an eye on the firings, hirings and retirements in college football listed on the sports pages and I hadn't seen anything about an opening at Akron. I didn't get the whole story during that phone call but I would, bit by bit, piece by piece. Unfortunately, I didn't know what I needed to know until it was too late to save either myself or Jim Dennison, whom I would learn had been football coach at Akron for 13 seasons.

"When I was hired in January 1985," Adams says, "the direction I had was that I would replace the football coach. The first day on the job I was told (by Akron President William V. Muse):'You can replace the football coach now and we will support you, or you can wait.'

"My comment was:'If you wanted the football coach replaced now, why didn't *you* replace him?' There was no way I could do that without any kind of justification. I had never seen the man coach.

"The reply I got was:'You have a year.'"

Dr. Muse's memory of this differs slightly from that of Dave Adams.

"I don't remember if that was something discussed with Dave from the outset," Muse says. "I would acknowledge that during the first year there was discussion about moving to I-A and continuing discussion of whether Jim Dennison was the appropriate person to take us to that next level."

Whatever the case, Dave Adams' year was up, and I was his answer.

"The direction was," Adams says now, "that we were going to go to Division I-A. We wanted a high-profile coach. We were the 54th largest university in the country but probably the least known among that group, even among the top 154. We wanted somebody who could bring some attention to our program. With that in mind, I already had a list.

"Knowing what we were trying to achieve, one person who came to mind was Gerry. Unless he went undefeated at Notre Dame in 1985, there was a question whether he would be retained. But with his outstanding record in high school and with it being in Ohio, I felt that he was somewhat of a natural. He had a great reputation in Ohio, a great reputation with high school coaches and good rapport with a lot of them. If he were going to have an opportunity to be really successful, I felt the greatest opportunity would be back in the state of Ohio."

I cannot quarrel with that assessment, but I didn't want to go to a I-AA school. I wasn't even sure I wanted to go to one that had ambitions of becoming the first school ever to move up to I-A. Right or wrong, it just didn't appeal to me. I felt the same way about the call from Dr. John F. Geletka, a Youngstown dentist and Youngstown State University trustee. Dr. Geletka had first called me in Fort Lauderdale before my final Notre Dame game against Miami. Now, he was inquiring again whether or not I'd be interested in Youngstown. I told him that as much as I respected the University and the people of the Steel Valley, having played against Youngstown Mooney during my Moeller days, I just wasn't interested.

Dr. Geletka asked a favor of me. Since one of Youngstown's objectives was to get some attention for its football program, could I at least come to visit? I told him I not only would do that but also that I would share with Youngstown my ideas concerning what I felt Youngstown needed to do to make the program a success.

What I was really interested in were the I-A offers, especially Rice, which wanted me in two capacities, coach and athletic director. The second week of December, Marlene and I flew to Houston. Our visit was not a surprise. The newspapers had dug up the story. Some coaches like it to be known that schools are interested in them. It raises their profile. Mine was high enough. I'd have preferred weighing job offers without a spotlight on me. It was one of those times when what I needed conflicted with what the sportswriters wanted.

I found the University to be beautiful, the stadium large — too large to fill at 80,000 seats. It loomed like a castle above a campus, which looked like a village below. The facilities were excellent. The people were nice. I liked everything I saw.

What's more, everyone seemed to have a realistic attitude about what accomplishments were reasonable. Rice, like Notre Dame, has lofty academic standards. Playing in the Southwest Conference, where not every university's academic standards were as demanding as Rice's, made it difficult to win. But the trustees and other important people didn't expect to win big every year. They wanted a team that was competitive, one that would represent them well on the field. They were willing to invest money in football because of the positive attention it could attract for the University. They wanted to be in contention for the conference championship every three years or so.

I had dinner with the trustees and then met the president, who, it was clear, placed his priorities on academics. As it turned out, he had been my nephew Vic Agruso Jr.'s advisor during his previous tenure at the Harvard School of Divinity. I knew after talking to the trustees and the president that this would be a different situation than the one with which I was familiar at Notre Dame. Father Hesburgh and Father Joyce ran the show, academic and athletic. At Rice, the trustees were going to make the decisions, which I didn't have any problem with. I liked them and felt I could work with them. As athletic director, I planned to hire an exceptionally able assistant to run the day-to-day operation while I coached and guided the athletic department philosophy by making the decisions that set the tone for the institution.

We met for two days. Marlene, though ill and scheduled to have a hysterectomy later in December, looked at homes for hours. After we returned to South Bend, I received a phone call offering me the job. I asked for a few days to think about it, but I told them that the combination of coach and athletic director was one that appealed to me and that I loved Rice. I just wanted to talk more to Marlene about it.

By this time, of course, Akron was in the picture, and returning to Ohio, even to the opposite end of Ohio from Cincinnati, appealed to Marlene. We had made a pact. If I were to remain in coaching, this time she would have a say in where we went. We were in this together. A coach with a family can't think of himself all the time. He can argue that by choosing the school at which he is most likely to win, he is doing the right thing for his family but, in many cases, that's just another excuse for selfishness. And I didn't want to be selfish. I had made the Notre Dame decision almost in isolation—my dad's input being the lone exception—and I was never sorry. There was no choice: I had to say yes to Notre Dame. But now, the situation was different.

When I talked to Dave Adams, he told me his coach had indicated an interest in moving to athletic administration.

"Who is your coach?" I asked.

He said it was Jim Dennison. I didn't know him. Akron never
came to Cincinnati to recruit, or at least not to Moeller. The only
thing I knew about the University of Akron was that we had played
four state championship games in its stadium, the Rubber Bowl.
On those four occasions, I'd never met either Gordon Larson, the
previous athletic director and former football coach, or Jim
Dennison. I'd met Herm Farley, the University's sports business
manager who ran the high school playoff games, and I'd met Akron
trainer Don Marshall and team doctor George Mallo. But I'd never
met Jim Dennison. That struck me as odd. Even Ohio State coach
Woody Hayes came to at least one of our championship games in
Akron's Rubber Bowl and stopped by to wish us luck.

Though I hadn't inspected it closely, the Rubber Bowl struck
me as a suitable mid-level college facility. Close inspection years
later would reveal the cracks in this veneer. But that inspection
came too late. I didn't know much about Akron except it was in the
right state. At the behest of my friend and former University of
Dayton teammate Bill Ricco, former coach and principal at Walsh
Jesuit High School, I spoke one year at the *Akron Beacon Journal*
Player of the Year Banquet. And, of course, I knew longtime and
since-retired *Beacon Journal* prep sports expert Milan Zban. But
that was it. At the outset of our conversations and before he told
me that the University wanted me to help it move up to I-A, I even
had to ask Dave Adams at what level Akron played.

"I-AA," Adams told me.

"What was your record this year?" I said.

"It was 8-4 and we got into the I-AA playoffs."

"Why do you want to talk to me then? That guy you have has
an excellent record. He took you to the playoffs. What more do you
want?"

"Well," Adams said, "he's really interested in going into athletic administration. In fact, a year ago, he expressed to our president, Dr. Muse, that he wanted to move up."

What everyone failed to mention is that Jim Dennison didn't
want just any job in athletic administration. He wanted the job that
Dave Adams got. He wanted to be athletic director. In fact, he wanted
to be athletic director and continue coaching. He didn't want to be
associate AD. All I knew was that Akron wanted to move up to I-A.

"We thought," Dr. Muse says, looking back, "that the community would respond to Division I-A football, that it would be a rallying point for Akron, a city down at the heels and looking for something to be proud of, that the University of Akron could give it that, that the football program could give it that."

That interested me. But with one important condition.

"I want to tell you something, Mr. Adams," I said for the first of several times. "I'm not interested in the job unless your football coach *wants* to move up. I don't know if I would be interested even if he *does* want to move up. I'm down to two or three possible jobs. But you can get back to me if he does want to go into athletic administration."

That would become a critical and improbable issue, whether I forced Jim Dennison out of his job. In fact, I did just the opposite. I said I didn't want Jim Dennison's job if he still wanted it.

"He did say that," Dave Adams agrees.

But Dave Adams, who is a true friend to speak up now, did not tell me then that Jim was as good as being removed. It was a matter of semantics to Dave. It was a matter of principle to me.

"Jim was going to be replaced regardless," Dave Adams says. "So in that sense, bringing Gerry here wasn't forcing someone else out. Gerry's hiring wasn't affecting that."

I received a call a day later from Dave telling me that Jim Dennison almost surely wants to move up to athletic administration and that Dr. Muse would like to meet me. I assumed they had talked to Jim, but from what I learned later, I know that was not the case. I told Dave that I didn't want any of this to get to the media. It wasn't important to me that people know I had been offered several jobs.

At this stage, if I had known Jim Dennison, I would have called him directly and asked him about the situation. Because I didn't know him, I was reluctant to do that. Instead, I told Dave Adams that I was going to visit another university (it was Youngstown, but I didn't tell him that) and could stop in Cleveland on the way since I would be using Notre Dame's airplane.

"We can talk at the airport," I said.

We actually went to a restaurant at a motel near the airport.

"When I first approached Dr. Muse with this," Adams says, "I told him that the media would follow Gerry's every move when he leaves Notre Dame, that it would get us the kind of attention Dr. Muse wanted.

"The fact Gerry hadn't done as well as expected at Notre Dame was not a turn-off, because he already had been very successful in coaching and the expectations at Notre Dame were far greater than they would be at another university. My contention has always been that it is very difficult to move from a high school to a major college. And to go from a high school to Notre Dame, with the expectations and pressures that exist there, would be almost impossible. I don't know that Gerry was prepared for it.

"To me," Adams continues, "it was a plus that he had done as well as he had, making that big a jump, without having college experience. He certainly had to have learned from that, and what the University was looking for—attention—he was going to bring with him."

Without attention, I met with Dr. Muse, Dave Adams and Dr. H. Kenneth Barker, chairman of the University's Athletic Committee. The first thing I told them was: "Now, if Jim changes his mind and is not interested in being in athletic administration, that's fine with me. You're not going to hurt my feelings one bit. I don't want the job unless he wants to go to athletic administration on his own. I don't want anyone being forced."

"Gerry was concerned about that," Muse says.

I wanted no extra baggage, such as having forced someone, especially someone who had been successful, out of a job. I was bringing enough baggage with me from Notre Dame. I didn't need any awaiting me on the dock.

I explained to Dr. Muse and Mr. Adams certain requirements I had. I even gave them a list. Then I said one more time: "I want to reiterate that I have other jobs I am more interested in and if Jim Dennison decides he doesn't want to be an athletic administrator, I don't want the man's job. I will not take the job. I hope you understand."

They said they did. But they didn't.

In an effort to help Akron no matter what happened, I left with Dr. Muse and Mr. Adams a list of things I thought it important for the university to do to make a successful transition to Division I-A. Even though Dr. Muse and Dave Adams impressed me, and I would eventually enjoy working for them, I wasn't interested in Akron. I went on to Youngstown and spent the day and then flew back to Notre Dame. I thought I was going to Rice.

Both Marlene and I had been impressed with the people we met at Rice. When they called and offered me the job, I also wanted to find out what the man whom I wanted to be my offensive coordinator thought. I didn't want to make the mistake I had made at Notre Dame. This time, I wanted to have Ralph Staub with me. Staubie had spent the five years I was at Notre Dame in Texas with the Dallas Cowboys and Houston Oilers. He had retired to Florida, but I had convinced him to join me if we could agree on a university. I wanted his input on the programs we might take over.

"Since I had been with the Houston Oilers and Rice is in Houston," Staub says, "I had been to a number of Rice games. Going to those games in Rice's big stadium with about a thousand people there, it looked like a hundred. Some of the teams that came in to play were well-known schools but still hardly anybody was there. Had it not been for the following from the other schools, I don't think Rice could have paid its bills. It was not an inviting situation.

"I told Gerry I was not interested in Rice."

That was strike one. Marlene was strike two.

"I was very much impressed with Rice and with the people there," Marlene says. "As far as Gerry's career, that would have been the perfect choice, because they wanted him as both football coach and athletic director. If things didn't work out as football coach, he could have remained as athletic director. Or, he could have gone somewhere else as athletic director with the experience he had gained.

"The problem was, Houston was another world to us. It was so far from our family. We felt we needed to be near our children and Gerry's parents. We're both very family-oriented."

Strike three became my doubts about competing in the Southwest Conference against a number of schools I knew were not on the up-and-up in recruiting situations we had encountered at Notre Dame. I wasn't going to cheat. At Notre Dame, we won over such great players as Tim Brown despite the unethical behavior of a Southern Methodist. Could we do that at Rice? Would it sell as well as Notre Dame? Despite the fact it is an institution with a tremendous academic reputation, the answer to that was a resounding no.

In addition, I sensed that in Texas I would feel like a coach in a foreign land. I don't know why, exactly. I'd spoken to Texas high school coaches conventions. I'd recruited successfully in the state and established good relationships with a number of coaches, but I just didn't think it would be a fit. I think it is difficult for a Midwest guy to be accepted in Texas or in the Deep South. I know John

Mackovic, who is from the Akron suburb of Barberton, has made a successful transition at Texas. But I wasn't sure I could.

With that in mind, at this stage I still had Marshall and a couple of other possibilities. Marshall had become my first choice. Staubie agreed to go there. Now it was up to Marlene. It didn't work. Because of the fogged-in airport, Marlene didn't make the scheduled trip to Huntington and didn't reschedule. Wives of other coaches told her that she wouldn't like it. I didn't want to put undue pressure on her because I'd given my word that she would be an equal partner in this decision. She knew, though, that I thought the chemistry at Marshall was right. I had had no intention of going to a I-AA school, but Marshall had done a great job of selling the University, and I saw a place where coaches had been successful and would be again.

"For Gerry's career," Marlene says, "Marshall would have been better. I feel really, really bad that I didn't give him that opportunity. But I wanted to be back in Ohio and he did, too."

So when we returned to South Bend from Houston and Dave Adams called again from Akron and asked where I was in my decision-making process, I told him that I was more interested in Akron than I had been but that I had to know in the next couple of days if Jim Dennison wanted to move to athletic administration.

"If he wants to move up, that's great. If he doesn't, that's great, too," I told Adams again. "But I've got to know."

At this point, I was considering calling Youngstown State back and renewing that conversation. Staubie said he would he happy to go to either Akron or Youngstown.

"My feeling about Akron," Staub says, "was based on my memory from having been on Woody Hayes' staff at Ohio State. I knew there was a lot of great high school football played in the Akron, Canton and Cleveland area. I knew there were athletes and a base from which to draw.

"I had always felt Gerry was a great organizer and nothing that happened at Notre Dame changed my mind. I felt with Gerry going into that base of people that if he brought in a good staff, there would be a fine possibility for more success at Akron than at either Marshall or Rice."

I never got to the point of calling Youngstown.

Dave Adams called on Sunday, December 15. He said he and Dr. Muse were going to meet with Jim Dennison the next day to find out what Jim wanted to do. I reiterated that I didn't want the job if Jim was being forced to give it up.

"I understand," Adams said.

The next morning, Monday, December 16, Dave called again to confirm that the meeting with Jim was set and that he would call me soon with the result.

"I didn't know they were even thinking of doing anything like this," Dennison says. "I went over to the president's office with Adams and thought I was going there to get a raise for our staff. That's when they broke it to me."

Three hours later, Dave Adams called again. He said Jim was thinking about his decision. Then came his final call.

"Jim has decided he wants to move up to athletic administration," he said.

"That's great," I said. "I'm happy for him."

"You've got to come to Akron now," Adams said. "It's already out that you're coming."

"Wait a minute, Dave," I said. "You haven't even talked to my lawyer to get things squared away."

"But it's already out, Gerry."

"How? How did this get out?"

"Jim Dennison told the media."

It turns out Jim told Denny Schreiner, a former Akron sportscaster who had moved up to national events, and then word spread to the newspaper. He also called Bo Schembechler at Michigan and Earle Bruce at Ohio State who spoke out in his behalf in subsequent stories and, by implication, damned me.

I'm not the one to judge Jim. If I had been in the same situation, I don't know what I would have done, but I was not pleased that a deal that wasn't yet a deal had become public. What I should have done is nix the deal right there. I was concerned about the handling of this, but the alarms going off were muffled by my need to find a job, and this one was in the right location. I think it happens to a lot of people when they are considering a job. They look at the positives and ignore the negatives.

"Dave," I said, "all I told you was that if Jim wanted to move up I would take the job if we could work things out. We haven't worked anything out."

"Well," Dave said, "he decided on his own to move up. You've got to come tomorrow morning. We've got to have a press conference announcing this."

"Dave, I can't. I have other obligations. Second, you have to talk to Ken Schneider, my lawyer. We haven't decided a thing. I'm not coming unless certain things are in place, and we haven't even talked about them. There's no way I'm coming until my lawyer tells me it's OK. All we've talked about are some of the things we would need in the program."

Then I made a suggestion.

"I think it would be smart," I told Dave, "if we waited a week. Since Jim wants to move to administration, this will make it clear that he wasn't forced to do so. I think you owe that to him. I just went through a similar situation. I know what happened at Notre Dame, but because Lou Holtz was hired the day after I resigned, some people no doubt think it must have been set up ahead of time. It wasn't. But I don't want that to happen to another coach. Let's wait a week and get things done behind the scenes."

"No," Dave said, "it's already out."

"How does Jim Dennison know," I asked, "that you're hiring me?"

"We told him if he wanted to move up, we had someone in mind to take his place: Gerry Faust."

I never have been good at telling people no. I should have been in this instance. Instead, I let my attorney, Ken Schneider, work out the details of the contract that Dr. Muse and Dave Adams had offered me. Ted Mallo, the University's talented general counsel and now vice president, finalized the contract with Ken, who phoned me at midnight to let me know it was a done deal. I called Dave Adams and said I would be in Akron, still all but sight unseen to me, the following day.

Was I ever in for an awakening.

Before Marlene and I left South Bend for Akron and the press conference where I was to be announced as the new coach, I stopped in to see Gene Corrigan to tell him that I had accepted the Akron job. He was shocked. I think he, like most people, thought I was going to Rice.

When Marlene and I got to Akron late on that December Tuesday morning, we went to the office of President Muse, and Marlene knew immediately that something wasn't right. It was a little thing, something that might not have mattered if we hadn't been coming from Notre Dame, a place where they went to great pains to do things right.

So what was wrong? Lunch.

"They aren't going to do things right, Gerry," Marlene warned me.

"Why, Marlene? What do you mean?"

"Because instead of taking us out to lunch, they've ordered McDonald's for the office."

It wasn't just an omen in retrospect. Marlene had this gut feeling before she knew what was going to happen next.

As we walked over a bridge from Memorial Hall on one part of campus to the Tommy Evans Lounge in the James A. Rhodes Arena on another, doubt, not burgers, filled Marlene.

"Hey, Mar," I told her. "Things are just rushed. It'll be OK."

But it wasn't OK.

When we got to the press conference, it reminded me of Notre Dame. The lounge was packed. Television cameras stood in the back of the crowd. People were clapping. I was thinking this is going to be great. Dave Adams was in the front of the room.

"Where's Coach Dennison?" I asked.

I'd never seen him before. So Dave pointed out Jim Dennison to me. When I looked in the direction Dave had indicated, I saw a man with tears in his eyes. That's when I knew Marlene was right. I said to myself: Something's wrong here. That was my first inkling.

But what was I going to do? I was sitting in front of a crowd of people, ready to be introduced as the Akron football coach. As I was trying to sort this out in my mind, the press conference began. I felt like a man going through the motions. They were familiar enough. I was enthusiastic. The reception was warm. But that didn't change the fact that something was wrong.

Afterwards, I went to Jim Dennison's office and asked if I could see him. Because of the circumstances of being hired for a job that wasn't open until 24 hours before I was named to fill it, it was the first opportunity I had had to see some of the football facilities—in this case the staff offices. I wasn't impressed. They reminded me of a high school, not a university with Division I-A aspirations.

Jim was kind enough to see me. I did what I always do. I plowed straight ahead, as honestly as I could.

"Jim," I said, "were you forced to move up to athletic administration or did you go on your own?"

"I was forced," he said.

"Well, Jim, the reason I came to see you is that I saw the tears in your eyes. I want you to know that I told Dave Adams and Dr. Muse that I wasn't a bit interested in the job unless you wanted to move up on your own."

"I tried for the AD job a year ago," he said. "I wanted it, and I wanted to continue to coach for a year or two and then become the full-time AD. But they told me in our meeting that I could go into the physical education department, I could quit and go somewhere else or I could become associate athletic director."

"They did what?"

"That's what they told me."

"Jim, I'll be back. I told them I would not take this job unless you were making this move on your own."

I went to see Dr. Muse, but he wasn't in. I don't know what would have happened if he had been.

"At the time Gerry took the Akron job," Marlene says, "he did not need that kind of challenge. He did not need the controversy involved in the Akron program."

I did locate Dave Adams and confronted him with this Dennison revelation.

"We also told him," Dave said, "that he could continue as football coach as long as we remained I-AA but when we moved to I-A, he would not be the football coach any longer."

That didn't amount to much of a stay of execution. Akron planned to apply for I-A status and make the move as soon as possible, which would be after one last season in the Ohio Valley Conference and I-AA. When I asked Jim if he had been given this alternative, he told me he didn't remember it. I probably wouldn't have remembered, either. It was a less-than-memorable alternative. The truth of the matter is this: The situation was a mess. It was the biggest mess I'd ever been in in my life despite the fact I had tried to be sensitive to Jim's position and handle the offer the right way. It didn't look that way to others, though.

At the press conference a guy wearing cowboy boots and a beard clomped up to me and said: "You're supposed to be a guy of integrity, a straightforward guy. What do you think of this situation?"

I had no idea who this man was but the tone of the question put me on edge.

"What do you mean, this situation?" I asked. "By the way, who are you?"

"I'm Tom Giffen," he said.

"Well, what right do you have to reproach me about my ethics and values?"

I was upset. It was not the way to begin a relationship with the person who, I was soon to discover, was the sports editor of the *Akron Beacon Journal*. When Akron sports information director Ken MacDonald told me that he expected a terribly negative story to result from this whole mishandled scenario, I suggested we visit the newspaper and talk to Tom Giffen confidentially and not for publication. We went the next morning after I was named coach and I explained the hiring process from my perspective, particularly my repeated admonitions of not wanting the job unless Jim Dennison's move to athletic administration was voluntary.

From Day One, the circumstances placed me in an awkward position. I didn't want to get off on the wrong foot with President Muse and Dave Adams, but neither did I want people at the newspaper and in the community to believe I had taken Jim Dennison's job away from him.

But that's how it looked. Explanations fell on deaf ears. I had to shoulder the blame.

"That surprised me," Muse says, "and I regretted it for two reasons. One, Gerry was not the individual who made that decision. He simply responded to the opportunity we offered him. I think he felt—and we felt—he was the right person for the job. The right person to give Akron national visibility. The right person to bring our football program along to where it could be competitive at the Mid-American Conference level and occasionally beat a well-known school.

"Gerry should not have been blamed for this at all. I was the major person in that decision-making process and the one who should have been criticized for it. And I absorbed an awful lot of it. But I still feel bad for Gerry today. He is one of the finest human beings I've ever known."

That was not a unanimously shared opinion as I began what would be the most difficult coaching job of my career. I had helped to start a high school football program. I had spent five years in the pressure cooker that is Notre Dame football. But neither of those jobs came with the obstacles I found awaiting me in Akron. Suddenly, people not only doubted whether I could coach college football, but they also questioned what kind of man I was if I would take another man's job from him.

It was too late to reverse my decision, though other coaches have done just that in situations where they have developed second thoughts after agreeing to contracts. Almost to the man, though, these coaches have had jobs to return to. I didn't. I had called all the schools with whom I had been talking, including Rice and Marshall, and told them I was going to accept Akron's offer.

Now I was to face resistance of both an immediate nature due to feelings about Jim Dennison and one that had deep roots.

"I think the people around Akron have been very slow to accept change," Dave Adams says. "Many times I heard that Division I-AA was just fine. There was no need to go to I-A. Why do we want to change? That's why Gerry's appointment would have been more readily accepted had there been an announcement about Jim when the season was over, followed by a search process and not all of it announced at once as Gerry was coming in.

"Gerry didn't force Jim Dennison out in any way, shape or form. When I've tried to say that to people, they've shut their ears. They've never heard a word I've said.

"I'm not sure I did Gerry any favors by targeting him as the person to do this job."

13

▪ DIFFERENT JOURNEYS: ▪
FROM AKRON TO LOURDES

During the nine seasons I would spend as its football coach, I came to regard the University of Akron as a heaven-sent hardship. No blueprint existed for what we were attempting—the construction of a I-A football program out of a I-AA program. No map marked the route to the top of this mountain made of troubles.

In fact, on the day I was introduced as football coach, I ran into a major obstacle in addition to Jim Dennison.

On the afternoon of the press conference, I had to meet a number of people at Buchtel Hall, the University's administration building. On the way, I wandered into the portion of Rhodes Arena where Bob Huggins' basketball team was practicing. I'd met Huggins only once, but I had had a close professional and personal relationship with Digger Phelps at Notre Dame. So I was looking forward to getting to know Bob, whom I realized was a respected and successful young coach.

I didn't want to bother him during practice, but I went over, introduced myself again and shook hands. He didn't smile. He didn't say anything. No, glad you're here. No, good luck. He just shook my hand. That was it.

I knew we weren't going to hit it off. You know how you can get that feeling from just meeting a person? But, Bob was busy. So I wrote off his reaction to that and just forgot it. I hadn't wanted to bother him, but to walk through without saying hello seemed to me to be both wrong and rude.

He would claim later in his autobiography that I told him I had called Jim Dennison, who told me he had resigned to go into athletic administration. I told Bob no such thing. That's either an out-and-out lie or Bob's memory is as crusty as his language. I have always told everyone that I *didn't* call Jim because I didn't know Jim and had no way of anticipating the situation was different from what I was being led to believe.

The reception I received from Bob Huggins becomes understandable in light of his status. He had turned around Akron basketball. He won. He went to the NCAA Tournament after I arrived in Akron. And in any case, basketball already was I-A. He couldn't see the benefits that upgrading football would bring him and his staff —salary increases, for instance. All he could see was a splitting of athletic emphasis and, most important, leaving him and other coaches without a conference affiliation. If I had been in Bob's sneakers, I'd have felt the same way. What I wouldn't have done, however, is blame the football coach.

Though many of my experiences at Akron would be positive, mainly because of the people who did so much to help me, there was, nevertheless, an undercurrent of negativism among some at the University and in the community. The undercurrent was two-fold: One element was Jim Dennison; the other was the belief that the new emphasis being placed on football detracted from basketball and was too costly. There were supporters in both groups who could not or would not accept the decision that the University had made.

I concede that the move to independent I-A football status created immediate problems for basketball because the University had to disassociate itself from the Ohio Valley Conference. But in the long run, Akron would not be a member of the Mid-American Conference today had Dr. Muse not made the decision he made.

Of course, by the time that happened, basketball had been briefly involved with a couple of other conferences, the Northeastern and Mid-Continent, and Bob Huggins had moved on to the University of Cincinnati, which he has restored to its previous status as a national basketball power. Bob's departure from Akron was what Jim Dennison had in mind for me and my staff from Day One. When Huggins hit the road for Cincinnati, I took the blame for that, too.

During a brief period in which I returned to Notre Dame to clean out my office and to prepare for the move to Akron, I hired half of the coaching staff, including the three key members, Ralph Staub, Bob Shaw and Andy Urbanic. Ralph, of course, already had agreed to come out of retirement to coordinate the offense. I called him, made a formal offer and he accepted. I also had messages from a number of coaches around the country, including Bob Shaw, who had just finished a season with the Portland Breakers of the United States Football League.

I had known Bob since he coached Niles (Ohio) High School. He had a resume as long as your arm with college experience, including coordinating Tony Mason's defenses at the University of Cincinnati and at the University of Arizona. He also had coached Lou Holtz's linebackers at Arkansas. He wanted to return to Ohio and said he was interested in a job at Akron.

"You got it, Bob," I said, without hesitation. "You're our defensive coordinator."

Andy Urbanic also called. I'd known Andy both when he was head coach at Penn Hills High School in Pittsburgh and at the University of Pittsburgh, where he coached the running backs for both Jackie Sherrill and Foge Fazio. I also offered Andy the job of coaching our running backs, but he said he would have to weigh it against other possibilities. I understood, but I wasn't going to give up easily.

When I took Marlene to lunch on the Saturday after I'd become Akron's coach, I asked if she would excuse me while I made a phone call. She probably thought it was deja vu with a twist. On our way to Notre Dame five years earlier, I had left the table during dinner at an Indianapolis restaurant to make a recruiting call to some of my former players at Moeller. Now, I was recruiting a coach.

I was gone for half an hour, but when I returned it became a lunch with cause to celebrate. Andy Urbanic had agreed to become our running backs coach. By hiring these three key coaches, I was able to involve them in the hiring of the other assistants. I didn't keep anyone from Jim Dennison's staff, and, frankly, they didn't want to stay. They were loyal to Jim. I was Public Enemy No. 1. I was always surprised when I didn't see my face hanging in the Akron post office.

The fourth coach I hired in South Bend was Jerry Lasko from Indiana State. He was from Cleveland and wanted to return to the area. I interviewed him in my makeshift office at Notre Dame and told him he had a job but that I hadn't decided on his specific assignment. He could coach several defensive positions. He wound up as our defensive line coach and gave us recruiting knowledge of the Cleveland area. Bob Shaw, of course, was strong in recruiting the Niles-Youngstown area. Andy Urbanic knew Pittsburgh and its coaches, and Ralph Staub gave us entree to Florida.

Over a four- or five-week period, I completed the staff. I wanted three levels of experience: older, experienced coaches who could help the younger coaches learn some of the secrets of the business; coaches with mid-level experience; and young coaches with unbridled enthusiasm.

To the very experienced coaches (Staub, Shaw and Urbanic), I added Jim Corrigall, who played at Kent State and went on to a distinguished career in the Canadian Football League, where he began his coaching career with the Toronto Argonauts. Most recently he had been teaching the outside linebackers at North Carolina State. With Jerry Lasko, he gave us two mid-level coaches.

The raw enthusiasm came from Terry Bowden (quarterbacks), Gerald Carr (receivers) and Mike Woodford (defensive backs). I knew Terry's father, of course. Bobby Bowden's Florida State team had beaten us at Notre Dame, and Terry had learned that offense from his father. When Denver Allen, who was a fundraiser at Akron, told me he knew the Bowden family well from the days they had shared at the University of West Virginia and suggested that Terry, then head coach at Salem (West Virginia) College, would be interested in a job, I called him. We talked and I offered him a job.

I talked to Bob Shaw about our remaining openings—receivers and defensive secondary—and Bob knew of two promising coaches, one personally and one by reputation. To show how these things work, Bob had heard of Gerald Carr from Carl Angelo, whom Bob knew and who would join us for our second season. Angelo had coached at Southern Illinois where Gerald had been an excellent quarterback. For three years Gerald had been at Davidson College. Mike Woodford also was at a small college, in his case Rhodes College in Memphis, but he had worked with Bob as a graduate assistant both at Arizona and Arkansas. Mike came for a visit, and I found in him the enthusiasm and intensity I was looking for. Bob LaCivita rounded out the staff as administrative assistant and recruiting coordinator, jobs he had held at Pittsburgh. Because this position wasn't funded until the following summer, Bob volunteered to come a couple of months early to prove how much he wanted to be in Akron. It earned him the job.

As much as people like Bob LaCivita wanted to be in Akron, Jim Dennison made it clear that not everyone wanted me and my staff there.

"Jim Dennison told Bob Shaw not to buy a house because he wasn't going to be there that long," Ralph Staub says.

"I don't know where Gerry gets this," Jim Dennison says when asked if he could recall the incident. "I would never, ever say anything like that. Someone from the (athletic) staff might have said that, but it wasn't me."

Someone's memory is on the slippery slope of time or convenience. I'm not saying it's Jim's, but I know that neither Bob nor Ralph, exacting men both, would be confused about who said what. In any case, the welcome mat had been put into cold storage.

"That's a tough thing to combat," Staub says. "If the president, the athletic director, his staff and the coaches are not pulling together, it's tough to establish a program."

If that was tough, it would get tougher.

Not everyone, however, welcomed us with closed arms. I had friends in this community and before I was through, I'd make more. Even Eddy Niam still liked me, despite the fact that I made him sit in the car outside Frank Stams' house when we were recruiting Frank Jr.

Ray Meyo was a friend before I came to Akron and he has become like a brother during my Akron years. We met at Notre Dame. Ray is a big booster. In fact, he donated the money for the field in Notre Dame's indoor practice facility. It's called Ray Meyo field.

Ray has one of the greatest hearts of any person I've ever met. Though he has since become a trustee at the University of Akron, he was not on the board when I arrived, and I hadn't told him I was coming. It happened too fast.

I had talked to Ray once or twice since I had resigned from Notre Dame, but I didn't say anything to him or anyone else about where I might land. As surprising as it may seem, when it's important to do so, I can keep my mouth shut. At the time I came to Akron, Ray was the chief executive officer of the Telxon Corporation, but he has since become president and chief operating officer of R&R International Inc., a very successful construction management, environmental systems and facilities operation and maintenance firm.

"No one will believe this, because they think I had a part in getting Gerry to come to Akron," Ray Meyo says, "but I swear I'll never forget this. We were in our old house in Brecksville. It was a cold night. I had been out of town when Gerry resigned and I picked up the paper at O'Hare Airport in Chicago and read about it. Now, I was finding out secondhand again about what he was doing. My wife, Marie, said: 'Take a guess what.'

"I don't know, Marie. What happened?

"She said: 'Gerry's coming to Akron.' "

"The next day he was named coach and everyone said: 'Oh, Ray, you arranged it.' Well, nothing could be further from the truth. But I was beyond pleased. I was thrilled.

"I think Gerry Faust would be good anywhere. I'm prejudiced, but I just happen to think he is the finest person I have ever met in my life. My wife says the same thing. That quality of individual, any school, any organization would be fortunate to have.

"There's an incident that exemplifies what I mean. In 1992 we played host to a party for then Israeli Prime Minister Shimon Peres. I was still with Telxon at the time and this event was arranged by one of the directors of our board, Raj Reedy, chairman of computer science at Carnegie Mellon. It was a beautiful affair. I had invited Gerry, prominent members of the Jewish community and others who would enjoy meeting Prime Minister Peres. Everyone seemed to have a wonderful time.

"When the Prime Minister was preparing to leave, everyone flocked to him, forming a makeshift line to shake hands and say goodbye. Gerry wasn't there. I looked around for him and discovered he was in the kitchen, signing autographs for the busboys and telling the kitchen help what a terrific job they had done.

"I almost cried. That's Gerry. He's just as interested in the guy at the bottom of the ladder as the one at the top. He's a throwback, I think, to the days when everything was good."

As Ray said, he is not impartial, but I will tell you something about this man: He doesn't just talk about being there when you need him. He is there.

The night I arrived, the University had a reception at Hower House, one of Akron's oldest homes, located on the edge of the campus. No Big Macs this time. It was a nice reception and later Dr. Muse and his wife, Marlene, Dave Adams and his wife, Barbara, and Dean Barker and his wife, Bev, took my Marlene and me to dinner at the City Club. At the reception, Ray Meyo was kidding me about not telling him I was coming to Akron. He said if there was anything he could do for me, he would.

Soon, I would have to seek his assistance. At Notre Dame, a coach didn't have to seek help. It sought him out. But Akron was

different. Our budget did not include any money for filming practices. This was in the period before cheap and easy video cassettes
were used. Every college team needed to film its practices so the
coaches could better see where things were going right and wrong.
When I told Ray that we had no film budget, he made a donation to
the University that covered a season's worth of filming. That's the
kind of man Ray is.

There were many people, both in the community and at the
University, like Ray Meyo. People like Bill Greenzalis and Dan
Marchetta, the late Dick Combs and the late Ron Fisher, Ron Tedeschi,
Dick Pitts, Dick Van Auken, John Piscitelli, Leo Starr, Joe Bolognue,
Rudy DiDonato, Paul Newman, Chuck Holland, Joe Petracca, Bill
Ellis, Jim Pier, Armand Dellovade, Ray Kapper, Dan Fuller, and Joe
Clapp who became benefactors and personal friends.

I needed all the friends I could get. When I showed up that
first fall at the coach's luncheon, it shocked me. I had come from a
situation in which 500 to 1,000 people would attend these func-
tions—even if you were losing. There were 13 people at the Akron
Coach's Luncheon and one of them was Bill Greenzalis. A friend of
mine from Cincinnati, Don Schmitt, had called me and told me that
a fellow in the same business he was in, cookies, wanted to invite
me over to dinner. That was Bill. He came to the luncheon and was
as appalled as I was by the turnout.

"I never knew Gerry until he came to Akron," Greenzalis
says. "I had followed his career and I had heard him speak once at a
sales conference in Philadelphia. That's why I called this mutual
friend. Gerry was something special. He came to the house for dinner and we've been good friends ever since.

"That day at the luncheon, I raised my hand and said: 'Coach,
who's in charge of this mess?' I never even knew Akron had a
football program until Gerry came. Apparently a lot of others didn't,
either."

If Bill wasn't alone, he was unique. He did something about
this. He asked to help and with our director of promotions, Joe
Dunn, who is one of the best in the business but is fighting long
odds, he recruited corporate sponsors for tables at Lunch with the
Coach. By the time I left there were 150 to 200 people attending in
the good times and 100 to 150 even in the bad. It was a tremendous improvement.

With Ron Tedeschi, who was president of the local Cleveland
Browns Backers, Bill helped to turn what had been a preseason

picnic into a full-blown dinner at which such captivating speakers as Akron attorney and entrepreneur Dave Brennan, New York Yankees owner George Steinbrenner and NBC sports commentator Bob Trumpy spoke. We not only were able to honor the seniors on that year's team but we also raised money. Likewise, for the postseason banquet, Dan Marchetta stepped in and turned a hamburger budget into a steak event. He and his wife, Helen, went to work and helped us do something for the team that the players would always remember.

I knew Dick Pitts, of course. He was one of the Stams' family friends who made Frankie drive to Notre Dame when we were trying to recruit him and then laughed about it. Some sense of humor, Dick Pitts. The only thing that exceeds it is his sense of what is right and wrong.

Before I agreed to come to Akron, I had been promised a membership in a country club, a place like Firestone, Portage or Fairlawn, the top clubs in the city. I didn't want the membership for myself, and if you'd ever see me play golf, you'd understand that. A country club membership is a tool. It allows a coach to take potential donors out for a round of golf where friendships are cemented. It gives him a place to take a prospective assistant coach. But Akron, because of the size of the athletic budget, wasn't used to allowing for this kind of expenditure.

"He was promised that," Dave Adams acknowledges. "It's invaluable. It's tough to be a fund-raiser or a promoter, and a coach is all those things. Gerry had to be the top-rated public relations person with the University because he had so much to overcome."

That's why it was so important that Dick Pitts stepped in.

Dick owns Green Hills Golf Course, a nine-hole facility east of Akron and one of the prettiest little places around. He said to just bring out whomever I wanted and he'd take care of it. In addition, he put on a scramble tournament each year to which I invited everyone but Jack Nicklaus. Green Hills didn't have the amenities or the status of a Firestone Country Club, where the NEC World Series of Golf is played each August, but it was a life preserver in a stormy sea and I'll be forever grateful.

Having to create my own golf course arrangements was typical. Akron, I quickly discovered, was a do-it-yourself place. Just when I had gotten beyond my Moeller pick-up-the-towels, turn-out-the-lights syndrome, thanks to Gene Corrigan's insistence at Notre Dame, I found myself in need of a refresher course.

When it came to the facilities with which I was confronted, I had no one to blame but myself. By not insisting that this hiring be done more step by step, which means a visit and inspection, I blew it. I reminded myself, in this instance, of the raw rookie who went to Notre Dame. At Akron, I had been able to put together the best staff I would ever have as a head coach. One reason was my experience at Notre Dame. But nothing about my time in South Bend prepared me for what I found in Akron. In fact, it lulled me into a false sense of what all Division I-A or I-AA wannabe programs were like.

It's a small thing but a tipoff: When I went into the football offices for the first time, I discovered the team's awards board hanging there. Awards boards, for things such as most tackles, best offensive line play and the like, serve a purpose. But they belong in the locker room where the players who have won these honors can see them. They don't fit in in a high-profile I-A program's anteroom. Recruits should be struck by the class and status of the offices. They give an impression of the entire program.

We revamped the offices as soon as we could. We tore down a divider and added three more offices and a staff room. That wasn't done until spring, but we got the pedestrian tile off the floor and replaced it with carpet. A couple of the coaches and I did the work ourselves during Christmas break when we weren't allowed to be out recruiting. The young men whom we were recruiting would be comparing our facilities with those of other I-A schools and we didn't want to lose a player because we appeared to be second-rate.

The offices were just the beginning. We had no practice field worth using, unless, of course, we covered sprinkler heads with knee pads. Our best bet was to use the field at the Rubber Bowl, but this presented two problems. The artificial surface proved hard on legs and knees and other body parts, and the locker room resembled the kind of torture chambers that Purdue's Ross-Ade Stadium and others of that Works Progress Administration vintage imposed on teams. The only difference was, at Akron it was both the visiting and home teams that suffered.

We needed to rebuild a locker room at the stadium. So again, coaches pitched in and we found help. These things didn't all happen during the first few months, but over time we managed to make the facilities as good as we could without any significant financial commitment for upgrading. It was a true team effort. A couple of University officials,Tom Goosby and Roger Ryan, found us some money in the stadium repair budget. Jim Dennis brought in his apprentices from the carpenters' union and they used the tearing out of walls and lowering of ceilings and other exercises as training.

To these kindnesses, Joe Petracca, who is in real estate and construction, added building and installing the lockers, and Dave Metro donated carpet. When we were finished, we had one of the better locker rooms in the country to show to recruits. No longer did we have to turn red from embarrassment.

Both facilities and the direction of the program offered re-cruiting challenges from the outset. We couldn't guarantee the play-ers we were trying to recruit initially that we would be accepted as a Division I-A team. Akron was trying to get into the Mid-American Conference and had, with business support, sold enough tickets the previous fall to qualify for I-A.

"When I came to Akron in January 1985," Dave Adams says, "I was assured everything was in place to move into the Mid-Ameri-can Conference. That all the background work had been done. That there had been a great deal of research done throughout the com-munity and everybody was behind the move and behind the sport going Division I-A and hiring a name coach.

"Well, to the best of my knowledge, very little was done. The feeling I had is that there hadn't been anything done. Nobody ever stood up and said: We did want a name coach. There was no own-ing up to it.

"And as far as the MAC is concerned, as I understand it there were assurances from a school or two that everything was OK to come into the MAC, but then one or two didn't want us once we were going to make the move."

That didn't bother me. I thought with the right support that we could move into I-A as an independent and then try to help create a Big East Conference or join a similar group. In fact, I talked with Akron Mayor Don Plusquellic about the possibility of being a part of a city-university built indoor facility similar to the Carrier Dome at Syracuse University. I wanted to see a facility that could be used the way the city's John S. Knight Center is used now for conventions but also one that could seat 30,000 for football and 20,000 for basketball. We also had architect's renderings of other facilities that we hoped to obtain financing for, but as time passed we had to put away our drawings and stop showing them to recruits. To continue when the odds for building these facilities were lower than for hitting the Ohio Lottery would have been dishonest.

We had to fight to get enough for our athletes to eat on weekends one year when the University changed the dining program to fit the majority of students who commute to school rather than live on campus. Our players, however, were a minority in number, but of major size and appetite. We also did not have an adequate tutoring program, academic study area or weight room. Heavy lifting for mind and body were necessary if we were going to play the big boys of college football.

For the weight room, which was run by Pat Ciccantelli, a hardworking, earnest young man who was just learning his trade after having been more involved with basketball than football, we made some deals that benefited the student body as a whole and the athletes in particular. We donated our weights to the student body, which found a suitable spot to use them in the natatorium, and in turn we had built for us a new weight room that Pat and I were able to furnish at cost. To facilitate funding, I made calls to state legislators whom I knew, including Stanley Aronoff from Cincinnati.

I seemed to be on the telephone almost as much as I was on the field. One of our first challenges was to put together a schedule of I-A schools. This isn't easy for an independent. In a league, such as the Mid-American or Big East, you have seven or eight games automatically in place against I-A opponents and you have to fill in three or four slots. We had 11 spots to plug. This was the other end of the spectrum from Notre Dame, the independent. Everyone wanted to play Notre Dame, and they would come to South Bend to do it because the payday was good. At Akron, we had to take who we could get and we had to go there to play them. Dave Adams and I worked for hours calling schools. He'd call the athletic directors, especially those he knew, and I'd call coaches. My Notre Dame exposure and connections proved an invaluable asset here.

We got games against schools with which we could be competitive—New Mexico, Oregon State, Temple, Rutgers—and with those we couldn't—Florida, Auburn, Tennessee. By playing the latter we not only generated some needed revenue for the program but we also created interest among high school players who were looking for the tremendous challenge that such games presented. In reality, though, no coach at a university such as Akron should be judged on these games. For instance, Akron opens its 1997 schedule at Nebraska. Coach Lee Owens should never be judged on that game or games against similar opponents. He should be judged on the nine or 10 games that he has a chance to win. In the end, of course, that isn't the way it works.

A potentially more devastating problem than the losses that result from such mismatches are the injuries. In 1990 when we played Florida, two-thirds of the way through the season, we lost five starters for the remainder of the year. That contributed significantly to losses to Rutgers (17-20), Northern Illinois (28-31) and Louisiana Tech (15-36).

There were other ways in which we lost players, including academic difficulties. This seldom occurred at Notre Dame, which sought out, and quite successfully based on our graduation rate, the more academically-gifted athlete and then supported him with tutors, study areas and anything else that might help him in the classroom.

Akron is different, which does not mean inferior. It is an urban university that caters to the student who commutes between home and school. It provides a quality education at an affordable price. In the football program, we gave opportunities to student-athletes whom we felt could play major-college football but who were not heavily recruited by major schools and those who showed academic promise.

Rather than look at such recruits as a gamble, I always thought of them as the young men who most needed the opportunity to prove that they could play the game and do the academic work. Our problem was, they often needed more help and guidance than the players who went to Notre Dame, yet our resources were fewer.

We were concerned about a tutoring program for our players. I found, however, that the University offered to all students free tutoring through the University College Developmental Program. It was a perfect answer—with one catch. There is a rule that if a person misses two sessions, he loses his tutor. It's a good rule, but sometimes student-athletes are tired or under-motivated. To prevent this, but most important to prevent a young man from throwing away his chance to succeed, we hired Rob Rardin as an assistant coach for our wide receivers but with the primary responsibility of keeping an eye on these situations. At Notre Dame, this was referred to as becoming too involved in the student's life. At Akron, I'd eventually hear the same criticism.

Coincidentally with my coming to Akron, the NCAA tight-ened its academic requirements. While it was an attempt to force schools that played fast and loose with the rules to show greater concern for the student-athlete, it also caught some well-intentioned programs, such as Akron, in its web. We wanted to help our athletes to succeed as students. But because many of them came from aca-demically disadvantaged backgrounds, the requirements sometimes worked not to improve their chances of success in college, but to diminish them.

If such rules were not demoralizing enough to coaches who had to try to recruit the caliber of athlete who could help in the move to I-A, there were people in Akron who made the circum-stances doubly difficult.

In the spring of our first year, I got a phone call from a local alumnus who had become a prominent businessman in the com-munity. He asked if he could come over to the athletic offices and talk to the football staff. I should have grilled him as to what he intended to say, but this guy had supported Akron athletics finan-cially, so I told him that he could come and talk to us. It seemed like the friendly thing to do.

His address was anything but friendly.

This man comes at you straight-ahead. No sugar coatings. No niceties. I don't think he means to be obnoxious or to try to hurt you, but he succeeds on both counts. In any case, he believes it is his responsibility to share with you what he thinks and to offer his interpretation of broad community feeling without a shred of evi-dence.

We were going through challenge after challenge, not the least of which was Jim Dennison's promotion to athletic director, a decision by Dr. Muse that had my staff in turmoil. Still, we gathered to listen to this community leader.

He announced that he and others felt the basketball program should be highlighted instead of football and that soccer, which he supported and which had been quite successful, deserved more financial attention and a higher profile. He felt our football pro-gram—which had just completed a 7-4 season—was detracting from the other programs and he made no bones about it.

I don't know how he thought we should react or what we were supposed to do. Maybe say: OK, Mr. Deep Pockets. We'll get out of Dodge now that you've told us. His address would have been better suited for an audience with the president, who had made this decision of emphasis.

The coaches were up in arms. A couple of them spoke up and challenged the man's assertions to his face. The others were fuming. So there was another situation in which I had to calm my coaches and it came on the heels of the ultimate disruption: Dr. Muse's decision to reassign Dave Adams to a job overseeing the construction of new buildings and the promotion of Jim Dennison to oversee, among other things, the football program that he was told he was not suited to coach on a I-A level.

Is this the definition of a nightmare, or what?

I got a call from Dr. Muse, who asked me to come to his office. The search for an athletic director had been on-going but I wasn't prepared for what I was about to hear. He told me that he was going to name Jim Dennison to the job.

"Dr. Muse," I said, "this puts me in a precarious position, a situation that will be difficult not only for me but also for Jim. I can understand why you're doing it, but two wrongs don't make a right. This is going to set the football program back four or five years."

It would, in fact, set it back to the point that it never recovered.

"I thought it would work better than it did," explains Dr. Muse, who now is president of Auburn University and has as his football coach Terry Bowden, one of my first staff members. "In a way it was an attempt to reach out to Jim and say: Look, maybe we made a mistake in the way we treated you. We're going to give you a chance to be the AD, to run this program. Let's let bygones be bygones."

From the outset, everyone had his own agenda and none of them meshed. Dr. Muse and Dave Adams wanted a big-name coach who would draw attention to a football program that had been well run and relatively successful on the Division I-AA level but off the radar screen. They didn't want to tell Jim Dennison he was no longer the coach until they found such a person and when they did, that person, me, kept saying that he didn't want the job if it would result in someone's ouster. As the sheriff said in the old Paul Newman movie, "Cool Hand Luke," there was a failure to communicate.

"When Dave Adams took me over to the president's office," Dennison says, "I didn't know what was going on until I sat down. So I can believe that Gerry wasn't told the entire truth."

When Ralph Staub learned that Jim Dennison had been named athletic director and thus was in charge of our fates, to one degree or another, he told me he wasn't staying. He said he had been through a similar situation at Cincinnati, where he had been head coach, and that it simply wouldn't work. I asked him to stay because I thought he was critical to our success.

He had turned the offensive line into a smart, effective unit and guided the offense to within one fluke play of the Division I-AA playoffs. Dennison was not sympathetic, saying at the time: "This was the year. We shot for Division II in '76 (and lost in the national final). This was the year we were shooting for I-AA. We were 10th in the country last year and we had most of those players back."

The unstated implication was clear. I had failed to do with Jim Dennison's players what he could have done: Win a championship.

"People expect miracles," Fuzzy Faust said then. "But Gerry's no miracle man."

If I had been, I'd have been able to convince Staubie to stay. And I couldn't.

"Gerry," he said, "I've been through too much of this. I can't handle it. If I was younger, maybe I'd attempt to do it."

A dozen years later, Ralph hadn't changed his mind about a situation he felt so strongly about that he not only quit, but he also sent Dr. Muse a letter.

"This was the dumbest thing I had ever seen," Staub says. "The president was just trying to pacify Jim. I didn't have anything against Jim. He was coach of the year in Ohio at one point and I voted for him. I didn't know him, but I thought he had done a helluva job. But if you have a coach who is coaching and he is not good enough to upgrade your program and then all of a sudden you put him in charge of another staff that you've brought in to do it, that doesn't make sense. My point is, I know he was bitter. It takes a helluva man to swallow something like that and forget it.

"I think Jim blamed the wrong person. I think he should have blamed the president of the University. I think what (Dr. Muse) did was completely wrong. It's like buying a store and putting a robber in your store to run it. I don't mean that Jim was doing anything wrong. It was just an extremely poor choice."

It was difficult for Jim not to blame me. Heck, I might have blamed me if I had been Jim. Dr. Muse was trying to solve a community split, a failed attempt I still respect.

"I know they were not going to make a change unless Gerry Faust was going to be that change," Dennison says. "I know that for a fact. Bill Muse told me: 'I have a good football coach. If I wanted a good football coach, I wouldn't make a change. The only reason I'm doing this is that Gerry Faust is a name and he's available.'"

It may be a matter of semantics, but that isn't exactly how Dr. Muse remembers it.

"It's pure speculation," Dr. Muse says, "but had Akron been admitted to the Mid-American Conference, we probably would not have made a change. We probably would have stayed with Jim. That would have been an easier transition to make."

So if Jim wants to blame someone, he should blame the MAC.

"Since we had to compete as an independent," Dr. Muse says, "to make that jump on our own, we felt we had to do something more dramatic."

I provided the drama. But I was available only because no one told me the truth when I kept asking for it. If they had, I might never have met Whitey Wahl and that would have been a shame. Whitey had been a great athlete at the University and very supportive of the athletic program. He not only gave the program money but he also was active in fund-raising. Most important, he was willing to give a new guy a chance. I'm grateful, because at that time, Whitey was doing the commentary on the radio broadcasts of our games. If he had reacted to me the way the local businessman I told you about had done, it would have been just that much worse. Instead, Whitey excused an initial faux pas of mine.

I didn't know Whitey from Adam. Or from Eve, for that matter. One day when I was really busy during about my fifth or sixth week in Akron, I bumped into Whitey in the hallway of Rhodes Arena where the athletic offices are located. I said hello but just kept walking.

"You don't remember my name do you?" Whitey said.

"Sir," I replied, "I apologize, but I don't."

"Well, it's Whitey Wahl and don't you forget it. I can either help you or hurt you, and I think you want me to help you."

Whitey got my attention.

When I found out who he was and got to know him, I came to realize what a special person he is and we became great friends. Never forgot his name again, either.

Whitey's friendship was not the only new one that I came to prize. I loved meeting for breakfast on Saturday mornings at Niam's Parkette, which is a lot like an old diner but without the car. Eddy Niam would be there, of course, along with Joe LaRose, who owns the House of LaRose, an Akron beer and wine distributorship, Joe

Petracca, Bill Greenzalis, Norm Singleton, Bobby Bruno, Ron Tedeschi, Paul Hummel, Bruce Romeo, Pat D'Andrea and Bill Doria. Whatever the problems at Akron, the people I met made them seem less consequential.

It's the same at the University. There are so many good people who tried to help us overcome the obstacles that it would not be fair to try to list them all. When I'm speaking, especially to high school students on behalf of the University, I tell them that if they take a look on the Hilltop in Akron where the University is located, they'll discover one of the best-kept secrets in America. It continues to amaze me that I live in this great city and work for this University that has a nationally known College of Polymer Science and Polymer Engineering and offers a tremendous education for a moderate price and when people approach me, they only connect me with Notre Dame and Moeller.

If the first year at Notre Dame required a great leap on my part, the first season at Akron demanded an even greater adjustment. Our staff, especially the older, more experienced members, had come from large college programs such as Pittsburgh or from the pros. The first game we coached on the road at Akron was at Eastern Michigan in Ypsilanti. As we were riding to Michigan in our buses, we stopped at a roadside park and had sandwiches, apples and Cokes. Here is Andy Urbanic, former backfield coach at Pittsburgh; Bob Shaw, who had been at Arkansas, Arizona and in the pros; and Ralph Staub, offensive coordinator at Ohio State, an offensive coach with the Dallas Cowboys and Houston Oilers and head coach at the University of Cincinnati, and myself, fresh off the griddle at the hottest, best football program in college football. We're sitting on a curb alongside the road with our sandwiches and Cokes.

"You know," I said to the coaches, "if you're in coaching long enough, you get humbled, don't you?"

They almost fell off the curb they were laughing so hard.

"We used to do this when we were high school coaches," they said of bus trips and box lunches.

"You know what else?" I said, smiling. "This isn't bad."

They laughed again.

"No," they said, "it's fun."

Those moments were priceless. I remember another such moment with Staubie. We were on a recruiting trip to Cincinnati, where we successfully tilled new recruiting ground for Akron. It was about 7 in the evening and we were driving through Columbus, near Interstate 71 and Highway 315. Woody Hayes lived nearby. Woody and I became close friends while I was at Moeller, and, of course, Ralph had been one of his most trusted assistants.

Ten or 12 players from Moeller must have gone to Ohio State to play for Woody over a 15-year period. His last year, he came down to see me. I was in the office. It was early December, about a week and a half before OSU played Clemson in the bowl game that would end Woody's career.

Woody always drove a pickup truck. He took me out to his truck to show me the Astroturf he had put in its bed. It was the same turf they had put down in Ohio Stadium. I always liked Woody to drop by, but this was unusual. He almost always called first.

"Coach," I said, "what are you doing down here?"

I thought he had come to recruit. But he hadn't. I asked if he needed a glass of water. I always had to get him one when he came by. He said he wanted to talk privately. I had a little locker room just for the coaches. We went in. There was a single bench with lockers on both sides. I sat at one end of the bench and Woody sat at the other. I shut the door.

"Coach," Woody said, "there's just something not clicking on my football team this year. Do you have any idea what it is?"

"Coach," I said, "I never get to see the team play. I don't get to watch on TV because I'm so busy with our season. So I can't answer that."

I was astounded that he had asked me. I mean, this is Woody Hayes, one of the greatest college football coaches who ever lived. But I was probably one of the high school coaches who was closest to him. And I did know something that had nothing to do with watching the Buckeyes play. I had heard from a trusted friend who would know that there were internal problems on Woody's staff. Even before the sideline incident in which Woody hit the Clemson player, there were people on his staff jockeying for his job, because he was getting up in years. They should have understood that at Ohio State, an assistant was unlikely to be elevated to head coach. It was like Notre Dame, where, of course, Bob Davie has just proved there are exceptions to every rule.

"Coach," I said to Woody, "I know for a fact that you have three or four people politicking for your job even though I know you're going to be there for years. You have to get it stopped."

Woody had a controlled temper and he used it for a reason —95 percent of the time. The other five percent caused him the trouble. He slammed his fist down on the bench.

"That isn't true," he said, and none too gently.

"Coach," I said, "it is true."

"What would you do?" he asked.

"I'd fire them. You have 10 to 12 families at stake on your staff and two or three guys might be ruining it for all of them."

Then Woody told me something I didn't know.

"I've never fired a coach in my life," he said. "They *all* have families."

"You have to be kidding," I said.

"Never. There is only one I would have fired, but he left on his own. He wasn't doing an above-board job."

I told him the names of the coaches I knew were causing problems. He thanked me, and we talked for another 15 minutes. He got up, thanked me again and left. Two weeks later the incident occurred at the Gator Bowl and it was Woody, not the assistants, who was fired. To this day, I think television failed to portray the incident fairly. There is no excuse for what Woody did, but there was more on that film than is usually seen. I've seen film clips of Clemson linebacker Charlie Bauman shoving the ball practically in Woody's face after he had intercepted. All you ever saw on the TV clips was Woody retaliating.

On this recruiting-trip night several years later, Ralph Staub said: "You know, Coach isn't doing very well. We ought to stop and see him."

"We have time," I said. "That's a great idea."

Woody lived in the house he had lived in when he began coaching at Ohio State. He was a great man of simple tastes. Mrs. Hayes opened the door and was surprised to see us.

"Ralph, Gerry," she said, "you couldn't have come at a better time. Woody will be happy to see you."

Happy isn't the word. We didn't get out of there until 12:30 a.m. Woody told story after story after story. Ralph had heard most of them a hundred times, and I'd heard a lot of them as well. But Woody was a great storyteller and when he was telling them, you didn't care how many times you had heard them before. He had a wonderful time, and we did, too. That's the coaching fraternity for you. One coach's health is failing and two others who knew him when he walked with the coaching giants stop to visit, because they have not forgotten who this man is. Not was. Still is.

We got to Cincinnati awfully late, but I wouldn't trade that time for anything. Time is the one thing that can't be replaced, and we had spent it wisely that night, because Woody died not long after that. That night was our goodbye.

Recruiting for Akron could be difficult compared to Notre Dame. Staubie was right, though, when he said that Akron sat at the core of a wealth of high school football talent. The problem was mining it.

When we arrived, the program had been built on a base of players who had promise but often were ignored by Division I-A schools. Under Jim Dennison's guidance, some of these athletes developed into fine football players, often with the coming of physical maturity. The old Division II and I-AA Akron could gamble on this physical and performance growth. The new I-A Akron had to widen its recruiting base and raise the talent bar. The new Akron offered full scholarships. The old Akron often split scholarships, not only for the benefit of more players but also with the hope that from greater numbers would emerge the few who could play. You can't recruit that way against I-A teams. If they offer a full scholarship and you offer a partial scholarship, you lose.

Because we became more selective and went after only the best of the Northeast Ohio players, we were accused of abandoning local recruiting, of not caring about the Akron and Canton and Massillon player. This never was true. But the illusion grew, in part from our initial recruiting. Because the players whom the previous staff had recruited had been recruited to play I-AA football and we intended to move up to I-A, we felt we had to re-evaluate each player who had been offered a scholarship.

I called every one of these 10 players personally and told them to send their game film to us again and we'd evaluate it. Of the 10, we offered two of them scholarships and one, Scott Brown from Parma, ended up starting for us for three years as a defensive tackle. Most of those to whom we didn't offer scholarships understood. We explained that we'd love to have them join us as walk-ons and if they proved themselves, we would give them full scholarships the following year. A couple of those we turned down were upset and felt we had reneged. We tried to explain that it wouldn't be fair to the University to give a scholarship to someone we didn't feel could play at Akron and neither would it be fair to them, because they wanted to play.

At the other end of the spectrum during the Akron years was Ricky Powers, the great Buchtel High School running back. Everyone wanted Ricky. He had been rated the top recruit in America. Many players of such talent from Northeast Ohio refused to even consider Akron, which was just getting started in I-A. They wanted the Big Ten. They wanted Penn State, which has turned the Big Ten into the Big Eleven. They wanted Notre Dame. They wanted what they considered the big time. We tried, nevertheless, to convince even the players of Powers' caliber to look closely at the advantages of going to school in Akron, where they not only could make a team but also could make a future career among people who would always remember their names.

Among other things, I mentioned this advantage to Ricky. But an *Akron Beacon Journal* story, written by Ralph Paulk, made it sound as if I had made false promises to Ricky and two other Buchtel players.

"I don't like what Faust did to (Michigan player Eric) Graves and Lester Carney (a freshman receiver at Northwestern)," Paulk quoted Powers as saying. "He told them he wanted them. Then, at the last minute, he said no to them. He may have done the same thing to me

"I remember when Faust came to our school, he told me that if I came to Akron they could get an indoor stadium and that people would come see me play at Akron U. He said I should stay home 'because you owe it to the people.' That really turned me off."

I was flabbergasted to read this. It seemed to confirm the suspicions that some people held about our program. The problem was it wasn't true. After this story appeared, I received a copy of a letter that Tim Flossie, Ricky's coach at Buchtel High School, had written to sports editor Tom Giffen. I quote, in part:

"In regard to the statements made by Ricky Powers concerning Akron University and Coach Faust, there were several errors and untruths printed. First and foremost, Akron University has always recruited Division I prospects at Buchtel and did it very aggressively and well within the rules provided. They have also always taken into consideration a player's wishes. In Ricky Powers' case, Ricky asked Akron U to delay contact with him because he was overwhelmed by all the other schools' attention. Akron U then contacted him when he was willing to talk to them. I know this is true because Ricky asked me to convey these messages to Coach Faust and his staff personally.

"In regard to Ricky and Ralph's comments concerning Eric Graves and Lester Carney's recruitments, I again take exception. Eric and Lester were both recruited by Akron U and Coach Faust and his staff.They never, ever said 'no to Eric and Lester at the last minute.' Eric and Lester were interested in other schools . . .What Ricky and Ralph were talking about was Akron U's interest in two other players at Buchtel whom Akron decided not to recruit because of the positions they played and other commitments by players to Akron University. At no time did Akron promise these young men anything other than an interest to see them on film.

"Coach Faust and his staff have done a fine and honorable job of recruiting at Buchtel. I have never heard one 'negative' remark about another school from them . . . .To give even less credence to the comments about recruiting Buchtel players, Akron U has signed Shawn Bagley to a full scholarship this year (1990).They also offered Robert Garnett the opportunity to sign and were interested in Kenya Ragsdale until he committed elsewhere.

"Coach Faust and Akron University, in my opinion, and to my knowledge, were falsely portrayed and done harm because of a lack of good, professional research and proper reporting techniques. Coach Faust, I am sorry and so is Buchtel High School."

I appreciated Tim's letter, but the recruiting of Ricky Powers was only the highest profile of problems we encountered.We never gave up on local players and as time went on, we began to get more and more of the better ones.Too often, however, players would blame us for some slight when they simply wanted to go away to school but did not want to say so directly.

If recruiting could cause a coach to gnash his teeth and pull out his hair, it also could offer magic moments, such as the "recruitment" of Mike O'Connor, who started four years for us at center.

Mike's dad, Jake, and I played football together at the University of Dayton.Jake moved to California and started a business in Orange County but we remained close and when I went to Notre Dame, he brought Mike to some games.They'd fly in and I'd get tickets for them.When I'd been at Akron for a couple of years, Jake, who's from Elyria, Ohio, was making a visit to his mother and brought his family. He called before the trip, and I told him that our freshmen were reporting for preseason practice the day after he arrived, but that I'd like to get with him for an hour or so.Jake said he was going to bring Mike, who was 6-foot-1 and about 220 pounds. He had played linebacker and guard for Mater Dei High School in Santa Ana, California, and was very good. He had attended junior college part-time in order to get into Boston College, where he was intending to become a walk-on with the football team.

After Jake and Mike got to Akron, we were shooting the bull and Mike was telling me his plan, I told him: "Mike, our freshmen start tomorrow. If you'll walk on here and you start or become a projected starter, I'll give you a scholarship."

"Coach," he said, "we're going golfing this afternoon with my uncles. Let me think about it and I'll call you late tonight."

The call came, and so did Mike.

The first week of practice, however, he broke his thumb and was sidelined. So we moved him to center and told him that he could probably be a starter after red-shirting his first year.

He worked so hard and was so dedicated. He was the toughest player and greatest student. He graduated with a 3.5 grade-point average in business. His final season, which was his fifth year in school, he was working on his MBA. I didn't know it would work out as it did. It was a spur of the moment suggestion. I just liked Mike. I knew he was a competitor. I knew he had good genes. His dad had been a great competitor on the field, too. Mike became our captain, and I got to see a lot more of his father, my friend. Jake flew to every one of Mike's games, home and away.

Mike O'Connor was in his first season of starting on the offensive line as a red-shirt freshman when we took one of our more memorable trips, this to Albuquerque to play the University of New Mexico. We had begun to play I-A schools with recognizable names outside the Mid-American Conference—Temple and Oregon State, for instance—but we had yet to win one of those games. We fell to 4-7 in 1987, competing on the I-A level for the first time after losing a good senior class and finding it difficult to recruit I-A caliber replacements when we could no more than promise that we had applied to the NCAA for I-A status. With two recruiting classes behind us, we began to make progress, which in this situation had to be measured in starts and stops. The NCAA refused to consider the uniqueness of what we were doing and would not allow us to catch up more rapidly with the number of scholarships offered by I-A schools. We had 62 players on scholarship and 92 slots available our first year in I-A. The NCAA had reduced the number of scholarships that could be offered annually from 30 to 25 and wouldn't allow us an exemption. We weren't trying to catch up in a single recruiting season, but we thought five more scholarships a year would not be unfair under the circumstances.

No steady climb to the top of the mountain existed, however, not even when we visited Albuquerque and rode the world's largest tram up a real mountain to a restaurant from which you could see El Paso, Texas. Overloaded with hefty football players, the tram stopped halfway to the top and had to be reversed and some of the players removed before it again began what would be a successful ascent.

The next night we scored what probably was Akron's most prestigious victory ever when Bob Dombroski kicked a 22-yard field goal with four seconds remaining to make it 30-28. Suddenly a team that had started 0-3 had created a moment from which it could draw faith in itself and relish the joy of winning. At the hotel after the game, we ordered about a million pizzas with the approximate circumference of the earth. I've never seen a happier group of young men, not to mention coaches. Of all our trips, and we always tried to make them enjoyable and educational for the team, that may have been the best.

I know without reservation which personal journey during the Akron years left an imprint on my life. It was a trip to Europe with Ken Schneider, my good friend. Ken loves to travel. Marlene and Ken's wife, Jan, don't care for these trips. So Ken and I headed off to visit three important religious sites: Lourdes in France, Fatima in Portugal and Medjugorje, a town in the former Yugoslavia at which an apparition of the Blessed Mother is said to still be appearing at the Catholic Church.

We flew first to Lisbon, Portugal and drove to Fatima, arriving one day after The Feast of Fatima. When we went to the basilica, the first thing I saw was a woman crawling on the concrete courtyard, carrying her baby. I'm convinced that something was wrong with her baby and that I was witnessing a great act of faith.

Though we could not speak Portuguese, we had a religious bond that I think allowed us to help a family of peasants who invited us to share their picnic lunch that day. In return we gave them $20 and were able to make them understand that our money was like the food they had so willingly shared with us: Not a handout but a small gift of friendship.

After flying to France and then driving another 200 kilometers, we arrived at Lourdes, where the Blessed Mother appeared to

Bernadette. When I saw the Grotto there, it was as if I had returned to Notre Dame. It was identical. Coincidentally, near Akron I had found another Grotto. It's located at St. Joe's Parish in Suffield and I drive there often, always finding the peace I found at Notre Dame. I bet there aren't 10 Grottoes in the United States. That I would pick this place with another Grotto to end my career seemed part of my destiny.

At Lourdes, we encountered some Irish priests from Dublin and asked if we might accompany the priests for Mass with the sick. After Mass, people helped to take patients from huge hospital wards in wheelchairs and even beds to the Grotto each night. There were maybe 80 male patients, ranging in age from 4 to 80. Ken and I got to talking to one man with an Irish brogue. I told him I was from Akron, Ohio.

"Where's Akron?" he asked.

I explained and he wanted to know what I did for a living.

"I'm an American football coach," I explained.

Then Kenny, my promotion manager, blurts out: "He was head coach at Notre Dame for five years."

"What's Notre Dame?" the man asked.

I said to myself: "Boy, it isn't that important, is it?" Then I explained about Notre Dame. It still didn't mean anything to the man.

"What are you doing here, Gerry?" the man asked.

"I'm on vacation. A holiday. We've been to Fatima and we're going to Medjugorje."

"That's great," he said.

"What are you doing here?" I asked. "Are you here to help the sick?"

"No, Gerry," he said, "I've got four months to live. I have lymphoma."

"You know," I said, "so many miracles happen here at Lourdes. Maybe one of those miracles will happen to you."

"Gerry, I'm 48 years old. I have four children. Two are out of high school and two are almost out. Four boys. I've lived my life."

Then he pointed to a group of children in wheelchairs.

"If a miracle is going to happen," he said. "let it happen to one of them. They haven't lived their lives."

I had to turn away. I couldn't say a word. All I could do was shed a silent tear and think: What a man of devotion. What a man of God. Here I am praying all these years to win a football game. That's so insignificant. To prove how insignificant, this man didn't even know what Notre Dame was.

I think the Good Lord was telling me that there had been a purpose for my having been at Notre Dame, a purpose other than winning football games. At that moment, a peace came over me that I had never known before, and it has remained with me ever since. From that point on, I never prayed to win a football game, and there were more than a few I needed to win. I just prayed for my family and for others. I didn't witness any miracles at Lourdes, but maybe the miracle was an Irishman who made me understand more fully what I had always known. There are more important things than winning football games.

At Medjugorje, we stayed with some peasants, went to St. James to Mass and then into the mountains to pray the Stations of the Cross. I even got to see Vicka Ivankovic, one of the visionaries to whom the Blessed Mother had appeared. It happened in a round-about way, for she had burned herself with some grease from a hot skillet and she wasn't seeing anyone. But when Ken and I happened upon a crew shooting a film on the miracle of Medjugorje, they allowed me to accompany them when they visited Vicka, who had agreed to keep her appointment with the crew. It was my birthday. This must have been the Lord's present to me. I sat and listened as she told the film crew of a vision in which the Blessed Mother came to Medjugorje and with four children set off to visit heaven, hell and purgatory. Two other children did not wish to see these places.

I didn't know if this could be true. Believing someone had been permitted to see heaven, hell and purgatory stretched my faith. But the more I listened, the more I began to believe. At the end of the session, I asked the interpreter if I could ask Vicka a question. Vicka agreed.

"What does a person do who is continually tempted in life, which I am?" I wondered. "What do you do to stop that?"

Vicka looked at me and spoke one word.

"Prayer," she said through the interpreter.

After our pilgrimage, I asked Ken Schneider, who had been skeptical about the Blessed Mother's appearance in Medjugorje, if he had come to believe.

"I'm not much on miracles and happenings," Ken says now. "I went as a Doubting Thomas."

Ken had decided, however, that the Blessed Mother had appeared at Medjugorje but that She was not appearing there when we visited. Back in America, Ken flew from Atlanta to Cincinnati and I came home to Akron. Then he called. I wasn't home, but he told Marlene that some of the links between the beads on the rosary he had taken to Medjugorje had turned gold.

When I called to say hello to my parents, I told them the story of Kenny's rosary and my mom said: "Did your rosary change?"

"No," I said.

"Why didn't it?"

"Mom," I said, "my rosary doesn't need to change. I believe. Kenny is the one who didn't believe."

The next day when Marlene and I were going to Mass, I reached over to my turn-signal bar where I keep my rosary and took it in my hand to pray and I noticed something different. The silver links around each Our Father had turned gold. I couldn't believe it. I called Kenny and asked where his rosary had changed color. It was the same place.

"Gerry went over there a true believer," Ken says, "but I came back as one. He had the knowledge and took us to the right place to change me."

The odd thing was that my rosary wasn't the one I had taken to Medjugorje. My dad showed the change to people after I had taken it to Dayton for him to see. I wanted him to have it, but he insisted that I keep this sign of faith.

Not long afterward, our assistant athletic trainer, Brian Sifferlin, borrowed my car to take an injured player to the hospital for an X-ray and somewhere along the way my rosary became dislodged from the turn-signal bar and was lost. I didn't discover this until the next day and my reaction, I admit, was out of proportion to the loss of a simple rosary. I was as mad as I've ever been, because to me it wasn't a simple rosary. It was a symbol that miracles do happen. What I didn't lose, though, was the feeling inside that this is so.

If the rosary was a wonder of a religious sort, Mike Woodford experienced one more secular. Because we had to watch how we spent our money, I limited the number of coaches who could be on the road in the spring at the same time. So Mike, who recruited Northwest Ohio and the junior colleges around the country, was home. He called me on a Saturday night.

"Coach," Woody said, "you'd better sit down."

I thought: "Oh no. What's happened? I'd just lost a couple of coaches. Don't tell me I'm going to lose another."

"What's going on, Woody?"

"Coach, I won the Lotto."

"That's fine," I said, not too excited because I didn't play or follow the Ohio Lottery. "How much did you win?"

"$16 million," Woody said.

That got my attention.

"Where's that ticket?" I asked.

"It's right here in my hand."

"Don't let it out of your hand," I told him. "You go to bed with that ticket. That's unbelievable."

Woody had always told us he was going to win the Lotto. He had faith, and faith of all kinds can work wonders. He had gone to a Dairy Mart, bought five tickets and sat down in front of the TV as they read the winning numbers. The numbers come up randomly. They put them in sequence later. Woody couldn't believe it. He slammed his fist on the table. He thought he had five of the six numbers. Then he went over them again. And he almost fell over onto the coffee table he had just slammed.

Woody kept coaching. I didn't know if he would. He gave $1.5 million to his mother and father, but I never saw a penny. I used to kid him about that. If it hadn't been for me, he might have been out of state recruiting and never had a chance to buy the winning ticket. We used to laugh about that. Some things are providential.

Though Mike did quit two years later, he has since returned to coaching at Walsh University with Jim Dennison. That doesn't surprise me. The money never affected his work. He worked just as hard as he ever had. Because of that, I felt I owed him a raise each year. We both knew he didn't need the money, but I needed to say with that raise that I respected his coaching and his contribution to our staff.

Early on, we hit a jackpot of another sort: national exposure. The spotlight I had been unable to dodge at Notre Dame cast an afterglow on Akron and its decision to hire me for the move to Division I-A.

"It was estimated in his first year here," Dave Adams says, "that Gerry brought us about $3 million worth of publicity. Someone sent me an article from Paris about his first spring football practice.

ESPN came in to do a Thursday-night game. Whoever was doing the national college game of the week would do cutaways to our game."

Television wasn't the only benefit. It filtered down to individuals.

"Dr. Muse and I were in New Orleans at an NCAA meeting right after the announcement that Gerry was going to be our coach and we took a cab to dinner," Dave Adams remembers. "The cabby asked us where we were from and Dr. Muse told him Akron, Ohio. The cabby, with one hand on the wheel, turned around to face us in the backseat. That caused him to jerk the wheel to the side.

"The cabby said: 'Akron, Ohio? You just hired Gerry Faust.'

"He damned near went up on the curb. We told him that yes we did and now look straight ahead, please. He was a guy who had never heard of the University of Akron before. But that's the way it was with Gerry. For a while, it was outrageous the number of letters Gerry was receiving daily. The secretaries were going crazy. They couldn't keep up with it. They couldn't believe it."

Records tell only part of any story. My record at Akron was 43-53-3, but until a disastrous final season of 1-10, we had been at the .500 level that might be expected of a program struggling to find itself on a new level of competition.

"I think Gerry did a tremendous job for Akron," Dr. Muse says. "Even today Akron benefits from Gerry having been coach. Everyone I meet asks me where I was before I came to Auburn. I tell them the University of Akron and the first thing they mention is Gerry Faust. They know that's where Gerry Faust went to coach. That's important because three-fourths of the coverage a university gets is athletic.

"There were two things we were trying to accomplish when we hired Gerry: No. 1 was to raise the visibility of the University of Akron and No. 2 was to move up to I-A. You didn't have to travel outside the state of Ohio to confront people who had never heard of the University of Akron. I believe we accomplished this goal. I hardly ever encounter anyone now who says they haven't heard of the University of Akron and it is always in association with Gerry Faust. The view today is that Akron is a major school playing on a major level. They certainly have not been as successful as they wanted, but the visibility aspect of that objective has largely been fulfilled and we did end up in the Mid-American Conference which is where we wanted to be in the first place."

The circuitous route to the MAC caused problems and misperceptions. It caused problems for coaches such as Bob Huggins, who lost the opportunity to have a conference's automatic berth into the NCAA Tournament, and it created the misperception that I felt my program was too good for the MAC. That's not how I felt at all. My interest in a conference, such as the Big East, was purely practical.

To be successful on the I-A level, and that means financially, I felt we had to be associated with a conference with a high-enough profile to attract television and bowl revenues. Most of the Mid-American athletic programs struggle financially. It was nothing against the MAC. The MAC plays a better caliber of football than most people realize, but it gets little support. I saw this when I was at Moeller. What upset me was not the MAC, but the fact that people don't support the MAC.

Historically, people never supported Akron football. You can look it up. The *Akron Beacon Journal* reported in December 1996, on the status of the program 10 years after going I-A. One of the alarming trends it suggested was the declining attendance overall and that of the Acme-Zip Game in particular. The Acme-Zip Game is sponsored each year by a local supermarket chain. Once, it was the social event of an Akron fall. But no more. I can't explain why, but I think it is coincidental, not because of the shift to I-A. While the newspaper's figures were accurate, they also were incomplete.

During our eight seasons in I-A, our home attendance averaged between a high of 17,818 (1993) and a low of 8,841 (1988). Removing the Acme-Zip Game, the highs and lows were 16,222 and 6,784. In 1996, the average attendance was 7,418 with Acme-Zip and 6,024 without. But, in fact, Akron had seldom averaged more than 10,000, even in the glory years of Jim Dennison, which, if you look that up as well, were few. High school football draws better in Northeast Ohio than Akron football. It always has.

When Dr. Muse and Jim Dennison called me in the summer of 1991 and told me that Akron was going to join the MAC, I told them that while I had continuing reservations, I would, of course, support the move. The irony is that I helped to make the move possible.

"If it hadn't been for Gerry Faust," says Karl Benson, then commissioner of the MAC and now commissioner of the Western Athletic Conference, "Akron might not have gotten into the Mid-American Conference at all. I told our members: 'Why not Akron? Gerry Faust has a great profile. It would help us.' "

I knew joining the MAC would help Akron's total athletic program, bringing together men's and women's sports under one umbrella. We had teams in three different leagues. I also knew it would be a hard sell to my staff. We had been telling recruits that we were going to play teams different from those in the Mid-American Conference. It affected the person we could recruit. We could sell ourselves to players with a vision of big-time football. Now when we talked to high school coaches, they would suggest different players to us, their MAC-caliber players, those they thought were not likely to make it in the Big Ten or at Pitt or even Cincinnati. We had to sell the advantages of the Mid-American Conference, and there were many. The MAC offered a championship, a bowl game (the Las Vegas Bowl, now replaced by the Motor City Bowl in Pontiac, Mich., and the Music City Bowl in Nashville) and the opportunity for players from Ohio and Pennsylvania to be close enough to home that parents could see at least eight of their games each season.

I also knew the MAC would not be an easy conference in which to win, week in and week out. Jim Dennison's teams had played MAC opponents but they had been in a position to treat each of those games as one meant to prove they belonged in the conference. We couldn't do that. During Jim Dennison's 13 seasons, he had great success against Eastern Michigan (7-2), during a period when it was on a losing streak of 28 games, but far less success (5-7) against other MAC opponents, including Ball State 2-2, Kent 2-3, Western Michigan 1-0, Central Michigan 0-1 and Bowling Green 0-1.

I'm not sure Bob Huggins would have been happy in the Mid-American Conference. He likes to say that he loves Akron and uses my coming to the University and the changes it brought to his basketball program as circumstances for the reason he left, but I have my doubts. Why would a guy who loved Akron so much twice ask me to put in a good word for him for other jobs?

When Bob arrived in Akron, he announced he wanted to win a national championship here. Everyone applauded. When I came, I just said I wanted to play as high a level I-A competition as we reasonably could. I got booed. I was looking down on the Mid-American Conference, people said. The truth is, Bob Huggins would never have stayed in Akron with the facility he had to recruit players. The James A. Rhodes Arena is nice. It also is a spruced-up, oversized high-school gym. That's why I longed for a downtown football/basketball arena connected to a convention center.

Bob got his excellent facilities in Cincinnati and has taken a team to the Final Four. He began the 1996-97 season ranked as the No. 1 team in the country and was the featured story in *Sports Illustrated*. That's success to some. But frankly, if a story in which the great Oscar Robertson accuses his alma mater's basketball program of having no real interest in the players means success, I don't want it. Before he got the Cincinnati job, Bob approached me in front of the athletic offices. I was talking to one of my assistants. We'd just come from the weight room.

"Gerry," Bob said, "the University of Dayton head basketball job is open."

"I know," I said.

"I'm interested in that job. Would you call? I know you have a lot of influence as a graduate of Dayton. Would you put my name in?"

"Bob," I said, "I won't do that. I'll be right up front with you. I'll help you with any job but the Dayton job. That's my alma mater. You're a great basketball coach, but I don't like the way you handle kids. I don't want you at my University."

He walked away. I think he was startled.

"Jeez, Coach," my assistant said, "you told him."

"I told him the truth. Just the way I'd tell you. This guy is a heckuva coach, and he's demanding on his players, which is fine. But I just can't take that language he uses. I think you can get your point across without it. He has his philosophy and I have mine. I just don't want that at my alma mater."

I had gone to Akron's game against Ohio State in the National Invitation Tournament. Bob Junko, Chris Ball, my buddy Bill Greenzalis and I had seats behind the Akron bench in Ohio State's St. John Arena. Akron played well, but it was embarrassing to sit behind the bench and listen to Huggins. I didn't say anything until a man in scarlet and gray sitting nearby asked: "Aren't you Coach Faust?"

"Yes, sir," I said. "I am."

"Well, do you coach like this?"

"No, sir, I don't."

"Thank God," he said.

I didn't say another word, but I agreed. If this is how you have to behave to win big, then I don't want to win big. The trade-off is too great.

About three weeks after Bob approached me concerning the Dayton job, I saw him in the hallway of Rhodes Arena, and he said: "The Cincinnati job is open."

"I know some people," I said. "I'll call for you."

Which is what I had promised to do. I called Barry Scholak, who had clout in the Bearcat Club. We had been neighbors when I coached at Moeller. He graduated from UC. I told him I was calling on behalf of Bob Huggins and if they wanted a coach who would make them a winner, Bob was their man. I told Barry that Bob was the guy I'd go after. I don't know that my call had anything to do with it, but Bob got the job.

There are, of course, ways to inspire a team other than screaming at it. I preferred the way my friend Ray Meyo demonstrated on an occasion when I asked him if he would speak to our players. Ray, as I've mentioned, is the president and chief operating officer of R&R International Inc. and a member of the University of Akron Board of Trustees. Since my Akron teams were comprised of many young men who had had to struggle to overcome disadvantages they had encountered in their lives, I thought Ray might serve as a role model. I know how much I admire him.

When a coach invites someone from outside the team to speak, in this case, following a practice, some players will be interested and others won't. You never know how it will go. But Ray's address to the team was one of the most sincere, hard-hitting I've ever heard given to a team. It couldn't have been more appropriate for young men, some of whom had come from environments or situations that weren't easy to escape.

Ray told them about America, about what a great country this is, about what tremendous opportunities we all have. Most important, he told them about his childhood. He came from a family of Italian immigrants.

"We lived in Cleveland," Ray said, "and I was born with a speech impediment. Every day for six or eight years I had to stand in front of a mirror and speak. I also had buck teeth. The kids used to make fun of me because of my appearance and my speech impediment. But I said to myself: 'Some day, I'm going to prove to all these kids and neighbors that Ray Meyo is a success.'"

He made up his mind when he was 10 years old and never deviated from that path. Now, he is very successful businessman. He's a philanthropist. He gives to more than 65 charities a year. He and his wife, Marie, have reared a wonderful family. He told the players if he could overcome his appearance and speech impediment, they could make something out of themselves as well.

Ray went to Notre Dame at age 16. He graduated from Case Western with a law degree and became a chief executive. The story struck a chord. I've never seen a team pay as much attention to an outside speaker. Some of the players went up to him afterward and shook his hand. A couple of them asked if they could talk further with him. These young men were from difficult environments, tough circumstances. But none, they realized, had had it any tougher than Ray Meyo.

When the end came at Akron, though, even Ray couldn't save me. Nobody could. Though in 1992, two years before, we had been picked to finish ninth in the MAC in our first season and ended up third and with a 7-3-1 overall record, we were 1-10 in 1994 and that's unacceptable.

"It was very difficult," Ray says. "I voted for one of my best friends to be replaced on the job. I thought it was best for the University of Akron and best for Gerry."

In the final analysis, Ray is right. It has been for the best. Accepting this, however, has not been easy.

I have worked for three presidents at Akron, two of whom, Dr. Muse and Dr. Marion Ruebel, are excellent administrators, and for four athletic directors, including Dean Richard Aynes from the University's law school. Dean Aynes served on an interim basis in 1993 when Jim Dennison left Akron and became athletic director and coach of a new football program at Walsh University in North Canton, Ohio. Two athletic directors, Dave Adams and Dean Aynes, believed in me. Two didn't. The two who didn't were in charge for seven and a half of my nine years as coach.

Under different circumstances, I think Jim Dennison and I could have been friends. The situation made it impossible.

"Personally, of course, I'm only human and there was hurt," Jim Dennison says. "But professionally, it was not a difficult situation. I look back on that and I really, really feel that I wouldn't change anything I did."

Others, and that includes the man who made Jim Dennison my boss, took a different view.

"It just didn't work the way I wanted it to work," Dr. Muse says. "No one should have any ill will toward Jim Dennison. I guess Jim could never really put it behind him. I hoped he would be a big enough person to say: OK, I was hurt by that. But here I have a new opportunity. I have an opportunity to make a school in which I have invested a lot of time and effort successful, and I'm going to do the best job I can in that role. That's what I was hoping would occur. But the things you want don't always materialize."

Jim Dennison speaks on what he calls PMA—Positive Mental Attitude. It's an easy concept to appreciate but a difficult one to apply to yourself. If a person listens to Jim now, he can gain an understanding of how complex and difficult this situation turned out to be. Jim thinks he did exactly what Dr. Muse anticipated, but neither Dr. Muse nor I found that to be the case.

"I would never want the football program to go under," Dennison says. "My life was such a big part of that. I felt in my administrative career that if we didn't have a strong football and basketball program, I was going to fail. So it would be ludicrous for me to want the major sport to fail. I never, ever wanted that. I fought for the football and basketball programs and I look back on that and am proud of it. Gerry didn't always believe that."

What I don't believe is that Jim wanted me to succeed. I have no doubt that he wanted a successful Division I-A football team. I would have wanted the same as athletic director, a job I might have had if I had not felt the same as Jim when he first sought the job and didn't get it. I wanted to continue to coach, to do both jobs, at least for a time.

During Dean Aynes' brief tenure as AD, he did a tremendous job. Under his leadership we finally got an area that offered a conducive, supportive atmosphere for our student-athletes to study in. I helped raise the money by reaching out to people but Dean Aynes pushed it through. He was one of the better athletic directors I've ever been around and it wasn't even a job for which he had been trained. Maybe that says how much attitude toward a job can count. He visited our offices and others in the athletic department three or four times a week. He didn't care who got the credit or where the ideas came from. He just wanted to run an efficient department. I asked him if he would take the job permanently but he wanted to have the chance to run the school of law, which he is now doing. I think Akron is lucky to have him in any capacity.

That meant I had to make a decision in 1993. Frank Kelley, dean of the College of Polymer Science and Polymer Engineering, which is world renowned, told me I had been recommended for the athletic director's job. I told him the only way I would be interested is if I could continue as football coach until we got the program on solid ground and then I would turn it over to Bob Junko, my assistant head coach and the defensive coordinator who replaced Bob Shaw when he left to be defensive coordinator at West Virginia. I knew we hadn't recruited well in 1990 and would have a weak senior class coming up in 1994. I didn't want to saddle Bob or anyone else with that responsibility. When the administration decided that it wanted to maintain the separation between the jobs, I opted to remain with football.

During this period, I got a telephone call from Mike Bobinski, who was an assistant athletic director at the U.S. Naval Academy and with whom I had worked at Notre Dame, where he had been ticket manager. He asked if I was seeking the AD job and I told him I wasn't. He said he was interested. I told him that he should apply and asked if he would like my help. He said that would be great. It came down to Mike and one other person and, knowing Mike, I went to bat for him. I talked to the people on the selection committee. I also talked to President Peggy Elliott, who had replaced Dr. Muse.

Mike got the job.

When I called to congratulate Mike, he said he was looking forward to coming to Akron. What he didn't say, however, was "thank you."

I thought that was interesting, but it didn't set off an alarm in my head, though maybe it should have. From the moment he got the job, Mike divorced himself from me because I think he knew even then that it was likely that he was going to fire me. I think he came here with that knowledge and some of my assistant coaches believe to this day that he relished the chance to make a name for himself as a tough-minded athletic administrator by firing someone with a name that was recognizable nationally.

When the alarm should have gone off was on Mike's first day of work at Akron. He went upstairs to the athletic director's office, without even bothering to stop by the football office to say hello to an old friend, a guy who had lined up on his side. I finally went upstairs to welcome him and found him in the academic study room. I told him how happy I was for him and hugged him.

He backed off. That's when I first had the feeling that something wasn't right.

This was in April 1994. Mike Bobinski did not visit our offices but once that summer. From April to November, in fact, the only time he set foot in the football office was when I asked him to meet the assistant coaches. People have told me since that Mike went to visit Lee Owens, the coach he hired, at least once a week. Maybe I should have used a better mouthwash.

Worse than this private snub, however, was his lukewarm comments about me to *Sports Illustrated.* In its preseason college football section, *SI* was doing a segment called Coach on the Hot Seat. If I had become the athletic director and had been faced with this situation, I would have supported my coach to the hilt publicly and called him into my office and told him exactly what problems I had with him and what he had to do to remain my coach. Instead, the segment became fodder for the local media and created doubt in the players' minds before the season even began. A coach doesn't need that. There are enough problems.

To make matters worse, *Sports Illustrated* wanted a photo to accompany the story. I'm surprised they didn't ask me to pose on a gallows. A photographer from Cleveland, Tony Tomsic, came to Akron to shoot the photo. He was honest enough to say that he didn't want me to smile. I said I couldn't agree to that. I knew what they were doing. They wanted a photo that supported their job-on-the-line theme. So I smiled. And smiled. And smiled some more. Tony must have taken 500 photos and once, when I exhaled from smiling until it hurt, he clicked off a shot and that, of course, was the one they used. I looked exasperated.

There wasn't much to smile about that last season of 1994. I could still find friendship and support at Eddy Niam's place on Saturday mornings. The gang still stood with me—Joe LaRose, Bill Greenzalis, Ron Tedeschi, Joe Petracca, Eddy. They always were there when I needed help. If it weren't for these relationships, we'd never have accomplished some of the things we did.

The coaches remained steadfast. No one had to tell me what I had had to tell Woody Hayes about some of the men on his staff. No one maneuvered for a chance at my job. I never had to check in the mirror at night for knives in the back. Guys like Bob Junko not only could coach but I also knew where they stood. Come to think of it, I almost always knew where Junk slept, too. At least when we were on the road.

During trips to out-of-town games, I always received a roster of which rooms the coaches and players were occupying. I never had to check it, though, to know which room Junk and Carl Angelo were sharing. I'd just walk down the hallway until I came to the room with four or five Domino's Pizza boxes outside the door. I'd knock. It never failed. Junk or Angelo would open the door. When they were nervous, they ate like men who had just discovered food. That last season, there was a lot to be nervous about, including where their next meals might be coming from.

They realized that we didn't have the support of the new athletic director, Mike Bobinski. When he finally came to the football offices during the last week of the season, it was to ask me to meet him on Sunday morning following our final game at Ohio University. As difficult a situation as it had been with Jim Dennison and as sure as I am that he did not want me to succeed personally, Jim never isolated football from that athletic director's office the way Mike did.

"I was always up-front with Gerry on anything we were doing," Dennison says. "I tried to deal with him as a football person. Very seldom was football denied anything. In fact, when I left as AD, I told a couple of guys on his staff: 'You guys are going to find it's not the same. You're going to have a non-football person as AD.' And that proved to be true."

Jim Dennison did know and appreciate a coach's problems and at times responded as an athletic director should. In 1992, for instance, Temple wanted us to move our game from the middle of the season to the opener so the game could be played in Hershey, Pennsylvania, and used as a special promotion, the Hershey College Football Game. They were going to give us a small bonus, $5,000, I think, to help defray the cost of beginning preseason practice earlier than we otherwise would have. I didn't want the game or its bonus.

Though Temple, much like Akron, has struggled, it nevertheless has a leg up on recruiting. It is a more recognizable name than Akron. It is, like Akron, an urban university but in a larger metropolitan setting. And it has a larger immediate population base of athletes. We had beaten Temple three of the last four times we'd played but, in part, we had done it by playing in the middle of the year. By then it had been banged up by some of the bigger-name teams it played, and its depth advantage over us had been neutralized.

When I told Jim I didn't want to move the Temple game and why, he stuck by me. I give him credit for that. It made a difference. We won.

The fact that Mike Bobinski went immediately to a neutral corner rather than to that of an old friend upon his arrival in Akron proved all the more noticeable because of people such as Marlene Muse, wife of excellent President Bill Muse. Before the Muses left for Auburn, Marlene Muse had supported me and the program as if she were the person who had hired me and put her neck on the line to upgrade Akron football.

I think she complements her husband better than any university president's spouse I've ever met. When Marlene Muse was at Akron, she was well-versed on the University's activities, academics and the community. She was so well versed, in fact, that she could intercede in any situation and handle it with diplomacy, dignity and knowledge. It was as if they were a tag team, a dynamic duo.

It was encouraging to have this quality of person on your side.

"I wanted Gerry to win so much and I watched him lose so often," Marlene Muse laments. "How could that be? This is a man who if Joe Smith is in trouble and he hasn't seen Joe in 12 years, he still will get a friend to fly him to Joe. If you need something, Gerry will do it. There aren't many people like him.

"How could that kind of man not have success? I think it was to teach me that the value is in the person, not in the outcome of a game. I know this: I learned so much more from Gerry Faust."

We all learn from those around us, some things good, others not. I heard from University friends that at halftime following what I admit was the most embarrassing half of football I've ever coached, Mike Bobinski told Roland Queen from the *Akron Beacon Journal* that I was good as history. Even if I had known this at the time, I couldn't have been much lower. During the week we had lost our best defensive lineman because of a discipline problem. Then, Phil Dunn, our four-year starting linebacker, got hurt in the game and, suddenly, we're without our best defensive players on a defense that is not playing well anyway. When Bobinski said I was gone, we were losing 50-0 to Miami.

The game was being televised. I was hoping no one was watching. Then a sideline reporter approached me for a prearranged halftime interview but said that, under the circumstances, I didn't have to do it. I said: "No, you'd have me on if I was up 50-0. I'll be glad to do it down 50-0." It was my obligation.

What happened following the game had nothing to do with obligation and everything to do with love. We played better in the second half. The final score was 50-14. This Miami tried to do just what that Miami in Florida had done in the last game of my Notre Dame career. But it wasn't able to run up the score. I had seen enough from the team during the second half to tell our players that they had given me a new belief in what they had inside themselves.

After I had talked with them and I went back to my locker in the visiting coaches' locker room, I found a bag. My son, Gerry, had had to work that Saturday morning in Richmond, Indiana, and hadn't made it to the game in Oxford, Ohio, until the fourth quarter. I'd seen Steve, who had come down from the Ohio State School of Veterinary Medicine. Julie and her husband, Steve Buzzi, had come with him. So all my children and my son-in-law had been there to witness all or part of a crushing defeat that was not exactly a Kodak moment.

In this bag, however, was a sincere and supportive note from Gerry and a football painting by Norman Rockwell. On the bus back to Akron, I turned to Frank Kelley, who had made the trip with us, and showed him the painting and the note.

"Read this," I said.

When Dean Kelley had finished he turned to me and said: "You know, Gerry, that loss doesn't mean a thing."

"You're right, Dean," I said. "Not when you have kids like this."

It put football in perspective. Faith. Family. Friends. Football. That's the order. It isn't, however, an easy one to remember when your professional world is crashing down around you. We lost to Miami on October 8. Through the coaches' grapevine I heard after the season that Ohio State assistant Lee Owens, who would become my successor, was contacted even before we had lost to Miami. The grapevine could be wrong, of course, but, I'm convinced it was as accurate as an arrow to the heart. The other rumor had Owens visiting Akron before the end of the season. I can't verify that one, but it doesn't matter. I was 1-10. That record wasn't anyone's fault but mine. What happens in those circumstances is part of the profession I chose.

What did matter, however, was the manner in which Mike Bobinski approached my firing. He not only got all of his ducks in a row, but he also reached for reasons that were unnecessary. He wanted no loopholes. One in particular that became the focus of public attention cut deeply into what I had tried to stand for as a coach. That was academic emphasis.

I had been proud at Notre Dame that almost without exception our players who remained with us for four years had graduated. Even at Notre Dame, where football means more than it does almost anywhere else, devotion to academics was not mere lip service. At Akron, it was impossible to consistently recruit the same caliber of student-athlete, but we had some wonderful exceptions —Frank Kelley Jr., Dean Kelley's son, for instance. Frank proved to be an excellent fullback at Akron and has become a doctor of internal medicine. Shannon Wolfe, a four-year starter in the secondary, is serving his residency in orthopedic surgery, and two other players, Harold Robinson and Jeff Junko, are in medical school.

Toward the end of the season, *USA Today* ran a story concerning the graduation rates of football programs. The NCAA figures cited were based on the freshman class that had entered six years before and ours was among the lowest, at 17 percent. Even more upsetting, the *Akron Beacon Journal* took a week to decide this was a pertinent story and then rekindled it. Maybe they don't read their NCAA news releases or *USA Today* in the *Beacon Journal* sports department. What neither newspaper mentioned, of course, is that while football's graduation rate was unacceptably low, the University's graduation rate as a whole—28 percent, as reported in the *Buchtelite*, the student newspaper—was only marginally better. Moreover, our subsequent recruiting classes had done better.

Never did we recruit players and abandon them to their fates. If anything, according to Mike Bobinski, we did too much for them. We held their hands, academically. We pushed them to go to class by taking them to the classroom door, something that had been known to happen even at Notre Dame before my time. Our coaches cared, but this wasn't about whether we cared. This was about systematically removing any arguments that might be presented on my behalf. To that end, I was not allowed to even talk with Ray Meyo, who was incorrectly viewed as having stepped beyond the bounds of a University trustee to interfere in the operations of the athletic department.

Until the last moment I thought there might be a chance for another season, for the memory of our 7-3-1 start in the Mid-American Conference to serve as much as an indicator of the direction of our program as our 1-10 final season. I even misread Mike Bobinski's final words to me when he told me he wanted to meet with me the Sunday morning after we played Ohio University.

"Win the last game," he said.

I thought that might mean a victory could give me a reprieve. If that remote possibility didn't make the last game difficult, playing against the team of Tom Lichtenberg, my old friend and assistant from Notre Dame, did. Tom had resigned as Ohio's coach. They hadn't won a game, either. So while I wanted to win for our sake, I didn't want to see Tom go out on a loss. We played well and won, but after the game, Marlene and Dick Pitts and some other friends told me that the *Cleveland Plain Dealer* had reported that morning that I would be fired. Someone had leaked the story.

If there were any doubt, it vanished when I saw Rainy Stitzlein, the president of the Board of Trustees, in a hallway near our locker room. She had tears in her eyes.

"This isn't right," she said.

"Don't worry," I told her. "Everything will be fine."

I had planned to give a game ball to Mike Bobinski after our first victory, his first as an athletic director. I just never intended for him to have to wait until the last game of the season. I still thought he should have the ball. He didn't want to take it, but finally did. It was a sad scene. In the locker room, I sat down with the assistant coaches and told them that I had a meeting the next morning with Mike. They'd heard. I told them it didn't look good.

Ken and Jan Schneider had come to Akron for the game and at supper, Ken decided he would stay overnight. He wanted to accompany me to my 9 a.m. meeting with Mike Bobinski.

"Bobinski did not object to my presence, which was nice because he did not have to let me be present," Schneider says. "The decision had been made. So we went through the ritual. It wasn't a very pleasant one. His position was that Gerry was not the disciplinarian that was needed."

Mike said the main reason he was firing me as coach, and the University was reassigning me as assistant vice president of university public affairs and development, was because I was too good to the young men who played for me. I gave too many second chances, too many breaks, including bringing in players who were not the right kind of people. That's where we have come in college athletics: helping young men, molding them, giving them an opportunity to become better people and the guidance needed to reach that end can be used against you as surely as can losing too many games.

I would have preferred it if Mike had just said: "Gerry, you haven't won enough games." I could have accepted that. But this...

"Mike," I said, "this isn't the Naval Academy or Notre Dame. We're recruiting a different kind of person. It often takes these young men two or three years to see the light at the end of the tunnel, to understand that they can graduate from college and what that can mean to them. They sometimes come here just wanting to play football and then learn to want something more. These young men need direction."

I told Mike that we had had a young team and that if I didn't win more games than I lost in 1995, I'd step down on my own. He hesitated. I suggested he contact President Peggy Elliott. We left his office and then returned. I don't know if he talked to her or anyone else. It didn't matter.

"It's irrevocable," he said of the decision.

"Fine," I said, "but I'm going to tell you one thing, Mike: I hope some day after you've helped somebody that they don't do to you what you've done to me."

"It'll probably happen," he said.

Marlene, my staunchest defender, regarded this as a personal betrayal and took it even harder than I did.

"I don't have any respect for Mike Bobinski," Marlene says. "I feel he had an agenda when he came to Akron, that in his heart he knew he was going to fire a high-profile person in Gerry and make a name for himself. He would never have gotten his job without Gerry. He never thanked Gerry. Then he fires him. The guy is smart. He's articulate. He presents himself well. But I do not like him."

I may have held on to hope until the last, but my assistants, including Rudy Sharkey, knew the end was at hand.

"I could see it coming those last few weeks," Rudy says. "But to understand it, you have to go back two years. We were coming off a 7-3-1 season. Things were looking good. Even the three games we lost, we were in. Then the next season, 1993, the number of injuries was unbelievable. When you are in transition from I-AA to I-A, not all of your players are I-A caliber. Despite the best efforts of the players left, we were shorthanded. That was the beginning of the end, I think."

Expectations had risen. Ours and everyone else's. The 5-6 dip we took because we lost 20 key players to injury looked even deeper because we had anticipated 1994 would be a difficult year. With two good years in a row, we felt we could have survived 1994 and gotten quickly back on track. Instead, I found myself at the end of the tracks. All my assistant coaches either found jobs in college or updated their teaching certifications and took high school jobs. I had two or three calls from Division II and III schools and one call from a Division I school, but I decided it would be unfair to Marlene if I made the financial sacrifice to continue coaching.

Though I didn't try to get myself another job, I did put in every good word I could for Bob Junko as my successor. I didn't think he had a chance, because he had been my assistant head coach and Mike Bobinski wanted to divorce himself from anything that smacked of association with me. Nevertheless, I lobbied with President Elliott, reminding her that not only did Junk know the players and have their respect but he also was the most experienced of the four finalists for the job.

On the day he was to go upstairs from the football offices to Mike Bobinski's office for his formal interview, Junk and I sat and talked. He had done his homework. There was nothing I could tell him. But I did give him one fashion tip.

"Junk," I said, "you aren't going up there in those cowboy boots are you?"

"Coach," he said, "these are the only shoes I have that fit."

They were top-of-the-line boots, but not my style.

"Ok," I said, "but those white athletic socks sticking up over the tops of your boots have to go."

"They're my only socks, Coach."

I was wearing some long blue socks. I took them off and gave them to him.

"Here," I said. "Take these."

He thanked me, and for the next couple of hours, I walked around without socks. It was too good a story to keep to myself. I called Andy Urbanic, who had coached with Junk at both Pittsburgh and Akron and now is the assistant athletic director at Florida State.

"Andy," I said, "you won't believe this."

Then I told him the story, and he started laughing.

"That's Junk," he said.

"Yeah," I said, "but, kidding aside, I really hope he gets the job. He's an excellent coach."

"I agree 100 percent," Andy said. "But you can tell him this: He may be able to wear your socks, but he can't fill your shoes."

Unfortunately, Andy was right. It wasn't because Junk wasn't good enough, though. Because he had been on my staff, he never had a chance.

I might never have had a chance for another job if those Division III university presidents who were interested in me had overheard my comments at the Las Vegas Bowl the month after I was fired. All the MAC coaches, including Tom Lichtenberg and I, attended the bowl to support Ball State, the conference champion which was playing Nevada-Reno. At one point, Nevada-Reno had the ball on the Ball State 44-yard line. It was fourth-and-two. We were sitting with the other coaches and the athletic directors, talking strategy.

"I'd go for it," Lichty said.

A majority of the other coaches agreed. Not me, though.

"I'd punt," I said.

I was a minority of one. Nevada-Reno went for the first down and made it.

"Well," I said to the coaches and ADs, "I guess that's why I got fired."

Everybody laughed, including Mike Bobinski. But I think talk of my firing made him uneasy, because five minutes later, he got up and left.

When the University announced that I had been reassigned —a nice word for fired—I did what I had tried to do throughout my career at Akron. I kept my mouth shut and supported the decision. Encouragement poured in from friends everywhere and kept coming for months. One letter in particular reminded me that from the worst situations can come good. Joan Schmitt wrote to me after I had spoken in Cincinnati at a meeting of the Shur-Good Corporation, the cookie company her husband owns. I'd told these business people that I didn't regret coming to Akron, despite the hardships and what happened. I had the opportunity to coach some great young men during nine seasons. Some of them have made it. Some haven't. But that's the chance you take in life. Even the ones who haven't graduated have gone on to jobs and to the rest of their lives with more discipline than they might have had otherwise.

"You know," Joan wrote after listening to this story, "you are more effective now that you have met adversity. When you were unbeatable at Moeller, people had to find it hard to relate. Now, they have to feel you are 'one of them,' and how you have handled it all is what makes the important impression. Isn't it strange how God is always working in our lives?"

That's why I'll always think of Akron as a heaven-sent hardship. It may not have enhanced my credibility as a coach, but it did add to my credentials as a person. I know what it is like to fail, to not win enough games. I know also that it is not the end of the world. A lot of coaches used to know this. So did their players and those watching them from the stands. Not enough remember this, because they don't have someone to deliver the message to them that my son, Gerry, delivered to me after that devastating Miami game.

It hasn't been easy living without football, without the camaraderie of the coaches, without the association with the young men who play the game. Faith has saved me. Friends have lifted me up when I've been low. But day in and day out, it has been family that has sustained me through Saturdays that aren't the same any more.

14

■ THERE'S NO PLACE ■
LIKE HOME

On the first worst night of my coaching life, I saw a vision of the future: a beautiful, petite brunette. Through all the rest of the best and worst days, she would be there. She just didn't know it yet.

Marlene Agruso wanted nothing to do with me. Not me personally. Me, the football coach. Me, the financially-challenged Catholic school teacher. She liked me so much she wouldn't even tell me her name.

A girl whom Marlene knew told her she once had gone out with the Moeller football coach.

"You're nuts," Marlene said.

"I was not interested in marrying a football coach or a high school teacher," she says, 34 years later. "They don't make a lot of money, and they're gone a lot of hours."

These were the days, the early '60s, when I lived in the House of the Eight Bachelors. We were famous or infamous. I'm not sure which. Everyone knew where the Eight Bachelors lived. There was Tom Rini, a Notre Dame graduate; Tex Meloy, Phil Gigliotti and George Markley, who taught and coached at Moeller; Vic Craft, who taught at Woodward High School; Jim Gaffney, a professor at Xavier University; and Jerry Rajewiski, a friend of Tom Rini's who had come to Cincinnati from Cleveland. The word around Pleasant Ridge, where we lived, was that no party was official until the Eight Bachelors showed up.

I didn't feel like going to a party the night in 1963 that we lost the only game of our first varsity season at Moeller. I had lost that game to Cincinnati Roger Bacon by raising our players to a psychological peak too early in the week and not being able to keep them there. Now, I was sulking. I was the worst loser in the world. I went home and went to bed. I didn't want to be around other people.The other Bachelors didn't care what I wanted.These guys came into my room about 11:30 and dragged me out of bed.

"We're going to a party," they said.

"No way," I told them.

"You're going," they said. "Change, or we'll take you in your pajamas."

I changed. I knew they meant it.It didn't mean I had to like it. I was still sulking when I saw this little brunette over in the corner of the room, talking with some guy. I went over, introduced myself and we talked.When she was ready to leave the party, I walked her outside but she wouldn't give me her name. I had to ask a girl I had gone out with who knew her what this brunette's name was. I had a feeling that it was important.

I'd been praying to the Blessed Mother for eight years to meet the right girl, and when I called Marlene and she agreed to go out, we discovered we both had a great love for the Blessed Mother. It seemed like fate that we would find each other.

I couldn't date much because it was football season. So Marlene would come to our Moeller games and I'd meet her about two hours afterward, after I'd mopped up and helped the managers get things in order. We'd have an hour or so together. Sometimes on Saturdays, I'd take her to a University of Dayton game.

"I always liked football," Marlene says. "That wasn't a problem. But Gerry would seat me in the stands at UD and then go about meeting, greeting and talking to people around the stadium while I sat by myself. At least he always picked me up at the end of the game. I never had to find a way home.

"Gerry is a unique person. He never tried to impress me. He would take me to eat at the local dives he and his housemates frequented. I had been dating this other young man before I met Gerry. I was very interested in this other man. He had a lot going for him. He was extremely good looking. He had a tremendous job. He was a fabulous dresser, and he took me to the nicest places in Cincinnati. He was the complete opposite of Gerry."

No wonder Marlene dumped me. I'd have dumped me, too. She told me she was going to get engaged to this other guy. I told her good luck.That was it. Or so I thought.

After a week, she called a couple of my buddies and asked if she could go to the Moeller game with them. I didn't find out until later that the reason was she had gone to a priest to discuss me and the other guy.

"I told him about these two guys and my dilemma," Marlene says. "He told me to pray about it and to follow my heart. So I did. There was just something about Gerry that made me go back to him. The other guy had to go away for a six-week training program and that gave me the chance to get to know Gerry better. The one thing that really impressed me was the way he treated his parents and his sister, Marilee, and his brother, Fred. There were all sorts of kisses and hugs and I-love-yous. I didn't come from a family like that. Mine was a good family, but more reserved. The way Gerry treated other people made me think he would make a good husband and a fantastic father. So I just overlooked all the things about him that didn't impress me and concentrated on the man underneath. It was the right decision."

And a lucky one for me. Marlene has been not only a great wife but also a great wife for a coach. She understood this career and its demands. Even though I am very, very close to our three children, she is the one who took the bulk of responsibility for them. She did such a wonderful job of rearing them while tirelessly supporting me. She even quit smoking when I told her I wouldn't date her otherwise. Of course, when she gets mad today, she does say she wishes she had never quit.

It was snowing on Christmas 1963 when I took Marlene to Moeller High School. Behind the school stands a statue of the Blessed Mother. I always prayed there. In the presence of the Blessed Mother I gave Marlene an engagement ring. The Blessed Mother had answered my prayer; we were married April 4, 1964. It was Easter break. Another coach's family had begun.

Marlene could have asked my mother what it would be like. Football had been my life. My father was a coach from the day I was born until the day I finished my career as a high school player. Others influenced me as a coach—Vince Lombardi, Woody Hayes and Bron Bacevich, legendary coach of Cincinnati Roger Bacon— but it was my dad who left the deepest imprint on me. Often, that imprint was made with a strap.

These were different times, in the late '40s and early '50s. Whenever a player made a mistake, my dad would crack him across the rear end with his strap. This was tough love. Everybody accepted it. It wasn't considered abuse, though sometimes it was difficult to understand why any mistake made by the offense was always the fault of the quarterback. And who was the quarterback? Me. One week we were preparing for a top opponent and I got that dog-gone strap 10 times in one day.

I was so mad that I didn't speak to my dad the rest of the week. We would ride home in the car from practice in silence. I wasn't going to say a word. But you know, we won that Friday night, and we won big. I was so mad and everyone else was so mad that we went out to prove we could play the way Dad had been trying to make us see we could play. Somewhere along the years, I drifted away from coaching with my modified version of that tough love, and it may have been the biggest mistake I made.

At Moeller, I was like my dad. I didn't use a strap but I was tough. Bob Crable still talks about how tough I was. He should know. Once, when Crabes was a junior, he popped off in class and then almost hit another kid. When his teacher told me about this, I threw Crabes up against a locker and stuck my finger into the point of his chin.

"Crable," I told him, "if you ever do that again, you'll never play another down for Moeller. I don't care how good you are. You're representing Moeller football and you're not going to behave that way."

We laugh about it today, but he told me he had never been so scared. You can't do that now. You'd be sued. At Notre Dame and Akron, I thought a coach should have no need to do it, that the players were mature and should be treated that way. I was wrong.

Regardless of the methods, I always tried to turn my teams into a family of coaches and athletes, the kind I saw my father create when I was a boy. I was lucky. I had a ringside seat to watch a master. It wasn't an easy life. We didn't have much money. I remember we sold Christmas trees when I was in the fifth grade to come up with enough money to buy our first television. That became our Christmas present. We pitched in together to allow the family to survive economically. That principle worked on the field as well. If everyone pitched in for a common goal, good things happened.

When I was young, and I barely remember this because it was in the '30s and early '40s, the brothers at Chaminade High School sometimes lacked the funds to pay the teachers their full salaries. So to make up for the money missing in the paychecks, they would invite the teachers and their families to eat with them. We had our share of meals with the brothers at Chaminade. I never thought about money, though. Old Doc Meyer, the druggist in our neighborhood, could attest to this.

I grew up four blocks from Shawn Acres Orphanage in Dayton. I used to go there to swim and to play on their football and basketball teams. I knew all the kids. There was a mix of races, which was unusual in the 1940s. I'd bring home friends from Shawn Acres for meals. We'd go to movies together on Saturdays. People thought I was an orphan I was with them so much. I think it helped me, though, to get to know people of other races and backgrounds. Of course, these were the same kids who led to my shortened career as a soda jerk.

My friends from Shawn Acres would come into the drug store and I'd make extra thick milkshakes for them. Old Doc Meyer would peer over his glasses at me when he heard the milkshake machine grinding away. Extra thick shakes made a different sound on the machine.

One day, Doc Meyer called me back to the pharmacy: "Gerry," he said, "I can't make a profit when you are charging 20 cents for a 30-cent milkshake."

"Doc," I said, "I'm just charging the minimum price you have listed."

"But you're making extra-thick shakes and they cost 30 cents."

"Doc, these kids are orphans. They're lucky if they have 20 cents."

"But I can't make a profit."

"Doc, you don't need to make a profit on these people."

Doc Meyer gave me a look.

"Just don't do it anymore," he said.

The next time my buddies from the orphanage came in they refused to let the other soda jerk wait on them. They wanted their special jerk—me.

"I've got to give you guys regular shakes," I told them.

"But, Ger," they said, "we only have 20 cents and we really need a thick one."

"Oh, OK."

So Mr. Will Power here starts the milkshake machine and it grinds and grinds and everyone can tell there is a thick shake on the machine. Old Doc Meyer just looked at me. He didn't say a word. Not then. Not for the rest of the summer. After the football season, I came back to see Doc Meyer and asked if I could work again. He said no.

"Gerry," he said, "I had you for one summer and that was enough. I lost money at the soda fountain."

"OK, Doc," I said.

We remained friends. He just couldn't afford me. I never was sorry, though, that I gave those kids extra-thick shakes. They were like family.

As I was growing up, all I thought about was football and the great athletes who played quarterback for my father—Billy Hoban, Jake Hagen, Babe Perkins. Billy Hoban, in particular, was my idol, and I got to know him because of whom my dad was. On Friday nights before games, he would bring the quarterback of the team over to the house for dinner. They'd talk strategy and I'd listen. I learned the game. I was on the sidelines with my dad from the time I was 7 or 8 years old. That didn't help, however, when I tried to make his team as a freshman.

Dad told me not to go out for football. He said I was too small. He was right, of course. I was only 5-foot-8 and 106 pounds. So many guys went out for football as freshmen that they immediately posted a list of those who had been cut. These were guys who didn't look like players, because that's all a coach could find out in one day. I didn't make it to the second day.

Forewarned doesn't lessen the hurt. I was mad. All I could do was to become manager of that 1949 team so that I could be around the game. I also became more determined than ever to make my dad's team the next season. Fortunately, I grew between my freshman and sophomore years. I was about 5-10. I made the team and by the time I was a junior I was 6-feet and 160 pounds and challenging for playing time.

John Spezzafaro, our backfield coach, wanted to make me the starting quarterback as a junior. Dad refused. We lost our first game. In the second game, we fell behind Cincinnati Roger Bacon 7-6. When I finally got into the game late in the second quarter, I took the team to a touchdown. Dad still wouldn't start me in the second half. Finally, the fans began screaming for him to put me in.

"It's time," he said.

From that moment on, I was his quarterback and we won nine consecutive games. My dad recognized how tough it could be on a coach's son, particularly a coach's son who played quarterback. He wanted people to see that I deserved the job. I never had a chance to feel self-important. For two years, Dad never said a kind word to me on the field.

In the stands, Mom would sit and pray the rosary. She wasn't praying for Dad to win. She was praying that neither I nor my brother Fred, who was a great running back, would be injured. She devoted her life to her family, her children. She and Dad are the ones from whom I got my philosophy. That's why I tried to treat my players as I would have wanted a coach to treat my sons and daughter.

If there were any doubt how I felt about my father after all this tough love on the football field, it would have disappeared at halftime of my final high school game. We were 8-1 and playing unbeaten Cincinnati Purcell. This was 1952, long before state playoffs. We were ranked fifth in the state poll, and Purcell was third. It looked as if those rankings might be right. We trailed 21-7 when Dad dropped a bombshell.

He announced at halftime that this was his last game. He was retiring. I hadn't had a clue. His son. His quarterback. Clueless in Dayton. It hit us hard. Tom Travis, our big tight end who played at Purdue, started to break down. Everyone did. It was a difficult moment for me, because it seemed obvious that my dad had decided he would coach until my high school career was over and then his career would be finished as well. He had been such a great coach for so many years. Now, in his last game, his team and his son, I felt, were letting him down. It broke my heart.

In that second half, we fought back like the team of a coach who had won 10 consecutive Dayton city championships. This man would be an Ohio High School Hall of Fame coach. We couldn't play dead. We didn't. We scored three consecutive touchdowns and took a 27-20 lead. Purcell responded and the game ended in a 27-27 tie. The Chaminade players who walked off the field that night knew they had played their hearts out for a man who had given his heart to so many young men for so many years.

The following week I was reading a column about my father written by longtime *Dayton Daily News* sports editor Si Burick. I had so much pride in my dad and reading the flattering things Si had written only stoked that feeling. In this moment when the spotlight shone brightest on his career, my father did something that startled me. He told Si that I had been one of the best quarterbacks he had ever coached. He had never said anything nice about me before and then he said this. I knew his other quarterbacks—Hoban, Hagen, Perkins. It amazed and gratified me that he would place me in their company. I knew one thing though: I wasn't the best football player in the family. Fred was.

Fred started when he was a sophomore. Without my father, however, Chaminade fell on difficult times and going into his senior season in 1956, Fred had not played on a winning team. Then he heard a rumor: Chaminade had asked Dad to return as coach during a transition season. Chaminade was going to hire Ed Reagan from Holy Name High School near Cleveland, but it wanted Dad to put the program back on the track first.

"Boy, Dad," Fred said, "I'd love to play on a winning team."

So Dad came back, and Chaminade finished 8-3 and won the city championship, Dad's 11th, by beating Dayton Roosevelt 33-7. I cannot tell you how proud I was sitting in the stands watching my father coach again and my brother score 27 of the 33 points in the championship game. It was an even more perfect ending to my father's career than our come-from-behind tie with Purcell.

My dad's coaching proved an obvious blessing in my life. It brought us closer when I was young. It set me on my life's course. It proved a bond in adulthood. My coaching, on the other hand, would appear to have worked a hardship on my children.

Appearances, however, can be deceiving.

There were occasions, though, when a father had to wonder if he was doing the right thing. For instance, when it came time for us to go from Cincinnati to South Bend and then again from South Bend to Akron, the moves affected Julie traumatically. She got caught in the middle. She had just finished her sophomore year at St. Ursula High School in Cincinnati when the first move occurred, and she was at Saint Mary's College in South Bend when the second one happened. Each time, it meant changing schools, making new friends, starting over. She didn't want to do any of these things.

"The day we left Cincinnati," Marlene says, "I went to lunch with some of my very dear friends and each of the children went out with their friends. We met back at our house, which was empty. I was sitting in the driver's seat of our station wagon, crying. Young Gerry and Steve were in the back seat with these depressed looks on their faces and our dog, Moe, a white poodle we had named after Moeller, lay between them, sleeping. We had had the vet tranquilize Moe for the trip.

"It took four people—Jan Schneider, Dr. George Wendt, Jane Wendt and Steve Walsh—to get Julie into that car. She just didn't want to go. I decided that we all probably should have been drugged, like Moe."

It was a big adjustment. Our family had been living in a fantasy world when I was at Moeller. There weren't many pitfalls. Life was one big victory party. No one criticized me at Moeller. Notre Dame and Akron were different. It gave us all a taste of reality. It helped the children to mature. It caused us to support one another. I know how my children felt during these moves and rocky days. There was a brief period when I first moved to Akron when I was sleeping on the floor of my office. I would lie there in the dark and reflect: Six months ago I had a nice home. I was at Notre Dame, the top of the college football world. Now, I'm sleeping on the floor of my office, trying to build a football program in a place where a segment of people don't even want me.

It would have been easy to dwell on the negative. But life is ups and downs. What matters is how we handle what we're dealt. How we react determines whether or not we survive and are happy.

Julie wasn't happy being dragged away from her lifelong friends and to South Bend, and she wasn't any happier when I told her she would have to transfer to the University of Dayton from Saint Mary's. If she wanted to live with us and teach in Akron after she graduated, she would be better off completing her education in the state in which she would be teaching. Ohio's requirements for teacher certification are different from Indiana's. It seemed logical to me, but illogical to Julie.

She had lifted me with her smiles and words of concern during the bad Saturdays at Notre Dame. She had been my most vocal cheerleader when we won, once welcoming me home from a victory at USC with a house decorated with banners and balloons. She had gone to dinner with me, just the two of us, and shared her special moments. Now, she wouldn't even talk to me.

I bought her a TV for her room at Dayton. I told her to give Dayton a week and if she didn't like it, she could return to South Bend. She still wouldn't talk to me. That lasted for the first three days she spent at UD. Then she called. She had decided she loved Dayton and wished she had gone there from Day One of her college career.

No one, it seemed, wanted to leave South Bend, where we had established family traditions after those Notre Dame games. Marlene and Julie would come out of the stands and hug me, win or lose. Gerry would bound up, tell me it was a great game or that we'd get 'em next week and then bound off just as quickly with his buddies. Steve would wait at the tunnel.

He was there after each home game. Standing. Waiting. I'd shake hands with the opposing coach and then look for Steve. He'd be beaming from ear to ear if we had won or have tears streaming down his face if we had lost. Too many times, I saw his tears.

That's what bothered me at Notre Dame. My family suffered. They were always there for me but they had to listen to what people said about me, to defend me when that wasn't their responsibility. It put them in awkward positions. It didn't end when I left South Bend, either. Akron proved more of the same, especially for Marlene and Julie, who were here through it all. And it may have been hardest of all on Steve, who stayed behind in South Bend. Father Hesburgh had been kind and generous enough to award Steve the scholarship that I had hoped he might receive even though I was leaving Notre Dame.

"In the four years that Steve was there," Marlene says, "he never went to a Notre Dame game. He couldn't bring himself to go into that Stadium again. He still hasn't. The very first game, he called me in tears and said: 'I don't think I can stay here.'

"There's just so much enthusiasm and tradition and he wasn't a part of that. He sat in his dorm room while all his friends went to the games. He heard and saw things—like those souvenir Oust Faust T-shirts."

Two people helped Steve: Mike DeCicco, the academic advisor for football, and Emil Hoffman, the dean whose name all freshmen shout out the dorm windows the nights before his legendary quizzes. Steve also found his own ways to handle the difficult situations that arose.

In one of his psychology classes, the teacher included on a test this question: Who was the most successful coach ever at Notre Dame and who was the least successful? He didn't know that Steve was my son. Steve, who graduated with high honors, answered all the questions except the one about the coaches. When he turned in his exam he told the professor he had left it unanswered and why.

"I'm Steve Faust," he said, "and my dad is Coach Faust."

Then he walked out of the classroom. The professor was shaken. Interestingly, they became great friends as a result of this incident. Steve also became a friend to Lou Holtz's daughter, Liz. After one particularly difficult loss, Liz called Steve and he went to her dorm and talked to her about what he had been through during the five years I spent as coach. He just encouraged her to hang in there and told her that everything would work out for her father —and, of course, it did.

"Football season always put me out of place," Steve told the *South Bend Tribune* when he was a senior. "I feel distanced from my friends."

It's like senior Dan Hynes said in that story about Steve: "Before I met Steve, the T-shirts and comments seemed kind of witty. But people forget about his feelings, his family's feelings and the people who are close to him."

My last season at Notre Dame, Steve risked his feelings in a way that surprised me: He told me he wanted to play football at St. Joseph High School. I told him not to do this because of me, that Marlene and I would be proud of him, his brother and his sister no matter what they did as long as they did it to the best of their ability.

"I don't know if you can make the team," I warned Steve, much as my father had warned me when I was a freshman at Chaminade.

Steve's circumstances were different from mine. He was a senior, and though a good athlete, he hadn't played high school football because of his size. Even as a senior he was only 5-foot-8 or 5-9 and slender. To compound Steve's challenge, St. Joe had a good high school football team. He wanted to try to become a receiver. I worked with him in the summer until our preseason practice began. Then our schedules conflicted. I was gone before he got up. He was in bed when I came home. I didn't know how it was going for him.

One night I pulled into the driveway at 11. The light was on in the living room and I could see Steve, waiting. I thought: Uh oh. He got cut or he wouldn't be up at this hour. I went in to comfort him.

"Steve," I said, "what are you doing up?"

"Dad," he said, "I've got to talk to you."

We went into the kitchen and sat down at the table. I had been in so many family kitchens, sat at so many tables and had so many important conversations with young football players about the game. I loved those. This was different. I dreaded this. What would I say? It always is more difficult when the person across the table is your own child.

"Dad," Steve said, "I made the team."

"You've got to be kidding me. That's great! Get out your schedule."

He got his schedule and I got Notre Dame's and we compared them. We had five home games on weekends when he played on Friday night. I promised I would be at those games. He also had a night game on the Saturday we played Purdue. I told him I'd get to that game as soon as I could.

"Dad," Steve said, full of sincerity and concern, "you don't have to go to any of my games. You've got to win this year or you may not have a job."

I had to laugh. Even my son knew the score.

"Steve," I said, "no job is more important than you. I'll be there. I want to be there. We're not going to win or lose because I take the time to see some of your games. Besides, I can always get another job."

At St. Joe games I would stand in the last row of the grandstands, trying to be as inconspicuous as possible and to avoid people. People make comments about the coach or about this or that and I don't like to listen. I know what the coach is going through. In fact, in one game, Steve's coach, who sent in plays with his receivers, grabbed Steve, who wore No. 6, and started to give him the play. Then he saw who it was, shoved Steve aside and grabbed another receiver.

"Boy," said a man near me, "that was terrible. Did you see what the coach just did to your son?"

"That wasn't terrible," I told the man. "That coach has a responsibility to every kid on the team to win and if he doesn't think my son is good enough to help him do that, that's fine with me. I'm just glad he's on the team."

This was no fairy-tale experience. Steve didn't go out in his senior year and become the star of the team, bringing glory and honor to the Faust name. In fact, he played only one down in 11 games and I didn't see that. I did, however, always make sure to tell him after each game, either walking to the bus or at home, how proud I was of him. After the post-season banquet, at which he received his letter, I asked Steve what he thought of his experience with high school football. I'll never forget his words.

"Dad," he said, "it was the greatest experience I've ever had."

I couldn't believe it.

"But Steve," I said, "you only played one down."

"That's true, Dad, but I helped the team. In practice I worked as hard as I could, simulating the opponents' plays. At the games, I'd pat the other players on the back when they did something good and offer encouragement when they did something wrong. I met a lot of great guys. It was a lot of fun. I really, really had a great experience."

I thought I was going to cry.

"Son, you could have made all-state as a wide receiver and I wouldn't be as proud of you as I am right now. You know the true value of athletics and teamwork."

It makes you proud when your children develop the right perspective on life, especially when, as in Steve's case, they do it by themselves. I never force-fed Steve or any of the children these values. They watched our family live them and then decided how our values might fit into their own lives.

Much of this, I think, is the result of my mother-in-law Angela Americus Acquaro Agruso. I know people like to joke about mothers-in-law, but mine is a super woman. She lived with us 28 years, all the time the children were growing up. They became close to her. They saw the love between Marlene and her mom, how they interacted. They saw how my parents loved each other. They watched Marlene and me. These things rub off. Example speaks louder than words.

Sometimes, however, words are all you have. I always seemed to be able to find the ones I needed when I was dealing with the sons of others. Finding them for your own children, when you love them so much, is another matter. When Gerry was a freshman at the University of Dayton, he wanted to quit school, head for the West Coast and have, I guess, an adventure. He came to Notre Dame to tell us this. He said he'd return to school later. I had heard this a thousand times before from a thousand different players.

"Gerry," I said, "once you are out of school, you seldom go back. I want you to finish school."

"Dad, I want to go to the West Coast."

"If you do, you can forget your car. You can forget everything."

We left it there, and Marlene and I went out. When we returned, Gerry's car was in the driveway but he was gone. It was 11:30 at night.

"Where's Gerry?" I asked Marlene's mother.

"Oh," she said, "he went back to Dayton."

"How did he do that? His car is in the driveway."

"He called one of his buddies to pick him up and drive him to Dayton."

He left behind the car that I said he could forget.

I climbed into his car and began driving. I got to Dayton at 4 in the morning and went to his house. He wasn't there. Then I spotted six guys playing basketball on a lighted court nearby. One of them was Gerry. I pulled him aside, told him I wanted him to keep the car, no matter what, and that after I went to church he could drive me to the airport so I could catch a flight home.

"Things will work out in the long run," I told him. "Not everything goes right all the time."

"But Dad, I just don't like school."

"Gerry, there are a lot of things I don't like that I've had to do. When you were younger, I had to support you. So I became a rod-buster, working with iron, in the summer. I was a pipe coverer. I stocked shelves at a grocery. I didn't like those things. I like coaching. But I had to do them to put food on the table. There are things in life all of us have to do that we don't like. We do them because there is a purpose to it and a reason for it. The purpose for you now is education. The reason for it is so it will open doors for you. It's not going to get you a job. But it will open doors to jobs."

Gerry didn't like it but he stayed at UD and finished in four years and one summer. I called Don Frericks, who was assistant dean of the School of Education and with whom I had taught at Chaminade, and asked if he could give Gerry some guidance. He became a mentor to him, and Gerry is still quick to recognize what Don did for him.

When Gerry graduated, a huge cheer went up in the UD basketball arena from all of Gerry's friends. He may not have liked school, but a lot of people at that school liked him. He became president of a fraternity. He knew everybody. He could have been president of partying and gotten a doctorate in social-eventing.

It's odd how things turn out. I've watched Gerry in the middle of the night giving out invoices and itineraries, getting things organized at the Roadway Express terminal in Richmond, Indiana. I have seen how he handled himself and the men working with him and it made me appreciate the skills he has with people. He used those same skills when he was promoted to a sales position with Roadway in Cincinnati. Now, he is considering one of the ultimate "people" jobs. He's participating in a six-month program at Franciscan University in Steubenville, Ohio. It's designed to help young men determine if they want to commit themselves to the priesthood, and to permit the Franciscans to decide if the person would fit into their order.

It would make me tremendously proud if Gerry decides this is his calling. The decision has to be his. I can't expect him to make a decision that I didn't make when I had the chance. People still say I should have been a priest.

"We've all said that," Father Joyce says. "Gerry himself has said to me more than once that he would have been a priest if they would have allowed him to also coach football. He would have been ideal. He is so solicitous of everybody in need. He will do anything for them. He would have been a marvelous missionary, a marvelous priest."

There is, of course, another view.

"Sure, you can say he would have been a good priest," Father Riehle says. "But he's a good father, too. Look at the influence he has had on so many kids, including his own."

All of our children have become giving young adults. Gerry spent a year and a half working with retarded and abused children in the Christian Appalachian Project in Kentucky, and Steve worked with my friend Father Robert Tobin in Yucatan and spent a year in Puerto Rico helping the poor as a part of the Notre Dame Outreach Program. Julie, as an everyday commitment, works with elementary students at an inner city school in Akron.

Julie supported me through the most difficult of times, both at Notre Dame and Akron. So when she found herself face to face with her own moment of truth as a first-year teacher, Marlene and I tried to be as supportive as she had been to me. Sometimes, though, another person, someone outside the family, can be the important influence that I tried to be with my players. For Julie, that person was Joanne Shippy, former principal at Akron's Voris Elementary School, where Julie began her career.

A teacher's first year can be traumatic. In hers, Julie discovered the difference between training as a student teacher and being on your own. Reality set in. She probably felt like I did during my first years at Notre Dame and at Akron. To teach at an inner city school is a challenge. To a first-year teacher, it can seem an insurmountable one. If it hadn't been for Joanne Shippy, Julie might not have made it.

Julie felt she couldn't do anything right. She had been teaching for only two or three months, and it wasn't turning out the way she had imagined. This sounded familiar to me. I'd lived this. Julie, who was teaching first grade, had gone into Mrs. Shippy's office, ready to quit. Mrs. Shippy told her to take the rest of the day off. To relax. Julie took her advice. She also came to my office, a shaken young woman.

I talked to her for an hour. I told her that I knew it didn't feel this way at this point, but that in eight or nine years she would look back on this moment and laugh. Teachers learn as much as students, and one of the things each teacher learns is that not every student will respond positively to what you're trying to do for them. Every teacher encounters negative situations. It's part of life.

Marlene also talked to Julie. She reinforced her in ways I couldn't. Then Mrs. Shippy took over. She refused to write off Julie. She helped her through that year. I think she saved Julie and her teaching career, and the reward is that Julie has become a respected, accomplished teacher in the Akron Public Schools system. Had it not been for Marlene and Mrs. Shippy, Julie may not have stayed in teaching and that would have been a tremendous loss, because Julie has a big heart and a capacity to help the most challenged child. A tremendous percentage of her students read above their grade level when they complete their year with her. Even in the summertime she remains close to her students. When one of her first-graders invited Julie to her birthday party after school was out, Julie and her husband, Steve Buzzi, went to the party, took the girl a gift and helped to make it a memorable day. Not every teacher would bother, but Julie is not just any teacher.

Julie did the same thing she always said she admired me for doing: She stuck it out when times got tough. I know that to most people it looks tough to have had to walk away from my Golden Dream at Notre Dame and then to be fired at Akron after trying to lift the football program to a new level in the face of opposition from within the athletic administration. Those things weren't the toughest things that ever happened to me. The deaths of my parents were.

My dad was suffering from prostate cancer when his doctors put him in the hospital during the 1991 season. I called the hospital every night from the football office. Despite our differences, Jim Dennison readily agreed I should do this. Many people would have taken time off and gone to be with their father, Jim said. So call, he said, and don't worry about the cost. I wanted to be with my dad. I also wanted to fulfill my obligation to my football team, something I knew my dad would have wanted me to do. So each night after practice I called him at the hospital and at 6:30 every Tuesday evening, I left from practice to drive three and a half hours to Dayton. By that point in the week, we had finalized our preparation for the upcoming opponent, and I could split my attention.

I usually got to Dayton about 10 o'clock. I would spend 10 minutes with Dad, telling him about the team, giving him a kiss on the cheek and telling him how much I loved him. Then I'd get back in the car and drive back to Akron. My dad made it out of the hospital, which didn't surprise me. Even when the foe was as unbeatable as cancer, Fuzzy Faust was a fighter.

I kept thinking about the summers we spent at Kiawah Island, S.C., at the vacation homes of my sister Marilee and her husband, Ken Oberhue, and my brother, Fred. Every morning after we went to church, we'd come back to Ken and Marilee's place and play the first half of our daily gin rummy tournament. We'd play from 10 a.m. until noon and then again from 8 p.m. until 10 p.m. We'd do this for five days. Total score won. We even had a trophy. Dad and Fred would play Ken and me, and it was smash-face gin rummy. Very competitive. My sister even had T-shirts made for us. They had the king of diamonds on them. This was serious.

At times, my dad wouldn't even speak to us. He was such a competitor. During one of these summers—we did this for at least 10 or 12—Dad and Fred were beating Ken and me so thoroughly after two days that Dad burst out laughing in the middle of one of the sessions. He tried to hold back, but he just couldn't. That afternoon, when we were out fishing, Ken and I decided we had to stage a comeback or face embarrassment that would last longer than forever. And we did come back. We came back enough to allow us to talk to Dad and Fred the way they had talked to us. In another words, between giggles. In the 10 or 12 years of the tournament, the score must have been 6-4 or 7-5 in favor of Dad and Fred.

Dayton Chaminade honored the competitiveness of my dad that 1991 season during halftime of its game against Kettering Alter. We had an open date in our schedule, and Chaminade coach Jim Place asked me if I would accept the award on behalf of my dad, who was too ill to attend. I said I would. I felt I owed it to Dad. I asked Rob Fournier, now assistant commissioner of the Mid-American Conference but then the University of Akron assistant athletic director in charge of compliance with NCAA rules, to tell the NCAA I was going attend the game and why. The NCAA said I couldn't go.

This was one of the more stupid decisions I had ever heard. We explained that I wasn't going to recruit, that I wouldn't talk to a single player during my trip to Dayton. The NCAA still said no.

I told Rob that I was going and that he could tell the NCAA that. I also told him that he could tell it that if the NCAA persisted in its objections, I would go to the media and tell them that the organization that runs college athletics was attempting to prevent a son from picking up an award for his dying father because the son happened to be a football coach. At least I knew what would make a good story after having been a good story myself for years. The NCAA knew, too. It decided I could go. That there was ever a moment's doubt is beyond my understanding. Family should always take precedence over arbitrary rules.

Marilee and Ken were there that night, as was Fred. My son, Gerry, came from Richmond, Indiana, because he had become especially close to his grandfather during the time he was attending the University of Dayton. Gerry and Dad even worked on an academic project that included Gerry interviewing Dad at length about his coaching philosophies. What I didn't know when I got to Dayton was that Dad had slipped into a coma. I was looking forward to seeing him and so was Gerry. When we got to Dad's house after the game, Gerry got to his room before I could and came running back down the stairs and out of the house. He was emotionally crushed. I'd never seen Gerry suffering in this way. When Mom told me that Dad had gone into a coma, I stayed by his side, except for going to church. On Saturday, I put a college football game on TV and talked to him about what was happening. On Sunday, I did the same thing with the NFL game. I don't know if he could hear me, but I knew that was what I had to do.

I also called my assistant head coach, Bob Junko, and told him to go ahead and begin preparation for the next week, that I was going to spend Sunday with Dad and that I'd drive home late Sunday night. I'll never regret deciding to stay another day.

As football droned on in the background that afternoon, I leaned over and told Dad that I loved him. I still don't know if he heard me, and I don't know if it was just a coincidence but there was a tear that rolled down his cheek.

He died three hours later.

I left for Akron that night. Dad's funeral was Thursday, November 7, 1991. I knew he'd want me to be with the team. I worked Monday and Tuesday and returned to Dayton for the Wednesday afternoon calling hours. I'd never seen such a long line of people. For four hours, there was a solid stream of friends of Dad's and also mine. For the Mass the following morning, my coaches came. Velma Bowen, my secretary and a Godsend if there ever was one as an administrative assistant, came. Ray Meyo and Marie were there. Frank Eck and his friend, Anne, came down from Columbus. Father Riehle flew in from South Bend and so did my secretary at Notre Dame, Jan Blazi, along with Brian Boulac, George Kelly and Bill Corbett. I hadn't been at Notre Dame for years, but they knew Dad and so they came and it meant the world to me.

The church was packed. There were 16 priests at the altar. Father Dave Porterfield came from Notre Dame, and then there were the priests who had once played for Dad: Fathers Ken Sommer, John Ceville, Tom Schroer and Frank Kenney.

My sister Marilee arranged the funeral, which was beautifully done, and my brother Fred gave the eulogy. Fred was great. In these circumstances I try to step back. I've always been in the limelight, the family focus because of my job. I thought others should be there on this day. In any case, there is no way I could have been as eloquent as Fred. He told a story I'll never forget.

"As you all came through the line, each one telling his or her own story," Fred said, "I noticed a very young man by himself spending a considerable time with Mom. Eventually he got to me, expressing his sympathy and sorrow. I couldn't help but be moved by the depth of this young man's sincerity, and as he said goodbye and started to move away, I reached out and grabbed his arm and asked his name. It was Tony, and since he was so young, 18 or 19, I asked Tony what his relationship with Dad was.

"Tony replied: 'Oh, I never met your father, but I have been studying Christianity with my teacher at school and trying to turn my life around, learning about ethics, morals, values and character and how to live a better life. And I read about your wonderful dad in the newspaper (a story which had been written by Ritter Collett, a close family friend and outstanding sports editor of the *Dayton Daily News*)...and I was compelled to come here...and view him. Since the wait in line was so long, an hour and a half, I got to hear some great stories about him from all the people around me, about what a wonderful man he was.'

"That story," Fred concluded, "was what Dad was all about."

Even strangers respected a man like Dad. That is as fine an epitaph as anyone could have.

After we buried the man who taught me more about love than he ever did about football, which was plenty, I returned to Akron. We played at Virginia Tech that weekend and on the long bus ride, I wrote thank-you notes to people. There were so many, and too soon, I would be writing others.

Mom died two and a half years later. She had gone to live with Marilee in an apartment attached to Ken and Marilee's home. My parents were just getting ready to move in when Dad died. It worked out well. Marilee and Fred both were there to look out for Mom and when in the summer of 1993 Marilee and Ken went to Europe and Fred was off at Kiawah, Mom came to spend several weeks at our house for the first time.

One day Mom wanted to get a present for Marlene. So I took her shopping and she picked out a cellular phone. It was the perfect gift. With it, Marlene, even away from the house, could call to complain to the newspaper sports columnist who was criticizing my record. I noticed that Mom became awfully tired during our shopping trip, but I thought it was just because she was 83 years old. When we got home, she said:"Gerry, I think I should go home to Dayton."

"Mom," I said, "you can stay as long as you want. We've really enjoyed having you here."

"No, Gerry, I think it's time to go home. I've been here five weeks."

I drove Mom home on the Saturday before the Fourth of July. I got her squared away in her apartment and drove back to Akron. On Monday the Fourth, I got a call from Marilee. She said Mom was dying. I went right back to Dayton and slept on the floor of her apartment. I was with her 56 hours, except for eating and going to church. Fred flew in from Kiawah. He got there on July 6. He had the chance to tell Mom that at 54, he had gotten engaged for the first time. When Mom found out he was marrying this wonderful woman named Laurie, she looked relieved. She had worried that once she was gone, there would be no one to look out for Fred.

At the end, we all were at the foot of Mom's bed. She sat up, focused on each one of us and smiled.Then she lay down and died. At her wake and funeral, there once again were huge crowds and six or eight priests were at the altar. Dad had lived in the limelight. More people knew him. But Mom was the other half of the equation of love that I spoke about the night of her funeral.

I previously had made a commitment to speak at the Camp of Champions which Andy Urbanic ran in Edinboro, Pennsylvania. My heart ached, but I knew Mom would want me to keep the commitment to these 600 high school players. Coach Urbanic told them that I had buried my mother that morning yet had come to be with them. I spoke from that aching heart of mine about family. The players seemed to understand. You talk about difficult, I said. Losing games is nothing. Losing a parent—that's a real loss. What I tried to explain to the players is that if you play your best and lose, there really isn't much to feel sorry about.

When I got home, I received a poem from the players who had been there from Penn Hills High School in Pittsburgh where Andy used to coach. It was titled: "Mothers Never Die. They Just Keep House Up in the Sky." It touched me.

That's what bothers me about collegiate athletics. There are so many young people who have great athletic potential but who haven't had the good fortune to be raised in families like Marlene and I were raised in and in a family such as the one we tried to create. We tried to guide and encourage our children, as our parents had tried to guide and encourage us. What happens to those young people who never have such guidance and encouragement?

I believe in standards. I think a person can see from the players I recruited at Notre Dame and the success they had in the classroom that I put a premium on education. I also believe, however, that there is a university for every person who wants to attempt higher education, that we should never establish such set-in-stone, high standards that we fail to accommodate those young people with the courage to try, to risk failure. Not every school can be Notre Dame. Others, and Akron is one, can open doors to new worlds, can help its students even if they do not graduate. Despite what the NCAA might have a person believe, graduation is just one criterion of success. It is not the true and only criterion.

The true criterion is: Did the person better himself by attending college—even if he did not get a degree? I've seen young men come through the University of Akron who have gotten degrees and done unbelievably well who would never have achieved this without athletics. I've also seen some who haven't gotten degrees who are very successful. I've also seen some who did not make it but at least tried. Learning about discipline, family—as in team and teamwork—sacrifice and a work ethic are my criteria of success.

A professor sent me a copy of a paper that had been written for his class by one of our successes at Akron, Odell Robbins. Odell is the director of the Grace Jones Day Care Center in Marathon, Florida. I took pride in Odell as a student-athlete. I take much more pride in him as a person.

"When I entered college," Odell said, "...at first I didn't agree with Mr. Faust's style of a role model. At the age of 18, I was stubborn and didn't want Mr. Faust to tell me anything. Now at 23, I realize how he is concerned with me becoming a worldly man. He preaches the importance of an education, character and giving that helping hand to those in need. He's lectured time and time again about the importance of life without athletics.... Mr. Faust truly is an inspirational person who is interested in the well-being of his athletes."

Odell Robbins is a kind, generous young man who learned there was more to life than games. It is easy to say this. It isn't as easy to live what you preach. I found that out. I no longer have my football family, but I still have Marlene and Julie, Steve and Gerry, my son-in-law Steve Buzzi, my daughter-in-law Patricia, whom we call Pij, Ken and Marilee and their children, Anne Marie, Ken III, Kristin and Molly, Fred and Laurie and our first grandchild, Megan Marie Buzzi.

I still have my family. I still have my friends. I just don't have football anymore.

15

■ SATURDAYS AREN'T ■ THE SAME

After being fired, I felt like the tree that shared my office. During the move from its prime, first-floor real estate in the James A. Rhodes Arena to an office tucked away on the top floor of the University of Akron's Martin Center, the tree was exposed to the cold winds of winter. It took a beating.

All that tree had ever known was the football office. It had no window, but it managed. A friend from Notre Dame, Dean Gongwer, who sold ribs outside the Stadium on football Saturdays, had sent the tree to me when I got the job at the University of Akron. Thanks to the tender, loving care of my secretary, Velma Bowen, it had survived nine years of my abuse. I had ignored it. I'd never taken care of a tree in my life. Heck, I didn't even mow my lawn. I had other priorities. Like football.

Now, this tree and I were alone in a new and shared world. Velma wasn't there to water it. The only company it had was me.

Its leaves turned brown and fell onto the floor around it. I didn't know what to do. I didn't know about watering, pruning and fertilizing. I didn't even know what kind of tree it was. I knew it was green. It had branches. It had leaves. It was just there, a piece of the furniture, only alive.

As the days passed, I began to mess around with my tree. I watered it. I cut away its dead branches. I gave it a spot in the office next to a window. This situation reminded me of the Birdman of Alcatraz. He didn't know anything about birds when they sent him away to that island prison in San Francisco Bay. But he learned. He became an expert on birds. I'm no expert on trees, but when I first moved to my new office and job, it felt as if I was being sent to Alcatraz. It was a whole new way of life.

I've been treated generously by the hard-working personnel in the University of Akron development department. But I was used to being around people. Lots of people. Especially at first, before I got into my new job and came to understand the contributions I could make, I felt alone. The only people I saw were the ones who came to use the unisex restroom two steps outside my office door.

The University offered to give me a month off after I was fired as coach. That was a kindness, but one I didn't want. I wanted to work. I came to the office every day for most of December 1994. I answered the many letters I received. I became my own secretary. It required a return to the old way of doing things. At Moeller, I had been my own secretary, my own janitor, my own laundry man. I'd been a Gerry of all trades. It took years to break the habit to which I now needed to revert.

During this period, I also began making contact with perhaps 30 people whom the folks in development wanted to reach to explain that even though Akron is a state university, it still needs the help of individuals if it is to support those students who most deserve it. My name sometimes provided entree where a lower-profile person's would not. I got through to most of the people on my list. Two or three wouldn't see me or talk to me. But that's no different from recruiting. Some young men wouldn't listen, no matter what a coach said.

Discovering the many needs of students makes it difficult to ignore those needs. An example of what can be done by caring people is the Robert E. Donovan Scholarship. Tim DuFore, the University's vice president for development, introduced me to Margaret Donovan during the summer of 1996 when she was visiting with Tim to discuss establishing a scholarship in her husband's name. Robert Donovan, 54, died April 3, 1996, aboard the plane that crashed in Bosnia, killing U.S. Secretary of Commerce Ron Brown and 32 other corporate leaders who were on a trade mission to the former Yugoslavia. Mr. Donovan, a West Point graduate who worked for Babcock & Wilcox for 17 years, part of that time living in Akron, was president and chief executive officer of ABB Inc., which offered manufacturing and engineering services in power generation and transmission, industrial systems and mass transportation. His daughter, Kara, graduated from the University of Akron School of Law in 1996.

Because Mrs. Donovan is a football fan, we talked and became friends, and I was invited to the ceremony honoring the first two recipients of scholarships for women studying engineering, law or business. What the winners of these awards—Emily Mills and Jennifer Love—told Mrs. Donovan, Kara and members of the University family who attended the scholarship awards luncheon affected me deeply.

Ms. Mills, who is a law student, told Kara that she could understand her feelings at the loss of her father because she had lost her own father when she was eight years old. It was a coincidence that a young woman with this background had been chosen, but, I thought, extremely appropriate. The other young woman, Ms. Love, is an engineering student. She explained that the Donovan Scholarship would mean that for the first time she would not be forced to drop classes because she couldn't afford to pay for them. As she thanked the Donovans, she began to cry.

There are many people like Ms. Mills and Ms. Love at the University of Akron, bright young people who would never have the opportunity they need were it not for the generosity of people such as the Donovans and the friends of Mr. Donovan who contributed to the scholarship fund.

I'd always understood and appreciated the scholarships that student-athletes received. In financially sound athletic programs, such as Notre Dame's, gate receipts, television appearances and bowl money supported those awards. But my association with the development office has given me a deeper appreciation of the work these people do to generate the same opportunities for students whose skills are no less significant but less obvious than those of Saturday's heroes.

The majority of my work falls in the field of admissions and public relations. I've spoken at dozens of high schools and to more than 11,000 students in each of the last two years. Instead of sitting in kitchens, across the table from a young football player and his parents, I visit with hundreds of young people simultaneously. Often these students don't know who I am until their principal introduces me. Many of them were little more than toddlers when I went to Notre Dame in 1980. I spend two or three minutes telling them about the University of Akron and letting them know that an admissions representative has accompanied me and has additional information if they want it. I soft-sell Akron, though. Hard sells don't work. I discovered this the hard way.

When I came to Akron to coach, I ran into the chief of the Ohio Highway Patrol and mentioned I'd be happy to visit prisons and talk to the inmates. I enjoy doing it and it became a regular part of my yearly calendar. The first time I went to the prison at Mansfield, Ohio, the state had not yet replaced the old dungeon they were using there. It was an ugly, scary place. I spoke in the gymnasium, where prisoners, on their free time, could attend. I had done more preparation than usual and when I took the stage, I thought I had a speech to which the inmates could relate. It was about second chances. I'd been at Notre Dame and had failed to do the job. Now, I had a second chance at Akron. I thought everyone deserved a second chance, but that what a person did with his was up to no one but the person you saw when you looked into the mirror.

The gym was packed. There must have been 3,000 prisoners there. I was excited. I was into my speech, really rolling. I thought I was downright spellbinding. That seemed to be the minority opinion, however. Doors started opening. Prisoners began walking. They didn't have to listen to me. They could go smoke in the yard rather than listen to someone they thought was blowing smoke. They could do something constructive, like whistle into the wind. I mean, this was a tough audience in more ways than one, and I was losing it. I jumped off the stage and plunged into the stands where the prisoners were sitting.

"Let's talk football," I said.

From that moment on, not one person left. Everyone, it seemed, had a question. They were walking encyclopedias of sports. I began telling stories, some of them about athletes who had had problems and how they solved them. Afterward, I shook a lot of hands and knew I had learned something important: People don't like a person who preaches to them. Stories work better.

I even visited the isolation area they call the hole to talk with the men. As I was walking through the area, I heard a guy yell out my name.

"Hey," he said, "aren't you Coach Faust?"

"Yes, I am."

"What are you doing down here?" he asked. "The real question is," I told him, "what are *you* doing down here?"

He laughed. We talked. Later, in the courtyard, I ran into two other prisoners who recognized me. They said they had been students at Warren Harding High School, which Moeller had played in the 1974 state playoffs.

"We beat you 20-10," they said.

They were right. Warren Harding was the only team we played during my Moeller years that we never beat. I did not have a history with the young men and women I have met while speaking at high schools during the last two years. I do tell them stories, though, fitting them into a speech titled: "How to Be Great at What You're Doing."

It's a streamlined version of the speech I give to business and industry groups. It's a philosophy. I hit upon the idea while driving to Newark, Ohio, to speak at a junior high school in the late 1980s. I talk about ethics, values, family, school spirit, togetherness and team work. I try not to preach. Some cons taught me that: No con jobs.

I haven't forgotten football, of course. I just try not to dwell on it. That became difficult a couple of years ago, when I learned that my friend George Steinbrenner was trying to buy the Tampa Bay Buccaneers. I called George. He wasn't in, but he returned the call, and I told him that if he got the team that I'd like to become his personnel director.

"You've got a job," he said.

"Gosh, George," I stammered. "Thanks a million. I've been in football all my life and ... "

"Gerry," he said, "you belong in football. You got screwed when they reassigned you."

I know that people, especially the media, don't like George. I think their judgment is faulty. George may become involved in the affairs of his teams right up to the top of his hip boots, but he cares about people. He may have fired Billy Martin a zillion times and others not quite as often, but he never failed to give them another job within his organization. Now, he was offering me one. He didn't promise me that I would become personnel director. He just said I had a job.

He knew how it felt to want to be in football and to suddenly find yourself out of the game. When he coached with Lou Saban at Northwestern, George lost his job when the University fired Saban.

I told him how much it meant to me for him to respond as he had. It didn't matter that, in the end, he didn't get the team and I didn't get a job.

"That's what friends are for," George said.

I'm lucky that I've found myself in a position to meet people such as George Steinbrenner, and I'm even luckier to have discovered when I lost the thing I loved most, coaching, that I could be useful to the University in other ways.

John Laguardia, then the executive director of the UA Alumni Association and of governmental relations and now vice president of public affairs and development, has invited me to accompany him to Columbus to talk about the needs of the University with Stan Aronoff and other legislators whom I know. I also know a couple of lobbyists. It was on this jaunt that John decided I knew more people in Columbus than he ever imagined.

We were on the street, going from one government building to another, when a panhandler came up to me and asked for money. He was a man in his 40s. I never ignore such people, but rather than giving them money, my practice is to take them to a diner and get them something to eat. That way I'm doing something for a person who needs help and I know that my contribution to his well-being is put toward food, not booze.

In this instance, I didn't have time to take him to lunch.

"I'm going to give you some money," I told him, "but I don't want you to use it on drink or drugs. I want your word."

"You've got it," the man said.

So I gave him $10 and turned to walk away.

"Hey," he said, stopping me, "aren't you Gerry Faust, the former Notre Dame football coach?

"Yes."

"Well, thanks a lot, Coach. I really appreciate this."

"You just make sure you get some food with that money."

"I will, Coach. I will. I promise."

John Laguardia just shook his head.

"Even the beggars know you, Gerry," he said.

For every George Steinbrenner in my life, there are a hundred working men and women, people just doing the best they can, trying to make it from one day to the next on faith and hope. One day as I was pulling into the parking lot at the Martin Center, one of the University maintenance men shouted out to me. These people receive little appreciation and less recognition, but they make the University the first-class place it is. I shouted back to him and asked how he was doing.

"Not very well," he said.

"How come?"

"They put me on the garbage truck this week to fill in," he said, "and I just can't stand it. This place just keeps doing these things to me."

Everything is relative when it comes to reaching our levels of frustration, but I may not have been the best person to tell about a place doing things to you that you don't like.

"Listen," I told the worker, "you ought to be happy you have a job. So they put you on the truck for a week. You still have my respect. And I'll bet you have the respect of other people, too. You're doing a job that needs to be done. You're helping in a significant way to make the University a better place.

"Look at me. I was at the top, in the limelight. Now I have an office up in the corner of this building. There's no limelight up there, but I'm happy to have a job. I have my health. I have my family, my faith. I live in a great country. You have all those things, too."

He looked at me for a minute.

"Boy," he said, "I'm glad I talked to you today."

I think he actually meant it. I know I can be up-tempo when I have some reasons to be down-beat but I can't help myself. What I worried about in my case was how I would handle the beginning of the first football season in 37 years that I hadn't coached. I worried about that a lot.

During my first winter away from the game, I missed recruiting. I'm not sure how many coaches would say that. But I did. The reason is simple: I enjoy meeting people, going to their houses, sitting around those kitchen tables. My speeches to high school students helped lessen my feeling of withdrawal, and Dick Pitts, my friend who owns Green Hills Golf Course, always was there for me.

I didn't have much free time, but when I did, I would meet Dick at his course and we would drive over to the Grotto in Randolph and then to lunch. He paved my way through those recruiting months. We talked about old times and football and golf. Spring, however, was just a preview of coming distractions.

When fall arrived, I wished I could turn into a cousin of the Birdman of Alcatraz's birds and fly south for the season. Just get away. The first Akron game turned my stomach inside out. I knew I should go to the game. I'm still a member of the University staff. I cared about the players whom I had been forced to leave behind. But I dreaded it.

Once again, Dick Pitts helped me through it. He met me on the first afternoon of the season and we drove to Kent for the Kent State-Youngstown State game. Watching this game was a breeze.

Coaches from my former staff had become the head coach at Kent (Jim Corrigall), the defensive coordinator (Bob Junko) and the defensive line coach (Jerry Lasko). They beat Youngstown, which pleased me. They'd been loyal to me, and I felt no less loyalty to them. Akron, however, was a different story.

Believe it or not, I wanted Lee Owens to do well, because I wanted my former players to succeed. What I didn't want was to attract attention to myself. Dick and I stopped to grab a bite to eat between games and then drove to the Rubber Bowl to watch the Zips play host to Eastern Michigan. I avoided the Akron section of the stadium and sat high up in the end zone.

I didn't want people to come up to me and feel they had to say they missed me and force me to say whatever it is the former coach is supposed to say in these circumstances. I wasn't even sure what I should say. Rather than encounter old friends and supporters at the end of the game, we left in the third quarter. I just couldn't handle the kindness of people saying: Gee, we wish you were back. We'd have won.

Akron did not win. When Pittsy pulled up to my car, which I had left at the restaurant, and let me out, I knew I owed him more than I could repay.

"I got through it, and I really appreciate that you helped me," I told him. "You're a real friend."

I watched more games on television, and told Marlene: This is the first opening day of a season in 37 years that I haven't coached a team. It sure felt odd.

As the weeks and weekends passed, I grew used to the feel of a season that was missing. I was like a man who has lost a limb, who grows used to its absence, yet can still feel it. Sometimes, it ached. The circumstances, however, allowed me to do things that I otherwise never would have had time to do. I had the time to be there for people who had meant something in my life.

I received a call that Ted Burwinkel, one of the members of my first Moeller team, was dying from Lou Gehrig's disease. Phil Gigliotti, one of my Moeller assistant coaches and a former resident of the House of the Eight Bachelors, called and asked if I could meet him and two of Ted's 1963 teammates, Mike Volle and Clyde Brenner, at the nursing home where Ted was on his deathbed. Ted had started at defensive back for that team and I'll never forget that he had to miss an important game because he got up the night before to get a drink of water and fell down the stairs at his house and hurt his back. That pain was nothing compared to what he had to endure now. But Ted never changed. He had this unyielding, upbeat attitude.

I told Phil I'd come to Cincinnati, but not to tell Ted I would visit. If I had been coaching, I wouldn't have been able to make the trip and would have had to live with that regret. Ted couldn't believe it when I walked in with Phil, Mike and Clyde and two of Ted's three sons, who had followed him to Moeller. We started laughing and telling football stories and before anyone knew it an hour had disappeared. Near the end of my visit, Ted said that his nose itched and asked one of his sons if he would scratch it for him. Ted, no longer able to control his muscles, couldn't do it for himself. I told Ted's son that I'd do it.

As I scratched Ted's itch, it salved the wound that my firing had left. How could I be depressed about getting fired when this man, whom I had coached, was dying at the age of 50 and couldn't even scratch his nose? I didn't have anything to complain about.

"Thank you for coming, Coach," Ted said. "I love you."

"Ted, I love you, too."

With that, I gave him a gentle hug, kissed his cheek and told him what I knew to be the truth: "You'll go straight to God."

Afterward, Mike and Clyde also thanked me for coming to see Ted.

"I should be the one thanking all of you for calling me," I said. "You're like my own kids."

Saturdays may not be the same for me anymore, but the young men with whom I spent my Friday nights and Saturdays will forever remain unchanged to me. It never was the game. It always was what the game allowed us to become to one another.

Ted died two days after my visit.

As fate would have it, I couldn't be there for the family of Joe Burnett, another of my former Moeller players who died too young. Joe was killed aboard the ValuJet aircraft that crashed into the Florida Everglades. His family wanted me to eulogize Joe, but I had two commitments at the University. What I was able to do was to write the eulogy and ask Phil Gigliotti to deliver it for me. He read it at the funeral service and I sent the original in a letter to the Burnetts' other son and told him to give it to his parents after the service. I thought it might be something they would want to keep.

It wasn't all sad times and empty Saturdays. With more free time, I got to do things I'd never done before, including attending the NEC World Series of Golf at the Firestone Country Club in Akron, the 1995 American League playoffs and World Series involving the Cleveland Indians, and a Cubs game the following summer. Ray Meyo took me to the Indians' post-season games and Frank Eck, my friend from Columbus, and Joe Chlapaty, president and chief operating officer of ADS, picked me up and flew me to Chicago to see the Cubs, which is my boy Gerry's favorite team. We also picked up Notre Dame baseball coach Paul Mainieri and in the process I got to fly directly above Notre Dame Stadium where the expansion was in progress.

The Cubs game was a thrill. I got Harry Caray, who once broadcast Notre Dame games out of St. Louis, to sign something for my son, and Ed Lynch, the Cubs general manager, even let me use his office to make a prearranged call to CBS for an interview with Rick Gentile and other CBS sports officials. They were considering me for a job as one of their college football commentators. I didn't get the job, but I'll keep trying. With a voice like mine and stories like these, how could they resist hiring me eventually?

Maybe they've been talking to some of the Akron assistant football coaches, who would not recommend me. I had asked Lee Owens if he would mind if I showed up on occasion at the Rubber Bowl to watch some of his spring practices. He said not only would that be fine but he also invited me to come down on the field. I told him I wouldn't do that, that it wouldn't be fair to him and might become a distraction.

I just wanted to watch how the players were developing. I'd go to practice late, and sit way up in the corner of the stands. Some of the players still would see me up there and wave, which I knew didn't do them any good with their new coaches.

Then one of my friends told me one day that he had heard some of Owens' assistants were objecting to my presence, that they were making a joke of it. So I called Lee and he came over to my office.

"Yeah," he admitted, "they don't want you out there. That's not the way I feel, but..."

"Coach," I said, "I won't be at another practice, and I won't be in your offices again. If I can ever help you in any way, just call. I'll root for you. I'll come to the games when I can, but I won't be around again."

As a coach I understand how they felt, and I haven't been back.

When I need a football fix, I visit high school coaches in and around Akron—Jack Rose at Massillon, Bill McGee at Akron Garfield, Tim Flossie, now at Barberton, or Dan Boarman at Copley. They allow me to share their practices and always act as if they're glad to see me.

The most excitement I had during my first free fall was generated by the opportunity to return to South Bend for a Notre Dame football Saturday. I had previewed the experience in the spring with Rudy Sharkey, one of my former Akron assistants and forever friends. We went to Detroit to visit my friend Tom Monaghan, owner of Domino's Pizza, and to speak to a group of men for Tom. Afterward, I called Lou Holtz to see it if would be all right if we drove over to South Bend for the start of the Irish spring practice. Lou, of course, said that I was always welcome and that he'd enjoy meeting Rudy.

Naturally the first place I stopped once I was back on campus was the Grotto. Rudy is a Lutheran, but I know he appreciated what this visit meant to me.

"Gerry," Rudy says, "is as fine a Christian person as you'll ever meet in your life. Just his attitude, his approach. Even his detractors, I think, appreciate the way he has gone about his life. Even though he's not coaching, there's a lot of be said for Gerry just being in the Akron community and doing the things he does behind the scenes—helping people and groups. He doesn't get the credit he deserves."

I don't believe Rudy thought I was going to receive much credit when I began banging on the door behind which the Rev. Edward "Monk" Malloy, president of Notre Dame, and the Rev. E. William Beauchamp, executive vice president, were conducting a cabinet meeting. Suddenly, there was silence where there had been voices. So I just barged in. There were 15 people around the table and I knew all but one or two of them.

"Hey," I said, "are you looking for a coach?"

They broke into laughter.

"Gerry!" they all said at once.

Who else? Right?

It was great seeing everyone. It brought back memories. After visiting with Father Hesburgh for 25 minutes—Father Joyce wasn't in—we stopped by to see Dick Rosenthal, Notre Dame's athletic director, and Brian Boulac. Then we went over to see Lou at practice, and I rode around in his golf cart. I told him the story of breaking in on the cabinet meeting and he just shook his head.

"Gerry," he said, "I could never do that."

"Hey, Lou," I reminded him, "what are they going to do, fire me?"

He almost fell out of the golf cart.

In the fall of 1995, I returned to South Bend for my first Notre Dame game in 10 years. The Irish were playing host to Texas, and I took my friend Bill Greenzalis and my former recruiting coordinator Bob LaCivita. They'd never been to Notre Dame, much less to South Bend on a football Saturday. We drove from Akron that morning and I used my influence as former coach and rounded up a parking pass that put us right in the middle of the tailgating parties. We hadn't gone 10 feet before people were coming up to me, grabbing my hand and telling me it was great to see me. I think they liked me more in the parking lot than on the sideline.

"It was like you had died and gone to heaven," Bill Greenzalis says. "Gerry put his foot on the pavement and there was a line for autographs. I'm telling you, coming from Akron, and knowing how he was received there, made this reception seem even more phenomenal."

"There was," says Bob LaCivita, now the assistant to head football coach Terry Bowden at Auburn, "a genuine feeling of love. Notre Dame is a great and special place. You can sense that. And Coach Faust is a special person, a great person. This love went two ways. He enjoyed it. The people at Notre Dame enjoyed it. I had the sense it was deep-rooted."

Bob is perceptive. I think what I went through at Notre Dame and thus what the Notre Dame supporters went through with me bonded us in a strange, wonderful way. They never seemed to hold against me the fact I didn't do as well as they and I wanted. I think they knew that as disappointed as they were, I was even more disappointed.

"Gerry's legacy," says Bob Crable, All-America linebacker, "will be that he is remembered as Gerry the man. If you go back to Notre Dame now and talk with people who were around during that time, they say that maybe he didn't take Notre Dame into the limelight in terms of its record but that he did put it there from a humanitarian standpoint.

"Maybe that was his downfall. To Gerry, it was still a game. It wasn't life and death. Now, at Notre Dame, football has become big business. I haven't been back to see a game in quite a few years, but

I heard this from a guy when I visited in the spring of '96: They didn't realize how lucky they were when Fuzzy was here."

Guess that proves memory can play tricks on a person.

"As far as Father Hesburgh and myself and I think Moose Krause, if he were still alive," Father Joyce says, "all the people who dealt with Gerry loved him. I can't really speak with authority but I think the general alumni, and it depends on whether they are fanatics on football or not, but maybe even the fanatics, hesitate to be very critical of him.

"I think it is a mystery to all of us why he didn't succeed. Winning all the time takes the fun out if. I don't mind losing. But then, every game I come to, I don't want to lose that particular game. I'm not *that* crazy, to say: Gee, I wish we'd lose this game because we'll enjoy winning the next one more.

"I do always want Navy to beat us. They've played us since 1927 and they haven't won a game since 1963, when Roger Staubach beat us. I wish they would beat us, but every year we come to the game and I say: We can't let Navy beat us this year. It would destroy our whole season. Let it be next year.

"I don't regret the Gerry experience. We go through these ups and downs. We expect them."

I guess I just gave Notre Dame too much of what it expected.

"Gerry as a person," says Notre Dame trustee Art Decio, "will make more contributions to the world than as a coach."

Rather than a condemnation, I consider that a compliment. As Bill Greenzalis, Bob LaCivita and I walked across the campus that football afternoon, I began to see more clearly how I was remembered.

"I wish all the people in Akron could see this," Bill Greenzalis said to me. "The city of Akron doesn't realize the respect you have around the country."

"Bill," I said, "when you're around all the time, you're just a friend. But when you haven't seen someone in 10 years, it's special. That's what's happening."

When we arrived at the Grotto, I ran into Notre Dame athletic director Mike Wadsworth and Phil Sheridan, a former Notre Dame player. It was wonderful to see them and to be able to visit on a football Saturday, like an ordinary Notre Dame fan. When I began to say some prayers, a group of people formed and quietly waited until I had finished before approaching me to talk, shake hands and have autographs signed. It was like this in the Stadium, too, where the ushers rushed to greet me, and in the press box and in some of the other boxes I visited. I saw my friends Ray Meyo and Jerry Hammes, who is an entrepreneur in South Bend. I visited Father Malloy's and Father Beauchamp's box and ran into my friend Regis Philbin, who dropped into a 3-point stance and seemed bent on going one-on-one with me. Regis was shouting: "Hike. Hike. Hike." I think it was a new monologue he was testing for his television show.

They gave me a seat in the press box with my former critics and the earth didn't move, though I have to confess a year later when I attended the Washington game and had a seat in the press box I decided I had better go outside because I couldn't seem to keep from breaking the press' one hard-and-fast rule: No cheering in the press box. The media were working. I was on a busman's holiday, cheering for ol' Notre Dame.

That wasn't my only embarrassing moment. When I was in the Stadium with Frank Kelley, Dean of the University of Akron's College of Polymer Science and Polymer Engineering, my knee gave out while I was climbing the steps. I fell, catching myself at the last second.

"Coach," the people around me asked, "are you all right?"

I looked like as if I had been drinking—except I don't drink.

I laughed and told them I was OK.

"It's no different," I said, "than any other time I was in the Stadium. I was always stumbling and bumbling and fumbling around."

Everybody got a kick out of that. This time, though, they were laughing with me. That's a memory I want to keep.

Notre Dame wasn't the only team that my changed circumstances allowed me to revisit. It has never been awkward going back to Moeller or watching it play when it comes to visit, say, Massillon. That first fall away from coaching, one of my former assistants, Bob Stanley, was helping Jack Rose coach Massillon and Bob got me tickets to the Tigers' game with Moeller. I warned him: I'm rooting for Moeller. He understood and put me on the Moeller side of the field. I ran into more people I knew, including, of course, Moeller coach Steve Klonne. Everyone was gracious and made me feel as if I were still welcome and important.

Although Dick Beerman, with whom I coached at Moeller, got me a sideline pass, I sat in the stands. The focus, I knew, should be on Steve and his team, and I didn't want to diffuse that. At halftime, Joe Asbrock, who is the only person living who has never missed a Moeller football game, heard I was in the stands. He came up from the sideline to find me. Joe is in his mid-80s and retired from his job as Moeller's janitor. We used to take Joe everywhere. He was as much a part of Moeller football as any of us coaches. We hugged and talked and laughed and when halftime was nearly over I walked him back down to the field. The steps were steep and Joe has become a little feeble. I didn't want him to fall like I had at Notre Dame.

When we reached the field, I asked a police officer if I could take Joe on down to the bench. The cop recognized me and said: "Sure, Coach, go ahead."

So I took Joe down and got him seated on the bench. While the bands finished playing, we said our goodbyes and I returned to the stands. The following Monday I got a call from the Akron athletic department. They said they had received a complaint. Someone said I was on the sidelines at the Moeller-Massillon game and that it was an NCAA violation, because I still represent the University.

Someone had reported it. I couldn't believe it. The University fired me and someone thinks I'm still recruiting its football players? I don't think Joe looked too much like a player and he was the only person I was talking to. It was ridiculous, but Ted Mallo, Akron's legal counsel, had to spend time to clear it up.

The most memorable Moeller game I've had the opportunity to attend because of my new schedule was made unforgettable not by today's players, as great as they are, but by yesterday's. Phil Gigliotti and Tom Backhus organized a 30-year reunion of the 1965 team, the first to go undefeated in school history. This team not only had talent but it also had the will to improve as the season progressed. It played great defense. It had a solid offense and kicking game. It was a team that made few mistakes. It may not have had as talented a group of athletes as some other Moeller teams, but the players and coaches believed in one another and that made it invincible.

Fifty-two players returned for the reunion, including 15 of the 19 seniors from that 10-0 team. As they came onto the field at the University of Cincinnati where the 1995 Moeller team was playing Cleveland St. Ignatius, they were wearing their old jerseys. The numbers before my eyes made memories dance in my head. But the moment belonged to the players so I sat in the stands with my former assistants Phil Gigliotti, Mike Cameron and Bill Clark and just watched. I probably looked like a toad I was so swelled up with pride. I've gotten so much credit for what I accomplished with Moeller football, but Phil, Mike, Bill and the other dedicated assistants deserve just as much attention and credit for building a great football tradition from scratch.

There was so much I wanted to say to these former players after 30 years. They looked different. I looked different. But, I think, in our hearts we are the same. Because I wanted to allow them the opportunity to talk about the things they wanted to share with one another, I didn't say much at their get-together. Later, though, I wrote them a letter, thanking them for what they had done for Moeller and for me.

"There was so much I wanted to say," I told them, "but just seeing all of you with a smile on your face was enough for me. I thank the Good Lord for having the opportunity to coach all of you. It has made my life better."

In addition to the occasional Moeller football game, other matters take me regularly to visit Cincinnati. There's my work on the board of BenchMark Federal Savings Bank and, of course, I have to get my hair cut. I may be the only guy who makes an eight-hour round-trip drive, in part, to get a free haircut. Morris Roberts, who owns Dillonville Barbershop, has cut what there is of my hair since the 1960s. We've gone through a lot together. My ups and downs. The death of one of Morris' and his wife Gladys' sons of stomach cancer. You don't appreciate how important your children are until you see what the death of a friend's child takes out of him.

When I was at Notre Dame, I couldn't get to Cincinnati for Morris to cut my hair. So Armando Femia became my South Bend barber, and even Morris would come to Notre Dame occasionally for games and bring his scissors. Now it's a routine. I drive to Cincinnati for the bank board meeting. Morris cuts my hair for free. Then Morris gets my money in a gin rummy game.

I don't have a lot of money to contribute to political campaigns. I do have time, however, when the politician is Rep. John Boehner from Cincinnati. John's staff called me during 1996 to ask if I would kick off a fund-raiser for the congressman. The date was Labor Day weekend; the time, Saturday night. Had I still been coaching, I'd never have been able to accept such an honor.

As it was, I could lend my support to a man who, during the '60s, was a linebacker and snapper for punts on my Moeller High School teams. I take satisfaction in seeing a man such as John not only doing well but also serving his country as a respected member of Congress. Politics and business have replaced football in my schedule.

I'm also a minor partner in Miller Buckeye Biscuit Company in Akron and Youngstown with Don Schmitt, Bill Greenzalis and Bob O'Leary, president and CEO, and now Steve and Pij have moved to the area to open a veterinary clinic. Pij is also a doctor of veterinary medicine. So I have both business and even more family events to fill the hours that I used to spend worrying about how to beat some coach who might just lose his job if I were successful.

During that first fall without a game of my own, I attended a game between the two schools from which my son, Steve, graduated: Notre Dame and the Ohio State School of Veterinary Medicine. My friend Frank Eck got me tickets and I was going to sit with Jim Kennedy, the Philadelphia man whom I had made my telephone recruiter when he was bedridden. As I walked to where Jim and a number of Notre Dame supporters were seated, high up in Ohio Stadium, the sea of Ohio State fans began booing me. Jim, however, seemed surprised.

"Those people were booing you," he said.

"Yeah, I'm in the wrong section for someone from Ohio."

A person has to follow his heart and make the best of a situation. So I just smiled at the booing. I always think of a friend of mine from Pittsburgh, Ray Anthony, when it comes to making the best of a situation. Ray grew up helping his father in his scrap yard, and on one occasion someone hauled in an old broken-down crane. Rather than scrap it, Ray asked his dad if he could try to fix it. His dad told him to give it a shot. So Ray did. When he got it working again, he began renting it out and from that scrap-metal seed grew the Anthony Crane Co., the largest crane company in the U.S.

Life is full of surprises. Now, some of them that I might have missed, I have time to appreciate. One surprise I almost missed occurred on a Saturday in April of 1994, my last season of coaching. Marlene and I had gotten an invitation to a surprise party for Patty Greenzalis, wife of my friend, Bill. It couldn't have been scheduled at a worse time. We had a spring scrimmage that Saturday morning and Bob O'Leary, one of my partners in Miller Buckeye Biscuit, also had asked me to speak to a Lions Club convention in Canton. I returned to the Akron football offices from the speech to review the film of the morning scrimmage. I was going to be late for the surprise party. I figured it didn't matter. Marlene would be there. The surprise would be over. I'd just show up when I could. They didn't need me.

Well, my coaches acted as if they were about to lose their minds. I'm watching the film and they're telling me I'd better get to that party—*now.* I didn't think anything of it. But after I'd watched film for about 30 minutes, Bob Junko convinced me that I should stop and go to the Martin Center, where the party was being held, and return later to finish watching the scrimmage. I had planned to watch the entire film first. Finally, I said OK.

When I walked into Martin Center, I discovered my brother Fred and sister-in-law Laurie, my sister Marilee and brother-in-law Ken and all the rest of my family and friends. The surprise party was in honor of Marlene and me. It was our 30th anniversary. I can tell you: It surprised the heck out of me. If it hadn't been for Junk pestering me, those people would have been waiting another hour or more. It turned out to be one of the more memorable days of my life.

Most people find it difficult to believe that the memories that last longest have more to do with faith and family and friends than with football. They figure I miss the game and that I'm pining away with my tree in my hidden office. I've run into a number of former coaches since I've been out of the profession and it's interesting to gauge their reactions to being out of the game. I saw Chuck Noll, the coach of Pittsburgh's Super Bowl championship teams, at the South Carolina Yacht Club when I was on vacation with Ken and Jan Schneider and Frank and Terri D'Andrea and we got to talking. We're both University of Dayton graduates and former football players. I asked him if he missed coaching, and he said he didn't, that he had had his time in it and now he was enjoying retirement, in Pittsburgh and at Hilton Head, South Carolina.

It was the same with George Perles, Chuck Knox and Hank Bullough, whom I was with at a golf outing in the summer of 1996. We talked about the pro and college game, where we had coached, and concluded that it is becoming increasingly difficult to win consistently on both levels. Not one of them missed coaching, which surprised me. But then, they had been successful. I think it was different for me.

I didn't have the success in college that I would have liked to have had. I think there still is doubt in some people's minds about whether or not I can coach on the college level—maybe in a lot of people's minds. But in my own mind, I feel good about the experience, good about what I accomplished. I know that as far as the public goes, I didn't fulfill the promise that I brought from Moeller. I didn't overcome the odds. I was a .500 coach.

The great college coaches win eight of 11 games each year. The good ones win seven of 11. Given the situation at Akron, it was difficult to do that. It wasn't difficult at Notre Dame. I should have won more.

Sometimes when I'm thinking about that, the telephone will ring and it will be one of my Notre Dame or Akron players or even someone who played for me a lifetime ago at Moeller. I got a call not long ago from Eddie Outlaw, who was the first minority player I ever coached. He called from Thailand, where he works for AT&T. He just wanted to tell me that he has a wife, a couple of kids and a great job and if it hadn't been for football and the things he learned during the 1964-'65-'66 seasons at Moeller, he wouldn't be where he is today. How could a coach win anything more than a call like that? Or win anything more important than the letter I received from Marty Klotz?

Marty was another of my Moeller players, which may speak to the question of at which level are young men the most impressionable and moldable. Marty joined the Marine Corps, got his bachelor's and master's degrees and served in five combat actions in four countries over 17 years. When he wrote, he and his wife and two children were living in Saudi Arabia where he was working for the Saudi army.

"Sir," Marty wrote, "you were a huge part of my success as a person. There are things much more important in life than winning in some game. You have always taught and personified character building. I am sure that I would not be the person that I am today if it were not for you. The intangible things that you taught me are priceless concepts. Ideas such as team building, character, honesty, integrity, sincerity, compassion, tenacity, and a solid work ethic were the things that turned me around from being a punk kid into a man.

"It was your teaching and your actions that I have used as a role model in my life. I am trying to instill those qualities in my children. The bottom line is that winning and losing football games do not remotely compare with winning and losing in life.You make young boys into men.You turn losers into winners.You mold men into model citizens.Those are concepts that few people in the world can lay claim to, much less turn from concepts to concrete results."

The goal, of course, is to do what Marty so generously suggests I did for him and still win games. I know it can be done, but sometimes a man has to wonder, and I'm not alone in that.

Auburn University president Bill Muse was wise enough to see that Terry Bowden, the quarterback coach on my first Akron staff, might be the man who could accomplish for Auburn these dual and sometimes conflicting goals of coaching. But Dr. Muse laments the scarcity of such coaches.

"That's the thing that bothers me tremendously about Gerry's situation," Dr. Muse says. "And I'll give you another example: Bill Curry. I've known Bill Curry since he was a student at Georgia Tech, where I had my first teaching job. Like Gerry, Bill is one of the finest human beings I've ever known. A good man to the core."

That good man was fired at Kentucky following the 1996 season.

"You wonder," Dr. Muse says, "can't goodness succeed? Isn't there somewhere out there a guiding hand who will let guys like Gerry Faust and Bill Curry achieve the kind of success they should have?"

Perhaps the problem is defining success by victories. Other definitions of success are more complex and subjective, more like moving targets.

Paul Daugherty, a sports columnist for the *Cincinnati Enquirer* whom I don't know personally, put it this way: "You could say Notre Dame's greatness returned with the win over West Virginia in the 1989 Fiesta Bowl; I'd say it peaked when the school honored its five-year deal with (Gerry) Faust.

"At Notre Dame, Faust was a beautiful loser. To see him in his fifth season in South Bend was to feel sad and ennobled at the same time.You knew he was gone after the season; so did he. But you could look at Faust and Notre Dame and see something grander at work than winning. It was the simple dignity of doing things honorably. Notre Dame football was a nobler thing when Faust was there."

If I have left the impression with persons like Marty Klotz and Paul Daugherty that I spent my coaching career on the moral high ground, then I have succeeded, record or no record. I know I felt as if I had succeeded when I attended Mass with Marlene at St. Hilary's on Thanksgiving following my firing at the University of Akron. At the end of the mass Father Gordon Yahner asked if anyone wanted to share why they were thankful on that Thanksgiving. Eight or 10 people did. I didn't. It wasn't that I didn't have anything to be thankful for. I just never say much in church. Elsewhere, I'm hard to shut up. In church, I try to hang back, out of the spotlight. This time, Father Yahner wouldn't let me.

When the parishioners had finished, Father Yahner stood at the altar and said: "Thank you for Gerry Faust. He may be taken away from the football field but he'll never be taken away from the table of our Lord." Then everyone stood—and applauded. I couldn't believe it. I was touched beyond words.

The exception to hanging back in church is when I'm invited to speak. I couldn't count the number of churches in which I've spoken. One of experiences I enjoyed most occurred when I still was coaching Akron football and the Rev. Ronald Fowler invited me to speak at the Arlington Church of God. Rev. Fowler, who leads one of Akron's black congregations, served as a team chaplain along with Rev. Knute Larson from The Chapel, Father Clyde Foster and Father John Miceli and did a wonderful job.

One Sunday morning after Mass I was in my office and we had just had a game ball inscribed with Rev. Fowler's name, the game, the score and the date to present to him in appreciation for his work with our student-athletes. On the spur of the moment, I decided to go over to the Rev. Fowler's church and give it to him. When I arrived I ran into the assistant pastor and asked if I could surprise Rev. Fowler when he was in the pulpit. She said she thought it was a great idea.

So as the offertory was being taken, I walked out into the filled sanctuary and the Rev. Fowler about came unglued.

"Coach!" he shouted, and came down from the pulpit to give The Hugger a hug.

He invited me to the pulpit, and I explained to the congregation why I was there and how much Rev. Fowler had done to help our young men.

"I can't tell you how lucky you are," I said, "to have Rev. Fowler as your pastor."

When he came up to receive the game ball, the congregation rose in a standing ovation.

"Since I'm up here," I continued, "I might as well give a little sermon."

The Hugger had turned into Mr. Pushy again. I told the congregation of my trip to Lourdes. I couldn't resist.

"Well," Rev. Fowler said, "you probably gave a better sermon than I will."

Everyone laughed. It was a wonderful moment. Sometimes we don't appreciate the people around us as much as we should. I just wanted to tell his congregation how much I appreciated Rev. Fowler.

As I look back on coaching, the things I miss are the practices, the games and being with the student-athletes. I don't miss the problems that can be associated with these things. I enjoy my work now and I still believe I'm helping the University. An example might be a call I fielded from Chuck Holland, one of the most generous, gracious men in Akron. Chuck owns Holland Oil and is a supporter of the University and many other deserving segments of the community. After I was fired, Chuck was approached by the Akron athletic department to help fund practice fields for the football team.

"Should I give it to them?" Chuck asked me.

"Chuck," I said, "by all means. Those kids need it. They deserve it. We've had so many injuries from being unable to practice on grass that they should have those fields."

"Well, I want you to come over and pick up the check and take it to them."

So I did. I took Chuck's check for $20,000 to the athletic department, to athletic director Mike Bobinski, the man who had fired me. No one knew I had a role. I don't mind being behind the scenes if it helps the students of the University.

Actually, a lower profile is not all bad. When I was coaching, a man imitating me would call Stan Piatt, a talk show host on WNIR radio. I didn't mind the guy imitating me. I have the kind of voice people love to imitate. The problem was, the man would say things I would never say. He was crude and borderline lewd. It got so bad that people would stop me and ask me why I had said these things. When I'd tell them I hadn't said such things, that it was someone imitating me, they'd tell me that I didn't know what I was talking about. They had heard me. Finally, I called Stan Piatt and he agreed to pull the plug on Radio Faust.

One of my buddies from high school, Lou "Hurricane" Krueger would appreciate the Radio Faust story. He has become a legendary caller to sports talk shows in Iowa. He lives in Davenport, and now that I have more free time in the evenings I talk to Lou often. Same with Larry Curk, a friend from Dayton. He calls regularly. The phone lines are open to the real Gerry Faust. I've met so many people in 37 years of coaching who have become friends and remain so. I call. They call. We talk. There's John "Jay" Jordan II, Fran Dugan, Robert Wilmouth, Chuck Lennon, Cy Laughter, Denny Spahn, Chuck Stimming, Tom O'Brien, Earl Bowen, Gerald O'Connor, Gerry Hammes, George Chimes, Art MacIntire, Alex Arshinkoff, Jack Breen, Ed McCarrick, Ron Lujan, Danny McCue, Pete Kostoff, Pete Spitalieri, Mike Lynch, Dan Williams, and Mike Lobalzo. The list could go on and on.

These are not friendships based on wins and losses. They are based on the same love and concern with which I tried to coach. Through it all, I tried not to lose touch with the principle that we were trying to help student-athletes recognize and embrace, the qualities that Marty Klotz addressed so eloquently: honesty, sincerity, compassion, tenacity. These qualities make not only for good players but also for good citizens, men who will stand by their families and lead in their communities, men who will be productive citizens.

To some it may appear I've failed. My record at Notre Dame was just over .500. My record at Akron was just under .500. But who in their lifetime has had more wonderful opportunities than I've had? I got to build from scratch a high school team into one of the most powerful programs ever. I got to jump from high school to the college football program with arguably the richest tradition in America. And I got to take the first football program from I-AA to I-A in NCAA history.

Along the way there have been successes and failures on the field, but in each of these places—Moeller, Notre Dame and Akron—I've made friendships that will last a lifetime, friendships not based on what's on the scoreboard but what's in the heart. These lives that have touched mine are what have made my career of 37 years a career without regrets.

I was the right man, if not the right coach, for Notre Dame.

I seized the day and it has never been a dark one—not even in its darkest moments. I still see the sun glinting off the Golden Dome, illuminating my Golden Dream.

The only shortcut I ever took in my life was to Notre Dame. How can that have been a mistake? It gave me a chance to walk the path I believe God intended me to take. I know He never once let go of my hand along the way. And one day, He will let me know how our walk went. I can live with that.

THE FAUST RECORDS

MOELLER HIGH SCHOOL

	Won	Lost	Tied
1963	9	1	0
1964	8	2	0
1965	10	0	0
1966	7	3	0
1967	8	2	0
1968	6	2	2
1969	10	0	0
1970	9	1	0
1971	9	1	1
1972	8	2	0
1973	10	1	0
1974	10	1	0
1975	12	0	0
1976	12	0	0
1977	12	0	0
1978	9	1	0
1979	12	0	0
1980	13	0	0
Totals	**174**	**17**	**2**

NOTRE DAME

	Won	Lost	Tied
1981	5	6	0
1982	6	4	1
1983	7	5	0
1984	7	5	0
1985	5	6	0
Totals	30	26	1

UNIVERSITY OF AKRON

	Won	Lost	Tied
1986	7	4	0
1987	4	7	0
1988	5	6	0
1989	6	4	1
1990	3	7	1
1991	5	6	0
1992	7	3	1
1993	5	6	0
1994	1	10	0
Totals	43	53	3

THE NOTRE DAME SEASONS

1981

Date		Opponent	
Sept. 12	27	LSU	9
Sept. 19	7	at Michigan	25
Sept. 26	14	at Purdue	15
Oct. 3	20	Michigan State	7
Oct. 10	13	Florida State	19
Oct. 24	7	USC	14
Oct. 31	38	Navy	0
Nov. 7	35	Georgia Tech	3
Nov. 14	35	at Air Force	7
Nov. 21	21	at Penn State	24
Nov. 28	15	at Miami	37

1982

Date		Opponent	
Sept. 18	23	Michigan	17
Sept. 25	28	Purdue	14
Oct. 2	11	at Michigan State	3
Oct. 9	16	Miami	14
Oct. 16	13	at Arizona	16
Oct. 23	13	at Oregon	13
Oct. 30	27	Navy (neutral)	10
Nov. 6	31	at Pittsburgh	16
Nov. 13	14	Penn State	24
Nov. 20	17	at Air Force	30
Nov. 27	13	at USC	17

1983

Sept. 10	52	at Purdue	6
Sept. 17	23	Michigan State	28
Sept. 24	0	at Miami	20
Oct. 1	27	at Colorado	3
Oct. 8	30	at South Carolina	6
Oct. 15	42	Army (neutral)	0
Oct. 22	27	USC	6
Oct. 29	28	Navy	12
Nov. 5	16	Pittsburgh	21
Nov. 12	30	at Penn State	34
Nov. 19	22	Air Force	23

Liberty Bowl

| Dec. 29 | 19 | Boston College | 18 |

1984

Sept. 8	21	Purdue (neutral)	23
Sept. 15	24	at Michigan State	20
Sept. 22	55	Colorado	14
Sept. 29	16	at Missouri	14
Oct. 6	13	Miami	31
Oct. 13	7	Air Force	21
Oct. 20	32	South Carolina	36
Oct. 27	30	at LSU	22
Nov. 3	18	Navy (neutral)	17
Nov. 17	44	Penn State	7
Nov. 24	19	at USC	7

Aloha Bowl

| Dec. 29 | 20 | SMU | 27 |

1985

Sept. 14	12	at Michigan	20
Sept. 21	27	Michigan State	10
Sept. 28	17	at Purdue	35
Oct. 5	15	at Air Force	21
Oct. 19	24	Army	10
Oct. 26	37	USC	3
Nov. 2	41	Navy	17
Nov. 9	37	Mississippi	14
Nov. 16	6	at Penn State	36
Nov. 23	7	LSU	10
Nov. 30	7	at Miami	58